"Scholarly in its technical foundations of theology and history, but written in language accessible to lay reader and scholar alike, this book is the best resource in print that provides trustworthy insight into a comparison of Arminianism and Calvinism. Scholars will admire the full footnoting of all sources, and lay readers will appreciate that technical language is avoided but explicated when needed. Pinson knows full well that there is no such thing as a single homogenous phenomenon of either Arminianism or Calvinism. This is where Pinson shines the brightest. He carefully guides the reader through nuanced differences and emphases, but he also honestly sets forth his own position on challenging differences. The careful reader will discern that Pinson is consequential in his pursuit, which means that no detail of difference is too small to set out. Simply put: this is the most comprehensive book available on the essentials of Arminian theology. The beauty of the book is that Pinson fulfills the ideal dialectic that he set out in his Introduction. He has produced an irenic apologetic for which Arminius himself would issue high praise. The spirit of Arminius shines through."

—W. Stephen Gunter,
Research Professor Emeritus, Duke Divinity School
and author of *Arminius and His "Declaration of Sentiments"*

"Matthew Pinson displays a broad and deep understanding of Arminius's theology, classical 'Reformed Arminianism,' and varieties of Calvinism. Here he ably answers questions about classical 'Reformed Arminianism' and demonstrates how it differs from both Calvinism and Wesleyan Arminianism. At the same time, in very irenic tones, Pinson acknowledges and celebrates areas of agreement between these lines of Protestant Christian theology. The novel contribution of this book is the author's insightful discussion of how Arminianism can be 'Reformed.' According to him, and I agree, classical Arminianism is a branch of the broad Reformed tradition even though Wesleyans are also Arminians. Although he does not mention this 'fun fact,' the original Arminian denomination, the Remonstrant Brotherhood of the Netherlands, is a charter member of the World Communion of Reformed Churches. That fact supports his theological argument for Reformed Arminianism. Anyone who wants to be thoroughly informed about Arminianism and also entertained in the process must read *40 Questions About Arminianism*."

—Roger E. Olson, Professor of Christian Theology
and Holder of the Foy Valentine Chair in Christian Ethics,
George W. Truett Theological Seminary, Baylor University

"Matthew Pinson has surely produced what may well rank as the best available exposition of evangelical Arminianism. I found the book enormously helpful in tracing the Arminian vision from the vantage point of Scripture, theology, and history. And while I remain unconvinced by his argument in a number of places, his book is a gracious and profoundly learned response to the biblical Calvinism that I embrace. In fact, reading it was not only a learning experience—it was a joyful exercise!"

—Michael A. G. Haykin, FRHistS,
Chair and Professor of Church History, Southern Baptist Theological Seminary

"Matthew Pinson in *40 Questions About Arminianism* has beautifully recaptured the classic question-answer format which framed the great historic theologies of the past in order to present the distinctives of Arminian theology and thought to a new generation. Rather than dividing Christians into theological camps, Pinson conveys a beautiful irenic tone, helping inform fellow brothers and sisters in Christ about many of the frequently misunderstood features of the great tapestry which makes up Christian theology."

—Timothy Tennent,
President and Professor of World Christianity,
Asbury Theological Seminary

"This work provides readers the perfect opportunity to get acquainted with a vibrant, evangelical Arminianism that is rooted and grounded in Reformation theology. This theology draws directly from Arminius himself. Through the centuries, the very best Arminianism—whether that of the early English General Baptists and their progeny in America or of Wesley and those who have followed his lead—has preserved the solas and the most important elements of that understanding of biblical truth. Pinson takes on all the questions involved, the hard ones included, and gives thorough, biblically based answers. You may be surprised!"

—Robert E. Picirilli, Professor Emeritus of New Testament and Greek and Former Academic Dean, Welch College

"I'm not an Arminian. However, I am deeply appreciative of the Arminian theological tradition and its contributions to the church catholic. As such, I'm thankful that Matt Pinson has written this important volume. The book is well written, the questions are well chosen, and the content is presented in an informative and winsome manner. Readers will benefit from learning more about the variations within Arminianism and the key differences between Arminianism and various forms of Calvinism. Perhaps more important, this book makes clear that orthodox Arminianism in its reformational and Wesleyan forms is distinct from the errors of semi-Pelagianism, the latter of which have been condemned by Arminians just as much as Calvinists. This book is a fine addition to a great series."

—Nathan Finn, Provost and Professor of Theological Studies and History, North Greenville University

"Arminius in particular and Arminians in general are often misrepresented or inaccurately defined by their detractors. Some people who write or speak about Arminianism evidently have never read Arminius himself. The great value of this work is that Matthew Pinson cogently articulates what Arminius and Arminians *actually believe*, and why they believe it."

—Steve W. Lemke, Vice President for Institutional Assessment and Professor of Philosophy and Ethics, New Orleans Baptist Theological Seminary

"By reading Arminius myself, I discovered how surprisingly Reformed Arminius himself really was. Through Matthew Pinson, I discovered to my surprise that this 'Reformed Arminius' has faithful followers through the seventeenth-century English General Baptists up to the present day. At the same time, the early 'Arminians' (Remonstrants), as well as those who pass for Arminians today, deviate more from Arminius than Arminius did from Calvin in many respects. It is easy to contrast this mainstream Arminianism with ultra-Calvinism by making the differences as great as possible. Yet it is much more exciting to confront Reformed Arminianism in the line of Arminius with 'mainstream' Calvinism. Pinson does the latter. Reformed Arminians profess the five solas of the Reformation in their emphasis on Christ, on grace and imputed righteousness by faith. Many Calvinists do not believe their eyes when they read an Arminian who writes about 'the rich Reformation portrait of our enslavement to sin and God's redemptive remedy for it' and about, for example, the need for penal substitutionary atonement. However, it is entirely in the spirit of Arminius. Calvinists can learn much from the clear, scriptural way Pinson sets forth questions regarding salvation, speaking warmly of the richness and necessity of God's grace in Christ. Pinson is very well versed in both Arminianism and Calvinism. In an honest and clear way, he lays out the differences without turning his theological 'opponents' into straw men with whom it is easy to 'win.' This book challenges both Arminians and Calvinists to rediscover their shared Reformed roots, to get a clear picture of the real differences, and to engage once again in the real conversation about them."

—William den Boer, postdoctoral researcher, Theological University Kampen, the Netherlands, and author of *God's Twofold Love: The Theology of Jacob Arminius (1559–1609)*

40 QUESTIONS ABOUT
Arminianism

J. Matthew Pinson

Benjamin L. Merkle, Series Editor

40 Questions About Arminianism
© 2022 J. Matthew Pinson

Published by Kregel Academic, an imprint of Kregel Publications, 2450 Oak Industrial Dr. NE, Grand Rapids, MI 49505-6020.

This book is a title in the 40 Questions Series edited by Benjamin L. Merkle.

The painting on the cover is *Allegory of Disputes between the Remonstrants and Contraremonstrants* (1618) by Abraham van der Eyk.

The Greek font, GraecaU, is available from www.linguistsoftware.com/lgku.htm, +1-425-775-1130.

ISBN 978-0-8254-4685-6

Printed in the United States of America
22 23 24 25 26 / 5 4 3 2 1

Dedicated to
F. Leroy Forlines (1926–2020)
and
Robert E. Picirilli,
who taught me Arminianism

Contents

Part 4: Questions About Election and Regeneration

Part 5: Questions About Perseverance and Apostasy

Acknowledgments

Too many people merit acknowledgment in a book like this, but I must mention a few key people without whom this work would never have come to fruition. I am thankful for my parents and grandparents, John and Linda Pinson and L. V. and Curro Pinson, for bequeathing to me the legacy of Christian teaching. I am grateful for Leroy Forlines and Robert Picirilli, to whom this book is dedicated, for teaching me Christian theology and Arminianism.

I thank Stephen Ashby for the innumerable hours of stimulating conversation on these matters. I owe gratitude to my Welch colleagues and friends Robert Picirilli, Matthew McAffee, Kevin Hester, and Richard Clark for reading the manuscript and offering invaluable suggestions for its improvement, as well as to my Calvinist friends Michael Haykin and Nathan Finn for reading the manuscript and helping me to be fair to my Calvinist brothers and sisters.

I appreciate my wife Melinda and my children Anna and Matthew more than I can express. All three of them share my love for Christian doctrine and the confessional commitments of this book and have been patient with me as I have written it in the midst of the COVID-19 pandemic. I am grateful to Ben Merkle for seeing the value of this project and for his excellence in scholarship and editing, as well as Laura Bartlett, Robert Hand, Kevin McKissick, Shawn Vander Lugt, and the entire team at Kregel Academic for all they have done to make this book a reality. Most of all, I thank the three-personed God for revealing to humanity his truth, which always and alone sets us free.

Introduction

I will never forget the crisp November day in Providence, Rhode Island, when my friend Michael Haykin and I were walking back to a meeting from lunch with a motley crew of Baptists from all over the soteriological map. Michael said, "I like my Calvinism like I think Matt likes his Arminianism." Then he paraphrased John Newton, who, after stirring some sugar into his tea, said: "I am more of a Calvinist than anything else; but I use my Calvinism in my writing and preaching as I use this sugar. I do not give it alone, and whole; but mixed, and diluted."[1]

I do not like what is normally called "polemics," defined as "an aggressive attack on or refutation of the opinions or principles of another. . . . From Greek *polemikos*, warlike, hostile."[2] However, I think Thomas Oden was right when he said that "irenics" and "polemics" are "sister disciplines" and thus polemics should always be irenic—characterized by a spirit that wants to foster peace and unity.[3] This is especially true when the differences are between brothers and sisters in Christ who have serious disagreements that might hinder ecclesiastical union but who agree on the gospel and the truths of Christian orthodoxy.

A little more from Newton is helpful in this context:

> I am an avowed Calvinist: the points which are usually comprised in that term, seem to me so consonant to scripture, reason, (when enlightened,) and experience, that I have not the shadow of doubt about them. But I cannot dispute, I dare not speculate. What is by some called high Calvinism, I dread. I feel much more in union of spirit with some Arminians, than I could with some Calvinists. . . . Not

---

1. Quoted in D. Bruce Hindmarsh, *John Newton and the English Evangelical Tradition: Between the Conversions of Wesley and Wilberforce*, Oxford Theological Monographs (New York: Oxford University Press, 1996), 168. In this book "Calvinism" will primarily refer to the doctrine of salvation that goes by that name. For more on this, see Question 2.
2. Merriam-Webster online dictionary, https://www.merriam-webster.com/dictionary/polemic. Accessed August 3, 2020.
3. Thomas C. Oden, *The Rebirth of Orthodoxy: Signs of New Life in Christianity* (New York: HarperCollins, 2002), 128.

because I think [their views] mere opinions, or of little importance to a believer,—I think the contrary; but because
I believe these doctrines will do no one any good till he is
taught them of God. I believe a too hasty assent to Calvinistic
principles, before a person is duly acquainted with the plague
of his own heart, is one principal cause of that lightness of
profession which so lamentably abounds in this day, a chief
reason why many professors are rash, heady, high-minded,
contentious about words, and sadly remiss as to the means of
divine appointment.[4]

The spirit Newton described toward the end of that passage is too
common in twenty-first century evangelicalism. Calvinists and Arminians
are more insular and less cooperative with each other than ever before. It
is sad when my hosting in the Welch College chapel pulpit, within a short
timeframe, Albert Mohler, president of the world's largest Calvinist seminary,
and Timothy Tennent, president of the world's largest Wesleyan Arminian
seminary, caused friends on both sides to raise their eyebrows, scratch their
heads in disbelief, and wonder why I would do such a thing.

Yet Newton's irenic mentality, the "catholicity of spirit" of which the
Anglican Calvinist Bishop J. C. Ryle spoke, was not always so unusual in the
evangelical Protestant tradition. Once a follower of George Whitefield asked
him, "Will we see Wesley in heaven?" to which Whitefield replied, "I fear not.
He will be so near the throne, and we shall be at such a distance, that we shall
hardly get a sight of him."[5]

Four of my favorite "running buddies" at Yale Divinity School were
a staunch Calvinist from the Presbyterian Church in America, a mildly
Arminian Anglican who was a postulant for the Episcopal priesthood, a "once-
saved, always-saved" Southern Baptist, and a conservative United Methodist.
We were all strongly committed to our respective confessional systems and
argued them vociferously among ourselves.

Yet we were thrown together by providence, in that pluralistic, Protestant-
liberal environment. We had far more conversations about our united witness
for Christian orthodoxy in its confessional Protestant form—and what that
witness could do to enliven not only gospel mission but also the public conversation in the West in the twenty-first century—than about our confessional
differences. We always agreed, however, that our full-throated confessional
commitments, about things like Arminianism versus Calvinism or paedobap-
tism versus anti-paedobaptism, made us much better cross-denominational

---

4. *The Works of the Rev. John Newton* (New Haven: Nathan Whiting, 1826), 4:369.
5. J. C. Ryle, *Christian Leaders of the Last Century, Or, England a Hundred Years Ago* (London: Thomas Nelson and Sons, 1869), 59–60.

dialogue partners. What was ironic was that our strong doctrinal commitments on matters like these made both our commitment to orthodoxy and our "catholicity of spirit" stronger.

This is the spirit in which I write this book. The reason I go into such great depth on this is that I want my Calvinist and Wesleyan brothers and sisters and dear friends in Christ to know where my heart is, even when my mind disagrees with them. In that vein, I have written this survey of Arminianism that is more didactic than polemical, but which every reader will see engages at times in hard-edged debate with scholars who are both on my Calvinist and Wesleyan sides.

That brings up the context from which I write. This volume will resonate with all Arminians because it explains the broad Arminian tradition to Calvinists and those from other traditions. Yet I am writing from a particular "social location" in the evangelical landscape. My perspective has been shaped more by a minority stream in the Arminian community that has come to be known as Reformed Arminianism. This tributary to the larger Arminian river has been more identified with Baptists. In our day it has been given the fullest expression by Free Will Baptist theologians such as Leroy Forlines and Robert Picirilli, heirs of the seventeenth-century English General Baptist tradition embodied by Thomas Helwys and Thomas Grantham. However, many Arminians who are part of the pan-Wesleyan movement—as well as non-Calvinists among Baptists and Bible churches who agree with Arminians on everything except the possibility of apostasy—concur with the broad outlines of Reformed Arminianism.

These and other in-house debates among Arminians are not the focus of this book, which intends to introduce Arminianism as a whole. Yet it will still be helpful to discuss the Reformed Arminian distinctives briefly here, since this less-well-known minority movement will come up at various places throughout the book. In short, Reformed Arminians are so named because Jacobus Arminius was a confessionally Reformed minister to his dying day who publicly affirmed the Belgic Confession and Heidelberg Catechism and drank as deeply as anyone from the rich fountain of Reformed theology.

Like all Arminians, Reformed Arminians diverge from Calvinism on *how one comes to be* in a state of grace (e.g., unconditional election, irresistible grace). Yet, unlike many other Arminians, they agree with Calvinists on *what it means to be* in a state of grace (e.g., penal substitution, imputation of the active and passive obedience of Christ; progressive as opposed to entire sanctification). This latter emphasis produces what they think of as a more *sola fide* emphasis with regard to falling from grace—so that a believer can apostatize, but only through a final, irremediable turning from Christ, not post-conversion sins and impenitence.

These differences transcend denominational and confessional boundaries: many Wesleyan Arminians, non-Calvinist Baptists, Anabaptists, adherents of the Stone-Campbell movement, and others have much in common with this perspective. There is also cross-pollination with some in the Lutheran Church who hold to a more conditional-election posture similar to older Lutheran scholastics such as Johann Gerhard. This is unsurprising, since Arminius found so much in common with the Lutheran soteriology of his day.

Still, most of this book will be about what brings all Arminians together and will serve as a primer to Arminians and Calvinists and others outside the Arminian community about the basics of this constellation of ideas. Yet I send it forth in the "spirit of catholicity" and irenic dialogue characteristic of the best of the evangelical Protestant tradition.

PART 1

Introductory and Historical Questions

Introducing Arminianism and Calvinism

Who Was Jacobus Arminius, and Who Were the Remonstrants?

Jacobus Arminius was born in 1559 in the city of Oudewater in the Netherlands and was named Jacob Harmenszoon, a Dutch name of which Jacobus Arminius is a latinized version.[1] His father died before he was born, and he and his brothers and sisters were raised by their mother. In 1575, Arminius went to study with Rudolphus Snellius, a professor at the University of Marburg. While Arminius was there, his family was killed in the Spanish massacre of Oudewater. The next year he enrolled in the new university at Leiden. It was there that he began his academic and ministerial career in earnest, as well as his serious interaction with the confessional theology of the Reformed Church in the Netherlands. After graduation from Leiden in 1581, he went to Geneva to study under Theodore Beza, Calvin's successor. He left there to study at Basel for a year but returned and studied at Geneva until 1586.

In 1587 Arminius began a pastorate in Amsterdam and was ordained the next year. Before assuming his pastorate, he traveled with his friend Adrian Junius to Italy and studied philosophy for seven months at the University of Padua. He said that the experience made the Roman Church appear to

---

1. Much of the brief summary information in this chapter relies on Carl Bangs, *Arminius: A Study in the Dutch Reformation* (Nashville: Abingdon, 1971); Bangs, "Arminius and the Reformation," *Church History* 30 (1961): 155–60; and Robert E. Picirilli, *Grace, Faith, Free Will: Contrasting Views of Salvation: Calvinism and Arminianism* (Nashville: Randall House, 2002), 3–17. For a valuable shorter introductions to Arminius's life, but longer than this sketch, see Stephen M. Ashby, "Introduction," *The Works of James Arminius,* 3 vols., trans. James Nichols and William Nichols (Nashville: Randall House, 2007). Some of the material in this chapter is adapted from J. Matthew Pinson, "Will the Real Arminius Please Stand Up? A Study of the Theology of Jacobus Arminius in Light of His Interpreters," *Integrity: A Journal of Christian Thought* 2 (2003): 121–39, reprinted in Pinson, *Arminian and Baptist: Explorations in a Theological Tradition* (Nashville: Randall House, 2015), chapter 1.

him "more foul, ugly, and detestable" than he could have imagined.[2] However, some of his later detractors used the trip to suggest that he had sympathies with Rome, "that he had kissed the pope's shoe, become acquainted with the Jesuits, and cherished a familiar intimacy with Cardinal Bellarmine."[3]

In 1590 Arminius married Lijbset Reael, a daughter of a member of the city council. About this time he became involved in theological controversy. He was asked to refute the teachings of Dirck Coornhert, a humanist who had criticized Calvinism, and two ministers at Delft who had written an anti-Calvinist pamphlet. The traditional view was that Arminius, in his attempt to refute these anti-Calvinist teachings, converted from Calvinism to anti-Calvinism. Yet Carl Bangs has shown that there is no evidence that he ever held strict Calvinist views. At any rate, he became involved in controversy over the doctrines of the strong Calvinists. In 1591 he preached on Romans 7, arguing (against many Calvinists' view) that the person described in verses 14–24 was regenerate.

A minister named Petrus Plancius led the charge against Arminius. Plancius labeled Arminius a Pelagian, alleging that he had moved away from the Belgic Confession of Faith and the Heidelberg Catechism, advocating anti-Reformed views on predestination and perfectionism. Arminius insisted that his theology was in line with that of the Reformed Church and its confessional standards, the Belgic Confession of Faith and Heidelberg Catechism, and the Amsterdam burgomasters sided with him. About a year later, after Arminius preached a series of sermons on Romans 9, Plancius again leveled accusations against him. The latter insisted that his teachings were in line with Article 16 of the Belgic Confession, and the consistory accepted his explanation, urging peace until the matter could be decided by a general synod.

For the next ten years, Arminius enjoyed a relatively peaceful pastorate and avoided theological controversy. During this decade, he wrote a great deal on theology (many things that were never published in his lifetime), including extensive works on Romans 7 and 9 as well as a long correspondence with the Leiden Calvinist Francis Junius. In 1602, there was an effort to get Arminius named to a post at the University of Leiden, but Leiden professor Franciscus Gomarus led an opposition to Arminius's appointment. Still, the Leiden burgomasters appointed Arminius as professor of theology in May 1603. Soon he was awarded a doctorate in theology.

Arminius would spend the last six years of his life at Leiden, struggling with tuberculosis but always in a firestorm of theological controversy. The primary source of the controversy was predestination. Another issue of dispute

---

2. Arminius, *Works*, 1:26. This quotation is from Peter Bertius, "An Oration on the Life and Death of That Reverend and Very Famous Man James Arminius, D.D.," reprinted in the London edition of Arminius's *Works*.

3. Caspar Brandt, *The Life of James Arminius, D.D.*, trans. John Guthrie (London: Ward and Company, 1854), 28.

was the convening of a national synod. Arminius's side wanted a national synod convened with power to make revisions to the Belgic Confession and Heidelberg Catechism, while the strict Calvinists relied more on local synods. In 1607 the States General brought together a conference to prepare for a national synod. Arminius recommended the revision of the confessional documents but was voted down. He continued to be accused of false teaching, which resulted in his petitioning the States General to inquire into his case.

Eventually, Arminius and Gomarus appeared before the High Court in 1608 to make their respective cases. This was the occasion for Arminius's famous *Declaration of Sentiments*.[4] In that work, Arminius forthrightly argued against unconditional election. He concluded by asking again for a national synod with hopes for a revision of the Confession. Gomarus appeared before the States General and accused Arminius of errors on not only original sin, divine foreknowledge, predestination, regeneration, good works, and the possibility of apostasy, but also the Trinity and biblical authority. While the States General did not support Gomarus, the controversy became more heated.

In August of 1609, the States General invited Arminius and Gomarus back for a conference. They were each to bring four other colleagues. Yet Arminius's illness, which had been worsening, made it impossible for him to continue the conference, which was dismissed. The States General asked the two men to submit their views in writing within two weeks. Arminius never completed his, owing to his illness, and he died on October 19, 1609.

Arminius's Theological Context

To understand Arminius's life as a theologian, one must understand the historical background of confessional theology in the Reformed Church in the Netherlands during his lifetime. Most of the interpretations of Arminius's theology have been based on misconceptions about Arminius's life and context.[5] Carl Bangs noted that interpreters of Arminius commonly misunderstand basic facts about him and his context.[6] They mistakenly think that Arminius was reared and educated amidst Calvinism and accepted Genevan Calvinism. They also misunderstand that as a student of Theodore Beza he accepted supralapsarianism and that, while preparing to refute Dirck Coornhert, he changed his mind and went over to Coornhert's humanism and that thus his theology was a polemic against Reformed theology. None of these things, as Bangs has shown, are true.[7]

---

4. W. Stephen Gunter, *Arminius and His Declaration of Sentiments: An Annotated Translation with Introduction and Theological Commentary* (Waco, TX: Baylor University Press, 2012).
5. The information in this section relies heavily on Bangs, "Arminius and the Reformation," 155–60.
6. These misconceptions arise from the Peter Bertius's funeral oration for Arminius and Caspar Brandt's *Life of James Arminius*.
7. See Bangs, *Arminius*, 139–42.

Arminius was not predisposed to a supralapsarian view of predestination. He rather shared the views of numerous Reformed theologians and pastors before him. The origins of the Reformed Church in the Netherlands were diverse, both historically and theologically. When Calvin published his views on predestination in the 1540s, many within the Reformed churches reacted negatively. When Sabastien Castellio disagreed with Calvin's view of predestination, he was banished from Geneva but was given asylum by the Reformed in Basel and soon offered a professorship there. It was said that, in Basel, "if one wishes to scold another, he calls him a Calvinist."[8]

Another Reformed theologian who reacted negatively to Calvin's doctrine of predestination was Jerome Bolsec, who settled in Geneva in 1550. When Calvin and Beza sent a list of Bolsec's errors to the Swiss churches, they were disappointed with the response. The church of Basel urged that Calvin and Bolsec try to emphasize their similarities. The ministers of Bern reminded Calvin of the many biblical texts that refer to God's universal grace. Even Heinrich Bullinger disagreed with Calvin's soteriology. Bangs notes that "the most consistent resistance to [Calvin's] predestination theory came from the German-speaking cantons." Even in Geneva there was a fair amount of resistance. This is evidenced by the presence of Charles Perrot, whose views diverged from Calvin's, on the faculty of the University of Geneva even during Beza's lifetime.[9]

"From the very beginnings of the introduction of Reformed religion in the Low Countries," says Bangs, "the milder views of the Swiss cantons were in evidence." Because of Roman Catholic persecution, the first Dutch Reformed synod was held at the Reformed church in Emden. The church's pastor, Albert Hardenberg, who was closer to Philip Melanchthon than to Calvin on predestination, exerted great influence on the early leaders in the Dutch Reformed churches—most notably Clement Martenson and John Isbrandtson, who openly opposed the spread of Genevan Calvinism in the Low Countries. At the Synod of Emden in 1571, the Heidelberg Catechism and the Belgic Confession of Faith were adopted. Both these documents allowed room for disagreement on the doctrines of grace and predestination, but some Geneva-educated ministers began attempts to enforce a stricter interpretation of them.[10]

Thus two parties arose in the Dutch Reformed Church. Those who were less inclined to a Calvinistic view of predestination tended to prefer a form of Erastianism (in which the magistrates controlled discipline in the church) and toleration toward Lutherans and Anabaptists, while the Genevan elements wanted strict adherence to Calvinism and Presbyterian church government.

---

8. Bangs, "Arminius and the Reformation," 157.
9. Bangs, "Arminius and the Reformation," 158.
10. Bangs, "Arminius and the Reformation," 159.

The laity, including the magistrates, tended toward the former, while more clergy tended toward the latter. However, a significant number of clergy clung to non-Calvinistic views of predestination. As Johannes Trapman notes, the States General "never wished to define the Reformed Religion so strictly as to exclude those who accepted only conditional predestination, that is 'some' ministers, 'many' magistrates, and 'countless' church members."[11]

As late as 1586, Caspar Coolhaes, a Reformed pastor in Leiden, after being excommunicated by the national synod at the Hague, was supported by the magistrates at Leiden.[12] The provincial synod of Haarlem of 1582 deposed and excommunicated him, an action opposed by the magistrates and some ministers of Leiden, the Hague, Dort, and Gouda. The Synod also attempted to force the Dutch churches to accept a rigid doctrine of predestination but did not succeed. As Bangs says, Coohaes "continued to write, with the support of the States of Holland and the magistrates of Leiden. A compromise reconciliation between the two factions was attempted, but it was not successful. This indicates something of a mixed situation in the Reformed churches of Holland at the time that Arminius was emerging as a theologian."[13] Thus there was no clear consensus on the doctrines of grace and predestination in the Dutch Reformed churches of Arminius's time.[14]

The Remonstrants and the Synod of Dort

While Arminius was still living, some of the local synods required their ministers to state their views on the Belgic Confession and Heidelberg Catechism.[15] This move concerned the States General, which saw this as a challenge to its power. Thus it ordered that the ministers in question submit their views to the States General. In 1610, not long after Arminius's death, some of his followers, led by men such as Johannes Uytenbogaert, Simon Episcopius, and Hugo Grotius, and supported by political leaders such as Johan van Oldenbarnevelt, issued an entreaty to the States General known as a Remonstrance. Thus they came to be known as "Remonstrants," and the Calvinists were dubbed "Counter-Remonstrants."

---

11. Johannes Trapman, "Grotius and Erasmus," in *Hugo Grotius, Theologian: Essays in Honor of G. H. M. Posthumus Meyjes*, eds. Henk J. M. Nellen and Edwin Rabbie (Leiden: Brill, 1994), 86.
12. Linda Stuckrath Gottschalk, *Pleading for Diversity: The Church Caspar Coolhaes Wanted* (Göttingen: Vandenhoek and Ruprecth, 2017), 106–10; Bangs, *Arminius*, 54–55. Coolhaes taught at the University of Leiden while Arminius was a student there. The first rigid predestinarian did not teach at the University until the arrival of Lambert Daneau.
13. Bangs, "Arminius and the Reformation," 160. See also Gottschalk, *Pleading for Diversity*, 114–15.
14. Bangs, *Arminius*, 51–55.
15. Much of this material about the Remonstrants relies on Picirilli, *Grace, Faith, Free Will*, 3–17.

Tensions continued to heighten after the publication of the Remonstrance. The States General desired peace, and the Remonstrants were protected by many in positions of political power. The Remonstrants continued to call for a national synod, as Arminius had, that would rationally and peacefully resolve the issue. Maurice, Prince of Orange, who had been mentored by Oldenbarnevelt, came increasingly to see the Calvinists as his political allies. Maurice wanted to go to war with Roman Catholic Spain, and he began to convince people that the Arminians were Roman Catholic sympathizers. This stacked the deck of the national synod, called in 1618, against the Arminians.

The States General called together this synod to begin May 1, 1618. Soon Oldenbarnevelt and Grotius were arrested, thus further predisposing the synod to oppose the Arminian party. The synod finally convened in Dordrecht—thus the name "Synod of Dort"—in November of 1618 and lasted to May of 1619. Although most of the delegates were from the Low Countries, twenty-seven of them came from elsewhere on the European continent as well as from the British Isles. Though it was directed that Remonstrants not be selected as delegates, three were initially, though they were required to yield their places to Calvinists. Thus the Synod essentially treated the Remonstrants as defendants, charged them with heresy, and required them to appear before the Synod and respond to the charges.

Episcopius, speaking for the Remonstrant party, attempted to work their strategy of starting with a refutation of Calvinism, especially reprobation, hoping to gain support. Yet the Synod would not allow him to do so, instead ordering the Remonstrants to "justify themselves, by giving Scriptural proof in support of their opinions." However, the Remonstrants would not give in to this method and were forced to withdraw from the proceedings of the Synod, which continued without them present.[16]

In January of 1619, the Synod dismissed the Remonstrants and denounced them as heretics.[17] The Belgic Confession and Heidelberg Catechism were officially adopted. However, a third document, the Canons of Dort, was added, which crystallized what are often known as the "five points of Calvinism" as the official teaching of the Reformed churches. Thus these three documents, which came to be known as the "Three Forms of Unity," formed the

---

16. Herman J. Selderhuis, "Introduction to the Synod of Dort (1618–1619)," in *Acta et Documenta Synodi Nationalis Dordrechtanae (1618–1619)*, vol. 1, *Acta of the Synod of Dort*, eds. Donald Sinnema, Christian Moser, and Herman J. Selderhuis (Göttingen: Vandenhoeck and Ruprecht, 2015), xvii–xviii; Thomas Scott, *The Articles of Synod of Dort* (Philadelphia: Presbyterian Board of Publication, 1856), 5.

17. Th. Marius Van Leeuwen, "Introduction: Arminius, Arminianism, and Europe," in *Arminius, Arminianism, and Europe*, ed. Th. Marius van Leeuwen, Keith D. Stanglin, and Marijke Tolsma (Leiden: Brill, 2009), xvii–xviii; see also R. Scott Clark's insightful essay, "Are the Remonstrants Heretics?" at https://heidelblog.net/2017/05/are-the-remonstrants-heretics-1. Accessed February 27, 2020.

confessional basis of the Reformed Church from that point forward. As will be argued in Question 8, the Canons of Dort were needed because neither the Belgic Confession of Faith nor the Heidelberg Catechism clearly taught the five points of Calvinism.

The Remonstrants were punished mercilessly. Two hundred ministers were stripped of their livelihood as ministers, and many were exiled. Many of the Remonstrants were imprisoned, yet some escaped to other countries that extended them more tolerance. Hugo Grotius, for example, escaped to England. As Th. Marius van Leeuwen says, however, this hostility backfired, causing many to have sympathy for the Remonstrants. Many of the English delegates to the Synod came to it against Arminianism but left in favor of it. One English visitor, reflecting on when he heard Episcopius speak, said, "There I bid Calvin good-night." The English "were shocked by the way in which the Remonstrants had been expelled from the church." After Prince Maurice's death in 1625, however, the Remonstrants were tolerated in the Netherlands. They started a school at which Episcopius and Grotius served as faculty members.[18]

Even at this early stage, Remonstrant theology had begun to move away from the more Reformed theology of Arminius.[19] Grotius's and Episcopius's views represented departures from the more Reformed views on original sin, atonement, and justification Arminius had taught, and later thinkers such as Philipp van Limborch diverged even farther from Arminius.[20] However, an approach more like that of Arminius would continue. During the seventeenth century, General Baptists such as Thomas Helwys and Thomas Grantham

---

18. Van Leeuwen, "Introduction," xviii–xx; G. J. Hoenderdaal, "The Debate about Arminius outside the Netherlands," in *Leiden University in the Seventeenth Century: An Exchange of Learning*, ed. Th. H. Lunsingh Scheurleer and G. H. M. Posthumus Meyjes (Leiden: Brill, 1975), 153.

19. See, e.g., William den Boer, *God's Twofold Love: The Theology of Jacob Arminius (1559–1609)* (Göttingen: Vandenhoeck and Ruprecht, 2010), who explains that there was a "significant theological shift from Arminius to Episcopius. This shift can be characterized as one from 'faith and justification' to 'repentance, sanctification and good works'" (39).

20. In addition to den Boer, *God's Twofold Love*, 38–39, see also, e.g., Mark A. Ellis, *Simon Episcopius' Doctrine of Original Sin* (New York: Peter Lang, 2006); W. Stephen Gunter, "From Arminius (d. 1609) to the Synod of Dort (1618–1619)," in *Perfecting Perfection: Essays in Honour of Henry D. Rack*, ed. Robert Webster (Cambridge: James Clarke and Company, 2016), 8–28; John Mark Hicks, "The Theology of Grace in the Thought of Jacobus Arminius and Philip van Limborch: A Study in the Development of Seventeenth Century Dutch Arminianism" (Ph.D. diss., Westminster Theological Seminary, 1985); Sarah Mortimer, *Reason and Religion in the English Revolution* (Cambridge: Cambridge University Press, 2010), 25–26, 119–25; Moses Stuart, "The Creed of Arminius," *Biblical Repository* 1 (1831): 303–4. As Gunter argues, "it was an altered form of Arminius's theology that we find on trial at Dort" (Gunter, "From Arminius (d. 1609) to the Synod of Dort (1618–1619)," 8n2).

were teaching views on the doctrine of salvation that were very close to those of Arminius.[21]

Summary

Arminius was a self-consciously Reformed pastor and professor who represented a broader approach to Reformed soteriology that was tolerated in his day but came under increasing scrutiny as Reformed theology began to be increasingly influenced by Genevan Calvinism. Arminius's theology must be pieced together from his scattered theological writings. He was not able to produce a fully formed theological system, which he could have perhaps produced had his poor health not cut his life short in 1609. Thus some of Arminius's theology is incomplete and ambiguous and does not answer all the questions that would be fleshed out in later Arminian theological systems. The Remonstrants soon began moving away from the Reformed caste of Arminius's theology.

One wonders, had Arminius lived another decade, if his conciliatory spirit and Reformed sensibilities might have brought about a different outcome in the theo-political situation of the Netherlands in the early seventeenth-century and thus the Synod of Dort. One wonders if Dort may have, in that case, allowed for more diversity in expressions of Reformed theology than it did.

REFLECTION QUESTIONS

1. What were Arminius's detractors' primary accusations regarding his theology?

2. Was Arminius reared and educated amidst Calvinism in a Calvinist country?

3. What does Arminius's being asked to refute Dirck Coornhert say about his alleged former commitment to Genevan Calvinism?

4. What became of Arminius's followers after his death?

5. Who in the seventeenth century were closer to Arminius's theology, the Remonstrants or the General Baptists?

---

21. For more on this stream of soteriology, see J. Matthew Pinson, *Arminian and Baptist: Explorations in a Theological Tradition* (Nashville: Randall House, 2015).

QUESTION 2

What Is Calvinism?

The words "Calvinism" and "Reformed" mean many different things. Calvinism is a subset of the Reformed movement, which started with Protestant Reformers (such as Huldrych Zwingli) on the European continent. In its early days, the use of "Reformed" came to be a demarcation from the Lutheran wing of the Reformation. However, in the sixteenth and seventeenth centuries, the use of "reformed" was not limited to Calvinists, because the term meant "reformed according to Scripture," in comparison with the Roman Church, which was unreformed. Thus various non-Calvinists, Amyraldians, English Dissenters, and Anabaptists thought of themselves as "reformed," as in "reformed according to Scripture."

Even among those in denominations that later came to be known officially as "Reformed," the word meant more than just holding to a Calvinist view of salvation. It often was ecclesiological, referring to a presbyterial form of church polity or a particular view of the sacraments. Thus, from this vantage point, the word "Reformed" describes something much broader than simply belief in the five points of Calvinism.[1]

Likewise, "Calvinist" carries connotations other than someone who affirms the five points of Calvinism. Many people today, especially in the Kuyperian "Neo-Calvinist" movement, think more about an approach to the Christian worldview or to society and culture when they call themselves Calvinists than about a given theology of salvation. People like Alvin Plantinga and Nicholas Wolterstorff come to mind. Plantinga, for example, says, "As for my view of

---

1. For two viewpoints that bear some similarities to this one, see Roger E. Olson, *Arminian Theology: Myths and Realities* (Downers Grove, IL: IVP Academic, 2006), 44–60, and Oliver D. Crisp, *Saving Calvinism: Expanding the Reformed Tradition* (Downers Grove, IL: IVP Academic, 2016), 25–46. The five points of Calvinism have typically been designated by the acronym TULIP: total depravity, unconditional election, limited atonement, irresistible grace, and perseverance of the saints. More information on these five points will be provided later in this chapter.

the Synod of Dort, I think that the Arminians should also be thought of as Calvinists. They thought of themselves as Calvinists. The synod declared that they weren't, but this was probably a mistake."[2]

As Question 6 will show, it is possible to be Arminian, demurring from the doctrines of particular and irresistible grace, and still be Reformed. For example, Jacobus Arminius saw himself as fully Reformed and affirmed the Reformed doctrinal standards, the Belgic Confession of Faith and Heidelberg Catechism. It is also possible to be Calvinistic in one's view of salvation but not be Calvinistic or Reformed with regard to any number of traditionally Reformed affirmations—the church or culture or eschatology or the charismatic gifts or religious epistemology (the knowledge of God). This book, however, deals with the doctrine of salvation. So the word "Calvinism" here will refer primarily to the "five points of Calvinism," or to less consistent permutations of Calvinism such as four-point Calvinism and the approach known as "once-saved, always-saved."[3]

Calvin and the Calvinists

Probably the most influential figure in the diverse phenomenon known as Calvinism is the man who gave the movement its name, the French Protestant reformer John Calvin (1509–1564).[4] Having studied classics at Paris and law at Orleans and Bourges, Calvin became a Protestant in 1533. Three years later, because of the mounting pressure against Protestants, he left Paris and moved to Basel, publishing his first edition of *Institutes of the Christian Religion*. Soon the reformer Guillaume Farel in Geneva convinced Calvin to come and assist him in the Reformation there.

---

2. Alvin Plantinga, "The Philosophy of Religion," in *God's Advocates: Christian Thinkers in Conversation*, ed. Rupert Shortt (Grand Rapids: Eerdmans, 2005), 53, quoted in Richard E. Clark, "The Calvinism of Arminius" (unpublished M.A. thesis, New Orleans Baptist Theological Seminary, 2018), 54.

3. I understand that many adherents of "once-saved, always-saved" who do not affirm unconditional election and irresistible grace will not like their position being termed a "permutation of Calvinism," but I am convinced that they never would have held that position had they not emerged from Calvinist confessional traditions. Thus I think it is accurate to refer to "once-saved, always-saved" as a "permutation" of Calvinism. I acknowledge my bias as one who is a member of a church body that has been confessionally Arminian on the "fifth point" for four centuries.

4. While "Calvinism," even in its soteriological form, received its character not just from Calvin but from diverse figures such as Huldrych Zwingli, Martin Bucer, Johannes Oecolampadius, Peter Martyr Vermigli, Heinrich Bullinger, William Perkins, and others, I will appeal primarily to the theology of Calvin as representative of this movement. For more on the fact that Calvinism is more than merely the theology of Calvin, see chapters 1 and 2 of Kenneth J. Stewart, *Ten Myths about Calvinism: Recovering the Breadth of the Reformed Tradition* (Downers Grove, IL: IVP Academic, 2011) and Carl Trueman, "Calvin and Calvinism" in *The Cambridge Companion to John Calvin*, ed. Donald K. McKim (Cambridge: Cambridge University Press, 2004).

From his post in Geneva, Calvin exerted an inestimable influence on Reformation thought and practice. This influence was not limited to the continent. It was also felt in the developing Reformation churches in England and Scotland, where many from these churches were exiled by Queen "Bloody Mary" of England in the 1550s, later known as "Puritans." Many of Calvin's views on the five "solas"—*sola Scriptura* (Scripture alone), *sola gratia* (grace alone), *sola fide* (faith alone), *solus Christus* (Christ alone), and *soli Deo gloria* (to the glory of God alone)—and on reforming the church according to Scripture were mediated through the Puritan movement even to many who demurred from the five points of Calvinism, such as the General Baptists and Arminian Puritans like John Goodwin.

Calvinism as a soteriological system arose from Calvin's views as expressed in subsequent editions of his *Institutes* and in his commentaries on the Bible. Yet followers of Calvin such as Theodore Beza and Jerome Zanchius almost immediately began to harden Calvin's doctrines into what later came to be known as the five points of Calvinism. However, other scholars such as Arminius and Moise Amyraut reacted against this crystallization, moderating Calvin's teaching in ways that they believed were consistent with the confessions and catechisms of the Reformed churches. This hardening of Calvinist theology can be seen most clearly in Calvinism's battle with Jacobus Arminius and his followers, the Remonstrants, whose views were condemned at the Synod of Dort in 1619. Seventeenth-century Reformed scholastics such as Francis Turretin and John Owen were a part of this development of Calvin's theology and that of other early Reformed thinkers like him.

There is a strong movement in modern scholarship that attempts to drive a wedge between Calvin and the Calvinists.[5] These scholars argue, for example, that limited atonement and supralapsarianism were introduced by later Calvinists and were not characteristic of the theology of Calvin himself. Whether Calvinism hardened in the years leading up to and following the Synod of Dort is beyond the scope of this book.[6] However, there is no

---

5. See, e.g., R. T. Kendall, *Calvin and English Calvinism to 1649* (Oxford: Oxford University Press, 1978); Holmes Rolston, III, *Calvin versus the Westminster Confession* (Louisville: John Knox, 1972); Tony Lane, "The Quest for the Historical Calvin," *Evangelical Quarterly* 55 (1983): 95–113 (which lists a number of other scholars of the "Calvin vs. the Calvinists" school); Basil Hall, "Calvin against the Calvinists," in *John Calvin: A Collection of Essays*, ed. G. E. Duffield (Grand Rapids: Eerdmans, 1968), 19–37; Brian G. Armstrong, *Calvinism and the Amyraut Heresy: Protestant Scholasticism and Humanism in Seventeenth Century France* (Madison: University of Wisconsin Press, 1969).

6. For an opposing view to the "Calvin vs. the Calvinists" perspective, see Richard A. Muller, *Calvin and the Reformed Tradition* (Grand Rapids: Baker Academic, 2012). Muller does not like to use the word "Calvinism" but instead prefers to use the word "Reformed" and, quite unlike the approach of this book, tightens the word to involve what most people mean by "soteriological Calvinism." These internecine Calvinist disputes regarding how Calvinist Calvin was are of limited interest for this study.

question that *Reformed* theology, as redefined by the Synod of Dort, hardened into a strict Calvinist system (see Question 8).

The system of Calvinism as it developed at and after the Synod of Dort has popularly been divided into five points explained by the acronym TULIP: T for Total Depravity, U for Unconditional Election, L for Limited Atonement, I for Irresistible Grace, and P for Perseverance of the Saints. In some ways, TULIP is a misnomer, because the first "head of doctrine" in the Canons of Dort has to do with unconditional election, the second with atonement, the third and fourth with total depravity and irresistible grace or effectual calling, and the fifth with perseverance.[7] This ordering at Dort is more coherent with the Calvinist system because it starts with unconditional election: The reason God chooses certain people unconditionally is because he directly foreordains every aspect of reality. Thus God's determination of all things, not depravity, is the reason for unconditional election.

Because TULIP is such a commonly used and easily remembered acronym for the "five points of Calvinism," this book will use it.[8] The remainder of this chapter will take each "petal" of the TULIP one-by-one, discussing primarily Calvin's *Institutes*, the Canons of Dort, and the Westminster Confession of Faith and Larger Catechism as representative Calvinist sources.[9] This is necessary because the Belgic Confession and Heidelberg Catechism do not affirm soteriological Calvinism (see Question 8).

Total Depravity

Calvin and his followers have consistently taught that human beings are totally depraved and unable to be converted apart from a radical intervention of God's grace, which they argue is irresistible.[10] Calvin said that Paul's intention in Romans 3 is to teach people that "they have all been overwhelmed by an

---

7. Herman J. Selderhuis, "Introduction to the Synod of Dort (1618–1619)," in *Acta et Documenta Synodi Nationalis Dordrechtanae*, ed. Donald Sinnema, Christian Moser, and Herman J. Selderhuis *(1618–1619)*, vol. 1, *Acta of the Synod of Dort* (Göttingen: Vandenhoeck and Ruprecht, 2015), xxxi.

8. Still, however, Richard Muller's concerns about the popular acronym are valid. See chapter 2 of his excellent work *Calvin and the Reformed Tradition*. See also Selderhuis, xxx–xxxii and chapter 3 of Stewart, discussing one of his myths of Calvinism, that "TULIP is the Yardstick of the Truly Reformed."

9. All quotations from the Canons of Dort and Westminster Larger Catechism come from the Puritan Reformed Theological Seminary website at https://prts.edu/wp-content/uploads/2016/12/Canons-of-Dort-with-Intro.pdf and https://prts.edu/wp-content/uploads/2013/09/Larger_Catechism.pdf. All quotations of the Westminster Confession of Faith come from the Westminster Theological Seminary website at: http://files1.wts.edu/uploads/pdf/about/WCF_30.pdf.

10. Muller correctly observes, "Whereas Calvin himself used phrases like 'totally depraved' or 'utterly perverse,' . . . the language of the Canons of Dort is more measured than that of Calvin." Muller is, rightly, attempting to avoid the "grizzly" concept of the "utter replacement" of the image of God in humanity (*Calvin and the Reformed Tradition*, 59–60). Total

unavoidable calamity from which only God's mercy can deliver them." People are sinful, Calvin argued, "not merely by the defect of depraved custom, but also by depravity of nature." Outside of God's mercy, "there is no salvation for man, for in himself he is lost and forsaken. . . . it is futile to seek anything good in our nature" (*Institutes*, 2.3.2).[11] Because the will is in "bondage to sin," Calvin held, it "cannot move toward good, much less apply itself thereto; for a movement of this sort is the beginning of conversion to God, which in Scripture is ascribed entirely to God's grace. . . . Therefore simply to will is of man; to will ill, of a corrupt nature; to will well, of grace" (2.3.5).

This doctrine is upheld by the Canons of Dort, which explain that, because "all men are conceived in sin, and by nature children of wrath," they are "incapable of saving good, prone to evil, dead in sin, and in bondage thereto." Unless God regenerates them, they are "neither able nor willing to return to God, to reform the depravity of their nature, or to dispose themselves to reformation" (heads 3–4, art. 3). These same doctrines are repeated in the Westminster Confession (9.3) and Larger Catechism (Q. 25).

Unconditional Election

To understand Calvin's doctrine of unconditional election, we must understand his doctrine of the divine foreordination of all things. Election has to be unconditional because God, to be God, must be the sole determiner of all things. Human beings "are governed by God's secret plan," Calvin averred, "in such a way that nothing happens except what is knowingly and willingly decreed by him" (1.16.3).

From eternity, God "decreed what he was to do, and now by his power executes what he decreed. Hence we maintain, that by His providence, not heaven and earth and inanimate creatures only, but also the counsels and wills of men are so governed as to move exactly in the course which he has destined" (1.16.8).[12] This is not the same thing as saying that God's providence upholds the universe and is guiding it to his divine ends, as Arminians and all orthodox Christians have always believed. Rather, it is the direct determination of every detail of reality to be exactly as God desires it to be. Calvin went on to say that "men can accomplish nothing except by God's secret command," that "they cannot by deliberating accomplish anything except what he has already decreed with himself and determines by his secret direction"

---

depravity does not entail that fallen people are as sinful as they can be, but simply that every aspect of a person is depraved.

11. Unless otherwise noted, Calvin quotations in this chapter come from John Calvin, *Institutes of the Christian Religion*, ed. John T. McNeill, trans. Ford Lewis Battles (Louisville: Westminster John Knox, 2006). It will be cited parenthetically in the text as *Institutes*.

12. This rendering is from the translation by Henry Beveridge, Jean Calvin, *Institutes of the Christian Religion*, trans. Henry Beveridge (Edinburgh: Calvin Translation Society, 1845), 1:242.

(1.18.1). In other words, every detail in God's universe will play out precisely as he wants it to.

Thus one can see why Calvin's view of predestination is unconditional: "We call predestination God's eternal decree, by which he compacted with himself what he willed to become of each man." For Calvin, "all are not created in equal condition; rather eternal life is foreordained for some, eternal damnation for others. Therefore, as any man has been created to one or the other of these ends, we speak of him as predestined to life or to death" (3.21.5). God "established by his eternal and unchangeable plan those whom he long before determined once for all to receive into salvation, and those whom, on the other hand, he would devote to destruction . . . he has barred the door of life to those whom he has given over to damnation" (3.21.7).

Why does God elect some people and reprobate others? Calvin answered that "we cannot determine a reason why he vouchsafes mercy to his own, except that it so pleases him, neither shall we have any reason for rejecting others, other than his will" (3.22.11). Despite assertions like these, there is debate among Calvinist scholars about whether Calvin believes that God directly reprobates people (double predestination) or simply passes over them (single predestination). However, one must bear in mind that, either way, God is directly foreordaining everything about them and arranging the world in such a way that they will be reprobate. "Therefore, those whom God passes over, he condemns; and this he does for no other reason than that he wills to exclude them from the inheritance which he predestines for his own children" (3.23.1). Thus the reprobate are "born destined for certain death from the womb, who glorify his name by their own destruction" (3.23.6).

The Canons of Dort concur with Calvin on unconditional election. In God's eternal decree, he "graciously softens" the hearts of the elect and "inclines them to believe." The Canons of Dort, however, are a bit softer than Calvin in avoiding double-predestinarian language, though, again, the difference does not really matter if God gets every detail of human choice exactly as he wants it. Still, the language of the Canons are softer in stating that God "leaves the non-elect in His just judgment to their own wickedness and obduracy" (head 1, art. 6).

Limited Atonement

Calvin did not unambiguously subscribe to a limited or definite atonement. David Allen's treatment of Calvin as believing that Christ died for all is more convincing than the views of those who agree with Roger Nicole that Calvin argued that Christ died only for the elect.[13] However, notwithstanding

---

13. See David L. Allen, *The Extent of the Atonement: A Historical and Critical Review* (Nashville: B&H Academic, 2016), 48–96; R. Nicole, "John Calvin's View of the Extent of the Atonement," *Westminster Theological Journal* 47 (1985): 197–225.

Calvin's views, the Synod of Dort certainly seems to have articulated limited atonement, and I think this is the most consistent Calvinist posture.

Still, there are differences of opinion on whether the Canons of Dort affirm limited atonement. The Canons state that the death of Christ provides redemption for "all those, and those only, who were from eternity chosen to salvation and given to Him by the Father" (head 2, art. 8). Furthermore, in its "rejections" under the second head of Doctrine, the Synod rejected as error the view that "God the Father has ordained His Son to the death of the cross without a certain and definite decree to save any, so that the necessity, profitableness, and worth of what Christ merited by His death might have existed, and might remain in all its parts complete, perfect, and intact, even if the merited redemption had never in fact been applied to any person" (head 2, rej. 1). These statements seem to affirm limited atonement. Yet even these sections, which are troubling to Arminians, have been interpreted by hypothetical universalist Calvinists such as John Davenant and Richard Baxter and their modern followers as allowing for unlimited atonement, strictly speaking (that the atonement is sufficient for the world but efficient only for the elect).[14]

Many Calvinists prefer to speak of definite atonement or particular redemption because, more than "limited atonement," these phrases highlight that the atonement is purchasing redemption expressly and only for the elect.[15] This involves reinterpreting the universal atonement passages that the consensus of the church catholic has interpreted universally. The Calvinist has to say that "all" or "the world" means "all kinds of people." For most Christians, even many strong Calvinists, this stretches the bounds of credulity.[16] Increasingly, limited atonement does not seem to be a viable option, even for those Calvinists who accept unconditional election and irresistible grace. However, Arminians believe that limited atonement is the only

---

14. See Lee Gatiss, "The Synod of Dort and Definite Atonement," in *From Heaven He Came and Sought Her: Definite Atonement in Historical, Biblical, Theological, and Pastoral Persepctive*, eds. David Gibson and Jonathan Gibson (Wheaton, IL: Crossway, 2013), 162–63. Cf. Allen, *The Extent of the Atonement*, 177–84, 200–4; Muller, *Calvin and the Reformed Tradition*, 70–106; Michael J. Lynch, *John Davenant's Hypothetical Universalism: A Defense of Catholic and Reformed Orthodoxy*, Oxford Studies in Historical Theology (New York: Oxford University Press, 2021).

15. See, e.g., R. C. Sproul, "Tulip and Reformed Theology: Limited Atonement," https://www.ligonier.org/blog/tulip-and-reformed-theology-limited-atonement).

16. This is indicated by the confessional standards of most of the world's Christian denominations, such as Lutheran, Wesleyan, Arminian, Catholic, Orthodox, Anabaptist, and Stone-Campbell Restorationist. Most Presbyterian and Reformed denominations explicitly affirm limited atonement and irresistible grace, while the Anglican Communion and most Baptist denominations have advocates of both limited and unlimited atonement and both *gratia resistibilis* and *gratia irresistibilis* within their membership. See Roger E. Olson, Frank S. Mead, et al., *Handbook of Denominations in the United States*, 14th ed. (Nashville: Abingdon, 2018).

consistent position to take on the extent of the atonement if one believes in unconditional election and irresistible grace as Calvinists do.

Irresistible Grace

Calvin certainly taught the doctrine of *gratia irresistibilis* (irresistible grace) or effectual calling.[17] Arminians believe that Calvin viewed divine grace in somewhat wooden terms, obscuring the biblical portrait of grace as a back-and-forth, relational dynamic between the divine person and the human persons he has created in his image as thinking, feeling, acting beings. For Calvin, the equation was clear-cut: Human beings are evil. Good cannot come from evil. So God, by simple fiat, has to change people's minds, hearts, and wills from evil to good. This, in short, was how Calvin portrayed irresistible grace. When human beings, "who are by nature inclined to evil" start to "will good," they do so "out of mere grace," because "nothing good can arise out of our will until it has been reformed" (2.3.8). Scripture does not teach "that the grace of a good will is bestowed upon us if we accept it and that He wills to work in us. This means nothing else than that the Lord by his Spirit directs, bends, and governs, our heart and reigns in it as in his own possession." Only those "on whom heavenly grace has breathed" seek after God. But this grace is only "the privilege of the elect, who through the Spirit's regeneration "are moved and governed by his leading" (2.3.10).

The Westminster Confession refers to this act as "effectual calling." Yet, while the language of "calling" bespeaks a wooing or persuading process, the Confession reiterates Calvin's cause-and-effect approach to grace. It says that God is pleased "in His appointed time, effectually to call, by His Word and Spirit, out of that state of sin and death . . . *determining them to that which is good*, and effectually drawing them to Jesus Christ: yet so, as they come most freely, being made willing by His grace" (10.1, italics added). This same tension between biblical motifs such as "drawing" and "calling" and more wooden, mechanical language such as "*powerfully determining* their wills" is present in the Westminster Larger Catechism (Q. 67, italics added).

Perseverance of the Saints

Calvin believed that those whom God unconditionally chooses and regenerates, and who therefore are determined to have faith, will continue in that regenerative grace and saving faith to the end of life. For Calvin, perseverance is

---

17. Some scholars discourage the use of "irresistible grace," perhaps because of its tie to popular polemics and the "TULIP" acronym. The fact is, however, that if one asks any Calvinist, "Do you believe one can resist divine prevenient grace?" he or she will always reply, "No." Many Reformed scholars acknowledge this. See, e.g., J. V. Fesko, "Arminius on *Facientibus Quod in Se Est*," in *Church and School in Early Modern Protestantism: Studies in Honor of Richard A. Muller on the Maturation of a Theological Tradition*, eds. Jordan J. Ballor, David S. Sytsma, and Jason Zuidema (Leiden: Brill, 2013), 353.

based on regeneration, which is based on election. Commenting on Matthew 15:13, where Jesus said that "every tree that my Father has not planted will be uprooted," Calvin said that "he conversely implies that those rooted in God can never be pulled up from salvation" (3.24.6). In his commentary on 1 John, Calvin stated that John "plainly declares that the Spirit continues his grace in us to the last, so that inflexible perseverance is added to newness of life. . . . the seed, communicated when God regenerates his elect, as it is incorruptible, retains its virtue perpetually."[18]

In discussing perseverance in the *Institutes*, Calvin reminds readers that perseverance, like election, is based solely on what God wants to happen to individuals and thus determines will happen to them. Sometimes Calvin almost sounds like an Arminian who believes people can fall from saving grace, but that the fall is caused by God, so that "only those whom it pleases the Lord to touch with his healing hand will get well. The others, whom he, in his righteous judgment, passes over, waste away in their own rottenness until they are consumed." This is the only reason why "some persevere to the end, while others fall at the beginning of their course. For perseverance itself is indeed also a gift from God, which he does not bestow on all indiscriminately, but imparts to whom he pleases" (2.5.3).

This perspective is more nuanced than the portrait most people have of Calvinist perseverance. It appears almost as though Calvin is saying that God causes certain regenerate people to fall away and others to persevere. Yet for Calvin, those who fall from grace have a temporary faith which is only a seeming faith. They were not truly regenerated by the Holy Spirit. As John Jefferson Davis remarks, for Calvin, the reprobate "may experience feelings of remorse for sin, make a public profession of faith, and yet not be truly regenerate." However, "such temporary faith is not to be confused with the genuine saving faith that endures to eternal life."[19]

While Calvin technically affirmed "once-saved, always-saved," he, unlike many modern-day advocates of that doctrine, insists on the perseverance of the *saints*. The Christian will necessarily persevere in faith *and holiness* until the end of life. Calvin averred that believers' hearts are "so effectually governed by the Spirit of God, that through an inflexible disposition they follow his guidance," and that the Spirit's power is "so effectual, that it necessarily retains us in continual obedience to righteousness."[20]

The Canons of Dort and Westminster Confession also bear out Calvin's doctrine of necessary perseverance. Once God has "conferred grace" on the

18. John Calvin, *Commentaries on the Catholic Epistles*, trans. John Owen (Grand Rapids: Eerdmans, 1948), 214. See John Jefferson Davis, "The Perseverance of the Saints: A History of the Doctrine," *Journal of the Evangelical Theological Society* 34 (1991): 213–28.
19. Davis, "The Perseverance of the Saints," 218.
20. John Calvin, *1, 2, & 3 John*, Crossway Classic Commentaries (Wheaton, IL: Crossway, 1998), 59.

saints, the Canons state, he "mercifully confirms and powerfully preserves them therein, even to the end" (head 5, art. 3). The Westminster Confession emphasizes the rootedness of perseverance in election and effectual calling: "They, whom God has accepted in His Beloved, effectually called, and sanctified by His Spirit, can neither totally nor finally fall away from the state of grace, but shall certainly persevere therein to the end. . . . This perseverance of the saints depends not upon their own free will, but upon the immutability of the decree of election" (3.17).

Summary

Though some people use "Reformed theology" as a synonym for "the five points of Calvinism," these terms mean different things to different people. While there is debate about how much later Calvinists hardened Calvin's doctrines into the five points of Calvinism, there is no doubt that they developed his doctrines with greater precision and imposed them with greater rigor on the Reformed Church.

Strong Calvinists hold that human beings are totally depraved and unable to be saved apart from a radical intervention of God's grace, which Calvinists usually say must be regeneration wrought by irresistible grace, not a resistible drawing grace. God chooses and predestines certain people for himself unconditionally and either directly reprobates the rest of humanity or leaves them in their sins. The most consistent Calvinists argue that Christ died only for the elect. Thus, if Christ purchased redemption only for them, and if this process is unconditional, then it follows that God will irresistibly draw them (or call them effectually) to himself and that this irresistible grace will of certainty continue to the end of life. These are the five points of Calvinism which offer an alternative to the Arminian theology that will be discussed in this book.

REFLECTION QUESTIONS

1. Are "Calvinism" and "Reformed theology" identical?

2. What are some of the ways in which later Calvinists differed from Calvin?

3. What is the relationship between God's direct foreordination of all things and the doctrine of unconditional election?

4. Why do many Calvinists believe that it is inconsistent to be a Calvinist yet believe that Christ died for everyone?

5. Is there a difference between Calvin's view that the elect will persevere in holiness and the modern view of once-saved, always-saved?

How Do Arminianism's Basic Doctrines Compare with Those of Calvinism?

A rminius was a Reformed theologian. Thus he agreed with the vast majority of what Calvin and his followers had taught. However, Arminius represented a strain of thinking in the Reformed churches prior to the Synod of Dort (1618–1619) that had always been broader than Calvinist predestinarianism (see Questions 7–8). In short, he agreed with Calvin and his followers on *what it means to be* in a state of grace, but he differed from them on *how one comes to be* in a state of grace. Thus, he agreed with Calvin on the depth of human sin and depravity and on *what it means to be* redeemed from sin: what Christ did to atone for sin, how that is applied in justification, and how Christians live it out in sanctification and spirituality. Yet he disagreed with Calvin on the details of *how one comes to be* in a state of grace: the doctrines of particular and resistible grace, and unconditional election.[1]

In reality, one could say that full-fledged Arminians are "one-point Calvinists." Recall the helpful way introduced in the last two chapters to remember the five points of Calvinism articulated at the Synod of Dort: TULIP—"T" for total depravity, "U" for unconditional election, "L" for limited atonement, "I" for irresistible grace, and "P" for perseverance of the saints. Most Calvinist authors have tended to see Arminians as denying all five of these points. However, Arminius strenuously argued for total depravity (see Question 15). Arminians who follow Arminius are fully Augustinian on what it means to be a sinful human being and what it means to be in a state of grace.

---

1. This broad approach is often referred to as "Reformed Arminianism," which, because of its agreement with Calvinism on the nature of atonement, justification, and sanctification, differs from classic Wesleyanism. For more detail on this, see the Introduction and the answers to Questions 3, 5, 9–11, 21, and 40.

In agreement with the Augustinian tradition, they affirm the Reformation doctrines of *sola gratia* and *sola fide*, wishing, as Arminius averred, to "maintain the greatest possible distance from Pelagianism."[2] Thus the notion that being an Arminian means being a semi-Pelagian, though often repeated in Calvinist circles, is a myth.[3]

Arminians, however, differ from Calvin on the other four points of Calvinism.[4] Instead of unconditional election, they believe that God sovereignly decreed that election be conditional; that is, God's election or predestination of a believer to eternal salvation is conditioned on God's foreknowledge of the believer in union with Christ. Instead of limited atonement, Arminians believe that Christ died for everyone and genuinely desires everyone's salvation. Instead of irresistible grace, Arminians believe that God, in his own mysterious manner and time, influences everyone with his enabling, calling, and drawing grace, without taking away their ability to resist it. Instead of the certain perseverance of the saints, Arminians believe that, just as divine grace is resistible prior to conversion, it continues to be resistible after conversion, thus making turning away from Christ a possibility.

This chapter and the next one will engage in a simple comparison and contrast of Calvinism and Arminianism. The next chapter will consider the differences between the two systems, while this one will discuss the things they have in common.

Total Depravity and Inability

Calvinism holds that humanity is radically depraved and thus has no natural ability to seek after God. This is why Calvinists say they believe that irresistible grace is necessary: God must, in their view, irresistibly draw to himself those he has unconditionally chosen and regenerate them. Then they will irresistibly be granted faith. Arminians also believe that humanity by nature is totally depraved and hence spiritually unable to desire the things of God without a supernatural, gracious intervention of the Holy Spirit. Thus, the difference between Arminians and Calvinists is not what they believe about humanity's total depravity and spiritual inability. Rather, it is about whom

---

2. Jacobus Arminius, "Apology against Thirty-One Defamatory Articles," in *The Works of James Arminius,* 3 vols., trans. James Nichols and William Nichols (Nashville: Randall House, 2007), 1:764.

3. That Arminians are not semi-Pelagians is affirmed not only by Arminians such as Roger E. Olson, but also by many Calvinists, e.g., Robert A. Peterson and Michael D. Williams. See Olson, *Arminian Theology: Myths and Realities* (Downers Grove, IL: IVP Academic, 2006), 18, 30–31; Peterson and Williams, *Why I Am Not an Arminian* (Downers Grove, IL: IVP Academic, 2004), 39.

4. Some advocates of eternal security who agree with Arminians on the other points of Calvinism have come to identify themselves as Arminians.

God graciously draws and influences and enables with his grace and whether they are able to resist that gracious drawing.

Still, Calvinists have for centuries characterized Arminius and his followers as semi-Pelagians who deny that humanity is totally depraved and thus wholly unable to be saved naturally without the intervention of the supernatural grace of the Holy Spirit. J. I. Packer is an example of this mischaracterization.[5] Quoting John Owen, he states that the earliest Remonstrants were "Belgic semi-Pelagians" who disagreed with the Calvinistic doctrine of human inability in salvation.[6]

This is a gross misrepresentation.[7] The earliest Remonstrants, following Arminius, said plainly that "man does not possess saving grace of himself, nor of the energy of his free will, inasmuch as in his state of apostasy and sin he can of and by himself neither think, will, nor do any thing that is truly good." Thus, without divine grace, humanity is characterized by utter depravity and inability in spiritual things. They went on to say that the "grace of God is the beginning, continuance, and accomplishment of all good, even to the extent that the regenerate man himself, without prevenient or assisting, awakening, following and cooperative grace, can neither think, will, nor do good, nor withstand any temptations to evil; so that all good deeds or movements that can be conceived must be ascribed to the grace of God in Christ."[8] In this sentiment, these earliest Remonstrants followed Arminius.

Wesleyanism also affirms this approach to depravity and inability. Richard Watson, the most influential early Methodist systematic theologian, stated that "the true Arminian, as fully as the Calvinist, admits the doctrine of the total depravity of human nature in consequence of the fall of our first parents." Watson said that, in this doctrine, Arminians and Calvinists "so well agree, that it is an entire delusion to represent this doctrine, as it is often done, as exclusively Calvinistic."[9] Thus, to argue that Arminianism is semi-Pelagian is to misrepresent Arminians, who clearly avoid the heresy of semi-Pelagianism

---

5. I hesitate to criticize Dr. Packer who, despite our differences on Arminianism, Calvinism, and other issues, had a tremendous impact on me when I took one of his courses—and took up too many of his office hours with questions and discussion!—at Regent College one summer nearly thirty years ago.

6. See Packer's otherwise superb book, *A Quest for Godliness: The Puritan Vision of the Christian Life* (Wheaton, IL: Crossway, 1990), 127.

7. An exception to the rule of Calvinists characterizing Arminians as semi-Pelagians is Peterson and Williams. They say that Arminians are "Semi-Augustinians" (40). I would say that, in the doctrines of the nature of sin and salvation, Reformed Arminians are fully Augustinian but that they are semi-Augustinian regarding questions of determinism, unconditional predestination, and irresistible grace. However, we must be careful with the term "semi-Augustinian" because of its synergistic undertones.

8. Five Articles of Remonstrance, in Philip Schaff, *The Creeds of Christendom* (New York: Harper and Brothers, 1877), 1:518.

9. Richard Watson, *Theological Institutes* (London: John Mason, 1829), 2:215. Not all those who call themselves Arminians affirm total depravity. For more information, see Question 15.

condemned at the Second Council of Orange (A.D. 529). On the doctrine of depravity and inability, most Arminians fall squarely in the Augustinian camp. Semi-Pelagianism is inconsistent with traditional Arminian theology of all varieties.[10]

The Nature of Atonement and Justification

Arminius and the Arminians who follow him have held strongly to a doctrine of penal substitutionary atonement and the imputation of the righteousness of Christ in justification. While atonement theories seem arcane to many people, it is at this point that one finds the most difference between Reformed theology and that of many Arminians. Some Arminians reject a penal satisfaction view of atonement, whereby Christ satisfies the justice of God by fulfilling the law in our stead and paying sin's penalty in our place. Their view issues forth in a more moralistic account of justification in which Christ's atoning work is not imputed to the believer; rather, the impartation of righteousness is the dominant theme. This doctrine of justification, unhinged from a thoroughgoing penal satisfaction understanding of atonement, results in legalistic and moralistic construals of sanctification, sin in the life of the believer, assurance, and perseverance.[11]

This is one reason Reformed Arminians place so much emphasis on a penal satisfaction approach to atonement. It brings the biblical themes of the Reformers back into the center of one's understanding of the priestly office of Christ: that he pays the penalty for sin and fulfills the law on one's behalf, and that perfect lawkeeping and penalty-payment is imputed to the believer through faith in him. That, and not believers' own righteousness, is what from start to finish makes them just and holy before God. Thus they can sing with the hymn writer, "Dressed in his righteousness alone/Faultless to stand before the throne."[12] There is no need for Arminians to jettison these beautiful biblical doctrines, throwing out the Reformed baby with the Calvinist bathwater.

Thomas Oden provides an example of a Wesleyan Methodist who retains the motifs of penal substitutionary and propitiatory atonement and the full imputation of the righteousness of Christ to the believing sinner. Oden argues

---

10. However, some who have *claimed* the Arminian label have said things that sound semi-Pelagian.

11. For more on the term "penal satisfaction," see footnote 25 in Question 10.

12. Edward Mote, "My Hope is Built on Nothing Less," *Rejoice: The Free Will Baptist Hymn Book* (Nashville: Executive Office, National Association of Free Will Baptists, 1988), no. 419. On the inextricable connection between penal substitutionary atonement and the imputation of the righteousness of Christ, see Forlines, *Classical Arminianism: A Theology of Salvation* (Nashville: Randall House, 2011), 211–21, and Stephen J. Wellum's important essay "'Behold, the Lamb of God': Theology Proper and the Inseparability of Penal Substitutionary Atonement from Forensic Justification and Imputation, in *The Doctrine on Which the Church Stands or Falls: Justification in Biblical, Theological, Historical, and Pastoral Perspective*, ed. Matthew Barrett (Wheaton, IL: Crossway, 2019), 351–86.

for "penal substitution as sufficient vicarious satisfaction" and states, "The benefits of Christ's obedience (active and passive) are accounted or reckoned to the believer."[13]

Sanctification

This Reformed approach to atonement and justification coheres with a Reformed approach to sanctification. Just because one is an Arminian on how people come to be in a state of grace, he or she does not have to disagree with the rich Reformed understanding of sanctification. The traditional doctrine of sanctification in Calvin and the larger Reformed tradition maintains a beautiful balance between antinomianism and legalism. It confesses a *sola gratia, sola fide* approach to sin in the believer's life that does not cause believers to despair of their justification in the ebb and flow of their growth in holiness, thus conflating justification and sanctification as many Arminian construals do.

F. Leroy Forlines's chapter on "Sanctification" in his *Classical Arminianism* is the best account of how one can achieve a biblical balance, benefitting from the Reformed doctrine of progressive sanctification propounded by Calvin as well as authors like John Owen and Sinclair Ferguson, yet still being Arminian.[14] This doctrine of sanctification also results in a more ordinary-means-of-grace approach to spirituality similar to that found in Puritan piety, as opposed to the mystical, crisis experience-oriented, higher life, and second-work-of-grace emphases of some Arminians.

Summary

Arminius, and many Arminians who followed him, agreed with Calvin and Calvinism on the basic teachings of the Reformed tradition. This included the theology of *what it means to be* in a state of grace. Yet, like others in the Reformed Church prior to the Synod of Dort who affirmed the classic Reformed confessional standards, the Belgic Confession of Faith and the Heidelberg Catechism, these Arminians have differed from Calvin and Calvinism on *how one comes to be* in a state of grace. Thus they have diverged from Calvinism on the last four points of the "TULIP," which the next chapter will consider.

---

13. Thomas C. Oden, *Classic Christianity: A Systematic Theology* (New York: HarperCollins, 1992), 409–10, 422.

14. F. Leroy Forlines, *Classical Arminianism: A Theology of Salvation* (Nashville: Randall House, 1999), 277–306. Cf. Sinclair Ferguson, *The Whole Christ: Legalism, Antinomianism, and Gospel Assurance—Why the Marrow Controversy Still Matters* (Wheaton, IL: Crossway, 2016); John Owen, *Of the Mortification of Sin in Believers*, reprinted unabridged with some of Owen's other works in John Owen, *Overcoming Sin and Temptation*, eds. Kelly M. Kapic and Justin Taylor (Wheaton, IL: Crossway, 2006), 41–140.

REFLECTION QUESTIONS

1. What is semi-Pelagianism and why are Arminians opposed to it?

2. What is meant by the terms "total depravity" and "inability"?

3. What did Arminius teach regarding penal substitutionary atonement?

4. What did Arminius teach regarding justification and the imputation of Christ's righteousness?

5. Can one be both Arminian and Reformed on sanctification and spirituality?

How Do Arminianism's Basic Doctrines Contrast with Those of Calvinism?

While Reformed Arminians and many other non-Calvinists agree with Calvin and Calvinism on the emphases discussed in the last chapter on *what it means to be* in a state of grace, they just as vigorously oppose them on *how one comes to be* in a state of grace. This chapter will discuss the last four points of the classic TULIP.

Unconditional Election

Arminians demur from Calvinism on the doctrine of unconditional election. As Questions 27–31 will discuss, Arminius believed in the doctrine of conditional, individual election. In this way he was much like the Lutheran scholastics of his day such as Niels Hemmingsen.[1] Arminius believed that, just as salvation was conditioned on being in Christ through faith *in time*, election was conditioned on being in Christ through faith *in eternity*. God knew his own individually and personally from all eternity because he foreknew them in Christ, according to his sovereignly decreed condition for that union.[2]

---

1. Henrik Frandsen, *Hemmingius in the Same World as Perkinsius and Arminius* (Praestoe, Denmark: Grafik Werk, 2013).
2. See Robert E. Picirilli, *Grace, Faith, Free Will: Contrasting Views of Salvation: Calvinism and Arminianism* (Nashville: Randall House, 2002), 53. Picirilli rightly points out that God *unconditionally* decrees that election be *conditional*. For an insightful account of conditional election from a Reformed Arminian perspective, see Kevin L. Hester, "Election and the Influence and Response Model of Personality," in *The Promise of Arminian Theology: Essays in Honor of F. Leroy Forlines*, eds. Matthew Steven Bracey and W. Jackson Watts (Nashville: Randall House, 2016), 55–80. For the difference between foreknowledge and foreordination, see Question 20.

Thus traditional Arminians such as Arminius and Wesley did not affirm the Calvinist notion of "election unto faith."[3] In their view, this doctrine involved God's embracing people with his elective love outside of Christ and then predestining them to be in Christ. Instead, God predestines persons to be his own for eternity *in Christ* via his foreknowledge of them in union with his Son. The reprobate are those whom God foreknows will not believe in Christ and continue in that unbelief. From eternity God *knew* those in union with Christ and, based on that foreknowledge, predestined them to be his chosen ones for eternity. Yet he did not foreknow those whom he comprehended, in his foreknowledge, would not be in union, and continue in union, with Christ through faith, and he predestined them to eternal separation from himself.[4]

Limited Atonement

Unlike some Calvinists who believe that it would be "wasteful" for Christ to die for the reprobate and that therefore God sent his son to die only for the elect, Arminians believe that God's desire that everyone be saved entails that Christ's atonement is for everyone (universal or general atonement, sometimes called general provision).[5] This gracious divine desire and provision is the basic thrust of Arminianism, which makes Arminians skeptical of the particularism of Calvinism. This is why it is so hard for Arminians to understand the notion of many Calvinists that there are, in essence, two wills in God for everyone's salvation. The latter distinguish between a revealed will that desires everyone's salvation and loves everyone and a secret will that desires the salvation of only the elect and salvifically loves only them.

Arminians likewise find the doctrine of two callings incommensurable with the overwhelming thrust of Holy Scripture. This is the teaching of Calvinism that there is one public calling that freely offers and preaches the gospel to all, just as most Christians always have, and another secret calling that only the elect can sense. All of this seems to the Arminian to fly in the face of the universal purpose of grace, the universal call of the gospel, and the

---

3. Many Arminian and Lutheran authors use this phrase to characterize Calvinism's view of election because Rejection 2 of the first head of Doctrine of the Canons of Dort suggests that "election unto faith" is the same thing as "election to salvation." https://prts.edu/wp-content/uploads/2016/12/Canons-of-Dort-with-Intro.pdf., accessed January 8, 2021; Matthias Loy, "Election and Justification," in *Lutheran Confessional Theology in America, 1840–1880*, ed. Theodore G. Tappert (New York: Oxford University Press, 1972), 209–22.

4. For treatments from this perspective, see Picirilli, *Grace, Faith, Free Will*, 19–84; Forlines, *Classical Arminianism: A Theology of Salvation* (Nashville: Randall House, 2011), 37–202; and Jack W. Cottrell, "Conditional Election" in *Grace for All: The Arminian Dynamics of Salvation*, eds. Clark H. Pinnock and John D. Wagner (Eugene, OR: Wipf and Stock, 2015), 69–92.

5. Roger E. Olson, *Arminian Theology: Myths and Realities* (Downers Grove, IL: IVP Academic, 2009), 223. The image of wastefulness is used, e.g., by Edwin H. Palmer in his widely read book *The Five Points of Calvinism* (Grand Rapids: Baker, 2010), 50.

universal atonement of Christ. This is exemplified in the seventeenth-century English General Baptist William Jeffery. Arguing against the Calvinist view of election, he said that it contradicted God's love for the world, because it entailed that God "did (before time) hate the greatest part of the world" and that

> (in time) he gives them up to hardness of heart (without grace at any time whereby to be saved) and at the day of Judgment will cast them into everlasting torments, because of their wickedness and hardness of heart; and yet declare in his Word, (which you say is a word of truth) that he is *good* to *all*, and that his "tender mercies are over *all* his works"; that he is "slow to anger, and of great mercy," (Ps. 145.8, 9), "patient, long-suffering," etc. (Ex. 34.6, 7), "not willing that *any* should perish" (2 Peter 3.9), swearing by himself, "that he desireth not the death of the wicked" (Ezek. 33:11) but "would have all men saved, and come to the knowledge of the truth" (1 Tim. 2.4), "forty years long grieving for the iniquity of his people" (Heb. 3.17), bemoaning their undone estate (Psal. 81.13), yea, even *weeping* for them (Luke 19.41), saying, "What could I have done more" (for your good) "that I have not done?" (Isa. 5.4), when as he knew (according to your tenet) that [he] himself had shut them up from all possibilities of believing unto salvation, and that by his own unresistible decree, and purpose of reprobation. Judge ye, friends, in this cause, and judge righteous judgment, and with fear and trembling, weigh these things.[6]

Because of his universal gracious purpose, or eternal counsel, Arminians confess, God sent his Son to atone, not only for the sins of the elect, but also for the sins of the entire world (1 John 2:2).[7]

Irresistible Grace

Calvinism affirms that if God loves and elects a certain number of people out of the mass of humanity, secretly desiring only their salvation and not the salvation of all people and thus sending Christ to atone only for their sins, he will give only them his special grace, and they will have neither the ability nor the desire to resist it. Another way of putting this is that he will regenerate

---

6. *The Whole Faith of Man* (London, 1659), 31–32. As with most of the other early modern English texts quoted in this book, the spelling, punctuation, and capitalization in this quotation have been modernized and some archaic words have been updated.
7. For arguments and references to works defending universal atonement, see Question 13.

them, and then they will desire salvation and will have no way not to desire it, no way to resist it.

Arminius and his theological descendants, however, believed that God reaches out to all humanity with his grace, without taking away their ability to resist. As the earliest Remonstrants stated:

> This grace of God is the beginning, continuance, and accomplishment of all good, even to the extent that the regenerate man himself, without prevenient or assisting, awakening, following and cooperative grace, can neither think, will, nor do good, nor withstand any temptations to evil; so that all good deeds or movements that can be conceived must be ascribed to the grace of God in Christ. But with respect to the mode of the operation of this grace, it is not irresistible, since it is written concerning many, that they have resisted the Holy Spirit (Acts 7, and elsewhere in many places).[8]

A passage from the nineteenth-century Free Will Baptist confession, the 1812 Abstract, expresses this doctrine:

> We believe that sinners are drawn to God the Father, by the Holy Ghost, through Christ His Son, and that the Holy Ghost offers His divine aid to all the human family, so as they might all be happy would they give place to His divine teaching; whereas, such who do not receive the divine impressions of the Holy Spirit, shall at a future day own their condemnation just and charge themselves with their own damnation, for willfully rejecting the offers of sovereign grace. (Matt. 11:17, John 6:44, 66; Ps. 1:1; Tit. 2:11, 12; Jer. 12:29)[9]

Thus Arminians, in contradistinction to Calvinists, believe that the grace by which God draws sinners to himself is not limited to the elect. That grace is sufficiently enabling, but resistible, by all those to whom it comes.[10]

---

8. Philip Schaff, *The Creeds of Christendom* (New York: Harper and Brothers, 1884), 1:518.

9. The 1812 Abstract is a confession of faith of the nineteenth-century Free Will Baptists in the American South that condenses the 1660 Standard Confession of their English General Baptist forebears. Art. 9, reprinted in J. Matthew Pinson, *A Free Will Baptist Handbook: Heritage, Beliefs, and Ministries* (Nashville: Randall House, 1998), 145.

10. Steve W. Lemke, though he does not prefer the designation "Arminian" but likes "traditional Baptist" instead, provides an insightful discussion of this doctrine in "A Biblical and Theological Critique of Irresistible Grace," in *Whosoever Will: A Biblical-Theological Critique of Five-Point Calvinism*, ed. David L. Allen and Steve W. Lemke (Nashville: B&H Academic, 2010), 109–62.

Certain Perseverance

Calvinists and their successors have historically embraced the doctrine of the certain perseverance of the saints. This includes those who emerged from Calvinist confessional backgrounds but jettisoned the predestinarian and irresistible-grace teachings of their tradition.[11] While historic Calvinists have believed that the true believer does indeed persevere in holiness (thus ruling out modern-day antinomian "pseudo-Calvinism"), they have held that all genuine believers will of necessity persevere in grace to the end of life. Another way of saying this is that grace continues to be irresistible after conversion. The historic Arminian confessional traditions have unanimously affirmed the possibility of the apostasy of genuine believers. However, differences of opinion have existed among Arminians on how apostasy occurs, or how often—that is, whether there is only one kind of apostasy and whether it is remediable.[12]

Reformed Arminians believe that the Bible teaches only one kind of apostasy: final apostasy, defection from saving faith (see Questions 33–40). This is a complete "shipwreck" of faith (1 Tim. 1:19). Such apostasy occurs only when the believer willfully turns away from faith. When that occurs, the apostate has departed from the very condition that brought him into union with Christ and the imputation of his righteousness which alone covers the believer's sins. And, as the author of the letter to the Hebrews makes clear, such individuals cannot be "renewed to repentance" (and thus, obviously, to salvation). Why? Because they have "trampled underfoot" the only thing that could save them, and there remains "no more sacrifice" for their sin (Heb. 6:4–6; 10:26–29).[13] While this is a distinctive of Reformed Arminianism, some scholars from the

---

11. Some of these advocates of "once-saved, always-saved" who have emerged from Calvinistic confessional backgrounds and yet agree with Arminians about predestination, unlimited atonement, and irresistible grace have adopted the label "Arminian" for themselves. The Society of Evangelical Arminians welcomes such individuals into its membership, while all confessionally Arminian denominations have not ordained ministers who accept eternal security. Many Baptists who believe in eternal security but agree with Arminians on other doctrines refuse to be labeled either Arminians or Calvinists, referring to themselves as traditional Baptists (with their detractors calling them "Calminians"). Interestingly, many such individuals demur from Arminius's own vigorously Reformed position on the first point of Calvinism, total depravity.

12. It is difficult to decipher where Arminius comes down on perseverance. He is so ambiguous on the subject that Reformed Arminians (who emphasize irremediable apostasy only by turning away from Christ through unbelief), conventional Arminians (who emphasize apostasy through sinning and regaining salvation through penitence), and once-saved, always-saved advocates all claim him as their own. I have almost given up on the possibility of ascertaining Arminius's position.

13. The best treatments from this perspective are Forlines, *Classical Arminianism*, 307–61; Picirilli, *Grace, Faith, Free Will*, 183–234; and Stephen M. Ashby, "A Reformed Arminian View," in *Four Views on Eternal Security*, ed. J. Matthew Pinson (Grand Rapids: Zondervan, 2002), 137–87.

Wesleyan tradition affirm this, including, for example, I. Howard Marshall.[14] Other Arminians believe that one can repeatedly lose one's salvation through sinful behavior and regain it through penitence (for examples, see Question 40).

Summary

Though Arminianism has often been caricatured, by friends and foes alike, as being anti-Reformed, it need not be so. One can, like Arminius, be an Arminian and still benefit from the broad Reformed tradition without subscribing to Calvinist views on particular redemption, unconditional predestination, and irresistible grace. The rich Reformation portrait of our enslavement to sin and God's redemptive remedy for it beautifully coheres with the historic church's testimony to the free provision of grace to all humanity. Holding these two emphases together—the former in harmony with Calvinism and the latter at variance with it—is what the Arminianism of Arminius is all about.

REFLECTION QUESTIONS

1. Can you explain the Arminian belief in conditional election?

2. How does the Arminian understanding of God's universal gracious purpose cause Arminians to differ with Calvinist doctrines other than limited atonement?

3. Do Arminians believe it is possible to come to God without his grace?

4. What do Arminians believe about the resistibility of God's grace?

5. Do all Arminians believe that Christians can lose their salvation when they commit sins?

---

14. See his classic *Kept by the Power of God: A Study in Perseverance and Falling Away* (Eugene, OR: Wipf and Stock, 2007).

Who Was John Wesley, and What Did He Believe About Salvation?

John Wesley is one of the leading lights in the history of Christianity. His Methodist movement not only helped spark an evangelical awakening but also led to a "reformation of manners" in the English-speaking world that had a profound effect on Western civilization and served as a check to the secularizing tendencies of the eighteenth-century Enlightenment.[1]

Wesley was born in 1703 at Epworth in Lincolnshire, England, the fifteenth of nineteen children, to Samuel and Susanna Wesley. Samuel was an Anglican clergyman. Though Wesley would eventually reject much of the high church Anglicanism of his parents, who had turned away from their own roots in English Nonconformity, he retained much of their Anglican Arminianism.

In 1735, after his education and ordination, Wesley went as a missionary to the American colony of Georgia. On his voyage there, he encountered some Moravians, whose piety made a deep impact on him. Three years later, with the Moravian Peter Bohler, he started a religious society in London known as the Fetter Lane Society.[2] In May of that year, Wesley had what was later termed his "Aldersgate Experience." He later remarked that he felt his heart was "strangely warmed" while hearing the reading of Luther's preface to the

---

1. Some of this chapter is adapted from J. Matthew Pinson, "Atonement, Justification, and Perseverance in the Theology of John Wesley," *Integrity: A Journal of Christian Thought* 4 (2008): 73–92, reprinted in Pinson, *Arminian and Baptist: Explorations in a Theological Tradition* (Nashville: Randall House, 2015), chapter 6.
2. William J. Abraham, *Wesley for Armchair Theologians* (Louisville: Westminster John Knox, 2005), 8.

Epistle to the Romans, in which Luther was speaking of "the change which God works in the heart through faith in Christ."[3]

Wesley was fascinated by reports of the Great Awakening surrounding luminaries like Jonathan Edwards in America. Soon he forged a deep comradeship with his old friend from Oxford days, George Whitefield. This led Wesley into open-air preaching, which launched him into a new phase of ministry and influence. The word "Methodist" started as an epithet to describe the methodical spiritual practices of Wesley and his compatriots. Yet he took it on and began using it as a moniker for his new movement.

Wesley declared that "the world is my parish" and spent the next five decades until his death in 1691 not only preaching but also writing and teaching. His *Sermons on Several Occasions* and *Explanatory Notes on the New Testament* were adopted by the Methodist movement as standards. His intellectual and cultural labors were as far-reaching as his preaching and evangelistic ministry. The Methodist movement he founded, and the many Wesleyan movements that sprang from it, would become one of the most vibrant evangelistic and missionary forces in the history of Christianity. He and his brother Charles also wrote hymns, Charles being one of the chief architects of the burgeoning movement of English hymnody that would transform the worship of Protestant churches. Few movements would have as much impact on Christianity as that birthed by John Wesley.

Wesley's Place in the Christian Theological Tradition

Scholars of Wesley's theology have divergent opinions about his place in the Christian tradition. Four main schools of thought have developed in Wesley studies: one highlights his Calvinist or "Reformation" tone; the second stresses the Catholic elements in his theology, while the third emphasizes Wesley as Anglican. A fourth school consists of those scholars who have recognized the eclecticism of his theology.

David Hempton is representative of the approach to Wesley's intellectual influences that emphasizes their eclectic nature. Wesley was influenced by "a bewildering array of Christian traditions," according to Hempton. These included "the church fathers, monastic piety, and ancient liturgies; continental mystics such as Jeanne-Marie Guyon," as well as Byzantine and Puritan spirituality, the "Moravians and other channels of European Pietism," Pascal and Thomas à Kempis, as well as various strains of Anglican theology, including Anglican Arminianism.[4] This interpretation is most accurate, with

---

3. John Wesley's Journal, May 1738, in *The Works of John Wesley*, 3rd ed., ed. Thomas Jackson (Grand Rapids: Baker, 1986 [1872]), 1:103.
4. David Hempton, *Methodism: Empire of the Spirit* (New Haven, CT: Yale University Press, 2005), 714. See also Albert C. Outler, "The Place of Wesley in the Christian Tradition," in *The Place of Wesley in the Christian Tradition*, ed. Kenneth E. Rowe (Metuchen, NJ: Scarecrow, 1976), 11–38.

the Anglican Arminian interpretation running a close second. Wesley did not selectively choose between Reformation and Anglican Arminian theological expressions of these doctrines. Rather he, seemingly unconsciously, absorbed central motifs from both traditions and amalgamated them into a unique theology that differed substantially from both systems.

Of the two most significant broad influences on Wesley's theology, the Reformation and Anglican Arminianism, the latter is more foundational. The most formative of influences was that of his parents, who were steeped in Anglican Arminianism. Their resistance to the rigid predestinarianism of their upbringings precipitated a vigorous acceptance of seventeenth-century Anglican Arminianism.[5] Wesley was immersed in that movement and its influences, especially Hugo Grotius, Jeremy Taylor, William Law's *Christian Perfection* and *A Serious Call to a Devout and Holy Life*, as well as the works of Thomas à Kempis.[6]

However, in addition to the Anglican Arminianism of the seventeenth century, Wesley was enormously influenced by two non-Anglican theologians whose views cohered with the moralism of his Anglican context. These were the Independents John Goodwin and Richard Baxter. Affirmative quotations of Goodwin and Baxter abound in Wesley's writings, especially their moralistic views on justification found in works such as Baxter's *Aphorisms of Justification* and Goodwin's *Imputatio Fidei, or A Treatise of Justification*, both of which Wesley reprinted. Goodwin had perhaps more influence on Wesley's doctrine of justification in the last thirty years of his life than any other single thinker, as is evidenced by his preface to Goodwin's treatise.[7]

Wesley and Arminianism

Wesley used the term *Arminian* to describe himself and even published *The Arminian Magazine*. However, he never quoted or extracted from Arminius himself, as he did so extensively from Anglican Arminians and other Arminians.[8] He was more influenced by Grotius and later anti-Calvinists such as the Anglican Arminians and John Goodwin.

As will be seen in subsequent chapters, Wesley agreed broadly with Arminius on total depravity and original sin. Yet his views on prevenient

---

5. Adam Clarke, *Memoirs of the Wesley Family Collected Principally from Original Documents,* 2nd ed. (New York: Lane and Tippett, 1848), 89.

6. Richard P. Heitzenrater, *The Elusive Mr. Wesley* (Nashville: Abingdon, 1984), 2:23; *Works,* XI, 366; John Deschner, *Wesley's Christology: An Interpretation* (Dallas: Southern Methodist University Press, 1985 [1960]), 197; Albert C. Outler, ed., *John Wesley* (New York: Oxford University Press, 1964), 7. See also the important work by C. F. Allison, *The Rise of Moralism: The Proclamation of the Gospel from Hooker to Baxter* (New York: Seabury, 1966).

7. Outler, ed., *John Wesley,* 148–49; Allison, *The Rise of Moralism,*193–94.

8. Luke L. Keefer, Jr., "Characteristics of Wesley's Arminianism," *Wesleyan Theological Journal* 22 (1987): 87–99.

grace placed more emphasis on humanity's being born into a state in which the effects of their depravity are unilaterally lessened by grace (see Question 21). Wesley also agreed with all Arminians on conditional election, unlimited atonement, resistible grace, and the possibility of resisting salvific grace even after conversion and thus apostatizing. His views on these standard Arminian doctrines are well known, summarized in his famous sermon, "Predestination Calmly Considered." Yet Wesley and his theological descendants differed from other Arminians in their views on the nature of atonement, the imputation of Christ's righteousness in justification, sanctification, and how one falls from grace.[9] A brief summary of Wesley's views on the nature of atonement, justification, and apostasy will aid in understanding his unique soteriology.

Wesley's doctrines of the nature of atonement and justification will be discussed in some detail in Questions 10–11. Though they differed from Arminius's views and were closer to those of John Goodwin, Richard Baxter, and later Wesleyans, Wesley's views on the nature of atonement and justification were distinctly his own. His understanding of atonement was similar to the penal satisfaction view of the magisterial Reformers. However, he believed it atoned only for *past* sins. Furthermore, Christ's active obedience in fulfilling the law is not a part of the atonement; only his passive obedience is. This affects Wesley's doctrine of justification, which demurs from the Reformed doctrine of the imputation of the obedience of Christ to the believer.

Wesley's divergence from the imputation of Christ's righteousness in justification is crucial for his doctrine of perseverance. For him, the possibility of falling from grace manifests itself in two ways: the first is through irrevocable apostasy; the second is through willful sin. In some of his writings, Wesley found examples of irrevocable apostasy in such scriptural passages as 1 Timothy 1:19–20 and Hebrews 6:4–6. He stated that the apostasy described there is irremediable, "for ships once wrecked cannot be afterwards saved."[10] This "total" or "final" apostasy is a result of the defection from faith—the renouncing of the atonement of Christ—and hence cannot be remedied.[11]

However, Wesley struggled with this notion. In his sermon "A Call to Backsliders," he indicated that even those guilty of the kind of apostasy described in 1 Timothy 1:19–20 and Hebrews 6:4–6 can still be restored. Responding to the question whether "real apostates" who have "made

---

9. As noted in Question 40, Arminius is ambiguous on the doctrine of perseverance and apostasy and is often claimed by Wesleyans, Reformed Arminians, and advocates of "once-saved, always-saved."
10. John Wesley, *Explanatory Notes upon the New Testament* (Peabody, MA: Hendrickson, 1986), 1 Timothy 1:20; cf. note on Hebrews 6:6.
11. "Serious Thoughts on the Perseverance of the Saints," in *Works*, 10:284–98.

shipwreck of faith" can "recover what they have lost," he responded, "Yea, verily, and not one or an hundred only, but, I am persuaded several thousands."[12]

The second, and most common, avenue of apostasy for Wesley, which he unambiguously taught, is sin in the believer's life. For him, it is absurd to say that God can forgive sins that have not yet occurred. Just as God pardoned the believer for past sins, the believer's future sins must be pardoned.[13] Failure to receive pardon for post-conversion sins results in apostasy.

Wesley used King David as an example of the pattern of apostasy through sin. Wesley gives a vivid description of David walking on his rooftop "praising the God whom his soul loved, when he looked down, and saw Bathsheba." Then he "felt a temptation." The Spirit immediately convicted him, and David heard the Spirit's "warning voice . . . but he yielded in some measure to the thought, and the temptation began to prevail over him." He still saw and loved God, "but it was more dimly than before . . . not with the same strength and ardour of affection." The Spirit continued to convict him; "his voice, though fainter and fainter, still whispered," but David "would not hear: He looked again, not unto God, but unto the forbidden object, till nature was superior to grace." Then "God vanished out of his sight. Faith, the divine, supernatural intercourse with God, and the love of God, ceased together: He then rushed on as a horse into the battle, and knowingly committed the outward sin."[14]

Wesley termed this second, remediable sort of apostasy "backsliding."[15] In his sermon "A Call to Backsliders," he described believers who "had fallen either from justifying or sanctifying grace" yet who "have been restored . . . and that very frequently in an instant, to all that they had lost."[16]

Summary

Wesley's views on predestination, the extent of the atonement, and the resistibility of prevenient grace are stock-in-trade Arminianism. Yet his understanding of the nature of atonement, justification, and continuance in the Christian life differ from that of some other Arminians. His modified penal satisfaction theory of atonement, which entails that Christ atoned only for the believer's past sins, results in a notion of justification and the Christian life that has imparted rather than imputed righteousness at its core. These doctrines in turn lay the foundation for an understanding of entire sanctification and Christian perfection that came to characterize the heart of Wesleyan Arminianism.

---

12. "A Call to Backsliders," in *Works*, 6:525.
13. *Notes*, 1 John 1:9.
14. "The Great Privilege of Those Who Are Born of God," *Works*, 5:230.
15. See, e.g. entries in his journals, *Works*, 2:33, 278–79, 337, 361.
16. *Works*, 6:526.

REFLECTION QUESTIONS

1. Which of the following characterizations of Wesley is best: Calvinist, Catholic, Anglican Arminian, or Eclectic?

2. What theological movements and individuals from the seventeenth century had the most influence on Wesley?

3. How did Wesley modify the penal substitutionary doctrine of atonement, and what difference did it make?

4. What did Wesley think about the doctrine of the imputation of Christ's righteousness?

5. What are the two ways Wesley thought one could apostatize, and what did his view of imputation of Christ's righteousness have to do with sin in the believer's life and its relation to apostasy?

Arminianism and the Reformed Tradition

Can One Be Both Reformed and Arminian?

I learned Christian theology from F. Leroy Forlines, my Reformed Arminian mentor at Welch College, an institution of the Free Will Baptist Church.[1] His theology was shaped by the broadly Reformed theological consensus of the Evangelical Renaissance in the mid-twentieth century. Under the tutelage of scholars like H. D. McDonald and Carl F. H. Henry in seminary, Forlines cut his teeth on such stalwart American mediators of confessional Reformed theology as William G. T. Shedd and Charles Hodge. Yet it was Shedd, whose Augustinian natural headship view, as opposed to Federalism, resonated most with Forlines. This is no mistake, because it is the same broad approach that Arminius and the seventeenth-century General Baptists Thomas Helwys and Thomas Grantham followed.

What was interesting about the kind of theology that Forlines taught was that it was so comfortable with the basics of broadly Reformed theology while very ill at ease with Calvinistic predestinarianism. In other words, Forlines's Reformed Arminian soteriology differed with Calvinism on *how one comes to be* in a state of grace but strongly agreed with Calvinism on *what it means to be* in a state of grace.

The "How" and the "What" of Salvation

How one comes to be in a state of grace involves questions of (1) libertarian freedom vs. divine determinism and how that comes to bear on (2) whether predestination is conditional or unconditional and (3) whether God's salvific grace is resistible or irresistible, both before and after conversion. Arminianism affirms the former, Calvinism the latter, in all three questions.

---

1. His most influential book is his systematic theology, *The Quest for Truth: Theology for a Postmodern World* (Nashville: Randall House, 2001).

What it means to be in a state of grace involves questions of (1) whether or not atonement involves penal satisfaction, (2) whether or not justification involves the imputation of Christ's righteousness to the believer, (3) whether one believes in progressive sanctification or entire sanctification, and (4) whether perseverance is by faith alone or faith plus works and penitence.

It is here where Reformed Arminian views veer from those of many other Arminians. Yet it is here where Reformed Arminianism provides a theological alternative to those who believe that the Bible teaches a Reformed understanding of what it means to be in a state of grace, as well as other Reformed doctrines, even though they demur from divine determinism, unconditional predestination, and concomitant doctrines.

Reformed Views on Sanctification and Spirituality

"What it means to be in a state of grace" also has a great deal to do with the way one sees sin in the life of the believer. Often anti-Calvinist traditions see sin in the life of the believer in moralistic terms that are very different from the gracious language that great Reformed confession, the Belgic Confession of Faith, uses:

> Though we do good works, we do not found our salvation upon them; for we can do no work but what is polluted by our flesh, and also punishable; and although we could perform such works, still the remembrance of one sin is sufficient to make God reject them. Thus, then, we should always be in doubt, tossed to and fro without any certainty, and our poor consciences would be continually vexed if they relied not on the merits of the suffering and death of our Saviour.[2]

Reformed Arminians believe it is possible to apostatize through a once-for-all, irremediable defection from Christ. Yet they very strongly see sin in the life of the believer as being non-imputed to the believer and Christ's active and passive obedience, which is imputed to the believer through faith, as the grounds for perseverance, assurance, and sanctification.

This agreement with Calvinism on what it means to be in a state of grace is also why Reformed Arminian spirituality is so different from the more mystical, crisis experience-oriented, pietistic, holiness, or Keswick spirituality that characterizes large swaths of the evangelical Arminian landscape.[3] That is why

---

2. Art. 24, in Arthur C. Cochrane, ed., *Reformed Confessions of the Sixteenth Century* (Louisville: Westminster John Knox, 2003), 206.
3. See Forlines's chapter on sanctification in *The Quest for Truth* as well as F. Leroy Forlines and Harrold Harrison, *The Charismatic Movement* (Nashville: Commission for Theological Integrity, National Association of Free Will Baptists, 1989). Though he disagrees with certain

Reformed Arminians love reading Puritan spirituality. Most of the passing references to divine sovereignty or predestination that authors such as John Bunyan or John Owen make in their works of piety are fully in keeping with Reformed Arminian thinking.

"Reformed" Is About More Than Soteriology

Reformed theology, as presented by theologians such as Forlines, is about much more than merely what it means to be in a state of grace. This is reinforced by reading the Belgic Confession and Heidelberg Catechism because they are the pre-Synod of Dort confessional documents of the Dutch Reformed Church of Arminius's day, which he eagerly and repeatedly affirmed.

These confessional standards that Arminius extolled represent a broader, pre-Dort Reformed theology that allowed more diversity in the details of how one comes to be in a state of grace. Today, people often define "Reformed" as the "TULIP" doctrines—five-point or at least four-point Calvinism. However, that is not how people in the historic communions that have "Reformed" in their name define the word. They define it as subscription to the "Three Forms of Unity," which are the Belgic Confession, Heidelberg Catechism, and Canons of Dort.

Prior to the Synod of Dort in 1618–1619, however, "Reformed" was not defined in this way. Dort represented a firming up or crystallizing of a scholastic predestinarianism that was growing in the Reformed Protestant intellectual community in the late sixteenth and early seventeenth centuries. One could even say that it had become the mainstream academic theology in the Reformed community at that time. However, it was not confessionally articulated and imposed on the churches until after the Synod of Dort.

That is why there were so many theologians, pastors, and laypeople prior to the Synod of Dort who fully subscribed to the Belgic Confession and Heidelberg Catechism but did not embrace *gratia particularis* (particular grace) and *gratia irresistibilis* (irresistible grace). There was sufficient ambiguity in these confessional documents to allow for this diversity. Therefore, someone like Arminius could self-consciously see himself as organically Reformed, as representing a stream of thought regarding soteriology that was within the bounds of confessional Reformed theology prior to the addition of the Canons of Dort to the confessional standards of the Reformed Church (see Questions 7–8).

Of course, Baptists, whether Calvinist or Arminian, could not have subscribed to even these pre-Dort confessional documents because of various ecclesial doctrines and practices they could not uphold. This is why James K. A. Smith, for example, in his book, *Letters to a Young Calvinist: An Invitation to*

---

perseverance, Forlines never says anything about sin in the life of the believer or assurance of present salvation that disagrees with the fifth head of Doctrine of the Canons of Dort.

the Reformed Tradition, laughs at the idea of "young, restless, and Reformed" pastors who accept the five points of TULIP and define Reformed theology in merely those terms but who refuse to baptize infants by sprinkling, who have a nonsacramental understanding of baptism and the Lord's Supper, and who practice congregational church government and other ecclesial tenets that break with the Three Forms of Unity: the Belgic Confession of Faith, the Heidelberg Catechism, and the Canons of Dort.[4] So, in a sense, all Baptists, if one uses the confessional tradition of the Reformed churches as a guide to what is "Reformed," whether pre- or post-Dort, must demur from the Reformed confessional documents on ecclesiological grounds.

It is even more complicated than that, however. Doctrines that all traditional soteriological Calvinists, whether Baptists or Paedobaptists, would have abhorred are now widely tolerated within Calvinist circles. Calvinists laud the seventeenth-century cleric Richard Baxter for his book *The Reformed Pastor.*[5] However, when I tell my Calvinist friends that Richard Baxter did not believe in the penal substitutionary view of the atonement or the imputation of Christ's righteousness in justification, I am often met with blank stares of disbelief. Similar things could be said about Jonathan Edwards. This is not confined to the past, however. There is an increasing number of four- and five-point Calvinists, in good standing in conservative Calvinist circles, who have embraced Baxter's approach to justification in their appreciation for the New Perspective on Paul or Federal Vision theology.[6] Another example of what all confessionally Reformed people would have thought was fanaticism until just recently is the doctrine that the apostolic/charismatic sign gifts are normative for today, something the rigorous Calvinist Sam Storms is articulating with increasing boldness.[7]

It is fascinating that one could be a tongues-speaking, slain-in-the-Spirit charismatic who has words of knowledge and claims the gift of healing, and yet does not believe in penal substitutionary atonement or the imputation of the righteousness of Jesus Christ in justification. Yet if that person could affirm TULIP, he or she would be considered "Reformed" in much of the current dialogue. However, Reformed Arminians can agree with the

---

4. James K. A. Smith, *Letters to a Young Calvinist: An Invitation to the Reformed Tradition* (Grand Rapids: Brazos, 2010).
5. Richard Baxter, *The Reformed Pastor* (Carlisle, PA: Banner of Truth, 1974).
6. David Van Drunen, "To Obey Is Better Than Sacrifice: A Defense of the Active Obedience of Christ in the Light of Recent Criticism," and Guy Prentiss Waters, "Introduction: Whatever Happened to *Sola Fide?*" in *By Faith Alone: Answering the Challenges to the Doctrine of Justification,* eds. Gary L. W. Johnson and Guy P. Waters (Wheaton, IL: Crossway, 2006), 127–46, 21–32, respectively.
7. See Storms's aggressive plan for teaching people how to use their charismatic gifts in his book *Practicing the Power: Welcoming the Gifts of the Holy Spirit in Your Life* (Grand Rapids: Zondervan, 2017).

pre-Dort Reformed understanding of every single doctrine (as much as any Baptist can). Yet because they do not accept the U, L, I, and P of soteriological Calvinism, they are theologically unacceptable and not "reformed according to Scripture" (the original meaning of "Reformed" embraced by the General Baptists and other offshoots from the Reformed movement). That is what comes from defining "Reformed" only as acceptance of the TULIP doctrines.

Creation-Fall-Redemption-Consummation

One of the things that strikes the reader of the Belgic Confession and Heidelberg Catechism is their broad Reformed approach to a worldview shaped by the schema of creation-fall-redemption-consummation. These documents articulate a Reformed understanding of the radical fallenness of humanity, which result in a more pessimistic *epistemology* regarding the possibility of human beings having knowledge of God outside redemptive revelation.[8] This understanding of how human depravity makes special revelation necessary for knowledge of God is also seen in the Reformed confessional tradition's *sola Scriptura* stance. It propounds a doctrine of the *sufficiency of Scripture* (intricately tied to the doctrine of the outward and ordinary means of grace), not just for doctrine but for ecclesial practice, even worship (what many call the regulative principle of worship).

Furthermore, the broadly covenantal inaugurated *eschatology* of Reformed confessional theology stresses the renewal of all things through a sovereignly guided redemptive process in humanity—the renewal of the image of God, whose lordship applies to all things.[9] This produces a more redemptive approach to *culture* than Thomism, Lutheranism (two kingdoms), Anabaptism, or Dispensationalism, while still emphasizing the radical depravity of fallen human culture (the antithesis, in Kuyperian terms).[10] Thus Reformed theology suggests an Augustinian-Kuyperian balance in culture between transforming and redeeming culture on one hand yet not seeing cultural engagement as merely accommodation to fallen cultural norms on the other.[11]

This creation-fall-redemption-consummation schema coheres with Reformed Arminianism. It sees a holistic cohesiveness between a broadly

---

8. For a "soft presuppositional" (non-Van Tilian) approach to epistemology and apologetics from a Reformed Arminian perspective, see F. Leroy Forlines and J. Matthew Pinson, *The Apologetics of Leroy Forlines* (Gallatin, TN: Welch College Press, 2019).
9. See Matthew McAffee's essay on Forlines's eschatology, "Forlinesean Eschatology: A Progressive Convenantal Approach," in *The Promise of Arminian Theology: Essays in Honor of F. Leroy Forlines*, eds. Matthew Steven Bracey and W. Jackson Watts (Nashville: Randall House Academic, 2016), 141–72.
10. See Richard J. Mouw, *Kuyper: A Short and Personal Introduction* (Grand Rapids: Eerdmans, 2001), 60–63.
11. For a Reformed Arminian/Kuyperian understanding of culture, see Matthew Steven Bracey and Christopher Talbot, eds., *Christians in Culture* (Gallatin, TN: Welch College Press, forthcoming).

Reformed view of what it means to be redeemed from a fallen state (*even though that does not involve predestinarianism*) and what it means for God's sovereign rule to govern creation, redemption, and consummation (*even though that sovereignty is about God's rule, his Lordship, not about his meticulous determination of every detail of reality*).

Summary

In short, reading the Belgic Confession and the Heidelberg Catechism confirms that most Arminians have thrown out the Reformed baby with the TULIP bathwater. So the "Reformed" in "Reformed Arminianism" need not be only about what it means to be in a state of grace. It can also encompass classic Reformed thought on the effect total depravity has on one's epistemology, approach to culture, and need for special revelation for knowledge of God and how he wants to be worshiped and served in his church. It is about a broadly Reformed kingdom eschatology and the way that impacts how one views the transforming impact Christianity can have on worldview, on culture, on knowledge, on the academic disciplines, and on human flourishing.

I often encourage my younger Reformed Arminian colleagues to read the Belgic Confession and Heidelberg Catechism from time to time. These documents open us up to everything that is beautiful about confessional Reformed theology, because they were written before Reformed theology was "tightened up," before it morphed from a theology of sovereignty—in terms of the extension of God's rule, his kingship, his lordship, as he redeems creation from its radically fallen state—into a theology of divine determinism.[12]

Arminius eagerly affirmed these confessional standards. He loved them and recommended them to his students. They commend to us the beauty of Reformed theology in its essence without the biblical and theological problems that accompany determinism, unconditional predestination, particularism, and irresistible grace.[13] Arminians of all varieties will experience renewal as they give Reformed theology, shorn of its TULIP elements, a fresh look and stop throwing the Reformed baby out with the TULIP bathwater.

---

12. As Calvinist Paul Helm points out, even compatibilist Calvinists are determinists: "The compatibilist is a determinist who argues that determined actions may be actions that the agent is responsible for, praised if good, blamed if bad" (Paul, Helm, "Foreword," in Michael Patrick Preciado, *A Reformed View of Freedom: The Compatibility of Guidance Control and Reformed Theology* [Eugene, OR: Pickwick, 2019], ix). For more on compatibilism, see Question 17.
13. Without the ecclesiological elements from which a Baptist like me, whether Calvinist or Arminian, would demur.

REFLECTION QUESTIONS

1. Do Arminians necessarily disagree with Calvinism on what it means to be in a state of grace?

2. What are some areas that Arminians can be Reformed regarding what it means to be in a state of grace?

3. What goes into a discussion of who is Reformed and who is not? Give examples.

4. What are some ways Arminians can affirm Reformed theology on subjects such as spirituality, epistemology, apologetics, worship, eschatology, worldiew, culture, and so forth?

5. Does Arminians' interpretation of divine sovereignty as God's kingdom, rule, or lordship over the whole of life, rather than determinism, keep them from affirming Reformed theology's application of that sovereignty to every area of life?

Was Arminius Reformed?

Jacobus Arminius has been the object of much criticism and praise from detractors and proponents during the past four centuries. Both, however, have often proceeded from partisan bias and rest on misinterpretations of his theology. Most Calvinist critics have portrayed him as a semi-Pelagian and a defector from Reformed theology, while many Arminians have cast him in terms of later expressions of Arminianism, failing to take seriously his theology and its context.[1]

Arminius and His Interpreters

Both Calvinist and Arminian scholars, especially in popular writings, have traditionally portrayed Arminius's thought as a departure from Reformed theology. Many Calvinist thinkers have portrayed Arminius as "a clever dissembler who secretly taught doctrines different from his published writings."[2] Some have gone as far as Roger Nicole, who, for example,

---

1. The best, most accessible source for becoming acquainted with Arminius's soteriology in the context of the Arminian-Calvinist debate is Robert E. Picirilli, *Grace, Faith, Free Will: Contrasting Views of Salvation: Calvinism and Arminianism* (Nashville: Randall House, 2002). Some of the material in this chapter is adapted from J. Matthew Pinson, "Will the Real Arminius Please Stand Up? A Study of the Theology of Jacobus Arminius in Light of His Interpreters," *Integrity: A Journal of Christian Thought* 2 (2003): 121–39, reprinted in Pinson, *Arminian and Baptist: Explorations in a Theological Tradition* (Nashville: Randall House, 2015), chapter 1.
2. Bangs, "Arminius and the Reformation," *Church History* 30 (1961): 156. Richard A. Muller and W. Robert Godfrey have recently resurrected this specter, leaving Arminius's honesty open to question. See Muller, "Arminius and the Reformed Tradition," *Westminster Theological Journal* 70 (2008): 41. Godfrey says Arminius "was likely more than a controversialist, however. He was likely a dissembler who abused the good will and efforts of the Calvinists to maintain peace with him in the church" (W. Robert Godfrey, "A New Look at Arminius, Part 6," *Tabletalk*, https://tabletalkmagazine.com/posts/arminius-a-new-look-part-6; accessed November 14, 2020). Yet this perspective is wholly based on a reading of

described Arminius as the originator of a slippery slope that started with Episcopius and Limborch (who were "infiltrated by Socinianism") and ended with Unitarianism, Universalism, and the philosophy of E. S. Brightman.[3] Most commonly, Calvinists have described Arminius as a semi-Pelagian.[4] These comments are remarkable given Arminius's often-stated aim to maintain "the greatest possible distance from Pelagianism."[5]

Most Arminians, while praising Arminius, have viewed him in the light of later non-Calvinist theologies and have described him in more synergistic or semi-Pelagian terms. Their tendency is to give a brief biographical sketch of Arminius, with the customary discussion of "Arminius as the Father of Arminianism," and then to offer an exposition of the five points of the Remonstrance. Or, as Carl Bangs says, the biographical sketch is many times followed by "copious references to Arminius's successor, Simon Episcopius, who, although in many ways a faithful disciple of Arminius, is not Arminius."[6]

None of these assertions, however, is true of Arminius, and only by bringing certain assumptions to his writings will one interpret him in these ways. "It is evident that such accounts of Arminius assume a definition of Arminianism which cannot be derived from Arminius himself," Bangs said. They start with a "preconception of what Arminius should be expected to say." Then they read Arminius and "do not find what they are looking for." They "show impatience and disappointment with his Calvinism and shift the inquiry into some later period when Arminianism turns out to be what they

---

the Belgic Confession and Heidelberg Catechism that rules out conditional election. For more on this, see Question 8. See also Stephen M. Ashby, "Notes on Arminius" (Lecture Notes, Randall University).

3. Roger Nicole, "The Debate over Divine Election," *Christianity Today*, October 21, 1959, 6.
4. For just a few representative examples, which could be multiplied, see Carl Trueman, "Post-Reformation Developments in the Doctrine of the Atonement," in *The Precious Blood: The Atoning Work of Christ*, ed. Richard D. Phillips (Wheaton, IL: Crossway, 2009), 184; Alan F. Johnson and Robert Webber, *What Christians Believe* (Grand Rapids: Zondervan, 1993), 223–24; W. Robert Godfrey, review of *Jacob Arminius: Theologian of Grace*, Reformation21. com, http://www.reformation21.org/shelf-life/jacob-arminius-theologian-of-grace.php. See Roger E. Olson, *Arminian Theology: Myths and Realities* (Downers Grove, IL: IVP Academic, 2006), for more examples.
5. Jacobus Arminius, *The Works of James Arminius*, 3 vols., trans. James Nichols and William Nichols (Nashville: Randall House, 2007), 1:764, "Apology against Thirty-One Defamatory Articles."
6. Carl Bangs, "Arminius and Reformed Theology" (Ph.D. diss., University of Chicago, 1958), 23. See also John Mark Hicks, "Theology of Grace in the Thought of Jacobus Arminius and Philipp van Limborch: A Study in the Development of Seventeenth-Century Dutch Arminianism" (Ph.D. diss., Westminster Theological Seminary, 1985). W. Stephen Gunter, "From Arminius (d. 1609) to the Synod of Dort (1618–1619)," in *Perfecting Perfection: Essays in Honour of Henry D. Rack*, ed. Robert Webster (Cambridge: James Clarke and Company, 2016), 8–28; Mark A. Ellis, *Simon Episcopius' Doctrine of Original Sin* (New York: Peter Lang, 2006); and Sarah Mortimer, *Reason and Religion in the English Revolution* (Cambridge: Cambridge University Press, 2010), especially pp. 25–26, 119–25.

are looking for—a non-Calvinistic, synergistic, and perhaps semi-Pelagian system."[7]

This approach fails to realize one of the most important things about Arminius's theology: that it is distinctively Reformed, and that it is a *variety* of Reformed theology rather than a *departure* from it. By focusing on Arminius's doctrine of predestination and its differences from both Calvin and post-Dort Calvinism, people have tended to emphasize Arminius's differences with Calvinism rather than his similarities with it.

Recent scholars have taken one of two broad positions on the soteriology of Jacobus Arminius. One group, following Carl Bangs, holds that his theology was a development of the Dutch Reformed theology of his day.[8] The other, following Richard Muller, says that it was a departure from Reformed categories.[9] The perspective of this book is the first. As will be discussed in Question 8, in Arminius's "multi-faceted" pre-Dort Reformed context, there was not "*the* Reformed theology," as William den Boer argues.[10]

Those who see unconditional election, *gratia particularis* (particular grace), and *gratia irresistibilis* (irresistible grace) as the essential core of Reformed theology find it necessary to classify Arminius as outside the bounds of Reformed orthodoxy, even semi-Pelagian. Generations of theological

---

7. Bangs, "Arminius and Reformed Theology," 14.
8. Following Carl Bangs, scholars such as Robert Picirilli, Roger Olson, Stephen Gunter, John Mark Hicks, Stuart Clarke, William Witt, William den Boer, G. J. Hoerdendaal, Bakhuizen van den Brink, Oliver Crisp, Alan P. F. Sell, Arthur Skevington Wood, Stephen Ashby, Mark Ellis, Sarah Mortimer, and Charles Cameron fall into this first category. In addition to the sources in the notes above, see especially Bangs, *Arminius: A Study in the Dutch Reformation* (Nashville: Abingdon, 1971); Roger E. Olson, *Arminian Theology: Myths and Realities* (Downers Grove, IL: InterVarsity, 2006); W. Stephen Gunter, *Arminius and His Declaration of Sentiments: An Annotated Translation with Introduction and Theological Commentary* (Waco, TX: Baylor University Press, 2012); F. Stuart Clarke, *The Ground of Election: Jacob Arminius' Doctrine of the Work and Person of Christ* (Milton Keynes, UK: Paternoster, 2006); William G. Witt, "Creation, Redemption, and Grace in the Theology of Jacobus Arminius" (Ph.D. diss., University of Notre Dame, 1993); and William den Boer, *God's Twofold Love: The Theology of Jacob Arminius (1559–1609)* (Göttingen: Vandenhoeck and Ruprecht, 2010).
9. Muller, "Arminius and the Reformed Tradition"; *God, Creation, and Providence*; Keith D. Stanglin, *Arminius and the Assurance of Salvation* (Leiden: Brill, 2007); Keith D. Stanglin and Thomas H. McCall, *Jacob Arminius: Theologian of Grace* (New York: Oxford University Press, 2012). Though they agree with the broad outlines of Muller's historiography, even Stanglin and McCall seem less committed at this point: "Whether one desires to label Arminius as 'Reformed' is not a question of great import to us" (Stanglin and McCall, 203). For more on why Muller believes Arminius's thought is a departure from Reformed categories, see Question 8.
10. *God's Twofold Love*, 43–44. Den Boer's perspective has much to commend itself over against the tendencies of Muller and colleagues to see Reformed theology as more of a monolith. Cf. Den Boer, "'Cum delectu': Jacob Arminius's Praise for and Critique of Calvin and His Theology," *Church History and Religious Culture* 91 (2011): 73–86.

students have received this picture of Arminius. However, the best way to understand Arminius, and thus to benefit from his unique and substantial contribution to Protestant theology, is to understand his theological context, his stated view of Reformed theology (specifically that of Calvin), his confessional beliefs, and his published writings. If one believes Arminius to be an honest man, rather than a treacherous one, one will see a picture of him emerge that is radically different from that of his detractors.[11]

Arminius's Confessionally Reformed Self-Conception

Arminius saw himself as Reformed and worked out his theology in the context of a Reformed theology that was broader than the rigorous Calvinism of the Synod of Dort. As a devout Dutch Reformed theologian, Arminius was loyal to the symbols of his church: The Heidelberg Catechism and the Belgic Confession of Faith. He reaffirmed on numerous occasions his faithfulness to these confessional standards. Responding to the consistory in Amsterdam in 1593, Arminius affirmed his loyalty to the Catechism and Confession. He repeatedly reiterated this loyalty, as in 1605, when he responded to deputies of the Synods of North and South Holland.[12]

In 1607, at the meeting of the preparatory convention for the national synod, Arminius and some other delegates, emphasizing the priority of the Word of God as the church's rule of faith and practice, argued that the confession and catechism should be open to revision by the Synod, to clarify certain doctrines (e.g., the use of the plural when discussing original sin in the catechism).[13] This did not mean, however, that Arminius disagreed with the documents. Arminius made this clear in a letter to the Palatine Ambassador, Hippolytus à Collibus, in 1608: "I confidently declare that I have never taught anything, either in the church or in the university, which contravenes the sacred writings that ought to be with us the sole rule of thinking and of speaking, or which is opposed to the Dutch [Belgic]

---

11. Though Muller and some of his former students (e.g., Stanglin, McCall, and Raymond Blacketer) place more emphasis on Arminius's differences with Reformed orthodoxy than most scholars do, in most respects they avoid the conventional stereotypes of Arminius characterized above. They are astute interpreters of Arminius and are more attentive to his historical and theological context than most scholars (e.g., their correct emphasis on Arminius's scholasticism vs. the older approach that portrayed him as a humanist; Stanglin's setting of Arminius's thought in the context of that of his Leiden colleagues).

12. Carl Bangs, "Arminius as a Reformed Theologian," in *The Heritage of John Calvin*, ed. John H. Bratt (Grand Rapids: Eerdmans, 1973), 216.

13. Arminius's *sola Scriptura* approach is not out of line with Reformed notions of the revision of confessions of faith, which has happened in Presbyterian and Reformed church bodies regarding church and state, for example. See R. Scott Clark, *Recovering the Reformed Confession* (Phillipsburg, NJ: P&R, 2008).

Confession or to the Heidelberg Catechism, that are our stricter formularies of consent."[14]

In his *Declaration of Sentiments* that same year, he challenged anyone to prove that he had ever made doctrinal pronouncements that were "contrary to God's Word or to the Confession and Catechism of the Belgic Churches."[15] Arminius lived and died loyal to the Heidelberg Catechism and the Belgic Confession of Faith. It is hard to believe that one could consistently lie both in public statements and in published writing after published writing (when it would have been much easier to enter another profession, as Caspar Coolhaes did, that was less emotionally strenuous). If Arminius was not dishonest and surreptitious, it may be confidently believed that he was a loyal defender of the symbols of his church to his dying day.[16]

Arminius's Appreciation for Calvin

In light of the fact that so many interpreters have cast Arminius as a foe of Calvin, Arminius's statements on Calvin are very interesting. Arminius made explicit references to Calvin throughout his writings—most of the time favorable ones. He had a high regard for Calvin as an exegete and theologian. His only important disagreement with Calvin was on the particulars of the doctrines of predestination and the resistibility of grace. Arminius did not, however, think particular, irresistible grace and unconditional election were the essential core of either Reformed theology or Calvin's version of it.

He expressed his high esteem for Calvin in a letter to the Amsterdam Burgomaster Sebastian Egbertszoon in May of 1607. The occasion of the letter was a rumor that Arminius had been recommending the works of the Jesuits and of Cornheert to his students. Arminius said: "So far from this, after reading the Scripture . . . I recommend the *Commentaries of Calvin* be read. . . . In the interpretation of the Scriptures Calvin is incomparable, and . . . his *Commentaries* are more to be valued than anything that is handed down to us in the writings of the Fathers. . . . His *Institutes* . . . I give out to be read after the [Heidelberg] Catechism. But here I add—with discrimination, as the writings of all men ought to be read."[17]

---

14. Arminius, *Works*, 2:690, "Letter to Hippolytus à Collibus."
15. Gunter, *Declaration of Sentiments*, 98; cf. Arminius, *Works*, 1:600.
16. In one place, responding to his hostile critics who were claiming he taught that unregenerate people's works can cause God to "communicate to them his saving grace," Arminius quipped that "these good men" misread a word in what he had stated, "unless, perhaps, since that time, having proceeded from bad to worse, I now positively affirm this, which, as I was a less audacious and more modest heretic, I then denied" (Arminius, *Works*, 2:17, "Apology against Thirty-One Defamatory Articles"). One could wish for this sense of humor in contemporary theological debate.
17. Quoted in Bangs, "Arminius as a Reformed Theologian," 216.

In his *Declaration of Sentiments*, Arminius, setting forth his doctrine of justification, says, in essence, that if he is wrong, then Calvin too must be wrong: "Whatever one might say about this, no one among us accuses Calvin or considers him heterodox on this point, and my position is not so different from his as to prevent my signing my name to the positions he takes in Book III of his *Institutes*. To these opinions, I am prepared to state my full approval at any time."[18]

Summary

Arminius's opinion of Calvin in these passages is not that of an antagonist, but rather one who has great respect for Calvin and is in agreement with him on most things. It is a mistake to exaggerate the importance of the doctrine of particular, irresistible grace to the point that it is essential to Reformed theology. The Belgic Confession of Faith and Heidelberg Catechism certainly did not do this, making it possible for Arminius to affirm them. As the next chapter will show, Reformed theology in Arminius's time was broad enough to have room for someone with his views. Though Arminius differed from Calvin and others in the Reformed Church on the doctrines of predestination and irresistible grace Arminius was—and believed he was—consistently Reformed.

REFLECTION QUESTIONS

1. How have most writers, especially popular ones, characterized Arminius's theology, as Reformed or anti-Reformed?

2. What was Arminius's posture toward the Heidelberg Catechism and the Belgic Confession of Faith?

3. What was Arminius's opinion of Calvin's writings?

4. What are some things on which Arminius agreed with Calvin?

5. What does Arminius's posture toward the Reformed confessions and Calvin indicate about his status as a Reformed theologian?

---

18. Gunter, *Declaration of Sentiments*, 149; cf. Arminius, *Works*, 1:700. Arminius's doctrine of justification will be dealt with later in this book. See William den Boer, "Cum delectu," 73–86.

Was Reformed Theology Less Calvinistic Before the Synod of Dort?

Arminius argued against his detractors was that he was a Reformed theologian within the bounds of the Belgic Confession of Faith (BC) and Heidelberg Catechism (HC). After his death the question would come to dominate the Reformed community: should the confessional standards of the Reformed churches be limited to the teaching of particular and irresistible grace? This was an open question until the Synod of Dort in 1618–1619, which decisively answered yes.

Most scholars of Arminius have seen him as representing an organic stream of sixteenth-century Reformed theology that was broader than it came to be after Dort. Carl Bangs was the dean of this school of thought.[1] He rooted his argument in Arminius's Reformed self-conception, maintaining that Arminius was simply giving voice to a *gratia universalis* (universal grace) stream of Dutch Reformed theology that dated to the earliest days of the Dutch Reformation and had always fit within the Dutch Reformed milieu.[2] While more sophisticated, Bangs's treatment runs along the same lines as the traditional Remonstrant interpretation.[3]

---

1. See primarily Carl Bangs, *Arminius: A Study in the Dutch Reformation* (Nashville: Abingdon, 1971). For examples of other scholars who support the broad Bangs thesis, see footnote 8 in Question 7.
2. G. J. Hoenderdaal bore strong similarity to Bangs. Among his many essays, see especially "The Debate about Arminius outside the Netherlands," in *Leiden University in the 17th Century* (Leiden: Brill, 1975), 137–59.
3. See, e.g., Peter Bertius, *An Oration on the Life and Death of That Reverend and Very Famous Man James Arminius*, reprinted in Jacobus Arminius, *The Works of James Arminius*, 3 vols., trans. James Nichols and William Nichols (Nashville: Randall House, 2007 [1609]), 1:13–47; Hugo Grotius, *Ordinum Hollandiase Ac Westfrisiae Pietas*, trans. Edwin Rabbie (Leiden: Brill, 1995 [1613]); Philipp van Limborch, *Historical Relation concerning the Origin and Progress of the Controversies in the Belgic League, upon Predestination and Its*

Scholars such as Richard Muller, the distinguished scholar of Reformed scholasticism, have argued that Arminius's soteriology was a "full-scale departure" from confessional Reformed theology in the sixteenth century.[4] Muller acknowledges that Arminius's clerical and academic appointments "indicate" that the Reformed leaders around Arminius "assumed" he was Reformed. However, Muller argues that it is "incontestable" that Arminius's views contradicted the "authorial intention" of the BC and HC and most Reformed clergy's "plain reading" of them.[5] Muller would be correct if he were arguing only that soteriological Calvinism characterized the majority of Reformed thinkers in the late sixteenth century. He argues, however, that Reformed *confessional* theology disallowed views like Arminius's.

There was growing support in the Reformed churches of the late sixteenth century for interpreting the confessional standards in a soteriologically Calvinist way. Yet one can still maintain that Arminius represented a strain of Reformed theology that was acceptable early on, though it became increasingly unacceptable, and completely unacceptable after Dort.

Most of Muller's arguments simply establish that Arminius's views were not in the ascendancy, not that they were disallowed. One of Muller's lines of evidence is that a national synod at the Hague disavowed universal grace in 1586.[6] Yet the argument that Arminius represented an earlier, broader approach to what was acceptable in the Reformed churches is unaffected

---

Connected Heads, trans. L. W. P., *Methodist Review* 26 (1844): 425–60, 556–87; Gerard Brandt, *History of the Reformation and Other Ecclesiastical Transactions in and about the Low-Countries* . . ., 4 vols. (London: John Nicks, 1723). Later advocates include Frederick Calder, *Memoirs of Simon Episcopius* (London: Simpkin and Marshall, 1835); Théodore van Oppenraaij, *La doctrine de la prédestination dans l'église réformée des Pays-Bas depuis l'origine jusqu'au synode national de Dordrecht en 1618 et 1619* (Louvain: J. van Linthout, 1906); H. D. Foster, "Liberal Calvinism: The Remonstrants at the Synod of Dort in 1618," *Harvard Theological Review* 16 (1923): 1–37.

4.   Richard A. Muller, *God, Creation, and Providence in the Thought of Jacob Arminius* (Grand Rapids: Baker, 1991), 281. See also Muller, "Arminius and the Reformed Tradition," *Westminster Theological Journal* 70 (2008): 19–48. Arminians Keith D. Stanglin and Thomas H. McCall sometimes emphasize dissimilarities between Arminius and his Reformed contemporaries. They say, however, "Whether one desires to label Arminius as 'Reformed' is not a question of great import to us." (One can see from earlier chapters why the question is of great import to Reformed Arminians.) See Keith D. Stanglin and Thomas H. McCall, *Jacob Arminius: Theologian of Grace* (New York: Oxford University Press, 2012), 203. Their language is much more restrained than Muller's, yet they say that Arminius "forged a new trajectory from within Reformed theology that veered in significant ways from it" (ibid.).

5.   Muller, "Arminius and the Reformed Tradition," 19, 21, 39. Freya Seirhuis concurs with Muller *contra* Bangs, but it is not within the purview of her subject matter to argue for it. (However, she mistakenly lumps William Den Boer into the Muller camp.) See Seirhuis, *The Literature of the Arminian Controversy: Religion, Politics and the Stage in the Dutch Republic* (Oxford, UK: Oxford University Press, 2015), 42–47.

6.   Muller, "Arminius and the Reformed Tradition," 29. Muller rightly criticizes Bangs's and Hoenderdaal's downplaying the national character of synods like the Hague in

by the fact that stronger Calvinist sentiments had become dominant by the mid-1580s. Muller also argues that the Remonstrant historian Gerard Brandt "reserves the term 'Reformed' for the opponents of universal grace," that he "does not claim the name 'Reformed' for his spiritual ancestors."[7] Laying aside this argument's anachronism, one can see that Brandt repeatedly used "Reformed" to describe people like Arminius.[8]

Muller's primary argument is that Arminius departs from the *confessional* theology of the Dutch Reformed churches. What Muller would need to establish, to sustain his argument, is *not* merely that most Reformed theologians of Arminius's day interpreted their confessional standards in a Calvinistic way, which Bangs acknowledges. Muller's focus on differences between the scholastic metaphysics of Arminius and some of his Calvinist contemporaries does not change the reality that the Reformed confessions transcended such speculative distinctions. Muller would need to show that the confessions clearly prohibited views like Arminius's.

To sustain the Bangs thesis, one would need to demonstrate the following: First, Dutch Reformed theology was broader and less carefully defined prior to the Synod of Dort. Second, the teaching of universal, resistible grace was present in the Dutch Reformed consciousness from the beginning. Third, the BC and HC were, and can be, interpreted in a less Calvinist manner, and their authors could have been soteriologically Calvinist without intending those documents to be.

The Breadth of Reformed Theology Prior to Dort

Advocates of the Bangs thesis posit the diversity of the Reformed tradition in the sixteenth century. As William den Boer says, "It is too simple to discard Arminius as a deviation from *the* Reformed theology."[9] Quoting Willem Van Asselt, den Boer explains that at that time there were "different trajectories" within Reformed theology. There "was not just one Reformed theology," but a "whole series of Reformed theologies in the sixteenth century."[10]

Scholars who advocate this view are too numerous to quote in this brief chapter. For example, Christine Kooi says that the Dutch Reformed Church at this time was "still figuring out what its orthodoxy was."[11] Willem Nijenhuis

---

1585–1586. Yet moving the dates of the controversy a little earlier does not affect the essential Bangs thesis.

7. Muller, "Arminius and the Reformed Tradition," 28.
8. See, e.g., Brandt, *History of the Reformation*, 1:308–09 364–65, 437, and 442.
9. Den Boer, *God's Twofold Love*, 43.
10. Den Boer, *God's Twofold Love*, 43–44. Cf. den Boer, "'Cum delectu': Jacob Arminius's (1559–1609) Praise for and Critique of Calvin and His Theology," *Church History and Religious Culture* 91 (2011): 73–86.
11. Christine Kooi, review of *Pleading for Diversity: The Church Caspar Coolhaes Wanted*, by Linda Stuckrath Gottschalk, *Church History and Religious Culture* 98 (2018): 166.

says its theology was characterized by "pluriformity."[12] Alastair Duke says it had an "ambivalent face." Its "unresolved differences," lying buried "like a bomb with a long fuse until it exploded in the last decade of the sixteenth century," were checked only by Dort. Both sides there claimed to be "the authentic heirs of the Dutch Reformation—and such was the diversity of the Reformed inheritance that, by careful selection of the evidence, they could both advance plausible cases."[13] Linda Gottschalk maintains that the Reformed Church in the sixteenth century was in a "plastic phase" in which "opposing theological views had not yet been co-opted by various interest groups." Thus "Calvinist" and "Reformed" were "often not used as equivalents." "Reformed" was frequently used to describe a theological persuasion "broader" than "Calvinist," which often described a "Genevan-influenced person of narrower views."[14]

Philip Benedict defines the Reformed movement in terms not of soteriology but of its differences with other movements.[15] Reformed confessions that were ambiguous on the finer points of soteriology unequivocally articulated a plethora of anti-Lutheran, anti-Catholic, and anti-Anabaptist views. If sixteenth-century Reformed confessional theology equated to Calvinistic soteriology, why were the doctrines at issue in the Synod of Dort not spelled out clearly like these other doctrines were?

This picture of diversity before Dort is unsurprising because of the cross-pollination between Lutherans (who were non-Calvinist) and the Reformed at this time. Arminius referred to this when he said that Luther and Philip Melanchthon had "later moved away from" their earlier Calvinist-leaning views on election, referring to the Lutheran theologian Niels Hemmingsen.[16] Indeed, Arminius's approach closely paralleled Lutheran views, affirming

---

12. W. Nijenhuis, "Variants of Dutch Calvinism in the Sixteenth Century," in *Ecclesia Reformata: Studies on the Reformation* (Leiden: E. J. Brill, 1994 [1972]), 167–68.

13. Alastair Duke, *Reformation and Revolt in the Low Countries* (London: Hameldon Continuum, 2003), 282.

14. Linda Stuckrath Gottschalk, *Pleading for Diversity: The Church Caspar Coolhaes Wanted* (Gottingen: Vandenhoek and Ruprecht, 2017), 54. Other scholars who support this thesis include Nicholas Tyacke, Peter White, and Silke Muylaert.

15. Philip Benedict, *Christ's Churches Purely Reformed: A Social History of Calvinism* (New Haven, CT: Yale University Press, 2002), xxiii–xxiv, 2, 27, 57, 142–43, 155, 181–85. Albert Hardenberg and Anastatius Veluanus, two of the earliest Dutch Reformed ministers, exemplify this. Their iconoclasm, eucharistic views, and other ecclesiological tenets were Calvinistic and put them out of fellowship with Lutherans, while they retained a more Melanchthonian soteriology.

16. W. Stephen Gunter, *Arminius and His Declaration of Sentiments: An Annotated Translation with Introduction and Theological Commentary* (Waco, TX: Baylor University Press, 2012), 128–9; Arminius, *Works*, 1:642. See Hendrik Frandsen, *Hemmingius in the Same World as Perkinsius and Arminius* (Praestoe, Denmark: Grafik Werk, 2013). The Bangs thesis does not need to show that Arminius and his predecessors were Melanchthonian in every scholastic point but simply that they agreed with him on soteriological Calvinism.

the *gratia universalis* and *gratia resistibilis* while eschewing synergism.[17] The seventeenth-century English Arminian Peter Heylyn thus spoke of the early Dutch Reformed as those "divines of the Belgic churches as were of the old Lutheran stock," who "were better affected unto the Melancthonian doctrine of predestination than to that of Calvin."[18] Melanchthon influenced the earliest Dutch Reformed ministers such as Albert Hardenberg, Joannes Anastasius Veluanus, Johannes Holmannus Secundas, Gellius Snecanus, Caspar Coolhaes, and Clement Martenson.[19]

As Stephen Gunter explains, those older Dutch Reformed ministers represented one of two groups: the *rekkelijken* and *preciezen*. The *rekkelijken* desired toleration on the finer points of soteriology and thought magistrates should have more involvement in church government.[20] In North Holland, "a strong majority of magistrates and a significant contingency of clergy" belonged to this group. As Gunter says, they were "the original shapers of Dutch Protestant ecclesial and political life, while the *preciezen* were the reactionary 'late comers.' It was not unusual to hear, 'Wij waren er eerder dan gij!' (We were here ahead of you!)"[21] This is why Heylen remarked that the Remonstrants' views were "ancienter than Calvinism, in the churches of the Belgic provinces, which being originally Dutch, did first embrace the Reformation, according to the Lutheran model."[22]

The characterization of the early, pluriform Dutch Reformed theology being tightened as Genevan Calvinists began to exert influence over the European Reformed movement has a strong pedigree among Lutheran,

---

17. See Heinrich Schmid, *The Doctrinal Theology of the Evangelical Lutheran Church*, trans. Charles A. Hay and Henry E. Jacobs (Minneapolis: Augsburg, 1961 [1876]), passim.

18. Peter Heylyn, *Historia Quinqu-Articularis . . .*, part I (London: Thomas Johnson, 1660), 38.

19. See, e.g., Bangs, *Arminius*, 93; Wim Janse, *Albert Hardenberg als Theologe. Profil. Eines Bucer-Schülers* (Leiden: Brill, 1994); Gottschalk, *Pleading for Diversity*; Erik A. de Boer, "Who Are the 'Predestinatores'? The Doctrine of Predestination in the Early Dutch Reformation (Joannes Anastasius) and Its Sources (Philip Melanchthon)," in *The Doctrine of Election in Reformed Perspective: Historical and Theological Investigations of the Synod of Dort 1618–1619*, ed. Frank van der Pol (Göttingen: Vandenhoeck and Ruprecht, 2019); Johannes Trapman, "Grotius and Erasmus," in *Hugo Grotius, Theologian: Essays in Honor of G. H. M. Posthumus Meyjes*, eds. Henk J. M. Nellen and Edwin Rabbie (Leiden: Brill, 1994); "Holmannus (Johannes) Secundus," in *Biographisch woordenboek der Nederlanden*, ed. Abraham Jacob van der Aa (Haarlem: J. J. van Brederode, 1862), 309; Jasper van der Steen, "A Contested Past: Memory Wars during the Twelve Years Truce (1609–21)," in *Memory before Modernity: Practices of Memory in Early Modern Europe*, eds. Erika Kuijpers, et al. (Leiden: Brill, 2013), 53.

20. Gunter, *Declaration of Sentiments*, 45–47.

21. Gunter, *Declaration of Sentiments*, 46. See also Bangs, *Arminius*, 54–55; as well as van der Steen, "A Contested Past." Van der Steen discusses this under the heading "Who Was First?" (53).

22. Heylyn, *Historia Quinqu-Articularis*, 38.

Arminian, and many Anglican scholars over the past four centuries.[23] Théodore van Oppenraaij, for example, meticulously argued that "rigid Calvinists" educated in foreign Calvinist universities influenced many Dutch ministers, but "preachers with more penetrating and independent minds continued to defend the ancient doctrine," continuing in the way of the "first Dutch Reformed."[24] This group included Hardenberg, Veluanus, Holmannus, Snecanus, Coolhaes, and Martenson, as well as figures such as John Isbrandtson, Cornelius Meinardi, Cornelius Wiggertsz, Cornelis Cooltuin, Tyco Sabrants, Hubert Duifhuis, and Herman Herbertsz.[25]

The Influence of Melanchthon and Bullinger

Melanchthon and Heinrich Bullinger influenced these proto-Arminians. Muller responds that Arminius and Brandt grouped them all together "as if these thinkers were all in agreement."[26] Yet neither Arminius nor Brandt had that ambitious a goal. They were simply arguing, as Bangs later did, that the earlier Reformed theology was broader and not as tightly defined as it was after Dort.

There is usually no disagreement that Melanchthon influenced these early Dutch Reformed ministers. The debate is over Bullinger's views. Grotius argued, according to Johannes Trapman, that "conditional predestination was not an innovation introduced by Arminius, but was to be found in the works of Melanchthon and the 'sweet explanation' of Bullinger."[27] Proto-Arminians as early as Clement Martenson and Cornelius Meinardi cited Bullinger's "mild exposition" as support for their views, and Arminius followed suit.[28]

There has always been a lively debate over Bullinger's doctrine of predestination. Calvinist scholars such as Cornelius Venema have revived the argument that, despite Bullinger's ambiguity on the doctrine, he, at least eventually,

---

23. Brandt, *History of the Reformation*, 1:308; Limborch, *Historical Relation*, 425–60, 556–87; Trapman, "Grotius and Erasmus," 82. For Lutherans see, e.g., Heinrich Ludolf Benthem, *Holländischer Kirch- und Schulen-Staat* (Frankfurt and Leipzig: Försters, 1698) 1:628; John Laurence von Mosheim, *Institutes of Ecclesiastical History, Ancient and Modern*, vol. 3, trans. James Murdock (London: Longman and Company, 1841 [1726]), 384–85, 401–02; see also Calder, 20; Van Oppenraaij, *La doctrine de la predestination*, 120.
24. Van Oppenraaij, *La doctrine de la predestination*, 120 (translation mine).
25. These preachers are cited early on by Grotius, Heylyn, Limborch, and Brandt. Bangs has the most extensive discussion of these figures in print, but Van Oppenraaij's treatment is the most exhaustive yet, although outside of Oppenraaij there are solid book-length studies of Hardenberg and Coolhaes and shorter treatments of Veluanus and Duifhuis. See, e.g., Janse, Gottschalk, De Boer, Trapman, and Benjamin J. Kaplan, *Calvinists and Libertines: Confession and Community in Utrecht 1578–1620* (Oxford: Clarendon, 1995).
26. Muller, "Arminius and the Reformed Tradition," 28. Muller correctly notes that Arminius was referring to Bullinger's Second Helvetic Confession.
27. Trapman, "Grotius and Erasmus," 86; Grotius, *Ordinum Hollandiase*, 454; G. Brandt, *History of the Reformation*, 1:308–9, 364–65; 437; 442.
28. Arminius, *Works*, 1:604 n. 3, 622.

adopted views similar to Calvin's.[29] However, a robust historiographical tradition insists that Bullinger diverged strongly from Calvin on grace and predestination. Scholars such as J. Wayne Baker and Richard Greaves have advocated this mainstream approach.[30] Baker, in his influential book *Heinrich Bullinger and the Covenant: The Other Reformed Tradition*, makes a convincing case that Bullinger held to a bilateral, conditional covenant and a moderate doctrine of predestination that bore similarities to Melanchthon's view of universal, resistible grace. Baker even says that Bullinger "sometimes sounds like a proto-Arminian."[31]

One can see why Arminius would appeal to Bullinger. In addition to advocating for universal grace, Bullinger said that "God has elected us, not directly, but in Christ, and on account of Christ, in order that those who are now ingrafted into Christ by faith might also be elected."[32] God "ordained and decreed to save all, how many soever have communion and fellowship with Christ, his only-begotten Son; and to destroy or condemn all, how many soever have no part in the communion or fellowship of Christ. . . . Higher and deeper I will not creep into the seat of God's counsel. . . . In Christ, by and through Christ, hath he chosen us."[33] Many scholars also emphasize that Bullinger was sympathetic to Jerome Bolsec when the latter was punished by Calvin for advocating universal, resistible grace.[34]

---

29. See, e.g., Cornelius P. Venema, *Heinrich Bullinger and the Doctrine of Predestination: Author of "the Other Reformed Tradition"?* Texts and Studies in Reformation and Post-Reformation Thought, Richard Muller, series ed. (Grand Rapids: Baker, 2002); Aureio A. Garcia Archilla, *The Theology of History and Apologetic Historiography in Heinrich Bullinger: Truth in History* (San Francisco: Mellen Research University Press, 1992).

30. J. Wayne Baker, *Heinrich Bullinger and the Covenant: The Other Reformed Tradition* (Athens, OH: Ohio University Press, 1980), 165–69. See also Richard L. Greaves, "The Origins and Early Development of English Covenant Thought," *The Historian* 21 (1968), 21–35. Scholars such as Leonard Trinterud, Jens Moeller, W. A. Clebsch, Kenneth Hagen, Charles McCoy, Peter White, Stephen Strehle, Oliver Crisp, and Mark A. Ellis strongly concur, with W. P. Stephens and G. Michael Thomas largely agreeing but being careful to emphasize Bullinger's ambiguity.

31. Baker, "Heinrich Bullinger, the Covenant, and the Reformed Tradition in Retrospect," *Sixteenth Century Journal* 29 (1998), 371.

32. Second Helvetic Confession, 5.053, 5.060, in *The Constitution of the Presbyterian Church (U.S.A.), Part I, Book of Confessions* (Louisville: Office of the General Assembly, 1999), 66, 68.

33. *The Decades of Henry Bullinger*, the Fourth Decade, ed. Thomas Hardin, trans. H. I. (Cambridge: Cambridge University Press, 1851), 186–87.

34. See G. Michael Thomas, *The Extent of the Atonement: A Dilemma for Reformed Theology from Calvin to the Consensus (1536–1675)* (Eugene, OR: Paternoster, 2006), 72; for a similar perspective, see Pieter Rouwendal, "The Doctrine of Predestination in Reformed Orthodoxy," in Herman J. Selderhuis, ed., *A Companion to Reformed Orthodoxy* (Leiden: Brill, 2013), 563.

The Ambiguity of the Reformed Confessional Standards

Bullinger's ambiguity parallels that of the sixteenth-century Reformed confessional standards. The great Reformed scholar John Williamson Nevin exemplified the common perspective that the Reformed confessions were ambiguous on the "knotty points of Calvinism" because of the "material differences in the Church itself." By not taking a position "on such points of divergent opinion," the HC "became a mirror for the true life of the Reformed Church as a whole."[35]

While Calvinist soteriology was allowed, even encouraged, in the Reformed churches, especially in academic theology, it was not required. Most of the confessional standards, designed for the pulpit and lay theological education and piety, did not wade into these disputes. Thus, as H. D. Foster remarked, "Before 1618 one looks in vain for any accepted national creed incorporating the exclusive teachings of this Synod [Dort]." The Remonstrants "were quite in harmony with all Calvin thought it necessary to put into creed or catechism." As Foster argued, the Reformed confessional documents prior to Dort left out the details of how one is elected. Irresistible grace was not seen in these confessional documents, and the certain perseverance of the saints is not found in any Reformed confession before Dort except the Irish Articles three years earlier.[36]

This ambiguity is why the early Reformed were so much warmer than their later counterparts to the Lutherans' non-Calvinistic Augsburg Confession. In the 1970s Nijenhuis commended Calvin's warmth toward Melanchthon and the Augsburg Confession as a good thing for Reformed-Lutheran ecumenical dialogue.[37] One is tempted to ask, might it have been a good thing for the dialogue at the Synod of Dort? As Grotius queried of the Counter-Remonstrants, "I ask those rigid critics who deem nothing tolerable but their own opinion, if Melanchthon were still alive, if he were to come to us, would they deny him the possibility to teach?"[38]

Jeffrey Meyers, examining how the doctrine of election "was *publicly confessed* by the Reformed church, not how it was *taught* or *argued* in the schools," finds "no substantial difference" between the Reformed confessions and those of the Lutherans, which were decidedly non-Calvinistic. While the sixteenth-century confessional standards were more "ecclesiastical" and "pastoral" and ambiguous on the finer points of soteriology, the seventeenth-century ones

---

35. John Williamson Nevin, *The History and Genius of the Heidelberg Catechism* (Chambersburg, PA: Publication Office of the German Reformed Church, 1847), 131; see also Heinrich Heppe, "The Character of the German Reformed Church, and Its Relationship to Lutheranism and Calvinism," *Mercersburg Quarterly Review* 5 (1853): 181–207.
36. Foster, "Liberal Calvinism," 19, 23, 27–28, 30.
37. W. Nijenhuis, *Ecclesia Reformata: Studies on the Reformation* (Leiden: E. J. Brill, 1972), 97–98.
38. Grotius, *Ordinum Hollandias*, 149.

were "more school-oriented, institutional or clerical, polemical, and cosmological" and clearer on these matters. Meyers does not argue that Calvin was more humanistic and biblical whereas later Reformed writers were more scholastic. He simply says that the earlier confessions did not ground their doctrine of election in speculative metaphysics nor "pry" into God's "secret counsels apart from the gospel of Christ . . . the secret, hidden will of God that is in contradiction to his revealed will in Christ and in the Gospel . . . denying or compromising the universality of God's grace."[39]

The Heidelberg Catechism and Belgic Confession

A careful reading of the BC and HC supports this argument. If there had never been "three forms of unity"—the BC (1561), HC (1563), and Canons of Dort (1619)—but only the first two, the Reformed Church on the continent after 1619 would not have been as consistently Calvinistic soteriologically. Dort was needed to narrow the definition of Reformed theology, bring people into line with that definition, and exclude those who would not be brought into line. Joel Beeke is correct when he says that Dort "addressed questions which were either not dealt with or were cursorily handled by previous confessional statements," particularly predestination.[40]

It is commonplace among all but the most rigorous of Calvinists to acknowledge this breadth in the sixteenth-century Reformed churches (and even rigorous Calvinists such as Joel Beeke acknowledge it; they just lament it). Nevin joined other Reformed titans like Philip Schaff and Heinrich Heppe in arguing that the HC neither rules out nor affirms the five points of Calvinism because its authors were attempting to bring harmony in a doctrinally broad Reformed spectrum.[41]

As Nevin explained, the reason Calvinistic soteriology "lies beyond" the HC's "horizon" is that "there was always a part of the Reformed Church which thought differently," and the Catechism was "so constructed as to allow this difference." Its ambiguity was "not by accident," but "with deliberate design." Its Calvinistic authors, such as Zacharias Ursinus, "seem to have held their

---

39. Jeffrey J. Meyers, "Light and Shadow: Confessing the Doctrine of Election in the Sixteenth Century," in *The Glory of Kings: A Festschrift in Honor of James B. Jordan*, eds. Peter J. Leithart and John Barach (Eugene, OR: Pickwick, 2011), 205, 211. 237–39. See also Oliver Crisp, *God Incarnate: Explorations in Christology* (London: T&T Clark, 2009), chapter 2, "The Election of Jesus Christ," 36–39.

40. Joel R. Beeke, *Debated Issues in Sovereign Predestination: Early Lutheran Predestination, Calvinian Reprobation, and Variations in Genevan Lapsarianism* (Göttingen: Vandenhoek and Ruprecht, 2017), 56.

41. Schaff is cited by Hendrikus Berkhof, "The Catechism in Historical Context," in *Essays on the Heidelberg Catechism* (Dayton, OH: United Church Press, 1963), 91. See Lyle D. Bierma, *The Theology of the Heidelberg Catechism: A Reformation Synthesis*, Columbia Series in Reformed Theology (Louisville: Westminster John Knox, 2013), 2–5, who discusses the myriad scholars who support this view.

own theological convictions purposely in abeyance, that they might be true to the objective church life with which they were surrounded. This we all know included much that could never have been satisfied with anything like extreme Calvinism, on the subject of the decrees. From all this, accordingly, the Catechism was made carefully to abstain." Thus not only did the HC not teach limited atonement, but on irresistible grace, Nevin said, it "refuses to give an answer. As it does not teach an unconditional election, so neither does it make salvation to be independent of all contrary motion on the part of the human will. The doctrine of the final perseverance of the saints, as it is called, it leaves in a great measure unsettled."[42]

Beeke laments that the HC "did not fill the Reformed need to grapple confessionally with the doctrine of predestination." Fifty-five years after its publication, Dort was "obliged, due to the challenge of the Remonstrants (Arminians) to spell out the biblical doctrine of predestination in greater detail. . . ." Beeke concludes that the reason for the HC's ambiguity is the theopolitical situation in the Reformed Church of that time.[43]

Lyle Bierma agrees that "the authors intentionally steered clear" of unconditional election, likely "for the sake of doctrinal harmony." Elector Frederick III had to deal not just with Calvinists, but also with followers of Melanchthon and Bullinger. Frederick's "Melanchthonian predilections and his desire to bridge the theological divisions in his realm" made him reluctant to "grant confessional status" to Calvinist soteriology.[44]

It would take the Synod of Dort, Beeke rightly argues, to "take up the task left undone by the Heidelberg Catechism." He asks, "Is Dordt merely a reinforcement for Heidelberg, propping up thicker braces at its weaker places, or is it in fact a coin of new minting . . . ?"[45] Even if Dort was simply "propping up thicker braces" at the Reformed confessional tradition's "weaker places," those weaker places provided the sort of ambiguity and breadth that allowed for Arminian views to be within the pale of Reformed confessional doctrine.

These observations mitigate Muller's most powerful argument: that since Ursinus was the main author of the HC and his commentary teaches unconditional election, the Catechism must be interpreted as excluding Arminius's reading of it.[46] However, scholars writing for groups of people with diverse views often produce consensus documents while still holding narrower views than the documents spell out. Den Boer is correct when he says that "the Catechism was composed so as to gain as wide an acceptance as possible. . . . It was intended

---

42. Nevin, *The History and Genius of the Heidelberg Catechism*, 131–32, 135–37.
43. Beeke, *Debated Issues in Sovereign Predestination*, 56.
44. Lyle D. Bierma, *An Introduction to the Heidelberg Catechism: Sources, History, and Theology.* Texts and Studies in Reformation and Post-Reformation Thought, Richard A. Muller, gen. ed. (Grand Rapids: Baker, 2005), 95–96.
45. Bierma, *An Introduction to the Heidelberg Catechism*, 57.
46. Muller, "Arminius and the Reformed Tradition," 34–35.

as a consensus document and remained silent on critical points of dispute—including predestination! Arminius's claim to be loyal to the Catechism is not entirely unusual given the wide net it cast."[47]

One sees the same ambiguity in the BC, which Arminius eagerly affirmed. Muller's argument is twofold: (1) most Reformed clergy at the time interpreted the BC as teaching unconditional election, and (2) he agrees with them.[48] There is no debate on the first argument, but the second one involves a hermeneutical, not a historical, question. Muller's interpretation is not self-evident. It is simply too much of a stretch to argue that Arminius's views were "conceived as an alternative to the plain and assumed meaning" of the BC.[49] Many scholars disagree with Muller on the article's "plain" meaning, and as far as its "assumed" meaning is concerned, it all depends on who was doing the assuming. As Edwin Rabbie quips, "that the Arminians never had much trouble signing Article 16 of the Confession, which, incidentally, was considered ambiguous (at least by the Arminians), is saying a lot."[50] As with the HC, to use Beeke's word picture, Dort had to "prop up" the "weaker places" of the BC with "thicker braces."[51]

The BC also does not clearly assert the doctrine of perseverance affirmed at Dort. Jay Collier argues that the doctrine simply "lacked widespread confessional status before Dort." As Collier notes, the BC and HC "never clearly state" it. He persuasively argues that the possibility of apostasy was a live option in the international Reformed community before Dort. When the Synod rejected the possibility of the apostasy of the regenerate, it "closed the gaps found in previous confessions and eliminated the possibility of any other Reformed position." This is one reason the Church of England came to be "at odds" with the developing "international trends of the Reformed churches" in the direction of Calvinism.[52]

Summary

The arguments against the Bangs thesis are that (1) there were national synods before Dort that were Calvinistic, (2) the fact that the authors of the confessional standards were Calvinistic means the standards themselves were, and (3) Calvinism was in the majority. I am not opposing argument 1. It does not add anything to the conversation to say that, in the mid-1580s, thoroughgoing Calvinism had become ascendant enough to dominate a national synod.

---

47. Den Boer, "'Cum Delectu,'" 85.
48. Muller, "Arminius and the Reformed Tradition," 39.
49. Muller, "Arminius and the Reformed Tradition," 46.
50. Edwin Rabbie, "General Introduction," in Grotius, *Ordinum Hollandiae*, 7n4.
51. Beeke, *Debated Issues in Sovereign Predestination*, 57; see also Den Boer, "'Cum Delectu,'" 85.
52. Jay T. Collier, *Debating Perseverance: The Augustinian Heritage in Post-Reformation England*, Oxford Studies in Historical Theology (New York: Oxford University Press, 2018), 10–12, 17–18.

This fact does not refute the existence of an earlier, broader, proto-Arminian Reformed approach. Argument 2 is implausible in light of the overwhelming evidence by Nevin, Beeke, Bierma, and others that all the opinions of the framers do not make their way into these documents because they are aiming to bring together diverse theological constituencies in a highly charged political context. Argument 3 is not in debate and is irrelevant to the Bangs thesis. The fact that a majority subgroup is gaining power at a given point in time does not prove that the minority subgroup was, before that point in time, an illegitimate or disallowed expression of the overall group. This is especially true when the confessional boundaries of the overall group are ambiguous on the points of controversy between the majority and minority subgroups.

REFLECTION QUESTIONS

1. What is the main reason Carl Bangs thought Arminius fit into the definition of "Reformed" in the sixteenth century?

2. How do Melanchthon and Lutheran theology figure into why the BC and HC were ambiguous on the finer points of Calvinist soteriology?

3. What are Richard Muller's arguments for why Arminius was not a confessionally Reformed theologian?

4. What have others scholars said about the ambiguity of confessional Reformed theology before Dort?

5. Why were the Canons of Dort necessary to shore up the Calvinism of the Reformed Church?

PART 2

Questions About the Atonement and Justification

The Nature of the
Atonement and Justification

Did Arminius Affirm Penal Substitutionary Atonement?

The Calvinist theologian Robert L. Reymond is representative of most Calvinists when he says that the Arminian theory of atonement is the governmental theory. That theory, he remarks, "denies that Christ's death was intended to pay the penalty for sin," and its "germinal teachings are in Arminius."[1] This opinion, however, is not unique to Calvinists. The Wesleyan scholar James K. Grider, in his article on "Arminianism" in the *Evangelical Dictionary of Theology* says, "A spillover from Calvinism into Arminianism has occurred in recent decades. Thus many Arminians whose theology is not very precise say that Christ paid the penalty for our sins. Yet such a view is foreign to Arminianism."[2]

Many Arminians concur with this statement, which has led Calvinists to assume that if someone differs from Calvinism on how one comes to be in a state of grace (determinism, unconditional predestination, and irresistible grace), it also entails the rejection of the classic Reformed penal substitutionary or penal satisfaction view of atonement. To see that this is not the case, one only has to study Arminius's doctrine of penal substitutionary atonement.[3]

---

1. Robert L. Reymond, *A New Systematic Theology of the Christian Religion* (Nashville: Thomas Nelson, 1998), 474.
2. J. K. Grider, "Arminianism," in *Evangelical Dictionary of Theology*, ed. Walter A. Elwell (Grand Rapids: Baker, 1984), 80.
3. I have dealt with this at length in J. Matthew Pinson, "The Nature of Atonement in the Theology of Jacobus Arminius," *Journal of the Evangelical Theological Society* 53 (2010): 173–85, reprinted as Chapter 2 of J. Matthew Pinson, *Arminian and Baptist: Explorations in a Theological Tradition* (Nashville: Randall House, 2015), 37–55. While, as with other Reformed theologians, penal satisfaction was not the only aspect of atonement Arminius emphasized, it was central.

The Priesthood of Christ

Arminius based his doctrine of penal substitutionary atonement on the classic Reformed doctrine of the threefold office of Christ as prophet, priest, and king. In his office as priest, Christ fulfills the demands of the law and suffers sin's penalty on behalf of the believing sinner.[4] Appealing to the letter to the Hebrews, Arminius established that Christ is the only possible priest or mediator between sinful humanity and a holy God. In his priestly office, Christ gives himself as an "expiatory," "propitiatory" "oblation" for sin and intercedes for believers at the Father's right hand.[5] To fulfill these "sacerdotal" duties of his priestly office, Christ fulfills the divine law in complete obedience to his Father in his life and death.[6]

Arminius asked the question, Who is qualified to atone for the sins of humanity? He must be both priest and sacrifice, priest and "victim." Yet "in the different orders of creatures neither sacrifice nor priest could be found." An angel could not qualify because a priest, according to Hebrews 5:1, must be a representative of the people. A human being could not qualify because sinners cannot approach God, "who is pure light," to make an offering. Yet, "the priest was to be taken from among men, and the oblation to God was to consist of a human victim." The all-wise God decided that a human being who shared humanity with "his brethren" and was "in all things tempted as they were" and "able to sympathize" with their sufferings must atone for sin. Yet he could not be sinful (Heb. 7:26); furthermore, this priest-victim must also be divine.[7]

Divine Justice and Wrath

For Arminius, God's most essential attribute is his justice, and it must be maintained inviolable in the salvation of humanity, which is an exhibition of his mercy. In his Oration "On the Priesthood of Christ," Arminius personified justice, mercy, and wisdom, discussing their role in God's decision to make Christ priest. Justice demanded punishment for sin. Mercy wanted to avoid that punishment.[8] It was Wisdom's role to decide how to accomplish this, how to please Justice and Mercy. She decided that it was only through "expiatory sacrifice" or "voluntary suffering of death," which would "appease Justice," opening up "such a way for Mercy as she has desired." Justice and Mercy agreed to these terms.[9]

---

4. Arminius's doctrine of the threefold office of Christ is that of the Belgic Confession of Faith, art. 21.
5. Arminius, *Works*, 2:219–21.
6. Jacobus Arminius, *The Works of James Arminius*, 3 vols., trans. James Nichols and William Nichols (Nashville: Randall House, 2007), 2:219–21. Public Disputation 24, "On the Office of our Lord Jesus Christ."
7. Arminius, *Works*, 1:414–15, Oration IV, "On the Priesthood of Christ."
8. Arminius, *Works*, 1:413.
9. Arminius, *Works*, 1:413–14.

One sees this relationship between justice and mercy in Arminius's notion of God's twofold love, his love for the creature and for his justice. God's love for the creature manifests itself in his desire to save sinners. His love for justice manifests itself in his "hatred against sin." Similar to Wisdom's meeting the terms of justice and mercy, Arminius said it "was the will of God that each of these kinds of love should be satisfied." Thus God "gave satisfaction to his love for the creature who was a sinner, when he gave up his Son who might act the part of Mediator. But he rendered satisfaction to his love for justice and to his hatred against sin, when he imposed on his Son the office of Mediator by the shedding of his blood and by the suffering of death (Heb. ii. 10; v. 8, 9)."[10]

God satisfies his creature-love through forgiveness of sin. He satisfies his justice-love by punishing sin, "inflicting stripes" on his son. Arminius said that "it was not the effect of those stripes that God might love his creature, but that, while love for justice presented no hindrance, through his love for the creature he could remit sins and bestow life eternal." In this satisfaction of God's love for the creature and for his own justice, Arminius explains, God "rendered satisfaction to himself, and appeased himself in the Son of his love."[11]

The idea of God's love for his justice was important to Arminius. Divine justice is rigorous and inflexible, making it necessary for the Father to "impose upon His son the punishment due from sinners, and taken away from them, to be borne and paid in full by Him."[12] In Christ's atonement, "the rigour of inflexible justice was declared, which could not pardon sin, even to the interceding Son, except the penalty were fully paid."[13]

Arminius also used this concept to argue against Calvinism's election *unto* faith rather than *in consideration of* one's in-Christ status. According to Arminius, in Calvinism's doctrine of unconditional election, God sets his elective love on people without respect to the merit of Christ or individuals' union with him. This, however, does damage to divine justice "because it affirms, that God has absolutely willed to save certain individual men, and has decreed their salvation without having the least regard to righteousness or obedience: The proper inference from which, is, that God loves such men far more than his own justice [or righteousness]."[14]

10. Arminius, *Works*, 2:221. William den Boer gives special treatment to this doctrine in his book, *God's Twofold Love: The Theology of Jacob Arminius (1559–1609)* (Göttingen: Vandenhoeck and Ruprecht, 2010).
11. Arminius, *Works*, 2:221. See also "Declaration of Sentiments," 1:653; Private Disputations 33–34.
12. Arminius, *Works*, 3:195. "Friendly Conference with Dr. F. Junius."
13. Arminius, *Works*, 3:195. With regard to rigor and inflexibility, see also Oration IV, "On the Priesthood of Christ" (1:409), where Arminius speaks of "the invariable rule of Divine Justice."
14. Arminius, *Works*, 1:624, "Declaration of Sentiments, On Predestination."

For Arminius, divine justice is essential to God's nature; it is not something outside God's nature but comes forth from it. "God is not bound by created laws," Arminius affirmed, "but He is a law to Himself; for He is Justice itself" and he is "bound by the immutability of His own nature and justice."[15] Thus divine justice requires three things: divine wrath, satisfaction, and payment. Wrath is an expression of divine justice against the human violation of law and gospel.[16] It culminates in punishment: "Punishment was consequent on guilt and the divine wrath; the equity of this punishment is from guilt, the infliction of it is by wrath."[17]

God loves his own nature and justice. So he is naturally repelled by injustice or sin. Arminius repeatedly emphasized the distinction between God's love for his creatures and their blessedness and his love of his essential nature and justice. The former is secondary to the latter. However, he explained, God also hates the misery sin puts the creature into and desires to take it away. However, if the creature insists on remaining alienated from the righteousness of God, God hates the creature and loves his or her misery. Yet this hatred does not arise from God's free will but from "natural necessity."[18] God's love for people finds a way for them to be shielded from the hatred for their unrighteousness that necessarily comes from his just nature.

Satisfaction and Payment

In his conception of atonement, Arminius viewed God as the divine judge whose just nature necessarily requires satisfaction. As quoted above, God "rendered satisfaction to his love for justice and to his hatred against sin, when he imposed on his Son the office of Mediator by the shedding of his blood and by the suffering of death."[19] God has the "right" to require satisfaction "for the injuries which He has sustained" because of sin. He is the "Divine Person in whose hands rest the right" to receive satisfaction for his justice. It is not fitting, Arminius argued, that God should "recede ... or resign any part of it," because of "the rigid inflexibility of his justice, according to which he hates iniquity and does not permit a wicked person to dwell in his presence."[20]

Another way of saying this is that this satisfaction is a satisfaction of God's law. All people owe God the duty to perform his law, but they cannot perform

---

15. Arminius, *Works*, 3:357, "Examination of Perkins's Pamphlet."
16. Arminius, *Works*, 2:157, Public Disputation 8, "On Actual Sins"; see also Public Disputation 7, "On the First Sin of the First Man."
17. Arminius, *Works*, 2:374; Private Disputation 31, "On the Effects of the Sin of Our First Parents. On punishment, see also Private Disputation 19, "On the Various Distinctions of the Will of God" (2:346).
18. Arminius, *Works*, 2:374.
19. Arminius, *Works*, 2:221. Cf. Ibid. 2:256, Public Disputation 19, "On the Justification of Man before God."
20. Arminius, *Works*, 1:12–13, Oration, "On the Priesthood of Christ."

it. So Christ, as mediator, must perform it for them. The law is twofold; it consists of both obedience and punishment. "That of obedience is first and absolute: that of punishment is the later, and does not take place except when obedience has not been rendered."[21]

In classic Reformed fashion, Arminius utilized the common theme of "paying the debt," "paying the penalty," and "paying the price" of sin. Humanity's "injuries" against God's justice accrue a debt sinners must pay.[22] Yet, no ordinary human being can pay this penalty. Only a sinless priest can.[23] The most common language Arminius used was "pay[ing] the price of redemption for sins by suffering the punishment due to them."[24] He speaks of "the price of our redemption paid by Christ," God being the one "who receives that price."[25] Arminius occasionally used ransom language without comment, but he never spoke of a price paid to the devil. God the Father is the one who receives the price of redemption from the divine Son.[26]

Summary

Contrary to popular belief, Arminius did not teach a governmental view of atonement, despite the fact that so many subsequent Arminians have. Instead, he held fast to the Reformed view of penal substitutionary atonement articulated in the Belgic Confession and Heidelberg Catechism. This view sees Christ's priestly sacrifice as a necessary response to human sinfulness and the inflexible justice of God, which cannot be set aside without doing damage to the divine essence. For Arminius, as for most other Reformed theologians of his day, God, by means of Christ's propitiatory sacrifice, extends his mercy to sinners while satisfying his justice. Through his oblation, Christ as priest and sacrifice suffers the divine punishment that is due for human sin. This suffering constitutes the satisfaction or payment to the divine justice for redemption of human beings from sin, guilt, and wrath. Arminius's understanding of the nature of atonement, in the context of his view of the priestly office of Jesus Christ, beautifully expresses the penal-substitutionary views of the Reformed theology of his day.

---

21. Arminius, *Works*, 3:477, "Examination of William Perkins's Pamphlet on the Mode and Order of Predestination"; 2:198, Public Disputation 12, "On the Law of God."
22. Arminius, *Works*, 1:406. See also 3:477, Examination of William Perkins's Pamphlet on the Mode and Order of Predestination. See also Public Disputation 12, "On the Law of God" (2:198).
23. Arminius, *Works*, 1:415, Oration IV, "On the Priesthood of Christ."
24. Arminius, *Works*, 1:419. Arminius's use of the imagery of paying a price is consistent with Francis Turretin's approach in Topic 14, question 10 of *Institutes of Elenctic Theology*, trans. George Musgrave Giger, ed. James T. Dennison, Jr. (Phillipsburg, NJ: P&R, 1994) 2:417–26.
25. Arminius, *Works*, 3:74, Sixth Proposition of Arminius: Arminius's Reply, or Consideration of [Junius's] Answer to the Sixth Proposition.
26. Arminius, *Works*, 3:74.

REFLECTION QUESTIONS

1. How does Arminius's understanding of the priestly office of Christ inform his doctrine of the nature of atonement?

2. Can you recount Arminius's image of Justice, Mercy, and Wisdom deciding on how God should atone for sin?

3. What does Arminius mean by the phrase "God's twofold love"?

4. Why do you think Arminius did not believe God could simply forgive sin without paying its penalty?

5. What does Arminius mean when he says that Christ's atonement satisfies God's law?

What Have Later Arminians Believed About Penal Substitution?

The penal substitutionary categories of Arminius's doctrine of the nature of atonement subsided in much of subsequent Arminian theology, such as that of Remonstrants like Hugo Grotius, English Arminians like the Puritan John Goodwin, and the Wesleyan movement that built on their thought. Yet penal substitution persisted in the theology of the English General Baptists, as seen in the writings of Thomas Grantham.

Thomas Grantham's Penal Substitutionary View

According to Grantham, "God having made a righteous law, it must be fulfilled; and none was able to do this but Christ, and he did fulfill it in our behalf." Thus, the "righteousness of the law is fulfilled in the children of God, because Christ's righteousness is made theirs through believing." Grantham later said, "The justice of God cried against us for sin committed; and sin must be purged by the blood of Christ; He bare our sins, that is, the punishment of our sins, in his own body on the tree."[1]

Grantham's theory of atonement is summarized in the following quotation from his book *Christianismus Primitivus*: "According to the will of God, and his eternal wisdom, Christ did, in the place and stead of mankind, fulfill that law, by which the whole world stood guilty before God." Here Grantham explained "how deeply mankind stood indebted to the righteous God of heaven and earth, and how unable he was to pay that score; and how consequently he must inevitably undergo the eternal displeasure of God, with the malediction of his righteous law." Humanity must undergo God's judgment and wrath because they "fall short" of God's law. Christ is "the only physician

---

1. Thomas Grantham, *St. Paul's Catechism: Or, A Brief Explication of the Six Principles of the Christian Religion, as recorded Heb. 6.1, 2* (London, 1687), 28.

to cure the malady of mankind," the only individual who can "pay the score" or the debt of sin that men and women have accrued to God.[2]

Like his modern-day descendants Leroy Forlines and Robert Picirilli, Grantham affirmed two aspects of atonement, passive and active obedience. Passive obedience is Christ's death on the cross, which satisfied the penalty for sin. Active obedience is Christ's satisfaction of divine justice by fulfilling God's law. "It is true, he was born under the Law," Grantham averred, "and so stood bound to keep the Law, yet for our sakes he was so born; and consequently all that he did in that capacity [active obedience], was on our account also, as well as his Sufferings [passive obedience]: For the Transgressions committed against the Law, was he crucified in our place and stead."[3]

John Goodwin's Governmental View

The Arminian Puritan John Goodwin, one of the most influential seventeenth-century Arminian voices outside the General Baptists, differed strongly from Grantham's views on the nature of atonement. Grantham's perspective aligned more with the Reformed and Arminius. Goodwin's views were more like those of Arminius's colleague Hugo Grotius who after Arminius's death, like most of the Remonstrants, developed his Arminianism in much more non-Reformed directions. One of these is the governmental view of atonement, the view toward which most Wesleyans have tended. Goodwin's own views were very important in the development of Wesleyan theology. Wesley himself promoted and republished Goodwin's writings on atonement and justification.[4]

Goodwin concurred with Grotius's governmental theory of atonement. Grotius held that God can pardon sinners without satisfaction for the violation of God's law. Such a pardon is within God's discretion as sovereign.[5] Thus, God accepts Christ's sacrifice in his role as sovereign or governor rather than judge. Christ's sacrificial death on the cross, according to the governmental view, symbolizes the punishment that results from sin. It is a deterrent to sin. So sin's penalty is not paid for or satisfied, as in the penal satisfaction understanding, but rather set to the side. God pardons the believing sinner as

---

2. Grantham, *Christianismus Primitivus, or The Ancient Christian Religion* (London: Francis Smith, 1678), Book II, 62–63.
3. Grantham, *Christianismus Primitivus*, 68.
4. Interestingly, however, Wesley's views on the nature of atonement fall somewhere between those of Arminius and Grantham on one side and Grotius and Goodwin on the other, though his anti-imputational views on justification are as rigorous as those of Goodwin (see Questions 10–11).
5. Grotius's governmentalism also influenced Richard Baxter and John Tillotson. See Alan C. Clifford, *Atonement and Justification: English Evangelical Theology, 1640–1790: An Evaluation* (Oxford: Clarendon, 1990).

a governor would pardon a guilty criminal, agreeing not to hold his past sins against him.

In his magisterial work *Imputatio Fidei*, which Wesley later reprinted and widely circulated, Goodwin articulated this approach to atonement (and the view that flows from it that the righteousness of Christ is not imputed in justification). He argued, "The sentence or curse of the law, was not properly executed upon Christ in his death, but this death of Christ was a ground or consideration unto God, whereupon to dispense with his Law, and to let fall or suspend the execution of the penalty or curse therein threatened."[6]

For Arminius and Grantham, the chief reason for the advent of Christ was to meet the inexorable demands of God's law. For Goodwin, on the contrary, Christ's main reason for coming was to set aside God's law, not holding it against the sinner who believes in him. Only when God dispenses with his law can he forgive sinners and not impute their trespasses to them. "But God in sparing and forbearing the transgressors (who according to the tenor of the law should have been punished) manifestly dispenseth with the law, and doth not execute it."[7] Thus, in Goodwin's theology, the atonement is not, strictly speaking, necessary. However, it is how God in his sovereignty or good government elected to administer salvation. Goodwin explained: "Neither did God require the death and sufferings of Christ as a valuable consideration whereon to dispense with his law towards those that believe, more (if so much) in a way of satisfaction to his justice, than to his wisdom. For (doubtless) God might with as much justice, as wisdom (if not much more) have passed by the transgression of his law without consideration or satisfaction."[8]

Goodwin agreed with Grotius's principle that "the law is not something internal with God or the will of God itself, but only an effect of that will. It is perfectly certain that the effects of the divine will are mutable," or that divine law is promulgated by God as "a positive law which at some time he may wish to relax."[9] This is why, as Goodwin stated, God could "dispense with his Law" in pardoning sinners. So, for Goodwin, the atonement is an exhibition of public justice. It is not a penal satisfaction, as Arminius and Grantham taught.

---

6. John Goodwin, *Imputatio Fidei. Or A Treatise of Justification* (London, 1642), part 2, 33.
7. Goodwin, *Imputatio Fidei*, 33.
8. Goodwin, *Imputatio Fidei*, 34–35.
9. Hugo Grotius, *A Defence of the Catholic Faith Concerning the Satisfaction of Christ, against Faustus Socinus*, trans. Frank Hugh Foster (Andover, MA: Warren F. Draper, 1889), 75. Statements like this show why Garry Williams's view that Grotius did not support what has come to be known as the governmental view of atonement is mistaken. See Garry Williams, "Grotius, Hugo," in *The Dictionary of Historical Theology*, ed. Trevor Hart (Grand Rapids: Eerdmans, 2000), 236. See instead Gert van den Brink, "Hugo Grotius," in *T&T Clark Companion to Atonement*, ed. Adam J. Johnson (Edinburgh: Bloomsbury T&T Clark, 2017), 523–25. I appreciate my interaction with my colleague Kevin Hester on this subject.

Wesleyan Views

In his doctrine of the nature of atonement, Wesley aligned himself with the penal satisfaction tradition of Luther, Calvin, and Cranmer. Despite his basic reliance on the seventeenth-century Anglican Arminians, Baxter, and Goodwin, who relied on Grotius's governmental theory, Wesley's doctrine of atonement was different from theirs.

Wesley speaks of God "showing justice on his own Son" so that he "might evidence himself to be strictly and inviolably righteous in the administration of his government, even while he is the merciful justifier of the sinner that believeth in Jesus. The attribute of justice must be preserved inviolate; and inviolate it is preserved, *if there was a real infliction of punishment on our Saviour.*"[10] Thus Wesley was at great pains to affirm a penal substitutionary view of atonement. However, he modified the penal substitutionary doctrine in two ways. First, for Wesley, the atonement consisted of Christ's passive obedience, his bearing the divine penalty for sin, not his positive fulfillment of the law: "Although I believe Christ fulfilled God's law, yet I do not affirm he did this to purchase redemption for us. This was done by his dying in our stead."[11] Wesley further modified the penal satisfaction view of atonement with his distinction between past and future sins. He asserted that Christ atoned only for the believer's past sins. Christ's atonement was not for the *condition* of sin, but it was a propitiation for "the remission of past sins."[12]

This concept is borne out in "A Dialogue between an Antinomian and His Friend," in which the antinomian says Christ "did then 'heal, take away,' put an end to, and utterly destroy, all our sins." Then his friend replies, "Did he then heal the wound before it was made, and put an end to our sins before they had a beginning? This is so glaring, palpable an absurdity, that I cannot conceive how you can swallow it."[13] Wesley's conception that Christ atoned only for past sins rather than for sin in general exerted great influence on his view of justification and perseverance.

Goodwin's understanding of atonement, which Wesley publicized, has been the majority view of Wesleyan theology. This is illustrated by Kenneth Grider's comments in his entry on Arminianism in the *Evangelical Dictionary of Theology*: "Arminians teach that what Christ did he did for every person; therefore what he did could not have been to pay the penalty, since no one would then ever go to eternal perdition. . . . [H]is death is such that all will

---

10. John Wesley, *Explanatory Notes upon the New Testament* (Peabody, MA: Hendrickson, 1986), Romans 3:26 (italics added).
11. John Wesley, "Some Remarks on Mr. Hill's 'Review of All the Doctrines Taught by Mr. John Wesley,'" in *The Works of John Wesley*, 3rd ed., ed. Thomas Jackson (Grand Rapids: Baker, 1979 [1872]), 10:386.
12. *Notes,* Romans 3:25. Wesley defines "past sins" here as "all the sins antecedent to their believing."
13. *Works,* 10:267.

see that forgiveness is costly and will strive to cease from anarchy in the world God governs. This view is called the governmental theory of atonement." He goes on to say that "Scripture always states that Christ suffered . . . and never that he was punished because the Christ who was crucified was guiltless and sinless." He explains that Arminians teach that God "would not be forgiving us at all if his justice was satisfied by the real thing that justice needs: punishment."[14]

One can see the contrast between Grider's doctrine and that of Arminius, despite his assertion that "Arminians teach . . . the governmental theory of atonement."[15] At least one Arminian did not do so: Arminius. Yet, as already discussed, others in the early modern period, such as Grantham, embraced Reformed views of atonement like those of Arminius rather than subscribing to the views of later Remonstrants such as Grotius, which John Goodwin and most of his Arminian heirs did.

One need not think that the doctrine of penal substitutionary atonement's minority status in the Wesleyan tradition means that Wesleyans do not or cannot articulate it, as Grider stated above. Modern examples of Wesleyan Arminian advocates of penal substitution include I. Howard Marshall and Thomas Oden, both of whom affirm robust versions of the doctrine.[16] Wesley's unique appropriation of the penal substitutionary view of atonement, mentioned above, makes it possible for Wesleyan Arminians to explore these more-Reformed motifs.[17]

The General/Free Will Baptist Tradition

The General/Free Will Baptist tradition has upheld the penal-satisfaction approach. One sees it no more clearly than in the seventeenth-century General Baptist confessional document, the Orthodox Creed. Its article, "Of Christ and his Mediatorial Office," elegantly summarizes the General/Free Will Baptist position:

> And being concerned by this office or appointment of the Father to make peace, it plainly appears, that he is the only fit mediator between God and man, who is very God and very man; yet one Christ, who was sanctified and anointed with the Holy Spirit above measure, and was superlatively and admirably fitted for and called unto this office by his

---

14. Walter A. Elwell, ed., *Evangelical Dictionary of Theology*, s.v. "Arminianism."
15. Walter A. Elwell, ed., *Evangelical Dictionary of Theology*, s.v. "Arminianism."
16. I. Howard Marshall, *Aspects of the Atonement: Cross and Resurrection in the Reconciling of God and Humanity* (Colorado Springs: Paternoster, 2007), 54–61; Thomas C. Oden, *Classic Christianity: A Systematic Theology* (New York: HarperCollins, 1992), 409–10, 422.
17. Thomas C. Oden, *John Wesley's Scriptural Christianity: A Plain Exposition of His Teachings on Christian Doctrine* (Grand Rapids: Zondervan, 1994), 216.

Father, who put all judgment into his hand, and power to execute the same, and he willingly undertook the same; and being made under the law, did perfectly fulfill or keep it, and underwent the punishment due to us, which we should have suffered, our sin, and the punishment of it being reckoned, or imputed to him; he being made a curse for us, and underwent and trod the wine-press of his Father's wrath for us, in dolorous pangs and agony of soul, and painful sufferings in his body, was crucified, dead, and buried, or remained in the state of the dead, yet saw no corruption, and on the third day he arose from the dead.[18]

This tradition continued in the Free Will Baptist Church in America, which originated from English General Baptists who moved across the Atlantic in the seventeenth century. It has been formulated in modern times by F. Leroy Forlines in his systematic theology, *The Quest for Truth*.[19] Forlines, a thoroughgoing Arminian, strongly contends for the Reformed doctrine of penal satisfaction and its consistency with Arminianism. In strains reminiscent of Arminius and Grantham, Forlines argues that, because God is by nature absolutely holy, sin by necessity must be punished. The sinner who violates God's holy law, which is an expression of the justice that is at the essence of his divine nature, must undergo the penalty of eternal death. "There are two things that the justice of God will not permit a departure from," Forlines argues. First, "sin can under no circumstances go unpunished." Second, "under no circumstances will a person stand justified in God's presence without absolute righteousness."[20]

No one can take that penalty away from humanity except the divine-human Christ. He is the only one who can bring the righteousness of God to bear on humanity through his fulfillment of the law on the sinner's behalf and his bearing of sin's penalty, thus paying the debt of sin. Utilizing traditional Reformed categories, Forlines refers to Christ's fulfillment of the law on the sinner's behalf as his active obedience. His suffering the penalty for sin on the cross, Forlines avers, is Christ's passive obedience. These two constitute the righteousness of God, a concept on which Forlines expands in his

---

18. A fresh transcription of this confession of faith by Madison Grace, with prefatory material that does not appear in earlier reprintings, can be found at Southwestern Baptist Theological Seminary's website: http://baptiststudiesonline.com/wp-content/uploads/2007/02/orthodox-creed.pdf.

19. See Jesse F. Owens's perceptive essay, "Forlines's Theology of Atonement and Justification," in *The Promise of Arminian Theology: Essays in Honor of F. Leroy Forlines*, ed. Matthew Steven Bracey and W. Jackson Watts (Nashville: Randall House Academic, 2016), 81–100.

20. F. Leroy Forlines, *Classical Arminianism: A Theology of Salvation* (Nashville: Randall House, 2011), 209.

commentary on Romans. He calls what Paul refers to as "the righteousness of God" as "a 'God-provided righteousness.' This righteousness is 'without works.'. . . . It is the righteousness of Christ."[21]

As Forlines teaches, the "righteousness and death of Christ" together satisfy the demands of God's law. They provide God a propitiatory sacrifice for sin, thus turning away his wrath and satisfying his intrinsic justice. Forlines explains:

> What the Old Testament sacrifice did in symbol on the day of atonement, Jesus Christ did in reality. He lived a completely holy life, thus fulfilling the demand for absolute righteousness. He paid the full penalty for sin, thus fulfilling the demands for a penalty. Propitiation is the full satisfaction of the demands of the law, for righteousness and the payment of a penalty, by Jesus Christ. This makes it possible for God to turn His wrath from the sinner who believes in Jesus, and to view him with favor, yet remain a God of justice.[22]

Forlines roots his doctrine of the penal satisfaction nature of atonement in careful exegesis of the New Testament in its redemptive-historical context. Christ's atonement is a playing out of what was foreshadowed in types and symbols by the old covenant sacrificial system. Christ, the Lamb of God slain from the foundation of the world, is our propitiation, our mercy seat (Rom. 3:25–26, Heb. 9:5). Foretold in prophecy as the one on whom God would lay the iniquities of all humanity (Isa. 53:6), he bore our sins in his body on the cross (1 Peter 2:24). Redeeming us from the law's curse, he was made sin and a curse on our behalf (Gal. 3:13, 2 Cor. 5:21).[23]

No Arminian since Arminius has theologically and exegetically made such an extensive and compelling argument for penal satisfaction or penal substitutionary atonement as Forlines.[24] He believes that this thoroughly

---

21. Forlines, *Classical Arminianism*, 213. See Forlines's more-detailed exegesis of the relevant passages in his *Romans*, Randall House Bible Commentary (Nashville: Randall House, 1987).

22. Forlines, *Classical Arminianism*, 214.

23. See, e.g., Forlines, *Classical Arminianism*, 210–13.

24. Forlines wants to revive the phraseology of "penal satisfaction," thus rescuing it from its shackles to Anselm. The Anglican scholar George Cadwalader Foley was correct when he stated that "the Reformers taught that our Lord's sufferings were *penal,* and Anselm expressly distinguishes between punishment and satisfaction. . . . As a *commutation,* satisfaction was instead of punishment; but they transformed it into satisfaction *by* punishment" (George Cadwalader Foley, *Anselm's Theory of the Atonement* [New York: Longmans, Green, and Co., 1909], 219). Many Reformed scholars have used the term *penal satisfaction* to describe this Reformational emphasis. Nineteenth-century thinkers such as Charles Hodge, Augustus Strong, William G. T. Shedd, and Robert L. Dabney used the term, taking it over from earlier Reformed scholastics like Francis Turretin and Stephen Charnock. In

biblical doctrine is crucial for an Arminian soteriology. One reason he thinks this, as the next chapter discusses, is that he sees it as the only way to free Arminian theology from the shackles of legalism and works-righteousness that have encumbered segments of it. Christ's satisfying the demands of God's justice is what, according to New Testament teaching, makes possible our justification by God's grace alone through faith alone. This has ramifications for an Arminian theology of perseverance, apostasy, sanctification, and spirituality, which subsequent chapters will consider.

Summary

    While Arminius held to a Reformed view of penal substitutionary atonement, most Arminians after him moved away from this view. Wesley's view of atonement employed themes from both the penal satisfaction and governmental views. However, most subsequent Wesleyans demurred from penal satisfaction, advocating a doctrine closer to the governmental view of Hugo Grotius and John Goodwin. Still, some Arminians adhered to the classic, Reformed view of penal substitutionary atonement as Arminius had done. This approach is most notable in the General/Free Will Baptist tradition, but one also sees Arminian examples of it outside that tradition. The doctrine of the nature of atonement has enormous effects on how Arminians understand justification, sanctification, perseverance, and assurance.

REFLECTION QUESTIONS

1. What is the governmental view of atonement?

2. What is the basic difference between the governmental view of atonement and the penal substitutionary view of the Reformers?

3. Why do you think Kenneth Grider says that some Arminians' articulation of penal substitution represents a Calvinist importation into Arminian theology?

4. What do Grantham and Forlines mean by the active and passive obedience of Christ?

5. What is meant by the term "penal satisfaction," and how does it further explain the doctrine of penal substitutionary atonement?

---

the twentieth century the term was employed by writers as diverse as James Orr, Lewis Sperry Chafer, and Cornelius Van Til. Recent scholars like J. I. Packer and Timothy George and the Methodist Thomas Oden have also employed the term.

Do Arminians Affirm the Imputation of Christ's Righteousness in Justification?

Wesleyan Arminians typically have answered no to this question, while Reformed Arminians have said yes. The doctrine of justification and how it relates to the doctrines of the nature of atonement, sanctification, perseverance, and assurance, constitute the main difference between Reformed Arminianism and Wesleyan Arminianism. These two systems agree on *how one comes to be* in a state of grace, but disagree on *what it means to be* in a state of grace.[1]

This is an important internecine debate today because of the divide between Reformation theology and the New Perspective on Paul associated with N. T. Wright. This discussion is encapsulated in an exchange between Wright and John Piper, with the latter articulating the classic Reformed position on justification and the former opposing it.[2]

---

1. As with the doctrine of atonement, imputation is only one aspect of justification but is the focus of this chapter because of the common notion that Arminius did not affirm it.
2. John Piper, *The Future of Justification: A Response to N. T. Wright* (Wheaton, IL: Crossway, 2007); N. T. Wright, *Justification: God's Plan and Paul's Vision* (Downers Grove, IL: IVP Academic, 2009). The New Perspective on Paul holds that Reformation theology has misinterpreted the Judaism of Paul's day as believing in salvation by works. This perspective argues that first-century Jews believed they were corporately elect because of their membership in the covenant community and not because of their works (though they must maintain membership through law-keeping). This perspective believes that the Reformation doctrine of justification by faith and the imputation of the righteousness of Christ is mistaken.

While many Arminians laud the New Perspective, the Wesleyan reaction to it has been mixed.[3] Yet when it comes to the doctrine of imputation and its implications for the Christian life, perseverance, and assurance, many Wesleyans have expressed appreciation for it. Joseph Dongell, for example, points out that "the New Perspective sets forth issues that bear an uncanny resemblance to those argued centuries ago by John Wesley." Though different from Wesley, the New Perspective's positing of a "distinction . . . in Judaism and Paul between 'getting in' (by grace) and 'staying in' (by works) . . . bears strong resemblance to the conjunctive instincts (faith and works) of the Oxford don."[4]

Reformed Arminians, however, have been highly critical of Wright and the New Perspective, agreeing with Piper that justification in Holy Scripture entails the imputation of both the active and passive obedience of Christ. The Methodist I. Howard Marshall, whose views were akin to Reformed Arminianism (though he did not use that terminology) agreed with it on the New Perspective. He believed that the "traditional perspective" is "essentially right" and that the New Perspective "must be regarded as flawed."[5]

Arminius's View of Imputation

Arminius's doctrine of imputation was Reformed. He agreed wholeheartedly with Calvin on justification: "My position is not so different from his as to prevent my signing my name to the positions he takes in Book III of his *Institutes*. To these opinions, I am prepared to state my full approval at any time."[6]

---

3. Matt Ayars argues that while Wesley and the New Perspective on Paul share a "mutual criticism of the Reformed tradition's configuration of the forensic metaphor for justification at the center of biblical soteriology," Wesley differs from the New Perspective on key points, primarily about the individual vs. collective nature of salvation. Ayars, "Wesleyan Soteriology and the New Perspective of Paul: A Comparative Analysis," *The Asbury Journal* 74 (2019): 385. Ben Witherington has lodged serious criticisms against Wright and the New Perspective, even having an article on it carried on the Calvinistic Ligonier Ministries website. However, regarding Wright's doctrine of imputation, he says, "I think Tom is 100% correct in this assessment." http://benwitherington.blogspot.com/2009/02/nt-wright-response-to-john-piper-on.html, accessed May 20, 2020.

4. Joseph R. Dongell, "The Pauline 'New Perspective' and Wesleyan Theology," https://www.catalystresources.org/the-pauline-new-perspective-and-wesleyan-theology, accessed May 20, 2020.

5. I. Howard Marshall, *New Testament Theology: Many Witnesses, One Gospel* (Downers Grove, IL: InterVarsity, 2004), 448. For a Reformed Arminian perspective on N. T. Wright, see Matthew J. McAffee, "The N. T. Wright Effect: A Free Will Baptist Assessment through the Theology of F. Leroy Forlines," *Integrity: A Journal of Christian Thought* 7 (2019): 25–50.

6. Gunter, *Arminius and His Declaration of Sentiments: An Annotated Translation with Introduction and Theological Commentary* (Waco, TX: Baylor University Press, 2012), 149; cf. Arminius, *Works*, 1:700.

Arminius said that justification is that act by which one, "being placed before the throne of grace which is erected in Christ Jesus the Propitiation, is accounted and pronounced by God, the just and merciful Judge, righteous and worthy of the reward of righteousness, not in himself but in Christ, of grace, according to the Gospel." Justification for Arminius was forensic. The righteousness that justifies believers "can on no account be called 'inherent'" but instead must be called "'imputed' . . . the righteousness of another, that is, of Christ, which is made ours by gracious imputation."[7]

Thus Arminius explained, "In his obedience and righteousness, Christ is also the Material Cause of our justification, so far as God bestows Christ on us for righteousness, and imputes his righteousness and obedience to us."[8] Arminius said that "the obedience of Christ is imputed to us," going as far as to say that "God reckons the righteousness of Christ to have been performed for us."[9] Arminius believed "that sinners are accounted righteous solely by the obedience of Christ, and that the obedience and righteousness of Christ constitute the only meritorious cause through which God pardons the sins of believers and accounts them as righteous, as if they had perfectly fulfilled the law."[10]

Some interpreters assert that Arminius denied the imputation of the active obedience of Christ because he wanted to stay out of the controversy in the French Reformed Church surrounding the strict Calvinist theologian Johannes Piscator, who denied outright the active obedience of Christ.[11] Arminius said, "I never took care to get involved in or attempt to resolve this dispute, for I deem it quite possible for those who confess the faith to differ on this point without any breach of Christian peace or unity."[12]

Arminius here made not a theological but an ecclesiastical statement in a period characterized by many "who are hot controversialists and too vehement in their zeal," with people being persecuted for their beliefs.[13] Arminius desired unity among brothers in the Reformed Church. Yet on this he was no different than the staunchest Calvinists, none of whom "resolved" the dispute. This explains why there were strong Calvinists at the Synod of Dort and the Westminster Assembly who denied the imputation of the active obedience of Christ. Almost none of the Reformed confessional documents required an

---

7. Arminius, *Works*, 2:256–57, Public Disputation 19, "On the Justification of Man before God."
8. Arminius, *Works*, 2:406. Private Disputation 48, "On Justification."
9. Arminius, *Works*, 2:702. "Letter to Hippolytus à Collibus."
10. Gunter, *Declaration of Sentiments*, 149; cf. Arminius, *Works*, 1:700. See William den Boer, *God's Twofold Love: The Theology of Jacob Arminius (1559–1609)* (Göttingen: Vandenhoeck and Ruprecht, 2010), 204–6.
11. John Hartley, "Justification and the Remonstrants," *Place for Truth*, https://www.placefor-truth.org/blog/justification-and-the-remonstrants.
12. Gunter, *Declaration of Sentiments*, 148; cf. Arminius, *Works*, 1:696.
13. Arminius, *Works*, 2:701, "Letter to Hippolytus à Collibus."

affirmation of it, not even the Canons of Dort and Westminster Standards.[14] It is ironic that one of the few confessional documents in the early modern period that directly affirms the imputation of the active obedience of Christ is an Arminian one: the Orthodox Creed, a General Baptist confession.[15]

Arminius never denied this doctrine. He articulated it in his statement above that both Christ's "righteousness and obedience" are imputed to believers. When Arminius stated that God "reckons" Christ's righteousness "to have been performed for us" and that "the obedience and righteousness of Christ constitute the only meritorious cause" of justification, through which God "accounts them as righteous, as if they had perfectly fulfilled the law," he was directly affirming the imputation of Christ's active obedience.[16] This is why the Calvinist historical theologian J. V. Fesko, in a chapter on Arminius's doctrine of union with Christ, states the following:

> Arminius affirms that justification is a forensic act, as he contrasts it with its antonym, *condemnation*. Moreover, there is indication not only from Arminius's definition of justification but also from his elaboration that justification involves the imputation of both Christ's active and passive obedience. . . . Arminius is clear; he identifies the meritorious cause of justification in the imputed righteousness and obedience of Christ.[17]

Arminius's view that God reckons Christ's righteousness to have been performed for believers, as if they had perfectly fulfilled the law, is the precise opposite of one of the things Wesley said in his disavowal of the imputation of Christ's righteousness: "Although I believe Christ fulfilled God's law, yet I

---

14. See Robert A. Letham, *The Westminster Assembly: Reading Its Theology in Historical Context* (Phillipsburg, NJ: P&R, 2009); and Alan D. Strange, "The Imputation of the Active Obedience of Christ at the Westminster Assembly," in *Drawn into Controversie: Reformed Theological Diversity within Seventeenth-Century British Puritanism*, eds. Michael A. G. Haykin and Mark Jones (Göttingen: Vandenhoeck and Ruprecht, 2011), 31–51.

15. Orthodox Creed, http://baptiststudiesonline.com/wp-content/uploads/2007/02/orthodox-creed.pdf. Accessed August 9, 2020. The Savoy Declaration (1658) and the Formula Consensus Helvetica (1675) also affirm it.

16. Arminius, 2:406. Private Disputation 48, "On Justification"; Arminius, 2:702. "Letter to Hippolytus à Collibus"; Gunter, *Declaration of Sentiments*, 148–9 ; see also Arminius, *Works*, 1:696.

17. J. V. Fesko, *Beyond Calvin: Union with Christ and Justification in Early Modern Reformed Theology (1517–1700)* (Göttingen: Vandenhoeck and Ruprecht, 2012), 277. Cf. where Fesko argues that, like Calvin, Arminius "affirms the active and passive obedience of Christ" (p. 282).

do not affirm he did this to purchase redemption for us. This was done by his dying in our stead."[18]

Arminius's detractors took statements he made out of context, using them to drive a wedge between his desire to deal seriously with the scriptural phrase "faith is imputed for righteousness" (Gen. 15:6; Rom. 4:3, 22–24; Gal. 3:6; James 2:23) and the truth that Christ's obedience is imputed to believers as the sole meritorious cause of their justification. Yet Arminius maintained that the Bible explicitly teaches both truths and that the scriptural phrase "faith imputed for righteousness" is "not repugnant" to his assertion that Christ's obedience alone is the "meritorious cause of justification."[19]

The General Free Will Baptist Tradition

The theology that produced the General Baptist Orthodox Creed is exemplified by Thomas Helwys, the first Baptist, as well as his theological descendant Thomas Grantham. The foremost modern proponents of this pre-Wesleyan Arminian tradition are Leroy Forlines and Robert Picirilli.[20] The doctrine of imputation is one of the reasons Thomas Helwys left his mentor John Smyth, who had veered into semi-Pelagianism. Among other things, Helwys opposed Smyth's teaching "that men are justified partly by the righteousness of Christ apprehended by faith, partly by their own inherent righteousness."[21] Instead, Helwys affirmed that "man is justified only by the righteousness of Christ, apprehended by faith."[22]

---

18. John Wesley, "Some Remarks on Mr. Hill's 'Review of All the Doctrines Taught by Mr. John Wesley," in *The Works of John Wesley*, 3rd ed., ed. Thomas Jackson (Grand Rapids: Baker, 1979 [1872]), 10:386.

19. See Arminius, *Works*, 2:50, n., letter to Johannes Uytenbogaert; 2:702, letter to Hippolytus à Collibus. Fesko and Aza Goudriaan have tried to resurrect this argument, despite most scholars' acknowledging that Arminius's doctrine is within the mainstream of Reformed thought. Curiously, Fesko argues this while in the above-cited chapter stating that Arminius affirmed the imputation of the active obedience of Christ. See J. V. Fesko "Arminius on Justification: Reformed or Protestant?" *Church History and Religious Culture* 94 (2014): 1–21; Aza Goudriaan, "Justification by Faith and the Early Arminian Controversy," *Scholasticism Reformed. Essays in Honour of Willem J. van Asselt*, eds. Maarten Wisse, Marcel Sarot, and Willemien Otten (Leiden: Brill, 2010), 156–78. Like Gomarus before them, they seize on a few isolated comments about the need to deal seriously with the biblical concept "faith counted for righteousness." They quote sparsely from Arminius and copiously from his detractors, failing to set his comments in the overall context of his robust affirmation of the imputation of Christ's obedience as the sole meritorious cause of justification.

20. See F. Leroy Forlines, *Classical Arminianism: A Theology of Salvation* (Nashville: Randall House, 2011); Robert E. Picirilli, *Grace, Faith, Free Will: Calvinism and Arminianism: Contrasting Views of Salvation* (Nashville: Randall House, 2002).

21. W. J. McGlothlin, *Baptist Confessions of Faith* (Philadelphia: American Baptist Publication Society, 1911), 93.

22. A Declaration of Faith of English People Remaining at Amsterdam in Holland, 1611, reprinted in J. Matthew Pinson, *A Free Will Baptist Handbook: Heritage, Beliefs and Ministries* (Nashville: Randall House, 1998), 125.

Grantham stated: "That God imputes righteousness to men without works, is so plain, that it can never be denied. What is thus imputed, is not acted by us, but expressly reckoned as a matter of free gift, or grace; and this can be the righteousness of none but Christ." Grantham argued: "Now whether the passive righteousness of Christ only, or his active righteousness also, be that which is imputed to sinners, is doubtful to some; but for my part I take it to be both. . . . The whole righteousness of Christ, active and passive, is reckoned as ours through believing."[23] This doctrine is carried over in the 1812 Abstract, which the heirs of the General Baptists, the Free Will Baptists of the American South, condensed from the General Baptist Standard Confession of 1660: "We believe that no man has any warrant in the Holy Scriptures for justification before God through his own works, power or ability, which he has in and of himself, only as he by grace is made able to come to God through Jesus Christ; believing the righteousness of Jesus Christ to be imputed to all believers for their eternal acceptance with God."[24]

These emphases lie at the heart of modern Reformed Arminianism. Leroy Forlines argues that the embrace of a penal-satisfaction understanding of atonement results in the affirmation of the imputation of Christ's active obedience to believers. "There are two aspects of atonement: active obedience and passive obedience. . . . Most of the discussion centers around passive obedience because it involved the payment of the penalty for our sins. A complete accounting of atonement also embraces the righteous life Christ lived on our behalf, which was His active obedience."[25]

Forlines points out that in Romans 3:20 Paul argues that "absolute righteousness," which totally depraved sinners do not have (Rom. 3:10), is necessary for justification. This is bad news, but verses 21–26 provide the good news that Christ meets sinners' needs by providing them his absolute righteousness. Through union with Christ, believers become "doers of the law," his lawkeeping being made theirs through gracious imputation. Thus the requirement of absolute righteousness, that human beings must be "doers of the law," is not "set aside by grace." Instead,

> the requirement, which we could not meet, was met for us by Jesus Christ. . . . Now, at this point in human and divine history, "the righteousness of God without the law has been manifested" (3:21). This righteousness is a "God-provided righteousness." This righteousness is "without works." It in

---

23. Grantham, *Christianismus Primitivus, or The Ancient Christian Religion* (London: Francis Smith, 1678), Book 2, 62, 67–8. On Helwys and Grantham, see J. Matthew Pinson, *Arminian and Baptist: Explorations in a Theological Tradition* (Nashville: Randall House, 2016), 57–127.
24. The 1812 Abstract, art. 15, reprinted in Pinson, *A Free Will Baptist Handbook*, 146.
25. Forlines, *Classical Arminianism*, 205–6.

no way takes into account our law-keeping or our failure to
keep the law. It is the righteousness of Christ.[26]

Relying heavily on the work of William G. T. Shedd, Forlines strongly emphasizes union with Christ, appealing to Romans 6:1–11; Galatians 2:19–20;
2 Corinthians 5:15–16; and 2 Timothy 2:11. In language similar to that of
Arminius, Forlines explains that, in union with Christ, the whole redemptive work of Christ becomes ours, and our sin becomes his. In that union
we engage in "identification with Christ" so that "his history becomes our
history" and "our history becomes his history." His fulfillment of the law becomes ours, and our sin is laid on him.[27]

Wesley and the Wesleyan Tradition

Wesley held to a penal substitutionary doctrine of atonement but asserted
that it was a propitiation only for "the remission of past sins."[28] However, most
later Wesleyans held to a governmental view of atonement or some other
approach that moved away from the views of the Reformers. This is why
Wesleyans have largely rejected the Reformed and Lutheran understanding of
justification that flows out of their forensic approach to atonement.

Wesley demurred from that forensic doctrine of justification.[29] As the traditionalist Methodist Vic Reasoner persuasively argues, "Wesleyan-Arminianism
denies the Calvinistic doctrine of imputation."[30] There are exceptions, such as
Thomas Oden, who affirmed the imputation of the active obedience of Christ.[31]
Yet most Wesleyans have agreed with Wesley that God never "judges concerning
us contrary to the real nature of things" or "esteems us better than we really are"
or "believes us righteous when we are unrighteous." Thus any doctrine of imputation, whether of the active or passive obedience of Christ, is suspect. An

26. Forlines, *Classical Arminianism*, 208–9.
27. Forlines, *Classical Arminianism*, 212–16. Forlines indicates that, while taking a college
    course taught by L. C. Johnson, he became convinced in his private study of Scripture of
    this doctrine of imputation, which was confirmed by his reading of Arminius, especially
    his oration "On the Priesthood of Christ," as well as Lorraine Boettner's then-recently pub-
    lished *Studies in Theology* (Nutley, NJ: Presbyterian and Reformed, 1947).
28. *Notes*, Romans 3:25. Wesley defines "past sins" here as "all the sins antecedent to their
    believing." For more on Wesley, see J. Matthew Pinson, "Atonement, Justification, and
    Apostasy in the Thought of John Wesley," *Integrity: A Journal of Christian Thought* 4 (2008):
    73–92, reprinted in Pinson, *Arminian and Baptist*, chapter 6.
29. Woodrow W. Whidden, "Wesley on Imputation: A Truly Reckoned Reality or Antinomian
    Political Wreckage?" *Asbury Theological Journal* 52 (1997): 63–70.
30. Vic Reasoner, "Imputed and Imparted Righteousness," *Light and Life*, https://lolministry.
    org/articles/articles-by-dr-vic-reasoner/imputed-and-imparted-righteousness, accessed
    May 19, 2020. Reasoner quotes other Wesleyans to this effect. Reasoner is a traditionalist,
    non-Holiness Wesleyan.
31. Thomas C. Oden, "A Calm Answer," *Books and Culture* 7, no. 2 (2001): 13.

all-wise God could never "think that I am innocent" or "judge that I am righteous or holy, *because another is so. He can no more, in this manner, confound me with Christ than with David or Abraham.*"[32] Thus Kenneth Collins argues that in Wesley, "the active obedience of Christ in fulfilling the law is *not* imputed to the believer. . . . It is clear, then, that Wesley disassociated the fulfillment of the law from atonement and justification."[33]

The early Wesleyan theologians agreed. Richard Watson unequivocally denounced any version of the imputation of Christ's righteousness as a legal fiction.[34] Adam Clarke averred, "I am quite of Mr. Wesley's mind, that once 'we leaned too much toward Calvinism,' and especially in admitting, in any sense, the unscriptural doctrine of the imputed righteousness of Christ. . . . In no part of the Book of God is Christ's righteousness ever said to be imputed for our justification."[35]

Wesley affirmed that the "plain scriptural notion of justification is pardon, the forgiveness of sins . . . the remission of sins that are past.'"[36] His main concern is that the doctrine of imputation results in antinomianism, and is thus "a cover for unrighteousness." Thus a believer with unconfessed sin can say, "I am unjust in myself, but I have a spotless righteousness in Christ." The problem with this, Wesley replied, is that, "if the very personal obedience of Christ . . . be mine the moment I believe, can anything be added thereto? Does my obeying God add any value to the perfect obedience of Christ? On this scheme, then, are not the holy and unholy on the very same footing?"[37]

While in some sermons Wesley used the language of imputation, his views on it in those sermons are ambiguous. When he does use "imputation," he defines it very differently from the Magisterial Reformers: "Negatively, God does not count our sins against us," as Reasoner states. "Positively, God counts our faith as righteousness, and we have peace with God."[38] Yet Wesley eventually gave up completely on even this use of the language of imputation. In his 1773 "Remarks on Mr. Hill's Farrago Double-Distilled," he insisted, "That phrase, *the imputed righteousness of Christ,* I never did use," and he advised everyone "to lay aside that ambiguous, unscriptural phrase."[39]

---

32. "Justification by Faith," *Works*, V, II, 4 (italics added).
33. Kenneth Collins, *The Theology of John Wesley: Holy Love and the Shape of Grace* (Nashville: Abingdon, 2007), 112–13.
34. Richard Watson, *Theological Institutes* (London: John Mason, 1829), 2:226, 241. See also *The Works of John Fletcher of Madeley* (London: John Kershaw, 1826), 2:145–46, 367–70; William Burt Pope, *A Higher Catechism of Theology* (London: T. Woolmer, 1885); 228.
35. Adam Clarke, *Christian Theology*, ed. Samuel Dunn (London: Thomas Tegg, 1835), 158.
36. "A Dialogue between an Antinomian and His Friend," *Works*, 10:267; "Justification by Faith," V, II, 5.
37. "The Lord Our Righteousness," *Works*, 5:244; "Thoughts on the Imputed Righteousness of Christ," *Works*, 10:315.
38. Reasoner, "Imputed and Imparted Righteousness."
39. *Works*, 10:430.

Thus Wesley's doctrine of justification differed from Arminius's in two key ways: First, Wesley believed that the atonement can be applied only to pre-conversion sins. In post-conversion sins, the believer must continually reappropriate the atonement through repentance to be rejustified.[40] Second, despite vague references to imputation in some of his earlier sermons, Wesley in the end rejected the entirety of the doctrine of imputation, of either the active or passive obedience of Christ. Thus he desired to avoid the language of imputation altogether, instead defining justification as simple pardon, the forgiveness or remission of sins.

Implications of Imputation

Why does this debate matter? The Reformed approach to imputation arises out of a penal satisfaction view of atonement. When one fully combines this approach to justification—*what it means to be* in a state of grace—with the broad Arminian narrative of *how one comes to be* in a state of grace, the result is a soteriology that affirms the full resistibility of grace (before and after conversion) but with a Reformed understanding of one's right standing before God. A denial of the imputation of Christ's righteousness to the believer results in a view of perseverance and assurance that is dependent on the ebb and flow of one's sanctification. At lower points in sanctification, believers fall from grace because of their sins and must regain it through penitence. This results in what I call a "light switch" soteriology—on and off, on and off—and thus provides a tenuous assurance of salvation. Christians are never really sure they are justified, because their justification consists of imparted righteousness, not Christ's imputed righteousness.

Woodrow Whidden encapsulates this approach in his *Asbury Theological Journal* article, "Wesley on Imputation": In Wesley's theology, "forgiveness of sins (both of nature and acts) is constantly available, but must somehow be constantly applied for by penitent ones experiencing salvation . . . they must continuously apply for pardon or face the loss of their salvation." Believers struggling with sin are like "high wire or trapeze artists" in that they can perform "with or without a safety net underneath." In the Reformed model, "the safety net is always underneath the faithful and one has to consciously move out of faith relationship with Christ to have such a net removed." In the Wesleyan model, "the incidentally falling performers must somehow appeal for the safety net to be put in place before they crash (through sin)."[41] This has enormous implications for the assurance of salvation.

---

40. Whidden, "Wesley on Imputation," 63–70; J. Steven Harper, "Wesleyan Arminianism," in *Four Views on Eternal Security*, ed. J. Matthew Pinson (Grand Rapids: Zondervan, 2002), 238–46.
41. Whidden, "Wesley on Imputation," 66.

The Wesleyan movement has emphasized a second work of grace and Christian perfection, which non-Wesleyan Arminians have avoided. These views are in harmony with other Wesleyan beliefs about salvation. If Christ did not pay the penalty for sin, and his righteousness is not imputed to believers, it makes sense that believers have less assurance of salvation until they reach a state of entire sanctification or Christian perfection, and that they must be "rejustified" through penitence when they fall into sin.[42]

While Reformed Arminians assert that the believer has the ability finally to resist grace and apostatize from the faith, their concept of assurance is grounded in the active and passive obedience of Christ imputed to believers, not in believers living out the imparted righteousness of Christ. Like the older Reformed and Puritan theologians, they have a strong view of sanctification and thus oppose antinomianism. Sanctification always accompanies justification; living in the practice of sin is inconsistent with regeneration. Yet Reformed Arminians believe that, because Christ's own active and passive obedience are imputed to believers for their right-standing before God, ebbs and flows in sanctification do not bring about apostasy. Only a one-time irremediable defection from justifying faith can do that (see Question 40).[43]

Summary

Arminius articulated a full-orbed Reformed doctrine of the imputation of the righteousness of Christ in justification. While this approach was carried forward by the English General Baptists and their heirs, many Arminians, including Wesley and many of his spiritual descendants, have eschewed the doctrine of imputation. This debate has continued in recent days, as seen in the debate between John Piper and N. T. Wright. Reformed Arminians have emphasized Piper's Reformed account. Most Wesleyan Arminians, like leading voices such as Joseph Dongell and Ben Witherington, have supported Wright's view while some thinkers in the Wesleyan orbit have, like Thomas Oden, have continued to affirm the imputation of the righteousness of Jesus Christ at the core of justification.

---

42. Wesley's intellectual progenitor John Goodwin referred to such individuals as "twice regenerate," saying that regeneration can be "reiterated" or "repeated." See Jesse F. Owens, "Scripture and History in the Theology of John Goodwin," paper presented at the Evangelical Theological Society Annual Meeting, November, 2015. On some of these themes in Wesley, see Pinson, "Atonement, Justification, and Apostasy in the Thought of John Wesley."
43. See Forlines, *Classical Arminianism*, 273–302.

REFLECTION QUESTIONS

1. How do New Perspective authors such as N. T. Wright and Calvinist authors such as John Piper disagree about the doctrine of imputation of the righteousness of Christ?

2. What was Arminius's perspective on the imputation of the active and passive obedience of Christ?

3. What does the General/Free Will Baptist tradition affirm regarding imputation?

4. What do Wesley and the Wesleyan tradition believe about imputation?

5. How does one's view of the imputation of the righteousness of Christ flow out of a given doctrine of the nature of atonement, and what are the implications of such imputation for other doctrines such as sanctification, sin in the life of the believer, and perseverance?

The Extent of Atonement

QUESTION 12

Does God Want Everyone to Be Saved?

Holy Scripture teaches that salvation results from three mighty works of the persons of the Holy Trinity: First, the Father is drawing everyone to himself because he desires everyone to be saved. Second, he sends the Son to die for everyone's sins. Third, he gives the Holy Spirit who calls everyone to salvation. This chapter will deal with the first of these truths, while the next two chapters will deal with the second and third respectively.[1]

The *Gratia Universalis*

Arminians believe in the *gratia universalis* (universal grace). The 1812 Abstract exemplifies this when it says that sinners are "drawn to God the Father, by the Holy Ghost, through Christ His Son," and that "the Holy Ghost offers His divine aid to all the human family, so as they might all be happy, would they give place to His divine teaching." Individuals who "do not receive the divine impressions of the Holy Spirit shall, at a future day, own their condemnation just and charge themselves with their own damnation, for willfully rejecting the offers of sovereign grace."[2]

The Abstract, repeating the 1660 Standard Confession of the General Baptists, says no one will "suffer in hell for want of a Christ who died for him, but as the Scripture has said, for denying the Lord that bought them." Because unbelief is "the cause why the just and righteous God of Heaven will condemn the children of men, it follows against all contradiction that all men, at one

---

1. The Spirit's calling and Father's drawing are part of the same thing, since the Father works through the agency of the Spirit.
2. The 1812 Abstract, art. 9. reprinted in J. Matthew Pinson, *A Free Will Baptist Handbook: Heritage, Beliefs, and Ministries* (Nashville: Randall House, 1998), 145. The 1812 Abstract, the confession of faith of the descendants of the English General Baptists in the American South, later known as Free Will Baptists, condensed the English General Baptists' Standard Confession of 1660, adding some new language.

time or another, are found in such capacity as that through the grace of God they may be eternally saved."[3]

Arminius had continued the consensus on universal grace found in the patristic, medieval, and mainstream Reformation understanding. Thus his view was that God desires the salvation of all people and so provides atonement for every individual, not just the elect. Arminius maintained that "Christ stood in the stead of all men universally . . . and not in the stead of the elect only."[4]

Arminius emphasized that redemption was "*obtained* for all the world, and for all and every man; but *applied* to believers and the elect alone."[5] His primary argument was that, unless God obtains redemption for all people, he cannot require faith in Christ from all people, nor can he blame people for "refusing the offer of redemption. For he refuses what cannot be his."[6] Thus "if Christ has not obtained redemption for all, He cannot be the Judge of all."[7] For Arminius, this was the only way to explain the New Testament passages that indicate God's desire for everyone to be saved. He spent several pages responding to Calvinism's explanation of the meaning of "all" (i.e., "all *kinds* of people") in New Testament passages that teach God's desire for all to be saved. Arminius believed this is the clear teaching of Scripture, and he wondered how those who believe Christ died only for the elect can explain Scripture passages like John 1:29; 6:1; Romans 14:15; 1 John 2:2; and 2 Peter 2:1, 3.[8]

The Biblical Witness

The reason Arminians affirm the *gratia universalis* is that they believe that biblical texts such as Jeremiah 22:29, Joel 2:28, Luke 2:10, John 1:9, John 6:44, John 12:32, John 16:8, Romans 2:4, and Titus 2:1 teach that God is reaching out to everyone, in some way, with his prevenient (pre-justifying, enabling) grace, pouring out his spirit on everyone, enlightening everyone, drawing everyone, convicting everyone, giving grace to everyone. These passages are about God's prevenient grace (see Questions 21–22). Why do Arminians think these texts teach that God is reaching out to everyone with his prevenient grace? Because Scripture passages such as Ezekiel 33:11; Acts 10:34; 17:30; 1 Timothy 2:4; and 2 Peter 3:9 teach that God's salvific purpose is universal. Thus Arminians, together with the vast sweep of the Christian tradition, believe that the reason Christ died for everyone, and the reason the Spirit is calling everyone, is that the Father's genuine desire is that everyone be saved.

3. 1812 Abstract, art. 6, 145.
4. Jacobus Arminius, *The Works of James Arminius,* 3 vols., trans. James Nichols and William Nichols (Nashville: Randall House, 2007), 3:332, "Examination of Perkins's Pamphlet."
5. Arminius, *Works,* 3:425, "Examination of Perkins's Pamphlet"
6. Arminius, *Works,* 3:425.
7. Arminius, *Works,* 3:426.
8. Arminius, *Works,* 2:9–10, "Apology against Thirty-One Defamatory Articles."

The Bible is replete with texts that discuss God's saving purpose for all humanity: God commands everyone to repent (Acts 17:30), specifying that he genuinely desires that everyone repent and not perish (2 Peter 3:9). Because he desires that everyone be saved (1 Tim. 2:4), he sends Jesus to give his light to everyone (John 1:9) and draw everyone to himself (John 12:32), and he pours out his Spirit on everyone (Joel 2:28) so that the Spirit can convict everyone (John 16:8). So the "good tidings of great joy" that the angels exclaimed to the shepherds of Bethlehem was not just for some but for "all people" (Luke 2:10): God's salvation-bringing grace has gone out to everyone (Titus 2:11) because God loved the entire world enough to give his Son for it (John 3:14–17), and because this kindness is intended to lead people to repentance, even people who will reject him (Rom. 2:4).[9]

Thus the good news of salvation meaningfully goes out to the whole earth (Jer. 22:29). God wants to give everyone an opportunity to be his—he even swears an oath that he does not take pleasure in the death of the wicked. Instead, he earnestly desires that they turn from their wicked ways and live, and there is absolutely no reason for them to persist in their sins and die (Ezek. 33:11). Therefore, since everyone is sinful, he extends his grace to everyone (Rom. 11:32), being no respecter of persons (Acts 10:34).

God's universal saving intent for humanity is encapsulated in 2 Peter 3:9 and 1 Timothy 2:4. These are the most important texts for understanding God's sincere, universal purpose to save all people, or, as the seventeenth-century Lutheran dogmatician August Pfeiffer put it, that "God wills seriously and earnestly that all men should be saved."[10] The will described in these texts is God's "antecedent will" as distinguished from his "consequent will."

This classic distinction introduced by John of Damascus is seen in every segment of the Christian tradition except Calvinism.[11] In his antecedent (beforehand) will, he desires everyone's salvation, but in his consequent (after-the-fact) will, he desires that those who reject his gracious offer of salvation be separated from him. It is important to note that these wills *are not opposed*: God does not desire the salvation of everyone unconditionally. He desires that everyone come to *repentance*. Those who do not, he wills (consequently) that his justice against them for their sin and refusal of his grace be enacted against them.

---

9. Calvinist responses to texts such as these will be discussed below.
10. August Pfeiffer, *Anti-Calvinism*, trans. Edward Pfeiffer (Columbus, OH: Joint Lutheran Synod of Ohio, 1881 [1699]), 86.
11. John of Damascus, *An Exact Exposition of the Orthodox Faith* in *A Select Library of Nicene and Post-Nicene Fathers* (Oxford: James Parker and Company, 1899), 9:42. Augustine and a few teachers such as Gottschalk of Orbais, Gregory of Rimini, and Thomas Bradwardine would see this differently from the majority of the Christian tradition. See Thomas C. Oden, *The Transforming Power of Grace* (Nashville: Abingdon, 1993), 82–88.

2 Peter 3:9

Second Peter 3:9 states: "The Lord is not slow to fulfill his promise as some count slowness, but is patient toward you, not wishing that any should perish, but that all should reach repentance." In saying that it is God's will, purpose, or desire (*boulomai*) that everyone should not perish but should repent, this passage means that God's strong purpose for everyone, his eternal counsel for them, is that they all should repent.

Calvin was willing to appeal to mystery on this: "So wonderful is his love towards mankind, that he would have them all to be saved." However, regarding why people perish if God does not wish it, Calvin remarked that this passage regards his public will revealed in the gospel, not his secret will: "No mention is here made of the hidden purpose of God, according to which the reprobate are doomed to their own ruin, but only of his will as made known to us in the gospel. For God there stretches forth his hand without a difference to all, but lays hold only of those, to lead them to himself, whom he has chosen before the foundation of the world."[12] Thomas Schreiner uses the phrase "'complexity' in the divine will" to describe this sort of explanation.[13]

Arminians insist that this passage should be read *as it stands*, that God wills everyone's salvation *through repentance* (thus ruling out universalism), and that positing two contradictory wills in God cannot legitimately be extruded from the text. It is not God's will to save those who refuse the grace he gives them to repent. In his antecedent will, God's purpose for humanity is that they all be saved through repentance. Yet in his consequent will, his purpose is that those who reject him will not be saved. One might refer to this as God's conditional will, and it is his public, revealed will. However, Calvinism's secret, decretive will goes directly against God's stated will in this text that he wants everyone to be saved *through repentance*.

1 Timothy 2:4

Arminians also appeal to 1 Timothy 2:4 to argue for God's sincere desire, which is both in his own mind and publicly revealed, to save everyone. God "desires all men to be saved and to come to the knowledge of the truth." Most Calvinists agree with Schreiner, who argues that in this text Paul is reminding his readers "of a fundamental truth of his gospel: God desires to save all *kinds* of people." Thus he introduces an "all without distinction, not all without

---

12. John Calvin, *Commentaries on the Catholic Epistles*, trans. John Owen (Grand Rapids: Eerdmans, 1948), 419–20.

13. Thomas R. Schreiner, "'Problematic Texts' for Definite Atonement in the Pastoral and General Epistles," in *From Heaven He Came and Sought Her: Definite Atonement in Historical, Biblical, Theological, and Pastoral Perspective*, eds. David Gibson and Jonathan Gibson (Wheaton, IL: Crossway, 2013), 393–94.

exception" formula, just as he does in his interpretation of Titus 2:11, "For the grace of God has appeared, bringing salvation for all people."[14]

However, as Robert Picirilli argues, "in none of these specific passages does the Calvinist's explanation of 'all' or 'world' seem correct. . . . [They] read the 'all' or 'world' in a way *not* justified by the context."[15] Charles Spurgeon agreed, appealing to mystery on texts like this: "'All men,' say they,—'that is, *some men*': as if the Holy Ghost could not have said 'some men' if he had meant some men. 'All men,' say they; 'that is, some of all sorts of men': as if the Lord could not have said 'all sorts of men' if he had meant that. The Holy Ghost by the apostle has written 'all men,' and unquestionably he means all men." To interpret the text differently is to apply "grammatical gunpowder" to it, Spurgeon said. It "explodes it by way of expounding it."[16]

So how did Spurgeon align his straightforward reading of this text with his Calvinism? He averred:

> I would sooner a hundred times over appear to be incon-
> sistent with myself than be inconsistent with the Word of
> God. . . . If we mind things too high for us we shall run
> great risks. . . . There stands the text, and I believe that it is
> my Father's wish that "all men should be saved, and come to
> the knowledge of the truth." But I know, also, that he does
> not will it, so that he will save any one of them, unless they
> believe in his dear Son; for he has told us over and over that
> he will not. . . . And I know, also, that he has a people whom
> he will save, whom by his eternal love he has chosen. . . . I do
> not know how that squares with this.[17]

John Piper on God's Desire for Everyone's Salvation

John Piper deals directly with this contradiction in his book *Does God Desire All to Be Saved?* At first his answer seems to be yes. Piper remarks that "Ezekiel 18:23, 32; 33:11; and Matthew 23:37 surely point to God's desire that all people be saved." Because he believes that, and also affirms unconditional election, his "aim is to show that this is not double talk." The reader cannot help but be struck by Piper's sincerity, compassion, and desire to communicate clearly to people what he genuinely believes the Bible teaches. Yet later in

---

14. Schreiner, "'Problematic Texts,'" 377 (italics added).
15. Picirilli, *Grace, Faith, Free Will: Contrasting Views of Salvation: Calvinism and Arminianism* (Nashville: Randall House, 2002), 111–12.
16. Charles Spurgeon, "Salvation by Knowing the Truth," in the *Metropolitan Tabernacle Pulpit* (London: Passmore & Alabaster, 1881), 26:50–51.
17. Spurgeon, "Salvation by Knowing the Truth," 26:51–52.

the book he states: "*There is a sense in which he desires that all be saved and a sense in which he does not.*"[18]

Piper's main solution to the problem is the classic Calvinist concept of two wills in God, what Jonathan Edwards called God's revealed will, his "will of command," and his secret will, his "will of decree." The upshot of this view is that, in his revealed will, God desires that the reprobate come to him and lovingly calls them to himself, but in his secret will, he is pleased to arrange the universe so that the reprobate can never come to him.[19]

Piper quotes the Arminian I. Howard Marshall as also supporting a concept of two wills when Marshall says: "The fact that God wishes or wills that all people should be saved does not necessarily imply that all will respond to the gospel and be saved. *We must certainly distinguish between what God would like to see happen and what he actually does will to happen, and both of these things can be spoken of as God's will.*"[20]

Piper dedicates the rest of the book to "undergird[ing] Marshall's point" by "drawing attention to the way Scripture portrays God's willing something in one sense that he disapproves in another sense."[21] The problem with this is that, for Marshall and other Arminians, what God "actually does will to happen" is not willed because it is his secret desire but because of the resistance of the unbeliever: God wills to punish unbelievers who resist his gracious overtures. Yet for Piper "what he actually does will to happen" is willed because he has a secret desire that, *by his design, goes against* "what God would like to see happen."

In other words, utilizing the classic distinction of John of Damascus, here are the two ways God wills:

Antecedent Will	**Consequent Will**
(what God would like to see happen)	(what God actually wills to happen)
"I *would like to see* everyone saved through repentance and will not withhold the grace necessary for this."	"I *actually will* that people who refuse my grace will be separated from me forever."[22]

A crucial feature of this formulation is that the antecedent and consequent wills are (1) both revealed and (2) not contradictory. In Calvinism, however, here are the two ways God wills:

---

18. John Piper, *Does God Desire All to Be Saved?* (Wheaton, IL: Crossway, 2013), 45–46 (italics added).
19. Piper, *Does God Desire All to Be Saved?*, 15–16.
20. I. Howard Marshall, "Universal Grace and Atonement in the Pastoral Epistles," *The Grace of God, The Will of Man: A Case for Arminianism* (Grand Rapids: Zondervan, 1989), 56, cited in Piper, 18 (italics added by Piper).
21. Piper, *Does God Desire All to Be Saved?*, 18.
22. This does not imply that there are things that God is incapable of doing but rather than this is the way God has sovereignly decided to set up his universe and his plan of salvation.

(Revealed) Will of Command	(Secret) Will of Decree
(what God would like to see happen)	(what God actually wills to happen)
"I *would like to see* everyone saved through repentance."	"I *actually will* to withhold the grace necessary for the nonelect to be saved."[23]

In Calvinism, one will is revealed while the other is secret. Edwards said that God's will of command, what he commands people to do, is his revealed will, but his will of decree, what he actually wills to happen, is secret.[24]

So how does Piper deal with this dilemma between Calvinism and the intent of these verses? He argues that these two wills—"God's willing (in one sense) a state of affairs that he disapproves (in another sense)"—are seen elsewhere in the Bible:[25] that God willed prophesied states of affairs that involved people sinning (e.g., Jesus's death), that God hardened Pharaoh, that God can "restrain evil" but chooses not to, and that God takes "delight in bringing ruin" on the wicked (Deut. 28:63).[26]

However, the Bible nowhere indicates that God causally determined the sins that led to Jesus's death or the fulfillment of other prophecies—that those sins were not committed freely (in a "libertarian freedom" sense) by individuals. God's hardening activity is always seen in Scripture as a response to individuals hardening their own hearts (see Question 29). God's taking delight in his justice in destroying the wicked is far more consistent with the non-Calvinist approach to God's will, in which both the antecedent and consequent sides of his will are revealed and in harmony. Piper's insertion of divine determinism into an argument over how God desires everyone's salvation is an exercise in begging the question. In essence, Piper's whole argument to explain the contradiction between God's secret and revealed wills is simply an assertion of determinism, not an explanation why, in Calvinism, God's two wills are *not contradictory*.

Piper's argument amounts to a case for a deterministic divine sovereignty in "willing that sin takes place." He fails, however, to see that simply asserting that God causally determines everything that comes to pass *does not solve the dilemma* of two contradictory wills in God—why God has revealed himself in a way that goes against what he is secretly pleased to do.[27]

---

23. In infralapsarian Calvinism, God is pleased both to bestow on the elect, and to withhold from the nonelect, the grace necessary for salvation.

24. "Miscellaneous Observations Concerning the Divine Decrees in General and Election in Particular," in *The Works of President Edwards*, 4 vols. (New York: Robert Carter and Brothers, 1881), 2:516.

25. Piper, *Does God Desire All to Be Saved?*, 19.

26. Piper, *Does God Desire All to Be Saved?*, 23. He makes this argument on pp. 19–30.

27. Piper, *Does God Desire All to Be Saved?*, 32–33, 37.

Piper explains that both Arminians and Calvinists "can say that God wills for all to be saved. And when queried why all are not saved, both . . . answer the same: because God is committed to something even more valuable than saving all." Piper believes that the Arminian thinks that "human self-determination and the possible resulting love relationship with God are more valuable than saving all people by sovereign, efficacious grace." The Calvinist believes that "the greater value is the manifestation of the full range of God's glory in wrath and mercy (Rom. 9:22–23) and the humbling of man so that he enjoys giving all credit to God for his salvation (1 Cor. 1:29)."[28]

God's desire, in Piper's view, has a narrow lens (his sorrow for sin and his desire to see everyone saved) and a wide-angle lens (his causally determining sin and, in another sense, not desiring everyone to be saved). "When God took counsel with himself as to whether he should save all people, he consulted not only the truth of what he sees when looking through the narrow lens, but also the larger truth of what he sees through the wide-angle lens of his all-knowing wisdom. The result of this consultation with his own infinite wisdom was that God deemed it wise and good to elect unconditionally some to salvation and not others." God's "emotional life" is "incomprehensibly complex." Thus "there is a sense in which he does not experience pleasure in the judgment of the wicked, and there is a sense in which he does. *There is a sense in which he desires that all be saved and a sense in which he does not.*"[29]

Piper gives the illustration of George Washington ordering the execution of the traitor John André. Justice demanded that Washington sign André's death warrant, though he felt love and compassion for André. This, however, is to confuse categories. The problem with Calvinism is not a conflict between God's love and desire for everyone's salvation on the one hand and his duty to exact justice in punishing sin on the other. Instead, the conflict is between, to use Piper's words, the "sense in which he desires that all be saved" and the "sense in which he does not." *There is* no *sense in which God desires that anyone* not *be saved through repentance!* Rather, God desires that all be saved and come to the knowledge of the truth, but people refuse his grace and continue in their sin, and thus he satisfies his justice in exacting punishment, though, like Washington, with sadness and lament.[30]

Piper quotes Robert Dabney as saying that Washington had "'plenary power to kill or to save alive.' Why, then, did he sign the death warrant?" Arminius's answer would be because he had no choice, owing to the demands of justice. Arminius affirmed a "twofold love" in God that consists of his love for "the creature" and for his justice. The only thing God loves more than

---

28. Piper, *Does God Desire All to Be Saved?*, 39.
29. Piper, *Does God Desire All to Be Saved?*, 45–47 (italics added).
30. Piper, *Does God Desire All to Be Saved?*, 47–50. This, of course, rules out universalism, since universalists believe everyone is saved, with or without the knowledge of the truth.

his human creatures is his justice. That is the *only* thing that keeps him from saving everyone, *not* his own secret will. The Arminian does not have to resort to Dabney's arbitrariness, because God's own just character demands that sin be punished.[31]

That is why there is no contradiction between the antecedent and consequent wills in God, why God can be just in punishing sinners who resist his grace while still having compassion on them and lamenting their resistance. Yet there *is* a contradiction between Calvinism's revealed and secret wills in God. In God's secret will, it is not justice that makes him choose to withhold his grace from the reprobate. It is some other, secret quality that is not revealed in Holy Scripture. Arminians agree with Luther when he said, regarding the so-called secret will of God, "Insofar as He has not been revealed, there is no faith, no knowledge, and no understanding. And here one must hold to the statement that what is above us is none of our concern. For thoughts of this kind, which investigate something more sublime above or outside the revelation of God, are altogether hellish."[32]

Summary

The mainstream of the Christian Church has interpreted passages such as 2 Peter 3:9 and 1 Timothy 2:4 as teaching that God unequivocally desires the salvation of all people through repentance and knowledge of the truth. However, Calvinists believe that this desire represents the revealed will of God, while his desire to save only those he unconditionally elects, and purposefully to deprive the rest of his grace, is his secret will. Arminians believe that these two wills are contradictory. Instead, they say, the revealed will of God is the only will of God. As the General Baptists' Orthodox Creed states, the "eternal election, or covenant-transaction between the Father and Son, is very consistent with his revealed will in the gospel. For we ought not to oppose the grace of God in electing of us, nor yet the grace of the Son in dying for all men (and so for us); nor yet the grace of the Holy Ghost in propounding the gospel, and persuading us to believe it."[33]

God's will is that everyone be saved through repentance and the knowledge of the truth. If people to whom he gives his grace wantonly refuse it, then his will is to uphold his justice, give them what they want, and separate them from himself. Both these wills are revealed, and both of them represent the authentic heart of a God who, as Arminius says, has a twofold love: his love of

---

31. Another factor is that Washington did not predestine that André would make the choices he did.
32. *Luther's Works*, ed. Jaroslav Pelikan (St. Louis: Concordia, 1968), 5:44. See also the Lutheran confession, the Solid Declaration of the Formula of Concord, 11:34–35, http://bookofconcord.org/sd-election.php, accessed June 19, 2020.
33. Orthodox Creed, art. 9; http://baptiststudiesonline.com/wp-content/uploads/2007/02/orthodox-creed.pdf, accessed June 29, 2020.

his justice and his love of the creatures he has made in his image and is lovingly calling to himself.

REFLECTION QUESTIONS

1. What did most of the church fathers, medieval teachers, and Reformers believe about the universal grace of God and his desire for everyone to be saved?

2. What do Arminians mean by God's antecedent will and consequent will?

3. What do Calvinists believe is God's revealed will and his secret will?

4. Why do Arminians believe that the revealed and secret wills of God that Calvinists affirm are contradictory?

5. Why do Arminians believe that the antecedent and consequent aspects of God's will that they affirm are both a revealed, noncontradictory whole?

Does Scripture Teach That Christ Died for Everyone?

Arminians are tempted not to spend much time answering this question, like the one about whether God desires everyone's salvation. Perhaps this is partly because most Calvinists they encounter already believe that Christ died for everyone. More importantly, they see how obvious it seems in Holy Scripture and note that the vast sweep of the Christian tradition bears overwhelming witness to it. Arminians are tempted to say what the seventeenth-century Lutheran dogmatician August Pfeiffer said, when considering Calvinist objections to the array of Scripture texts that seem so plainly to teach universal atonement: The doctrine "is so clear and simple that, if I were to attempt an extended exposition, it would appear like an attempt to illuminate the sun with a candle."[1] However, every theological system has difficult passages it must deal with; five-point Calvinists are not alone in this.

Because the Father desires that everyone be saved and is drawing everyone to himself, he sent his Son to atone for everyone's sins. Thus, as Robert Picirilli is fond of saying, to understand the *extent* of the atonement, one must really understand God's *intent* in the atonement. The most important issue in answering the question for whom Christ died is, why was Christ sent to die? Classical Calvinists argue that the intent of the atonement is to save only the elect. The wider Christian tradition, including Arminians, has argued that the intent of the atonement is to provide salvation for both the elect and everyone else. Or, as Picirilli states it, God "intended to provide a basis for the salvation of every person and to apply it to all who receive that provision by faith."[2]

---

1. August Pfeiffer, *Anti-Calvinism*, trans. Edward Pfeiffer (Columbus, OH: Joint Lutheran Synod of Ohio, 1881 [1699]), 92.
2. Robert E. Picirilli, "The Intent and Extent of Christ's Atonement," in *Grace for All: The Arminian Dynamics of Salvation*, eds. Clark H. Pinnock and John D. Wagner (Eugene, OR:

Four-Point Calvinism

Consistent Calvinists get so far from the consensus of the church catholic on this doctrine that many Calvinists do not hold to limited atonement.[3] While four-point Calvinists, sometimes called hypothetical universalists, hold that Christ died for the sins of the elect and everyone else, they believe that it pleased God to offer his grace only to the elect and to withhold it from everyone else.[4]

Consistent Calvinists and non-Calvinists ask four-point Calvinists: How can you coherently assert *both* (1) that God's intent in giving his grace is to save only the elect and to deprive everyone else of grace and (2) that God sent his Son to die not just for the elect, the only people he really purposed to save, but for everyone else? Thus five-point Calvinists and the rest of Christianity believe that four-point Calvinism is incoherent. They argue that if one believes that God sincerely desires to draw everyone to himself and give everyone an opportunity to be saved, universal atonement follows. However, if one believes that God intends to give his grace only to the elect and deprive everyone else of it, limited atonement follows. Pfeiffer was right when he said that four-point Calvinism makes God the Father say, "Here is the blood of my Son that was shed as a ransom for you, by which you can be saved, only on the condition, however, that you accept it by true faith; but the power to believe and through faith to come to me I have determined never to give you."[5]

As the next chapter will argue, in some sense all Calvinists, except Hyper-Calvinists like John Gill or Herman Hoeksema or modern Primitive Baptists, have the problem Pfeiffer raises: most five-point Calvinists believe in the free offer or "well-meant" offer of the gospel. Thus God is earnestly beckoning people to come to himself, lamenting when they do not, and punishing them more severely for their refusal to respond to his call. But there is another call,

---

Resource, 2015), 66. That chapter is the best brief explanation of the doctrine of universal atonement. For a more detailed discussion, see Robert E. Picirilli's, *Grace, Faith, Free Will: Contrasting Views of Salvation: Calvinism and Arminianism* (Nashville: Randall House, 2002), 85–138. For an exhaustive study of the matter, see David L. Allen, *The Extent of the Atonement: A Historical and Critical Review* (Nashville: B&H Academic, 2016).

3. While I have no hard data on this, four-point Calvinism seems to becoming the most popular form of Calvinism today, despite strong efforts among consistent Calvinists to argue for definite atonement.

4. Often hypothetical universalists say that the atonement is sufficient for everyone but only efficient for the unconditionally elect. Many use "Amyraldianism," named after the moderate Calvinist Moise Amyraut, for four-point Calvinism, yet many traditional Amyraldians, unlike other four-point Calvinists, affirm the governmental view of atonement and do not believe in the imputation of Christ's righteousness. See Alan C. Clifford, *Atonement and Justification: English Evangelical Theology 1640–1790* (Oxford: Clarendon, 1990).

5. Pfeiffer, *Anti-Calvinism*, 111.

an inner, irresistible call, that reaches only the elect, the only people whom God, in his secret will, is truly pleased to save.

However, four-point Calvinists have an even greater consistency problem: Jesus is not merely weeping over Jerusalem, wanting them to come to him and imploring them to do so, when in the secret counsel of the divine will it pleases the Lord to deprive most of them of his grace. He is also saying, "I died for you. Your sins have been atoned for. Your penalty has been paid, if you will only cease your resistance to me and your refusal of me." Still he has meticulously arranged their personal universe so that they cannot.

The Arminian Position

Arminius, in arguing against Bezan Calvinism's limitation of the atonement to the elect, was simply arguing what virtually every other Christian outside of Calvinism had always believed: the *intent* of the atonement determines its *extent*; God's universal salvific intent for the whole world and everyone in it is what makes him send his only Son to give his life. That is why it is difficult to understand the Arminian doctrine of the extent of the atonement (this chapter) without understanding God's universal salvific desire (the previous chapter).[6]

Essentially, Arminians start with the understanding that no text of Scripture states that Christ died only for the sins of the elect. That proposition is a theological construct imposed on the universal atonement texts. When addressing the extent of the atonement, Arminians emphasize that this is not a "battle of the proof texts," because there are no texts that Calvinists bring to the table that they claim directly assert that Christ died only for the elect. Thus the exegetical case against universal atonement consists almost entirely of interpretation of a large number of texts that unequivocally state that Jesus died for all or for the whole world.

Incidentally, some Calvinists argue that the insistence that Christ atoned for everyone's sins fails to reckon with the "corporate" categories of the ancient world in which the biblical authors were functioning. Yet this will not do, since the ubiquitous position of the church fathers, who shared that same ancient milieu, was universal atonement.[7] The remainder of this chapter will examine the biblical teaching on universal atonement.

What It Means to Say "Jesus Died for the World"

The apostle John emphasizes what the New Testament everywhere reiterates: Jesus died for the sins of the world. For John, this has special significance, because he uses "the world" repeatedly to indicate the unbelieving world that

---

6. See Question 12.
7. For a discussion of the overwhelming Patristic position on the extent of the atonement, see Allen, *The Extent of the Atonement*, 3–24, 62–66.

has set itself up against the knowledge of God, as indicated by 1 John 5:19. That verse contrasts the elect and the world: "We know that *we* are from God, and the *whole world* lies in the power of the evil one."[8] So when John says that God loves the world in such a way that he sent his son to die for "the world" (3:16), or the "whole world" (1 John 2:2), he is indicating the opposite of the Calvinist view that Christ died only for the elect.

He says in John 3:16, "God so loved the world, that he gave his only Son, that whoever believes in him should not perish but have eternal life." This strong statement appears against the backdrop of two prior statements in his gospel. First, John the Baptist exclaims, "Behold, the Lamb of God, who takes away the sin of the world!" (John 1:29). Then, in the immediate context of John 3:16, John likens Christ's being "lifted up" in his death to Moses's "lifting up" of the bronze serpent so that everyone who looked on it would be healed (3:14). This in itself is a vivid illustration of the universality of the atonement. The only thing that would keep people from being healed was their refusal to look on the bronze serpent and live.[9] Then, right after John 3:16, in verse 17, he states that the reason Christ died was to save the world.

In his first epistle, John clarifies even more what he means when he says that "the Father has sent his Son to be the Savior of the world" (1 John 4:14). Calvinists must say this means that Christ is the Savior of *all kinds of elect people in the world*. However, that is not what the text says. It states clearly that the intent of the Father in sending his Son is so that he might save "the world." The meaning of this is clarified by John's statement in 1 John 2:2 that Christ atoned not only for the sins of the elect but also for those of the "whole world."

So when one asks, "What does John specifically mean in John 1:29 and 3:16 and 1 John 4:14 when he says that Jesus died to save the world?," 1 John 2:2 states: "He is the propitiation for our sins, and not for ours only but also for the sins of the whole world." Jesus atoned not just for the sins of his readers—the elect, believers—but also for the sins of "the *whole world*."[10] If John were arguing that Christ died for the sins of the elect in all the classes and cultures of the world, he would not have distinguished between the sins of the elect and the sins of the whole world. Chrysostom touches on this notion in his homily on Hebrews: Christ "taste[s] death for every man, not for the faithful only, but even for the whole world: for He Himself indeed died for all."[11]

---

8. Italics added. See Picirilli, "The Intent and Extent of Christ's Atonement," 58; see also Allen, *The Extent of the Atonement*, 702–3.

9. W. Brian Shelton, *Prevenient Grace: God's Provision for Fallen Humanity* (Anderson, IN: Francis Asbury, 2015), 39.

10. See Picirilli, *Grace, Faith, Free Will* (126–28) for a detailed discussion of how "we/us" means the elect, not just the "we elect" compared with "other elect people in the world."

11. *Homilies of S. John Chrysostom on the Epistle of S. Paul the Apostle to the Hebrews* (London: Walter Smith, 1883), 51.

The Calvinist conclusion that "whole world" means "all kinds of elect people in the world" is further ruled out by the fact that 1 John 5:19 defines the "whole world" as those who lie "in the power of the evil one." This verse plainly distinguishes the whole world from "we" who are "from God" or "of God." Picirilli points out that, in his first letter, John consistently uses *kosmos* (world) "in a sense antipathetic to the church or Christians," as in 2:15–17, which makes readers choose between loving God and loving the world.[12]

Paul uses the word "world" in this same way in 2 Corinthians 5:18–19: "In Christ God was reconciling the world to himself." In 1 Corinthians 11:32, Paul distinguishes between "we" and "the world" as John does in 1 John: "we are disciplined so that we may not be condemned along with the world."[13] One sees the same distinction in Paul's first epistle to Timothy: God wants everyone to be saved (2:4); thus he sent Jesus to give himself as "a ransom for all" (2:6; cf. 2 Cor. 5:15, "He died for all"). Then in chapter 4 Paul, like John in 1 John 2:2, distinguishes between the world and the elect: God is "the Savior of all people, especially of those who believe" (1 Tim. 4:10). Why would Paul make this distinction if God was the Savior of *only* those who believe? Paul makes it clear here that God is "the Savior" not only of those who believe, but also of everyone else.[14]

Everyone Is Sinful, and Christ Died for Everyone

Neither John the Apostle, John the Baptist, nor Paul are using this language in a vacuum. Rather, they are taking note of the prophetic witness to the coming Messiah, especially in Isaiah 53:6[15]

> All we like sheep have gone astray;
> > we have turned—every one—to his own way;
> and the Lord has laid on him
> > the iniquity of us all.

John's theology is in line with this prophetic witness: Everyone has gone astray, and the Lord has laid on the Messiah everyone's iniquity.

This same dyad is seen throughout the New Testament: *Everyone is sinful, and Christ has died for everyone.* This is especially clear in Paul's letter to the

---

12. Picirilli, *Grace, Faith, Free Will*, 125.
13. Picirilli, "The Intent and Extent of Christ's Atonement," 62.
14. Obviously, in saying that Jesus is everyone's savior, Paul is not teaching universalism, but that Jesus *provides* salvation for all—but that only those who "come to the knowledge of the truth" (1 Tim. 2:4) will actually be saved.
15. Craig A. Evans, "Isaiah 53 in the Letters of Peter, Paul, and John," and Michael J. Wilkins, "Isaiah 53 and the Message of the Four Gospels," in *The Gospel according to Isaiah 53: Encountering the Suffering Servant in Jewish and Christian Theology*, eds. Darrell L. Bock and Mitch Glaser (Grand Rapids: Kregel Academic, 2012), esp. 113–14, 144.

Romans, in which he says, "Therefore, as one trespass led to condemnation for all men, so one act of righteousness leads to justification and life for all men" (Rom. 5:18) and "God has consigned all to disobedience, that he may have mercy on all" (Rom. 11:32).

These verses are troublesome for the doctrine of limited atonement precisely because they use "all" in a context that makes it impossible to deny that "all" means "all," everyone—or, as Calvinists often say, all without exception (*all* people), not all without distinction (all *sorts* of people). All partake in Adam's trespass, thus Jesus makes salvation available for all who partake in Adam's trespass. All are disobedient, so God has mercy on all by sending Jesus to provide salvation for them if they would not resist him. It is implausible to argue that the first "all" in these passages means "all" and the second "all" does not. Augustine supported this view when he said, "Thus all, without one exception, were dead in sins . . . and for all the dead there died the one only person who lived, that is, who had no sin whatever, in order that they who live by the remission of their sins should live, not to themselves, but to Him who died for all."[16]

Other Texts

The author of Hebrews unmistakably affirms universal atonement, saying that Christ "taste[d] death for everyone" (Heb. 2:9). The verse comes right after a quotation from Psalm 8, which is clearly speaking of all without exception, not just all without distinction. It is a painfully strained interpretation that would require reinterpreting the clear statement that Christ experienced death for "everyone" (*pantos*) to make it "everyone of the elect," which imports an alien theological concept into the chapter.[17]

Calvinists claim that when 1 Timothy 1:15 and Luke 19:10 say that Christ died to save sinners, or the lost, they mean only elect sinners. However, nothing in the text of Scripture, or in these particular texts, indicates this. These are the same lost sinners spoken of throughout the Bible. They are lost humanity for whom Christ died. Certainly a Calvinist can use the words "Christ died to save sinners" without contradicting limited atonement, but that does not explain the extent of the atonement.

Examples of People Who Are Finally Lost for Whom Christ Died

Lastly, the New Testament gives examples of people who were finally lost for whom Christ died. One sees an example of this in 2 Peter 2:1, which refers

---

16. Augustine, *The City of God*, vol. 2 of *The Works of Aurelius Augustine, Bishop of Hippo*, ed. Marcus Dods (Edinburgh: T&T Clark, 1881), 354.
17. See David L. Allen, *Hebrews*, New American Commentary (Nashville: B&H Academic, 2010).

to false teachers whom Peter says were guilty of "denying the Master who bought them" and thus have brought "upon themselves swift destruction."[18]

It is hard to avoid the force of this description. Whether the false teachers Peter describes in this text were believers who became false teachers and thus apostatized from salvation, or whether they never were genuine believers, this passage describes people who experienced "swift *destruction*,"—were finally lost—yet whom the Master had "bought" (italics added). As Luther argued, everywhere in the New Testament where God or Christ are said to "buy" or "purchase" someone, it means redemption, atonement.[19]

Two other examples from Paul's writings, both very similar, are Romans 14:15, "By what you eat, do not *destroy* the one for whom Christ died," and 1 Corinthians 8:11, "And so by your knowledge this weak person is *destroyed*, the brother for whom Christ died" (italics added). These are yet other examples of individuals who experience eternal destruction but for whom the text says Christ died.

Calvinist Objections to Universal Atonement

Particular Redemption

The most common theological argument for limited atonement is that if the atonement paid the world's penalty for sin, then everyone would be saved, because the atonement saves people.[20] This is why most Arminians reject the penal satisfaction view of atonement. However, this analysis fails to distinguish between the fact that on the cross redemption, as Arminius noted, was *accomplished* or "*obtained* for all the world, and for all and every man; but *applied* to believers and the elect alone."[21]

A person might say, "The prescription the doctor gave me saved my life," but what really saved the individual's life is the fact that he or she took the medicine the doctor prescribed.[22] As the Calvinist William G. T. Shedd remarked, "Vicarious atonement without faith in it is powerless to save. It is not the *making* of this atonement but the *trusting* in it, that saves the sinner."[23] Besides, most Calvinists acknowledge that not all elect people are saved

18. Douglas W. Kennard, "Petrine Redemption: Its Meaning and Extent," *Journal of the Evangelical Theological Society* 30 (1987): 399–405.
19. Martin Luther, *The Epistles of St. Peter and St. Jude*, trans. E. H. Gillett (New York: Anson D. F. Randolph, 1859), 272–73, 321.
20. J. I. Packer, "What Did the Cross Achieve? The Logic of Penal Substitution," *Tyndale Bulletin* 75 (1974): 37.
21. Arminius, *Works*, 3:425, "Examination of Perkins's Pamphlet."
22. This illustration is derived from a similar one Picirilli gives in "The Intent and Extent of Christ's Atonement," 64. Jacobus Arminius, *The Works of James Arminius*, 3 vols., trans. James Nichols and William Nichols (Nashville: Randall House, 2007), 3:425, "Examination of Perkins's Pamphlet."
23. William G. T. Shedd, *Dogmatic Theology* (New York: Charles Scribner's Sons, 1888), 2:440.

(though they will be), thus distancing themselves from the doctrine of the Hyper-Calvinist Antinomians, "eternal justification."[24]

"All" Does Not Mean "All"

Most Calvinist objections to the non-Calvinist reading of the above texts is to assert that "all" means not "all without exception" but "all without distinction"—not all people, but all *kinds* of people. This is seen most recently in the most comprehensive modern defense of limited atonement, *From Heaven He Came and Sought Her*.[25] An example of this is Thomas Schreiner's interpretation of 1 Timothy 2:4–6: "It seems, then, that Paul is saying here that God is potentially the Savior of all kinds of people . . . but that he is actually the Savior of only believers."[26]

David Allen, in his book *The Extent of the Atonement*, the most extensive modern study of universal atonement, gets to the heart of the problem with Schreiner's interpretation. He explains that the fact that "all" modifies "men" in 1 Timothy 2:4 makes it impossible "to change 'all' into 'some men of all kinds,'" because to do so would be to make "all" modify "kinds" rather than "men," which it does not. Yet Calvinists engage in this "semantic shift. . . . 'all' becomes 'some.' Apparently for some Calvinists, since 'all' sometimes means 'all of some sorts' or 'some of all sorts,' it can never mean in any atonement context all humanity including each and every person. The logical fallacy is evident."[27]

Phenomenological Language

Regarding the texts that say that Christ died for people who would ultimately perish, Calvinists say that these refer to what *appears* to be the case, not what is the case in reality. Thus Schreiner states that Romans 14:15 and 2 Peter 2:1 refer to believers "phenomenologically"—that they "*gave every appearance* of knowing Jesus Christ."[28] Yet how can he be so sure? As Picirilli observes, this is "another example of reading in to the sentence something manifestly not implied. These words, too, are straightforward: The Lord Jesus, by His death, bought them. They deny Him. Nothing else is justified by the

---

24. Robert J. McKelvey, "'That Error and Pillar of Antinomianism': Eternal Justification," in *Drawn Into Controversie: Reformed Theological Diversity and Debates within Seventeenth-Century British Puritanism*, eds. Michael A. G. Haykin and Mark Jones (Göttingen: Vandenhoeck and Ruprecht, 2011), 223–62.

25. David Gibson and Jonathan Gibson, eds., *From Heaven He Came and Sought Her: Definite Atonement in Historical, Biblical, Theological, and Pastoral Perspective* (Wheaton, IL: Crossway, 2013), 267–397.

26. Thomas R. Schreiner, "'Problematic Texts' for Definite Atonement in the Pastoral and General Epistles," in *From Heaven He Came and Sought Her*, 385–86.

27. Allen, *The Extent of the Atonement*, 707–8.

28. Schreiner, "'Problematic Texts,'" 390 (italics in original). Roger Nicole is another example of this approach; see his article "The Case for Definite Atonement, *Bulletin of the Evangelical Theological Society* 10 (1967): 205.

text." In the same verse, Paul says these people were "false teachers" and says the Lord "bought them." "It seems strange that in the same verse one statement would represent them according to their profession and the other according to God's true understanding."[29]

Other Arguments

Finally, Calvinists object to the doctrine of universal atonement with three other arguments: First, they contend that texts that discuss Christ dying for the elect prove limited atonement. Yet what does asserting that Christ died for the elect have to do with whether or not he died for others as well? Even Calvinist Matthew Harmon, in his argument for limited atonement, states: "True, the claim that Jesus laid down his life for his sheep does not logically demand that he died only for the elect."[30] All Christians, not just Calvinists, rejoice that "from heaven he came and sought her to be his holy bride."[31] As Augustine's mentor Ambrose of Milan said, "Although Christ suffered for all, yet He suffered for us particularly, because He suffered for the Church."[32] Furthermore, Paul says in Galatians 2:20, "Christ loved me and gave himself for me." That no more means that Christ died only for Paul than these texts mean that Christ died only for the elect.

Second, Calvinists argue that since the Bible says that Christ gave himself a "ransom for *many*," that means he did not give himself a ransom for all (italics added). Yet Pfeiffer was right when he argued that "it does not follow at all that what pertains to many can not be restricted to a few elect ('*many* be called, but *few* chosen,' Matt. 20:16), but may be predicated for all. . . . All men are, indeed, not few, but many."[33]

Third, some Calvinists argue that John 17:9 proves limited atonement because Christ prayed for his people but not the world in his high priestly prayer. However, this is called his high priestly prayer because he is praying, in this particular prayer, for his people. But in other places, Christ does pray for people who are not his people. For example, Isaiah 53:12, in the context of some strong universal-atonement language, says he "makes intercession for the transgressors." Besides, just because Jesus is not praying for the reprobate in one prayer does not prove that he did not die for them.

---

29. Picirilli, *Grace, Faith, Free Will*, 114–15.

30. Matthew S. Harmon, "For the Glory of the Father and the Salvation of His People: Definite Atonement in the Synoptics and Johannine Literature," in *From Heaven He Came and Sought Her*, 277 n. 30.

31. Samuel J. Stone, "The Church's One Foundation," in *Rejoice: The Free Will Baptist Hymn Book* (Antioch, TN: National Association of Free Will Baptists, 1995), no. 340.

32. Ambrose, *Exposition of the Holy Gospel according to Saint Luke*, trans. T. Tomkinson (Etna, CA: Center for Traditionalist Orthodox Studies, 1998), 201–02, cited in Allen, *The Extent of the Atonement*, 12.

33. Pfeiffer, *Anti-Calvinism*, 118. Italics in original.

Summary

If one is a Calvinist who believes that God, in his secret will, does not desire that everyone be saved through repentance, limited atonement must follow. Only limited atonement and Arminianism are theologically coherent. However, the doctrine of limited atonement or particular redemption is hard pressed to find exegetical backing. John's understanding of "the world" precludes the understanding that the statement "Christ died for the world" means he died only for all the elect in the world. Universal atonement is also borne out in texts that distinguish between the world and the elect—that essentially say that Christ died not only for the elect but also the whole world, or that he died for everyone, especially the elect. Furthermore, there are just too many passages that clearly teach, as Augustine averred, that "all, without one exception, were dead in sins . . . and for all the dead there died the only person who lived, that is, who had no sin whatever."[34] And if Christ died only for the elect, it is hard to see how Paul could say that people for whom Christ died could be spiritually destroyed. It is exceedingly difficult for the theological argumentation of five-point Calvinism to respond to this clear and consistent teaching of the New Testament.

REFLECTION QUESTIONS

1. Why do both classical Calvinists and non-Calvinists believe that four-point Calvinism is incoherent?

2. What do Arminians think John meant by "the world" and "the whole world" in passages such as 1 John 2:2; 2:15–17; 4:14; 5:19 and John 1:29 and 3:15–17?

3. How do 1 John 5:19 and 2:15–17 affect the Calvinist view that "the world" in John's writings refers to "all the elect in the world"?

4. How do texts like Romans 5:18 and 11:32 that indicate that Christ died for everyone who has sinned inform the doctrine of the extent of the atonement?

5. What does Paul mean when he says a person "for whom Christ died" can be "destroyed"? Is this problematic for the doctrine of limited atonement?

---

34. Augustine, *City of God*, 354.

Are Calvinists Inconsistent in Freely Offering the Gospel to Everyone?

In short, the Arminian answer is, yes.[1] This chapter will have special reference to Jonathan Edwards, the theological hero of the "Young, Restless, and Reformed" movement whose portrait graces T-shirts along with the message "Jonathan Edwards is my homeboy." What makes Edwards so important in answering this question is that he was an ardent Calvinist, but he strongly preached the gospel freely and indiscriminately to all sinners. In fact, Edwards portrayed the grace God gives to reprobates as a careful, personal influence of the Holy Spirit, who is graciously giving the sinner repeated, special opportunities to be saved. Yet gospel preaching belongs to what Edwards saw as the external call of God. Edwards sharply distinguished that gospel call from the internal call God gives to the elect, that "divine and supernatural light" that dawns on them because of God's special—not common—grace.[2]

Edwards believed that conviction and spiritual awakening—the strivings of the Spirit—are necessary beginning steps in the conversion of the elect. They are part of that internal call to the elect. Yet this convicting and awakening grace is not peculiar to the elect, according to Edwards. God also works

---

1. It is important to emphasize that this is an honest critique of Calvinists' theological consistency, not their hearts. While Arminians will argue that Calvinist theology is inconsistent with the free offer of the gospel, they should not caricature Calvinists as lacking a heart for evangelism and mission. See Michael A. G. Haykin and Jeff Robinson, Sr., *To the Ends of the Earth: Calvin's Missional Vision and Legacy* (Wheaton, IL: Crossway, 2014); and Nathan Finn, "Southern Baptist Calvinism: Setting the Record Straight," in *Calvinism: A Southern Baptist Dialogue*, eds. E. Ray Clendenen and Brad J. Waggoner (Nashville: B&H Academic, 2008), 171–94.
2. John E. Smith, "Religious Affections and the 'Sense of the Heart,'" in *The Princeton Companion to Jonathan Edwards*, ed. Sang Hyun Lee (Princeton, NJ: Princeton University Press, 2005), 106–7, 110–11.

this way in the reprobate. One sees this grace and calling on full display in Edwards's sermons.

The Reprobate Are Recipients of God's Offer of Mercy, Goodness, and Hope

Edwards's sermon "Pressing into the Kingdom of God" is one of the clearest examples of his free-offer preaching.[3] In it, as he urged his hearers to receive Christ now, he utilized the imagery of the reprobates who pounded on the door of Noah's ark after it was shut: "They may stand at the door and knock, and cry, Lord, Lord, open to us, in vain; they will be thrust back; and God will have no mercy on them; they shall be eternally left of him. . . . all offers of mercy and expressions of divine goodness will be finally withdrawn, and all hope will be lost. . . . God will . . . be their dreadful enemy, and will execute wrath with fury."[4]

What Edwards described here was the case of a reprobate person, someone who, by divine design, is outside the bounds of God's saving grace, who is without hope and never had any hope. God had planned from eternity past, according to his own good pleasure, that this person, of necessity, would be outside the scope of his eternal elective love, beyond the compass of his final salvific mercy. Thus God carefully arranged it so that this person would be "without this inclosure" of the kingdom and thus would be "swallowed up in an overflowing fiery deluge of wrath."[5] However, Edwards says that this same reprobate person, whom God has purposefully designed to be outside the scope of his saving mercy, is a recipient of an offer of divine mercy.[6]

In this sermon Edwards presents a scenario that any other Christian preacher would present: Dear sinner, God has offered you mercy. He has expressed to you his divine goodness. He has given you hope. But if you resist and reject that divine offer of mercy and goodness, you will be deprived of that hope. The trouble is that, while most Christians would not see this sinner's being, by God's design, outside the scope of God's saving mercy and goodness from before the foundation of the world—and thus without hope in God's eternal plan, Calvinism believes just that. Arminians ask, how can Calvinists say that the reprobate are recipients of an offer of divine mercy? Arminians see this as a gross inconsistency. (This concern remains even with

---

3. Jonathan Edwards, "Pressing into the Kingdom of God," *The Works of President Edwards*, 4 vols. (New York: Robert Carter and Brothers, 1879), 4:381–402.
4. Edwards, "Pressing into the Kingdom of God," 4:386.
5. Edwards, "Pressing into the Kingdom of God," 4:386.
6. Thomas Schreiner similarly says of the reprobate that God is "merciful and loving in . . . offering them salvation." Thomas R. Schreiner, "Does Scripture Teach Prevenient Grace in the Wesleyan Sense?" in *Still Sovereign: Contemporary Perspectives on Election, Foreknowledge, and Grace*, eds. Thomas R. Schreiner and Bruce A. Ware (Grand Rapids: Baker, 2000), 245.

single predestination, which has God withholding from the reprobate the grace they need to cease their resistance to his call.)

God Pours Out His Spirit on the Reprobate, Giving an Opportunity to Be Saved

Edwards directly stated that God is giving people who will never be saved an "opportunity" and in fact pouring out his Spirit on them for that express purpose. The difficulty with this is that Edwards was imploring people to take advantage of this special moment of the pouring out of God's Spirit. They have the opportunity now, "if [they] have but a heart to improve it."[7]

Why is Edwards implying that those who turn a deaf ear to God could have done otherwise and will be held accountable for not having done so? And for what purpose, to what end, is God pouring out his Spirit on them, giving them an opportunity to be saved, if he has arranged the universe in such a way as purposefully to prohibit them from "improving it"? Why is God—not just the human preacher—calling the reprobate "now . . . in an extraordinary manner"? Why is God coming to these sinners "in a very un-usual manner amongst us," by the "particular influences of the Spirit of Christ awakening" them? Why is Christ making a "special offer" to them: "You are not passed over. Christ has not forgot you; but has come to your door and there as it were stands waiting for you to open to him"?[8]

Edwards was not only talking to those who will eventually be converted but also to the reprobate, stating, "Doubtless there are many now seeking that will not be able to enter." In fact, he said he had "no reason to think any other, than that some of you will burn in hell to all eternity." The Arminian asks, why do Edwards and Calvinists think God works in this way? Why all the free offers of the gospel when God has always had every intention of reprobating these people? The reason lies in the next feature one sees in Edwards's preaching.[9]

Hell Will Be Hotter the More They Resist, and This Will Give God Glory

The reason God calls so freely to the reprobate, only to turn them away when they bang on the door of the ark, is to enlarge their punishment to give himself greater glory. Those who spurn Christ's gracious calling, Edwards preached, will be held more accountable for not "improving" the "special op-portunity" he is now, in freely offering the gospel to them, giving them to be saved. They have had every opportunity, Edwards said. God "set upon the fountain of his grace." He "so loudly called upon them." He came to them and "strove with them in particular, by the awakening influences of his Spirit."

---

7.   Edwards, "Pressing into the Kingdom of God," 4:392–93.
8.   Edwards, "Pressing into the Kingdom of God," 4:393–94.
9.   Edwards, "Pressing into the Kingdom of God," 4:395.

Thus they will "have no good account to give to the Judge, but their mouths will be stopped, and they will stand speechless before him."[10]

In fact, after times of "extraordinary effusion of God's Spirit," Edwards explained, God often leaves the unconverted in a harder condition than before these gracious times. Therefore, Edwards exhorted his listeners to "improve this opportunity, while God is pouring out his Spirit . . . and you yourself have the awakening influences of it." God will increase their judgment because they refuse to respond to the gospel, and believers "will rise up as witnesses, and will declare what a precious opportunity you had, and did not improve" and because they "continued unbelieving and rejected the offers of a Saviour, when those offers were made in so extraordinary a manner." Yet they were "negligent and slack, and did not know the things that belonged to your peace, in that your day."[11]

"God's Spirit Shall Not Always Strive with Man"

Edwards often appealed to Genesis 6:3, "God's Spirit shall not always strive with man," to emphasize the shortness of the opportunity people have to be converted.[12] This verse was commonly used in traditional Arminian preaching, in which the preacher would call on the sinner not to resist the striving of the Holy Spirit.[13] Edwards urged on his hearers: "Men must . . . be diligent in the use of the means of grace" now, while they have an opportunity, for "the Spirit of God will not *always* strive with you."[14] For the people who rejected Noah's message, "it was a day of grace with them. . . . All this while they had an *opportunity* to escape, if they would but hearken and believe God."[15]

> So it will be with you, if you continue to refuse to hearken to the warnings which are given you. Now God is striving with you. . . . Now the door of the ark stands open. But God's Spirit will not always strive with you. . . . Though now warnings are continued in plenty, yet there will be *last* knocks and *last* calls, the last that ever you shall hear. When the appointed time shall be elapsed, God will shut the door. . . . If you improve not your opportunity before that time, you will cry in vain, "Lord, Lord, open to us." . . . While you shall stand at the door with your piteous cries, the flood of God's wrath will

---

10. Edwards, "Pressing into the Kingdom of God," 4:396.
11. Edwards, "Pressing into the Kingdom of God," 4:396–97.
12. Edwards, "Pressing into the Kingdom of God," 4:400.
13. See, e.g., John Wesley's protégé, Adam Clarke, *The Holy Bible . . . The Text . . . with a Commentary and Critical Notes* (New York: T. Mason and G. Lane, 1837), 1:66.
14. Jonathan Edwards, "The Manner in Which the Salvation of the Soul Is to Be Sought," *The Works of President Edwards*, 4 vols. (New York: Robert Carter and Brothers, 1881), 4:371.
15. Edwards, "The Manner in Which," 4:373 (italics added).

come upon you, overwhelm you, and you shall not escape. The tempest shall carry you away without mercy, and you shall be forever swallowed up and lost.[16]

These themes are evident throughout Edwards's sermons. He preached again and again that, in conviction, the Holy Spirit enlightens, influences, and illuminates both elect and nonelect people.[17] Edwards even described a back-and-forth exchange that goes on between the Holy Spirit and those he is calling, some of whom are reprobates and thus for whom the call is ineffectual because it is merely external. In this back-and-forth activity, the Spirit is graciously giving them a strong conviction of sin, and they are becoming miserably sorrowful over their sin and seeking him more diligently. "But these affections are but short-lived, they quickly find that they fail." Even though the Holy Spirit is busy influencing them and convicting them of sin and making them feel miserable for it—even though he has created this special opportunity for them and is calling them—they can never be converted. In this cycle that Edwards refers to as a "labyrinth," he makes it clear that it is not "their own experience only," but the Holy Spirit's convicting influence, that produces these effects.[18]

Free Offer Preaching
Edwards is not as concerned as some modern-day Calvinists seem to be about letting some "loose ends" dangle. He is not ashamed to engage, *as vigorously as any Arminian preacher*, in the free or "well-meant" offer of the gospel. Hyper-Calvinists do not believe in the free offer of the gospel and, like Arminians, criticize Calvinists such as Edwards for being inconsistent. Most contemporary Calvinists, not being Hyper-Calvinists, support the notion of the free offer of the gospel and the revealed will and external call of God universally.[19]

Edwards's emphasis that the Holy Spirit is working graciously and repeatedly with people, repeatedly knocking at the door of their hearts, giving them special opportunities to be saved, is typical of non-Calvinist preaching. The difference between the Arminian preacher and Edwards is that the latter believed that God may not indeed, with his secret will, desire his hearers' salvation, even though he is perfectly justified in calling them to salvation, pleading with them to come, according to his revealed will. And he is doing

---

16. Edwards, "The Manner in Which," 4:379.
17. Jonathan Edwards, *A Treatise Concerning Religious Affections*, in *The Works of President Edwards*, 4 vols. (New York: Robert Carter and Brothers, 1881), 3:135–36.
18. Jonathan Edwards, "Narrative of Surprising Conversions," *The Works of President Edwards*, 4 vols. (New York: Robert Carter and Brothers, 1881), 3:243–244.
19. See, e.g., Schreiner, "Does Scripture Teach Prevenient Grace?" 245; see also John Piper, *God's Passion for His Glory: Living the Vision of Jonathan Edwards* (Wheaton, IL: Crossway, 1998).

this to enlarge their damnation, to make hell hotter for them, so that he can bring greater glory to himself.

One might think that this emphasis of Edwards is peculiar to his Great Awakening context. However, Calvin avers that God "vouchsafes his blessing, for a time, even to reprobates, with whom he is justly angry, in order that he may *gently invite and even allure them* to repentance; and may render them more inexcusable, if they remain obstinate; meanwhile, he curses their felicity. Therefore, while they think they have reached the height of fortune, their prosperity, in which they delighted themselves, is turned into ruin."[20]

Arminians love the kind of straightforward free-offer preaching in which Edwards engages. They believe that modern-day Calvinists would do better to let loose ends dangle in their theology, as Edwards did, and preach the gospel as freely as he did, if they really affirm the free offer of the gospel.

Like Edwards, Arminians preach to sinners indiscriminately that Jesus is pleading with them to repent of sin and trust him for salvation. They believe the Holy Spirit is graciously coming to sinners—elect and reprobate alike—and pressing home the call of Christ. They agree that the Holy Spirit is influencing people, convicting them of sin and the truth of the gospel, that he is awakening and enlightening and illuminating them spiritually, striving with them repeatedly, giving them special opportunities over and over again to respond to God's grace. They believe that the reprobate are recipients of divine offers of mercy. They believe there is hope for them. They believe that God is knocking on the door of the reprobate's hearts, opening a special door for them. They believe that the Holy Spirit is graciously influencing sinners. And they are urging sinners not to spurn these gracious invitations. And they believe that, without this grace from the Holy Spirit, no sinners can come to God in their own natural ability. *All the precise Edwardsean phrases* in this paragraph fit very well into traditional Arminian theology, preaching, and piety.

Yet Reformed Arminians, like many other Arminians, do not believe that these repeated, individualized strivings of the Spirit can be relegated to the category of "common grace" in terms of the divine grace that keeps the planets spinning and people breathing and gives unbelievers the ability to do good deeds. They think there must be a category between common grace of that sort and regeneration. They believe that this is the most natural reading of Holy Scripture—the best way to make sense of the contradiction Edwards has between his theology and his preaching. This they call prevenient or enabling grace, whereby the Holy Spirit calls, convicts, woos, influences, and enables unbelievers to come to him, a grace that God gives them the freedom to resist.

What if Jesus were preaching the gospel today? What would Jesus's free-offer preaching look like? How would he deal with his secret divine will in

---

20. John Calvin, *Commentaries on the First Book of Moses Called Genesis* (Edinburgh: Calvin Translation Society, 1850), 2:292 (on Genesis 39:1; italics added).

conversations with the reprobate as he "gently invited and even allured them to repentance"? Would he look a reprobate person in the eye and gently invite, allure, and plead with the individual, "Come, follow me," implying that that is what he genuinely wanted the individual to do, when in his mind he was thinking the following?

> I don't want this person to come to me. I am telling him to come and follow me simply to "render him more inexcusable." I know full well what I have always desired for this individual whom I·am gently calling to myself. My earnest desire for him is that he should spend eternity in hell, and I have from eternity carefully orchestrated the circumstances of his birth, life, and death so that my desire for him will, of necessity, come to pass. Still, it is good and right and just and honest for me to look him in the eye and gently invite and allure him to come to me.

Thus Thomas Helwys said that "this lamentable opinion of particular redemption and reprobation saith [the reprobate] can have no part nor portion in Christ. So is their judgment enlarged for not receiving Christ, with whom they have nothing to do." Thus, Helwys said, Calvinism makes "Christ to offer himself to them that he would not have receive him, and which he hath decreed shall not receive him, nor believe him, and make the words of the Lord feigned words, and words of dissimulation."[21]

Arminians believe that Calvinism's "two wills in God" doctrine demands a split-personality Jesus, and they see it as flying in the face of the natural reading of Holy Scripture. Instead, they believe that the Bible teaches that there is one will in God: that he is not willing that any should perish but that all should come to repentance (2 Peter 3:9). They believe that he wants all people to be saved and come to the knowledge of the truth (1 Tim. 2:4). They believe that he is commanding all people everywhere to repent (Acts 17:30) and in his own mysterious time and way will graciously enable them to repent, while also giving them the ability to resist (Matt. 23:37). This view comports much better with the kind of theology and free-offer preaching we see in the Bible and the mainstream of the Christian tradition. And it is the only way to remove the contradiction between a Calvinist like Edwards's theology and his biblical gospel preaching.

---

21. Thomas Helwys, *A Short and Plaine Proofe by the Word and Workes of God that Gods decree is not the cause of anye Mans sinne or Condemnation* (London, 1611), sig. B2v; repr. in Joe Early, Jr., *The Life and Writings of Thomas Helwys*. Early English Baptist Texts (Macon, GA: Mercer University Press, 2009). For more on Helwys's soteriology, see J. Matthew Pinson, *Arminian and Baptist: Explorations in a Theological Tradition* (Nashville: Randall House, 2016), chapters 3–4.

Summary

Arminians like the sort of strong free-offer preaching of the gospel they see in traditional Calvinists like Edwards, which offered "mercy" and "hope" to all sinners, assuring them that God has poured out his Spirit on them and is giving them an opportunity to be saved. This is the simple teaching of the Bible, and preaching and evangelism should reflect this. Still, Arminians believe that God's revealed will seen in these offers of mercy and hope cannot be reconciled with a secret will that contradicts these offers. Rather than simply letting the antinomies hang out there as Edwards did, or just toning down the free-offer language, as many modern-day Calvinists seem to do, Arminians wish that Calvinists would posit a holistic divine will and desire in God's consciousness that accord with the will and desire he reveals in his own invitations to everyone and the Christian preacher's assurances that they do indeed have an opportunity to be converted.

REFLECTION QUESTIONS

1. What does Edwards mean by the terms "awakening," "illuminating," and "enlightening"?

2. According to Edwards, what does God, and the Christian preacher, offer to sinners?

3. What opportunity does Edwards say God gives sinners?

4. Why does Calvin believe that God "gently invites and even allures" the reprobate "to repentance"?

5. What do Calvinists mean when they describe what they call "two wills in God," and what are the Arminian concerns about this doctrine?

PART 3

Questions About Free Will and Grace

Free Will and Determinism

Are Arminians Semi-Pelagians Who Deny Total Depravity and Inability?

One of the caricatures many Calvinists make of Arminians is that they are semi-Pelagians. R. C. Sproul, in referring to Arminianism as semi-Pelagianism, went as far as to state that "the 'semi' is a thin patina" and that the "essence of Pelagianism" is "carried through into Arminianism."[1] J. I. Packer characterized the early Remonstrants as "Belgic semi-Pelagians" who disagreed with the Calvinistic doctrine of human inability in salvation.[2] He was quoting the Puritan John Owen, who, discussing the early Remonstrants, said:

> Hence hath been the rise of all our miseries, of all our dissensions, whilst factious men labored every day to commend themselves to them, who sate aloft in the temple of God, by introducing new Popish Arminian errors, whose patronage they had wickedly undertaken. Who would have thought, that our church would ever have given entertainment to these Belgic Semipelagians, who have cast dirt upon the faces, and raked up the ashes, of all those great and pious souls, whom God magnified, in using as his instruments to reform his church?[3]

---

1. R. C. Sproul, *What is Reformed Theology?* (Grand Rapids: Baker, 2016), 208–9.
2. J. I. Packer, *A Quest for Godliness: The Puritan Vision of the Christian Life* (Wheaton, IL: Crossway, 1990), 127.
3. John Owen, *A Display of Arminianism, Being a Discovery of the Old Pelagian Idol Free-Will, with the New Godless Contingency . . .* , in *The Works of John Owen, D.D.*, ed. William H. Goold (London: Johnstone and Hunter, 1852), 10:6.

These harsh accusations do not stand up under the thinnest scrutiny. Pelagians and semi-Pelagians believe that there is, to a greater or lesser degree, some sort of natural free will or ability to respond to the gospel without special grace from the Holy Spirit. It, is however, a gross mischaracterization to say that Arminians believe this. While some who mistakenly claim the name Arminian believe it, traditional Arminians do not.

As Rebecca Harden Weaver observes, semi-Pelagians had stepped back from the teachings of Pelagius on the absence of original sin and the completely unfettered free will. Still, they believed that "in the case of some persons, grace will assist the will that already desires the good, whereas in the case of others, grace will arouse the will to good when it is not so inclined. The beginning of faith may have its source in the human agent, although it will not always have its source there."[4] The second Council of Orange repudiated semi-Pelagianism in A.D. 529, but, as Harden correctly notes, "in subsequent centuries variations of their teaching have functioned as the operative theology of the church."[5]

Robert A. Peterson and Michael Williams are among the Calvinists who agree that Arminians are not semi-Pelagians. Peterson and Williams correctly define semi-Pelagianism as holding that, while individuals cannot be saved "apart from the supernatural assisting grace of God," they can, apart from divine grace, "take the first step toward salvation." Thus "*God helps those who help themselves*."[6] As this chapter will show, Arminians have always been in line with the Second Council of Orange in their strong aversion to semi-Pelagianism.

Arminius on Human Depravity and Inability

Because Arminius has usually been incorrectly associated with semi-Pelagianism, most writers, both Arminian and Calvinist, have tended to dissociate his theology from that of Augustine. An investigation of his theological

---

4. Rebecca Harden Weaver, *Divine Grace and Human Agency: A Study of the Semi-Pelagian Controversy*, North American Patristic Society Patristic Monograph Series (Macon, GA: Mercer University Press, 1996), 72. As Hugo Grotius pointed out in 1613, the Second Council of Orange also condemned double predestination. See Hugo Grotius, *Ordinum Hollandiae ac Westfrisiae Pietas*, trans. Edwin Rabbie (Leiden: Brill, 1995), 131. Richard Clark first made me aware of this, and I later saw it in Grotius's *Pietas*.

5. Grotius, *Ordinum Hollandiae*, ix. Some scholars think that applying the term "semi-Pelagian," with its sixteenth-century origins, to sixth-century council is anachronistic; see, e.g., Irena Backus and Aza Goudriaan, "'Semipelagianism': The Origins of the Term and Its Passage into the History of Heresy," *Journal of Ecclesiastical History* 65 (2014): 26–46. Furthermore, often the term can be rather slippery—e.g., "anyone who is less Augustinian than I am." However, this book uses the term in its customary modern way.

6. Robert A. Peterson and Michael D. Williams, *Why I Am Not an Arminian* (Downers Grove, IL: InterVarsity, 2004), 35–37; see also Bruce A. Demarest, *The Cross and Salvation* (Wheaton, IL: Crossway, 2006), 59.

writings, however, reveals that he held to an Augustinian view of depravity and inability that was within the bounds of Reformed confessional theology.

Arminius openly affirmed and defended the Reformed statements on original sin and total depravity in the Belgic Confession of Faith and Heidelberg Catechism. He was clear in his affirmation of the Reformed account of what would later be called total depravity. Thus he desired to maintain "the greatest possible distance from Pelagianism."[7] He rooted his views on total depravity in an Augustinian doctrine of original sin. His position on the effect of Adam's sin on the race was that "the whole of this sin . . . is not peculiar to our first parents, but is common to the entire race and to all their posterity, who, at the time when this sin was committed, were in their loins, and who have since descended from them by the natural mode of propagation."[8] According to Arminius, all humanity sinned in Adam and are guilty in Adam, apart from their own actual sins.

When asked the question, "Is the guilt of original sin taken away from all and every one by the benefits of Christ?" Arminius said that "deliverance from this guilt" is a benefit of union with Christ and thus "believers only are delivered from it."[9] Furthermore, Arminius said that God "imput[ed] the guilt of the first sin to all Adam's posterity, no less than to Adam himself and Eve, because they also had sinned in Adam."[10]

A brief look at Arminius's perspectives on grace, free will, and human inability also reveal his loyalty to Reformed categories. Arminius believed that people have no ability to seek God or turn to him unless they are moved by his special grace. Arminius's view of human freedom does not mean freedom to do anything good in the sight of God or to choose God on one's own. For Arminius, the basic freedom that characterizes the human will is freedom from necessity (see Questions 16 and 20). Indeed, "it is the very essence of the will. Without it, the will would not be the will."[11] Though Arminius taught that the human will is free from necessity, he stated unequivocally that it is not free from sin and its dominion: "The free will of man towards the true good is not only wounded, maimed, infirm, bent, and (*nuatum*) weakened; but it is also (*captivatum*) imprisoned, destroyed, and lost: And its powers are

---

7. Jacobus Arminius, "Apology against Thirty-One Defamatory Articles," in *The Works of James Arminius*, 3 vols., trans. James Nichols and William Nichols (Nashville: Randall House, 2007), 1:764.
8. Ibid. It may be inferred from this statement that Arminius would accept (in the terminology of later Protestant Scholastic theology) a "natural headship" view of the transmission of sin, rather than a "federal headship" view. Rather than Adam being "federally" appointed as head of the race, he was naturally the head of the race, and individuals are sinful as a natural consequence of their being "in Adam" or in the race.
9. Arminius, *Works*, 2:65, "Nine Questions."
10. Arminius, *Works*, 3:224. "Friendly Conference with Junius."
11. Bangs, *Arminius,* 341.

not only debilitated and useless unless they be assisted by grace, but it has no powers whatever except such are excited by divine grace."[12]

Fallen human beings have no ability or power to reach out to God. Arminius details "the utter weakness of all the powers to perform that which is truly good, and to omit the perpetration of that which is evil."[13] He argued that the whole person—mind, affections, and will—is completely sinful. One would be hard-pressed to find a more thorough definition of total depravity than what Arminius articulated.

He stated that the human mind "is dark, destitute of the saving knowledge of God, and, according to the Apostle, incapable of those things which belong to the Spirit of God," having no perception of the things of God.[14] The affections and the heart are perverse, with a hatred and aversion to the true good and to what pleases God, and with a love for evil and the pursuit of it. In their deceitful, perverse, uncircumcised, hard, and stony hearts, unregenerate people have set themselves up as enemies of God.[15] The will has no power to perform the true good or keep from committing evil, because the unregenerate are slaves of the devil and under his power.[16] The entire life—mind, heart, and will—is submerged under sin and dead in sin.[17] These views led Moses Stuart to aver that "the most thorough advocate of total depravity will scarcely venture to go farther in regard to man in his unregenerate state, than . . . Arminius goes."[18]

Divine grace is the only power that can bring persons out of this state. That grace alone gives individuals the ability to come to God.[19] Grace for Arminius is necessary and essential to salvation from start to finish. The difference between him and Calvinism is simply that he believed that the grace of God comes to elect and nonelect alike but can be resisted. Though Arminius differed from Calvin and the mainstream of Reformed theology on the particulars of grace, he still maintained that salvation is *sola gratia*. Arminius can by no means be considered a semi-Pelagian.[20]

---

12. Arminius, *Works*, 2:192, Public Disputation 11, "On the Free Will of Man and Its Powers."
13. Arminius, *Works*, 2:193.
14. Arminius, *Works*, 2:192.
15. Arminius, *Works*, 2:193.
16. Arminius, *Works*, 2:193–94.
17. Arminius, *Works*, 2:194. Cf. 2:700, "Letter to Hippolytus à Collibus."
18. Moses Stuart, "The Creed of Arminius," *Biblical Repository* 1 (1831): 271. Stuart said Arminius went even further than most of the "orthodox" theologian of Stuart's own day. See John Mark Hicks, "The Theology of Grace in the Thought of Jacobus Arminius and Philipp van Limborch: A Study in the Development of Seventeenth-Century Dutch Arminianism" (doctoral dissertation, Westminster Theological Seminary, 1985), 22. Charles Hodge said similar things; see *Systematic Theology* (New York: Charles Scribner's Sons, 1888), 3:187.
19. Arminius, *Works*, 2:194–95. Public Disputation 11, "On the Free Will of Man and Its Powers."
20. Much of this section is adapted from J. Matthew Pinson, "Will the Real Arminius Please Stand Up? A Study of the Theology of Jacobus Arminius in Light of His Intrepreters,"

Other Arminians on Depravity and Inability

The early Arminians concurred with the anti-Pelagian sentiments of Arminius, as seen in the earliest Arminian confessional documents. The Remonstrant Confession of 1621, a confession produced by Arminius's followers shortly after the Synod of Dort, stated that "because Adam was the stock and root of all mankind, therefore, he involved and entangled, not only himself, but also all his posterity (who were as it were shut up in his loins, and were by natural generation to proceed from him) in the same death and misery with himself."[21] This caused the intellect, will, and affections of Adam's descendants after the fall to be radically depraved, as explained in the Five Articles of Remonstrance: "That man has not saving grace of himself, nor of the energy of his free will, inasmuch as he, in the state of apostasy and sin, can of and by himself neither think, will, nor do anything that is truly good."[22] The Remonstrant Hugo Grotius, who early on departed from Arminius in many ways, staunchly opposed semi-Pelagianism. He said that "no less dangerous" than the "Scylla" of absolute predestination is the "Charybdis" of "Pelagianism or Semi-Pelagianism," which he defined as teaching things such as that there is "no depravation of human nature," that "the beginning of faith, invocation, humility, obedience are not gifts of grace," and that "by nature's strength some good pertaining to salvation can be thought, made available, and chosen, or we can concur with the salutary, i.e., evangelical preaching without the illumination or inspiration of the Holy Ghost." Grotius believed that these "errors" should be "condemned."[23]

The General Baptists also articulated Arminius's approach to depravity and inability, as illustrated by the Orthodox Creed (1678), which said that original sin "is the fault and corruption of the nature of every man that naturally descendeth from Adam by natural generation; by means of which man has not only lost that original righteousness, that God created him in, but is naturally inclined to all manner of evil." Thus, while God "hath endued the will of man with that natural liberty and power, of acting upon choice, that it is neither forced, nor by any necessity of nature determined, to do good or evil," after the fall, man "wholly lost all ability, or liberty of will, to any spiritual good, for his eternal salvation, his will being now in bondage under sin

Integrity: A Journal of Christian Thought 2 (2003): 121–39, reprinted in Pinson, Arminian and Baptist: Explorations in a Theological Tradition (Nashville: Randall House, 2015), chapter 1. See also W. Brian Shelton, Prevenient Grace: God's Provision for Fallen Humanity (Anderson, IN: Francis Asbury, 2014), 106–9.

21. The Confession or Declaration of the Ministers and Pastors Which in the United Provinces Are Called Remonstrants (London: Francis Smith, 1676), 117–18.

22. Philip Schaff, The Creeds of Christendom (New York: Cosimo Classics, 2007), 3:545–49, art. 3.

23. Grotius, Ordinum Hollandiae, 133, 135.

and satan; and therefore not able of his own strength to convert himself, nor prepare himself thereunto, without God's grace. . . ."[24]

Finally, one sees this approach to depravity in the Wesleyan movement. The Methodist Articles of Religion (1784) state that after the fall, "man . . . cannot turn and prepare himself, by his own natural strength and works, to faith, and calling upon God" because human beings "have no power to do good works, pleasant and acceptable to God, without the grace of God by Christ preventing us, that we may have a good will, and working with us, when we have that good will."[25]

This Reformation understanding of total depravity is not limited to the early Arminians but is seen in many Arminians today. Not all who call themselves Arminians affirm total depravity. Jack Cottrell, for example, does not affirm it.[26] The Wesleyan theologian W. Brian Shelton does not deny total depravity like Cottrell. He does, however, contend that "the term 'total depravity' forever smacks of Calvinism" and that Arminians, therefore, "should avoid the use of the term."[27]

Traditional Wesleyans, however, affirm the doctrines of total depravity and inability. For example, the Wesleyan Timothy Tennent states: "It may come as a surprise to some of our Reformed readers that the doctrine of total depravity (the famous T in the Calvinistic TULIP) is shared by Wesleyans and Methodists just as ardently as by Calvinists." Tennent affirms a strong doctrine of total depravity. Because we are dead in trespasses and sins, he avers, we "cannot help or assist ourselves." We are "totally void of any ability to save ourselves . . . spiritually dead people have no capacity to respond."[28]

Reformed Arminians resonate with the statement above from the General Baptist Orthodox Creed. For example, F. Leroy Forlines affirms a Reformed doctrine of total depravity, stating that "total" means that "the corruption has extended to all aspects of man's nature, to his entire being." "Depravity" means that, "because of that corruption, there is nothing man can do to merit saving favor with God." Before Adam and Eve sinned, it was within what Forlines calls the "framework of possibilities" for their free will either to commit sin or not. After the fall, however, they and their posterity no longer had this choice

---

24. Orthodox Creed, articles 15 and 20. http://baptiststudiesonline.com/wp-content/uploads/2007/02/orthodox-creed.pdf, accessed September 17, 2020.

25. Art. 8, quoted in Henry Wheeler, *History and Exposition of the Twenty-five Articles of Religion of the Methodist Episcopal Church* (New York: Eaton and Mains, 1908), 190; cf. *Book of Common Prayer* (Oxford: Clarendon, 1793), art. 10, 320.

26. See Jack Cottrell, "Depravity: Total, Partial, or None at All?" http://jackcottrell.com/notes/depravity-total-partial-or-none-at-all.

27. W. Brian Shelton, *Prevenient Grace: God's Provision for Fallen Humanity* (Anderson, IN: Francis Asbury, 2014), 117. Interestingly, Shelton goes on to indicate the forceful manner in which Wesley affirmed total depravity (pp. 125–130).

28. Timothy Tennent, "Prevenient Grace: Why I Am a Methodist and an Evangelical," https://timothytennent.com/tag/grace, accessed April 16, 2020.

within their framework of possibilities: "Jesus makes it clear that it does not fall within the framework of possibilities for a sinner to respond to the gospel unless he is drawn by the Holy Spirit."[29]

Human depravity, as Robert Picirilli defines it, is "total." Human nature in its totality is affected by the fall, "whether the mind, the desires, or the will." Fallen humanity does not have the ability to "understand spiritual things. . . . Left to themselves, no persons will ever turn to God." Because of the radical estrangement from their creator, human beings "do not want to know" God. "In their separation from God they cannot understand and do not find appealing the vision that God has for them. They are blind and deaf and dead." Thus, totally depraved humanity, "faced with a mere 'gospel' offer of deliverance by the redemptive work of Jesus, is helpless and entirely unable to respond."[30]

Are Arminians Synergists?

One main concern Calvinists have with Arminianism is that it constitutes synergism, which means "working together." Thus, they say, rather than regeneration being monergistic, the work of God alone, Arminian theology makes it synergistic. Somehow, they say, Arminians believe that people are "working together" or cooperating with God to bring about their salvation. Many Arminians, while they would disagree with the above characterization, still use the term "synergism."[31] But Reformed Arminians such as Thomas Helwys, Thomas Grantham, and Arminius himself, would not have wanted to be called synergists.

Keith Stanglin and Thomas McCall even argue that Arminius himself was a synergist. "Some scholars," they say, "have denied that Arminius is a 'synergist,' yet his definition of subsequent grace is precisely 'synergistic,' which is simply the Greek equivalent of 'cooperative' (derived from Latin)."[32] Picirilli is correct when he intimates that Arminius never called himself or would ever have called himself a synergist because of the semi-Pelagian implications of the term.[33] It implies that people are working together with God in bringing about their salvation. Stanglin and McCall themselves quote Augustine himself a few paragraphs later using the same language of subsequent cooperating grace as Arminius used. Arminius's use of this Augustinian phrase does not

---

29. F. Leroy Forlines, *Classical Arminianism: A Theology of Salvation* (Nashville: Randall House, 2011), 17, 22.

30. Robert E. Picirilli, *Free Will Revisited: A Respectful Response to Luther, Calvin, and Edwards* (Eugene, OR: Wipf and Stock, 2016), 94–95.

31. Roger Olson, "Must One Agree with Arminius to Be Arminian?" http://www.patheos.com/blogs/rogereolson/2013/11/must-one-agree-with-arminius-to-be-arminian.

32. Their main culprit, whom they cite in the footnote, is me. Stanglin and McCall, *Jacob Arminius: Theologian of Grace* (New York: Oxford University Press, 2012), 152–53.

33. See Robert E. Picirilli, *Grace, Faith, Free Will: Contrasting Views of Salvation: Calvinism and Arminianism* (Nashville: Randall House, 2002), 162.

render him a "synergist" any more than it does Augustine, and he would not at all have been comfortable with the term. As Carl Bangs rightly argued, "Although Arminius speaks of 'cooperation,' it is not 'co-earning,' as has been pointed out. The cooperation is a *result* of renewal, not a means toward it."[34]

Arminius concurred with Luther's associate Philip Melanchthon. Conversion for him was, as Gregory Graybill argues "a passive *reception* of merit rather than an active cooperative work that earned merit. It was *not* synergism!" Just as it is unfair to attribute a term to Melanchthon that was associated with some of his later followers, it is unfair to saddle Arminius with a term that he did not employ and that was foreign to his theological context.[35]

The approach of Picirilli and Arthur Skevington Wood is preferable—that Arminius's views do not represent "a form of synergism in which God's work and man's work cooperate, but rather a relationship in which God's will and work within man [are] welcomed in an attitude of trust and submission."[36] Arminius would have been much more comfortable with the language used by Leroy Forlines, who uses the terminology of "conditional monergism" rather than synergism.[37] Forlines comments, "While there is an important difference between my view of regeneration and the view of Calvinism, the difference is not monergism. In both views, regeneration is solely the work of God."[38] This approach is shared by Bangs, who boldly stated, "Arminius was a monergist."[39] It is also affirmed by the Arminius scholar William den Boer, as well as scholars such as Mark Ellis and Oliver Crisp.[40] This perspective concurs with what Richard Muller, earlier in his career, said of Arminius's approach: "It is difficult to label it synergism in the sense of an equal cooperation between the divine and human wills in the movement of the individual toward grace."[41]

---

34. Bangs, "Arminius and Reformed Theology" (doctoral dissertation, University of Chicago, 1958), 166–67 (italics added).
35. Gregory Graybill, *Evangelical Free Will: Philipp Melanchthon's Doctrinal Journey on the Origins of Faith* (Oxford: Oxford University Press, 2010): 297.
36. Picirilli approvingly quoting Wood in *Grace, Faith, Free Will*, 162. See Wood, "The Declaration of Sentiments: The Theological Testament of Arminius," *Evangelical Quarterly* 65 (1993), 111–29.
37. F. Leroy Forlines, *Classical Arminianism*, 264, 297.
38. Forlines, *Classical Arminianism*, 260.
39. Bangs, "Arminius and Reformed Theology," 166.
40. William den Boer, "'Cum delectu': Jacob Arminius's Praise for and Critique of Calvin and His Theology," *Church History and Religious Culture* 91 (2011): 83–84; see also den Boer, *God's Twofold Love: The Theology of Jacob Arminius* (Göttingen: Vandenhoeck and Ruprecht, 2010); Mark Ellis, *Simon Episcopius' Doctrine of Original Sin* (New York: Peter Lang, 2006), 84; Oliver D. Crisp, *Deviant Calvinism: Broadening Reformed Theology* (Minneapolis: Fortress, 2014), 27–28.
41. Richard Muller, "The Priority of the Intellect in the Soteriology of Jacobus Arminius," *Westminster Theological Journal* 55 (1993): 70. In a later article, however, Muller

This same train of thought is pursued by scholars such as Kenneth Keathley, Jeremy Evans, and Richard Cross. In his article "Anti-Pelagianism and the Resistibility of Grace," Cross asks, "Suppose we do adopt . . . that there can be no natural active human cooperation in justification. Would such a position require us to accept the irresistibility of grace?"[42] Cross, along with Keathley and Evans, thinks it would not. Evans calls this "monergism with resistibility of grace." Keathley and Evans cite Cross's "ambulatory model," according to which the sinner is like an unconscious person who is rescued by EMTs and wakes up in an ambulance and does not resist the EMTs' medical actions to save his life.[43]

This attempt to maintain libertarian free will while avoiding the notion of synergism hearkens back to Arminius's desire to maintain "the greatest possible distance from Pelagianism."[44] Arminians who want to maintain the biblical balance between libertarian freedom on the one hand and the graciousness of God in salvation on the other need to find ways to avoid the terminology of synergism. I think scholars such as Forlines, Picirilli, Wood, Bangs, den Boer, Ellis, Crisp, Cross, Keathley, and Evans have good instincts in wanting to stay away from it. Arminius would have agreed.

Arminians who avoid the label are much like Lutheran theologians. Despite the fact that many modern scholars neatly divide Lutherans into "monergistic" and "synergistic" camps, no good Lutheran ever wanted to be known as a synergist. This includes famous scholastic Lutherans such as Aegidius Hunnius, Johann Gerhard, and Johannes Andreas Quendstedt. Most Lutherans throughout history have believed, like Melanchthon, that election is *intuitu Christi meriti fide apprehendi* (in consideration of the merit of Christ apprehended by faith). Election is always in view of Christ and his mediatorial work, which is of course apprehended by the individual's faith. God personally elects individuals in eternity past *intuitu Christi meriti fide apprehendi*. This is precisely what Arminius believed.

Scholars such as the Dane Henrik Frandsen emphasize the fluidity between Lutheran Scholasticism and the less-Calvinistic wing of Reformed theology in the late sixteenth and early seventeenth centuries.[45] These early

---

characterized Arminius as a synergist: "Arminius and the Reformed Tradition," *Westminster Theological Journal* 70 (2008): 29.

42. Cross, "Anti-Pelagianism and the Resistibility of Grace," *Faith and Philosophy* 22 (2005): 204.

43. Keathley, *Salvation and Sovereignty: A Molinist Approach* (Nashville: B&H Academic, 2010), 88, 103–8; Evans, "Reflections on Determinism and Human Freedom," in *Whosoever Will: A Biblical-Theological Critique of Five-Point Calvinism* (Nashville: B&H Academic, 2010), 253–74; see also Kevin Timpe, "Grace and Controlling What We Do Not Cause," *Faith and Philosophy* 24 (2007): 284–99.

44. Arminius, *Works*, 1:764. "Apology against Thirty-One Defamatory Articles."

45. Henrik Frandsen, *Hemmingius in the Same World as Pekinsius and Arminius* (Praestoe, Denmark: Grafik Werk, 2013). See also Frederick Calder, ed., *Memoirs of Simon Episcopius* (London: Simpkin and Marshall, 1835).

modern Lutherans and their descendants strongly demurred from the label "synergist" that their opponents placed on them. They believed that divine grace could be resisted even after conversion, that one could fall from grace. Yet they strenuously contended that they were not synergists.[46]

An aversion to being labeled synergists is not unique to Arminius, the General Baptists, or the Lutherans. Kenneth Collins confirms that Wesley himself would not have felt comfortable being called a synergist.[47] This is also confirmed by the well-known Wesleyan theologian and founding president of Boston University, W. F. Warren. He argued that synergism contradicts the Wesleyan view that "no man can come unto Christ without a divine drawing; none can even call Jesus the Lord but by the Holy Spirit." Warren said that, it is a mistake to think of salvation "as the product of a joint action of divine and human agency," and he excoriated "the error of synergism," which he said "predicates of man a natural and ethical independence which he does not possess; it ignores the fact that in God we live, and move, and have our being."[48]

Citing the great Wesleyan theologian John Fletcher of Madeley for support, Warren emphasized that "any undue stress upon the human element in the appropriation of salvation logically leads to a Pelagian anthropology, and a doctrine of salvation by the merit of good works." There are "fatal consequences" that result from the teachings of "Calvinistic monergists on the one hand, and by Pharisaic moralists and synergists on the other."[49]

In short, an affirmation of synergism, working together or cooperating with God in salvation, is not necessary to hold to be an Arminian. Many contemporary Arminians want to distance themselves from the word "synergist," and they are in good company. They have learned this sensibility from Jacobus Arminius, Thomas Helwys, John Wesley, Carl Bangs, Leroy Forlines, and Robert Picirilli, but also from some of Lutheranism's leading lights.

Summary

The accusation that Arminians are semi-Pelagians, though well-worn, has no foundation in Arminius and traditional Arminian authors. It reflects

---

46. These anti-Calvinist Lutherans will be surprising to the vast majority of Arminian and Calvinist evangelicals. For a stimulating polemic aimed at what its authors called the "crypto-Calvinism" of the Luthern Church, Missouri Synod, see George H. Schodde, ed., *The Error of Modern Missouri: Its Inception, Development and Refutation* (Columbus, OH: Lutheran Book Concern, 1897). Much of this book was translated from the German by the well-known Lutheran biblical scholar R. C. H. Lenski.

47. Kenneth Collins, *The Theology of John Wesley: Holy Love and the Shape of Grace* (Nashville: Abingdon, 2007). 163–64. William J. Abraham agrees with this in his article "Monergism" in the *Beacon Dictionary of Theology*, ed. Richard S. Taylor (Kansas City: Beacon Hill, 1983), 344.

48. W. F. Warren, "The Methodist Doctrine of the Appropriation of Salvation," *The Methodist Review* 68 (July 1886): 595–96.

49. Warren, "Methodist Doctrine," 596–97.

a reading of later semi-Pelagianism back into early Arminianism. Far from teaching the semi-Pelagian doctrine that divine grace simply assists humans who already desire God, Arminius and the confessional Arminian denominations have taught that the human will is totally depraved and cannot desire God without the interposition of special divine grace. Likewise, the mainstream of traditional Arminianism demurs from the notion of synergism or any idea that suggests a working together of God and the human will in regeneration.

REFLECTION QUESTIONS

1. What does the semi-Pelagianism that was declared heterodox by the second Council of Orange affirm?

2. How does Arminius's view of depravity and inability compare and contrast with semi-Pelagianism?

3. Are there any differences between the early confessional statements of the Remonstrants, General Baptists, and Wesleyan Methodists and the theology of Arminius on the questions raised by semi-Pelagianism?

4. Explain why some Arminians do not want to be associated with the term "synergism."

5. What is meant by the term "conditional monergism" and the "ambulatory model" of divine grace and the human will?

What Do Arminians Mean by "Free Will"?

If traditional Arminians do not affirm the semi-Pelagian account of free will, what do they mean when they say they believe in free will in salvation? In short, they mean *freedom from necessity,* not *freedom from depravity.* What does "freedom from necessity" mean?[1] Calvinists typically believe that everything that comes to pass is necessary, because for anything to occur that could have been otherwise than it is detracts from God's control over the universe.[2] That is why God must determine who is going to be saved and who is not, and human beings in those two categories cannot do otherwise than what God has determined (and will not, because God has determined that they will not desire to do otherwise than he has determined).[3]

---

1. See Robert E. Picirilli, *Free Will Revisited: A Respectful Response to Luther, Calvin, and Edwards* (Eugene, OR: Wipf and Stock, 2017). Picirilli deals with Luther's view of necessity on pp. 38–48, Calvin's on pp. 50–58, and Edwards's on pp. 62–74.
2. Arminians oppose what is referred to as *necessitas inevitabilitatis*—anything that makes a choice inevitable so that the individual could not have chosen otherwise. For the purposes of this book, the primary fact to keep in mind is that, despite Calvinists' disagreement on various complex philosophical distinctions regarding necessity, they all agree that, if God causes something, whether directly or indirectly, it is necessary. For different views on this, see Willem J. van Asselt, J. Martin Back, and Roelf T. te Velde, *Reformed Thought on Freedom: The Concept of Free Choice in Early Modern Reformed Theology,* Texts and Studies in Reformation and Post-Reformation Thought, Richard A. Muller, series ed. (Grand Rapids: Baker Academic, 2010); Paul Helm, *Reforming Free Will: A Conversation on the History of Reformed Views* (Christian Focus, 2020); and Richard A. Muller, *Divine Will and Human Choice: Freedom, Contingency, and Necessity in Early Modern Reformed Thought* (Grand Rapids: Baker Academic, 2017).
3. One must bear in mind that the dispute among Calvinists about single versus double predestination does not affect the question of God's determining who is going to be saved and who is going to be damned, since according to both systems he purposefully predestines everything.

Thomas Helwys on Free Will

Mainstream Arminians do not believe that fallen humanity is free from sin and its dominion, outside of the intervention of divine grace. For example, one of the first Arminians was Thomas Helwys, a Reformed Arminian and the founder of the first Baptist church on English soil. His view of the fall and its ramifications for humanity shaped his understanding of free will.[4]

Helwys disliked the recurring accusation from Calvinists that his doctrine of God's universal provision of salvific grace entailed a semi-Pelagian understanding of free will. He insisted that the common conception of freedom of the will was erroneous. Furthermore, such a view was not only logically unnecessary to the doctrine of God's general provision of salvific grace but was also inconsistent with it.

This idea is strongly reflected in Helwys's appendix to his *Advertisement or Admonition,* which was addressed to the Waterlander Mennonites, whose views were semi-Pelagian. In it, Helwys lamented the Calvinist suspicion that those who hold that Christ freely provides salvific grace for all "do, or must, hold free will." He stated, "We desire to testify unto all, for the clearing of ourselves from the suspect of that most damnable heresy." Those who hold to the general provision of grace to the entire human family, he argued, "cannot hold free will" because "free will doth utterly abolish Christ, and destroy faith and set up works: for free will is to have absolute power in a man's self to work righteousness and obey God in perfect obedience; And such men need no Christ."[5]

This is likely surprising to many, coming from the founder of the General Baptists, some of whom moved to the American colonies and would later be named Free Will Baptists. Helwys, however, was responding to abuses and misunderstandings of the term. He was combatting the semi-Pelagian notion of free will that characterized John Smyth and the Waterlander Mennonites. Like Arminius, Helwys believed that individuals have free will in the sense that they are free from necessity and are able freely to resist and reject divine grace. He did not, however, believe that human beings have the ability

---

4. For more on Helwys's soteriology, see J. Matthew Pinson, *Arminian and Baptist: Explorations in a Theological Tradition* (Nashville: Randall House, 2015), chapters 3–4. While "Reformed Arminianism" is obviously anachronistic, Helwys would have liked the term, because he was elated that the light of "general redemption" was "daily break[ing] forth" in the "the best reformed churches." Thomas Helwys, *A Short and Plain Proofe by the Word and Workes of God that Gods decree is not the cause of anye Mans sinne or Condemnation* (London, 1611), sig. A4v.

5. Thomas Helwys, *An Advertisement or Admonition, unto the Congregations, which Men call the New Fryelers, in the Lowe Countries, Written in Dutch, and Published in English* (London, 1611), 91–92. Both this work and *A Short and Plain Proofe* are reprinted in Joe Early, Jr., *The Life and Writings of Thomas Helwys*, Early English Baptist Texts (Macon, GA: Mercer University Press, 2009).

to choose the good without divine grace, thus retaining the same free will as Adam and Eve possessed before the fall.[6]

Arminius on Free Will

Though one cannot prove that Helwys relied on Arminius for his doctrine of free will, the similarities are striking. Arminius believed that while human beings have basic creaturely freedom and that God does not govern the universe deterministically, their wills are still in bondage to sin and depravity without the special intervention of divine grace. Key to his doctrine of free will was his differentiation of necessity, contingency, and certainty. In his "Apology against Thirty-One Defamatory Articles," he explained, "No contingent thing,—that is, nothing which is done or has been done CONTINGENTLY,—can be said to be or to have been done NECESSARILY *with regard to the Divine decree*."[7] Contingent things are things that do not have to turn out the way they in fact will. Necessary things are things that do have to turn out the way they in fact will. In God's universe, Arminius believed, there are necessities and contingencies, and for an act to be truly free, it has to be a contingency—it has to have been able to go one of two or more ways.[8]

In this way Arminius differed from Calvin, who, quoting Augustine, remarked that "'the will of God is the necessity of things' . . . what he has willed will of necessity come to pass."[9] Jonathan Edwards agreed that everything occurs because of "an infallible previous fixedness of the futurity of an event," according to a "universal, determining providence" that imposes "some kind

---

6. Helwys, *An Advertisement or Admonition*, 92.
7. Jacobus Arminius, *The Works of James Arminius*, 3 vols., trans. James Nichols and William Nichols (Nashville: Randall House, 2007), 1:755. "Apology against Thirty-One Defamatory Articles." As William den Boer correctly points out, "for Arminius an act can only be imputed if there is real freedom. Real freedom excludes all forms of necessity, not only the necessity of coercion but also the *necessitas inevitabilitatis*; for, this *necessitas inevitabilitatis* may not do away with spontaneous assent, but it does destroy freedom." William den Boer, "'Cum delectu': Jacob Arminius's (1559–1609) Praise for and Critique of Calvin and His Theology," *Church History and Religious Culture* 91 (2011): 73–86.
8. See esp. articles V and VI of Arminius's "Apology against Thirty-One Defamatory Articles," Arminius, *Works*, 750–60. This book uses the words "necessity" and "contingency" the way Norman Swartz does. He says that necessarily true propositions are "true in all possible circumstances," whereas contingent propositions are "true in some possible circumstances" and "false in some possible circumstances" ("Foreknowledge and Free Will," *The Internet Encyclopedia of Philosophy*, ISSN 2161–0002, https://www.iep.utm.edu, accessed September 18, 2020). Thus something cannot be contingent in this sense and necessary in this sense at the same time. Linda Zagzebski distinguishes "causal necessity" from "logical necessity" and "temporal necessity" (the necessity of the past). "Necessity" in this book refers to "causal necessity." See Linda Trinkhaus Zagzesbski, *The Dilemma of Freedom and Foreknowledge* (New York: Oxford University Press, 1991), 18–21.
9. *Institutes*, 3.23.8, p. 956.

of necessity of all events."[10] As Picirilli has shown, Edwards did not distinguish adequately between certainty and necessity.[11] For Arminius, however, something cannot be both necessary and contingent, but something can be both certain and contingent.[12]

Thus Arminius agreed with the idea that is known as "libertarian freedom." This is freedom, not from the power of sin or depravity, but from necessity. God has created his universe in such a way as to maintain creaturely freedom. Therefore, Arminius taught that the fall of humanity was contingent and not necessary. That is, God did not decree that Adam and Eve would fall by necessity. They fell as a result of their free choice to disobey God. After the fall, though the human will is free from deterministic necessity, it is in bondage to sin. Arminius said that, if left to themselves, without divine grace, human beings will be completely sinful: "The will, indeed, is free, but not in respect of that act which cannot be either performed or omitted without supernatural grace."[13]

Arminius believed that *arbitrium*, Latin for free will or free choice, is a God-given capability of the human mind to judge things presented to the mind, but the mind and the will have a "very close connection." Thus the "liberty" of the human will refers to an affection of the will that has its root in the mind ("understanding and reason").[14]

Arminius discussed five "modes" of the will's liberty: (1) freedom from "control or jurisdiction of one who commands, and from an obligation to render obedience," (2) freedom from the "government of a superior," (3) freedom from "necessity," whether from "an external cause compelling" or "a nature inwardly determining absolutely to one thing," (4) freedom from "sin and its dominion," and (5) freedom from "misery." Only God possesses free will in the first two senses, Arminius said. The third kind of freedom, freedom from necessity, is the sort of free will God has given humanity. Freedom from necessity "exists naturally in the will, as its proper attribute." Indeed, "there cannot be any will if it be not free." The fourth and fifth modes of freedom, freedom from sin and misery, pertain to the will only before the fall and after glorification.[15]

---

10. Jonathan Edwards, "On the Freedom of the Will," in *The Works of President Edwards* (New York: Robert Carter and Brothers, 1879), 2:177.

11. Picirilli, *Free Will Revisited*, 83–84 . See pp. 79–85 for a careful discussion of these distinctions from a Reformed Arminian perspective.

12. As William Witt points out, Arminius still makes the technical metaphysical distinction that, while contingency is incompatible with the "necessity of the consequent," it is compatible with the "necessity of the consequence." For more on this technical distinction, see William G. Witt, "Creation, Redemption, and Grace in the Theology of Jacob Arminius" (Ph.D. diss., University of Notre Dame, 1993), chapter 8; cf. Van Asselt, et al., *Reformed Thought on Freedom*, 113. I have enjoyed my interactions with Richard E. Clark on this subject.

13. Arminius, *Works*, 3:178, "Friendly Conference with Francis Junius."

14. Arminius, *Works*, 2:190. Public Disputation 11, "On the Free Will of Man and Its Powers."

15. Arminius, *Works*, 2:190.

Arminius spent most of the time in his discussion of free will on the question of the freedom from sin and its dominion. When Adam and Eve were in a "state of primitive innocence" before the fall, their wills possessed the "power" which was "abundantly qualified or furnished perfectly to fulfill the law which God had imposed on him." However, *after* the fall,

> the free will of man towards the true good is not only
> wounded, maimed, infirm, bent, and weakened; but it is also
> imprisoned, destroyed, and lost. And its powers are not only
> debilitated and useless unless they be assisted by grace, but it
> has no powers whatever except such as are excited by Divine
> grace. For Christ has said, "Without me ye can do nothing."
> St. Augustine, after having diligently meditated upon each
> word in this passage, speaks thus: "Christ does not say,
> without me ye can do but Little; neither does He say, without
> me ye can do any Arduous Thing, nor without me ye can do
> it with difficulty. But he says, without me ye can do Nothing!
> Nor does he say, without me ye cannot complete any thing;
> but without me ye can do Nothing."[16]

Since man's fallen mind is spiritually "dark," the will and affections are "perverse," having a "hatred" and "aversion" to what is good and pleasing to God, instead loving and pursuing evil. "The Apostle was unable to afford a more luminous description of this perverseness, than he has given in the following words: 'The carnal mind is enmity against God. For it is not subject to the law of God, neither indeed can be. So then, they that are in the flesh cannot please God' (Romans 8:7)."

Because the mind is so dark and the heart so perverse, Arminius averred, the will is powerless "to perform that which is truly good, and to omit the perpetration of that which is evil." Arminius remarked that Christ describes this "impotence" when he says, "A corrupt tree cannot bring forth good fruit" (Matt. 7:18) and "How can ye, being evil, speak good things?" (12:34). This utter powerlessness of the will in religious matters is why Jesus says, "No man can come to me, except the Father draw him" (John 6:44.), and why Paul says, "The carnal mind is not subject to the law of God, neither indeed can be" (Rom. 8:7). "Therefore, that man over whom it has dominion, cannot perform what the law commands."[17]

This view of free will explains why Arminians can believe in total depravity yet still reject unconditional election. What makes strong Calvinists believe in unconditional election is *not* that they believe in total depravity.

---

16. Arminius, *Works*, 2:192.
17. Arminius, *Works*, 2:193.

Instead, it is because they disagree with the notion of freedom from necessity. Calvinism morphed the biblical concept of divine sovereignty into an unbiblical concept of determinism.[18] Calvinists use sovereignty and determinism as synonyms. For them, the only way for God to be truly sovereign is if he determines every aspect of reality. The only way for God to be sovereign is for every action to be *necessary*, not contingent.[19]

Free Will and Determinism in Biblical Perspective

Arminius ended his disputation on free will by quoting Bernard of Clairvaux: "Take away FREE WILL, and nothing will be left to be saved. Take away GRACE, and nothing will be left [*unde salveteur*] as the source of salvation." For Arminius, if the will is not free from necessity—if it cannot do otherwise than what it does—it is not the will. Again, Arminius is clear that apart from grace the will is bound in spiritual matters. The mind is dark, the heart perverse, but grace allows free resistance, without which humanity would cease to be human.[20]

Arminius believed this because he thought that the biblical portrait of grace and free will is not of God as an absolute determiner of every choice, of people's choices being determined by God to be, of necessity, one way. The whole sweep of Scripture assumes that people, not God, are solely responsible for their choices. This includes the choice to resist God: When God gives people grace, and they refuse it, they alone are held responsible for their choice. God is not responsible for their choice.

Arminians see the passages in Scripture that Calvinists cite as teaching that God absolutely determines every human choice as not establishing that assertion. Calvinists appeal to strong divine sovereignty texts such as Genesis 50:20; Psalm 115:3; 135:6; Proverbs 16:9; Isaiah 10; 14:27; 46:9–10; Daniel 2:21; 4:35; John 9:3; and Acts 2:23; 4:28. Yet passages such as these argue for God's ultimate, sovereign power over individuals and the universe. They do *not* indicate that he necessitates all human choices and events and that people have no choice but to do what they do by necessity. Exodus 9 says that God hardened Pharaoh's heart, but as Question 29 discusses, he did this in response to Pharaoh's own self-hardening. Calvinists often point to texts such as Proverbs 21:1 that God sets up kings and can turn them wherever he will. Yet these passages do not establish that God always determines the decisions of kings, a principle contradicted by Hosea 8:4.

---

18. See Question 19. Some Calvinists have attempted to affirm libertarian freedom in non-soteriological matters, but they are few and far between in church history.
19. See Kevin L. Hester, "'Choose You This Day': Free Will and Determinism," Lecture, Annual Session, National Association of Free Will Baptists, July 2019.
20. Arminius, *Works*, 2:193, 196.

As will be discussed in detail in Question 24, Arminians emphasize that throughout Scripture God laments that people to whom he has given his grace wantonly refuse it, and he holds them solely responsible for their choice to refuse the grace he has given them. Nowhere does Scripture suggest that God is responsible for people's sin or refusal of divine grace.

Arminians point to texts such as Genesis 4:6–7; Leviticus 26:3–4, 12, 14–17; Deuteronomy 11:26–28; 30:15–19; Isaiah 30:1; Jeremiah 32:35; Matthew 6:24; Mark 10:17–27; 11:20; John 5:40; 1 Corinthians 10:13; and Galatians 5:7–8 to argue that people *did not have to* do what they did. While they could never have acted virtuously apart from God's grace, their decision to sin was wholly their own. God did not necessitate it.[21]

This whole discussion boils down to the question of *necessity*: Does the Bible give the impression that God makes it *necessary* for people to make the choices they make, or does the Bible indicate that people could have made different choices and are held solely responsible by God for the choices they make? While abundant Scripture passages teach God's sovereignty over his creation, no text establishes that he necessitates human choices and thus human beings have no choice but to do what they do. Instead, Holy Scripture consistently presents an influence-and-response dynamic in which the divine person relates to human persons created in his image as thinking, feeling beings who make authentic choices.

Summary

Arminianism's view of freedom of the will holds strongly to total depravity and the lack of free will after the fall, in the sense of freedom from sin and its dominion. Yet it affirms free will in the sense of freedom from necessity—that when I make a choice, it is a real choice and I could have done otherwise. I am not completely determined in every choice I make. People's day-to-day choices (say, whether to go to the hardware store or the ice cream shop) are genuinely free, and God maintains his creatures' freedom to resist his special grace, which is necessary for them to be converted.

REFLECTION QUESTIONS

1. What did Thomas Helwys, the progenitor of the Free Will Baptists, mean when he called "free will" a "damnable heresy"?

2. What is freedom from necessity, and what did Calvin and Arminius believe about it?

---

21. For more on the exegetical argument for free will, see Robert E. Picirilli's chapter, "Free Will in a Biblical Perspective," in *Free Will Revisited*, 18–34.

3. What is the definition of necessity, certainty, and contingency, and how do they differ?

4. What do you think Arminius meant when he said that if the human will is not free from necessity, it is not really a will?

5. How is it that Arminians hold to free will in salvation without saying that humanity is free from depravity and its effects, or free to desire God naturally, after the fall?

What Is Compatibilism, and How Do Arminians Respond to It?

While Classical Calvinists believe that God determines everything that comes to pass, some are hard determinists, but most are soft determinists.[1] Another word for this is *compatibilism*, because of its attempt to make God's foreordination of all things compatible with free will. Many compatibilist Calvinists do not like the word "determinism," because, like R. C. Sproul, they identify it with "external coercion" and thus want to distance themselves from it.[2] Yet, by the lexical definition of the term, Calvinism is a theological form of determinism. Curiously, despite wanting to distance himself from the language of determinism and coercion, in the same book, Sproul, in defending the doctrine of irresistible grace, argued that the Greek word for "draw" in the Gospel of John, *helkuō*, means to drag by force.[3] By any definition, Calvinism is a theological form of determinism.[4]

---

1. Stephen T. Davis, *Logic and the Nature of God* (London: Macmillan, 1983), 52; see his thoughts on soft determinism.
2. R. C. Sproul, *Chosen by God* (Wheaton, IL: Tyndale, 1986), 59. This is known as freedom from the necessity of coaction, which traditional Calvinists usually affirm, though they say that the will's movements are inevitable. See Question 16, n. 6.
3. Sproul, *Chosen by God*, 69.
4. Respected Calvinist scholars acknowledge that Calvinists are determinists. See Paul Helm, "Foreword," in Michael Patrick Preciado, *A Reformed View of Freedom: The Compatibility of Guidance Control and Reformed Theology* [Eugene, OR: Pickwick, 2019], ix). James N. Anderson states: "I think it's beyond reasonable dispute that *Calvinism is committed to divine determinism*, since historic Calvinism teaches that God actively foreordains all things" (*Analogical Thoughts*, https://www.proginosko.com/2014/07/calvinism-and-determinism, accessed February 16, 2020). Some scholars have historically affirmed soteriological Calvinism alongside full libertarian freedom in nonsalvific matters, but their numbers have been exceedingly few. See Oliver D. Crisp, *Deviant Calvinism: Broadening Reformed Theology* (Minneapolis: Fortress), 71–96.

Two Definitions of Free Will

Though they claim to affirm free will, many Calvinists are wary of using the term because of the way most people have always used it. When most people say free will, they think in terms of the freedom to choose a course of action or refrain from it. Today scholars often refer to this as *libertarian free will* (which seems to be redundant, like saying "free will free will").

Let me give an example of libertarian free will: If I went to the hardware store yesterday at noon, and that decision is said to be a free decision, then I could have chosen not to go to the hardware store. That is the way most people use "free will." So, if God decided that it was *necessary* that I go to the hardware store yesterday at noon, then, according to the way most people have defined free will, my decision to go to the hardware store would not be free but would be *determined* by God.[5]

Compatibilist Calvinists want to redefine free will so as to make it compatible with determinism—that every choice is determined by God and at the same time free. So they define free will differently from the way it is commonly defined. For them, free will is not the freedom to choose otherwise. Instead, it is doing what one wants to do.

Some scholars refer to these two definitions of free will as the "liberty of spontaneity" and the "liberty of indifference." As Anthony Kenny notes, individuals exercise the liberty of spontaneity when they do what they desire; they exercise the liberty of indifference when they could have done something else.[6] So most Calvinists would define free will as merely the liberty of spontaneity. Arminians, however, would define it as the liberty of indifference.

Compatibilism: "Choosing What We Want"

Sproul represents most Calvinists when he defines freedom as "the ability to choose what we want." The definition of freedom, he said, "rests on the important foundation of human desire. To have free will is to be able to choose according to our desires." He approvingly says that, according to Jonathan Edwards, "a human being . . . *must* choose what he desires to be able to choose at all." He affirms what he calls *Edwards's Law of Choice*: "The will always chooses according to its strongest inclination at the moment." What

---

5. See Robert E. Picirilli, *Free Will Revisited: A Respectful Response to Luther, Calvin, and Edwards* (Eugene, OR: Wipf and Stock, 2017), for a discussion of why Calvinism entails the idea that "God must *change* [one's] will *against* [his or her] will" (100–1, italics added). See also Kevin L. Hester, "'Choose You This Day': Free Will and Determinism," Lecture, Annual Session, National Association of Free Will Baptists, July 2019.
6. Anthony Kenny, *The God of the Philosophers* (New York: Oxford University Press, 1979), 73. See also Davis, 52.

this means, Sproul affirmed, is that "every choice is free *and* every choice is determined."[7]

Sproul, however, was quick to attempt to distance himself from hard determinism: He said that his use of the word *determined* does not imply that "some external force coerces the will." Instead, it "refers to one's internal motivation or desire." Human choices are "determined by our desires. They remain our choices because they are motivated by our own desires." Sproul called this "*self-determination*," stating that it is "the essence of freedom."[8]

Thus every choice human beings make is "for a reason. The next time you go into a public place and choose a seat (in a theater, a classroom, a church building), ask yourself why you are sitting where you are sitting . . . the seat that you choose will always be chosen by the strongest inclination you have at the moment of decision. That inclination may merely be that the seat closest to you is free and that you don't like to walk long distances to find a place to sit down."[9] According to the compatibilist definition of free will, let us say God determined that I would go to the hardware store yesterday at noon, and he gave me no choice but to go to the hardware store yesterday at noon. My decision to go there would still be free if the way God determined it ensured that I would *want* to go.

Thus, in soft determinism or compatibilism, God determines every event that will come to pass, but it comes to pass in such a way that we desire to do the thing we are doing. That desire makes the action a free action, according to the Calvinist. So the primary phrase is Sproul's discussion above is "[what] you choose will always be chosen by the strongest inclination you have at the moment of decision."

Robert Picirilli explains that the key word in compatibilism is *motivation*, using the illustration of a man tempted to steal a banana at a grocery store. Our instinct and experience tell us that he could have chosen to take it or leave it. The compatibilist responds that there was only one way he could have chosen, and that choice is determined by his predetermined motivation. That motivation is determined by any number of factors—his hunger, his parents' teaching on stealing, his previous experiences with theft or the thrill it gave him, and any number of other things. "It is a choice," Picirilli explains, "that is made necessary—that is, *caused*—by everything leading up to it, the only one he can actually make; yet it is a 'free' choice, since the person is not coerced and decides without constraint." We rely on our instinct and experience; it seems as if we *do* have the ability to make more than just one choice. When

---

7. Sproul, *Chosen by God*, 39–40. See also Oliver D. Crisp, *Jonathan Edwards and the Metaphysics of Sin* (Hampshire, England: Ashgate, 2005), 12.
8. Sproul, *Chosen by God*, 40.
9. Sproul, *Chosen by God*, 40–41.

we debate with ourselves in our minds about the course of action, we think the debate is real, that either option could win out.[10]

Not so, says the compatibilist. "Regardless how much we *think* we could have made the other choice, we really did not have the freedom. If we just understood the weight of all the factors that affected our thinking and feelings at the time (our motivation), we would realize that only one choice was possible: namely the choice we made. Indeed, some of the contributing factors we were not even conscious of."[11]

An Unfalsifiable Position

So what is wrong with this definition of free will? First, as Picirilli points out, the compatibilist's rebuttal is an *unfalsifiable* argument. No matter what the advocate of libertarian free will says, the compatibilist's answer will be, "It *seems* that way, but you just aren't aware of all that's affecting you. You only *think* you could have made the other choice, but you really couldn't. You must act in accord with your own desire, even when you think your desire is different from the way you decide." Thus there is no way to demonstrate to compatibilists that they are wrong, because they always "know better" than the way ordinary people experience things.[12]

No matter how much the compatibilist tells ordinary people they just *thought* they could have decided otherwise in a given decision, most people will still think they have genuine free will, and even compatibilists behave as though they do. As philosopher John Searle says in his argument against secular forms of determinism, compatibilism's main problem is that it does not satisfactorily answer the ordinary question of everyday people: "Could we have done otherwise?" He uses as an example a person who voted for the Tories in a British election who could have chosen to vote for one of the other parties. Compatibilism, he insists, "doesn't really answer that question in a way that allows any scope for the ordinary notion of the freedom of the will." He rightly states, "Compatibilism, in short, denies the substance of free will while maintaining its verbal shell."[13]

The assertion that our choices are always determined by our motivation belies the complexity of human experience and how that is exemplified over and over in Scripture. It is an unfalsifiable assertion, and there is no reason to accept it based on reason or our experience. Yet most importantly, there is every biblical reason not to accept it. As Roger Olson rightly argues, its core belief that people can act only according to their strongest desire contradicts Paul's statement about himself in Romans 7:15: "For I do not do what

---

10. Picirilli, *Free Will Revisited*, 14–15 (italics added).
11. Picirilli, *Free Will Revisited*, 16.
12. Picirilli, *Free Will Revisited*, 16.
13. John Searle, *Minds, Brains and Science* (Cambridge, MA: Harvard University Press, 1984), 89.

I want, but I do the very thing I hate."[14] Furthermore, it is difficult to see how 1 Corinthians 10:13 ("God . . . will not let you be tempted beyond your ability, but with the temptation he will also provide the way of escape, that you may be able to endure it") supports a compatibilistic rather than a libertarian-freedom understanding of the moral choices people make.[15]

Ultimate Responsibility

This brings up a second biblical and common-sense notion: We can be *held responsible* for something only if it is a genuinely free decision that we could have chosen *not* to make. Robert Kane is a philosopher who opposes philosophical and scientific determinism. He states that some freedoms would be important even if determinism were true, such as freedom from "things such as physical restraint, addiction or neurosis, coercion, compulsion, covert control, or political oppression." However, he states that "there is at least one kind of freedom worth wanting that is incompatible with determinism": libertarian free will.[16]

Kane correctly explains, "to be ultimately responsible for an action, an agent must be responsible for anything that is a sufficient reason (condition, cause, or motive) for the action's occurring." For instance, if, as compatibilists maintain, our choices are a result of our character and motives, still we are not ultimately responsible for them unless we are "responsible by virtue of choices or actions voluntarily performed in the past for having the character and motives" we now have.[17]

Kane cites Aristotle's notion that "if a man is responsible for wicked acts that flow from his character, he must at some time in the past have been responsible for forming the wicked character from which these acts flow." As Kane states, "Often we act from a will already formed, but it is 'our own free will' by virtue of the fact that we formed it by other choices or actions in the past for which we could have done otherwise." If that is not true, "there is *nothing we could have ever done differently in our entire lifetimes to make ourselves different than we are*—a consequence, I believe, that is incompatible with our being (at least to some degree) ultimately *responsible* for what we are."[18]

---

14. Roger E. Olson, "Why Compatibilism Is Unbiblical," https://www.patheos.com/blogs/rogereolson/2019/06/why-compatibilism-is-unbiblical, accessed April 26, 2020.

15. I owe this insight to Richard E. Clark.

16. Robert Kane, "Rethinking Free Will: New Perspectives on an Ancient Problem," in *The Oxford Handbook of Free Will*, 2nd ed., ed. Robert Kane (Oxford: Oxford University Press, 2011), 382–83.

17. Kane, "Rethinking Free Will," 383.

18. Kane, "Rethinking Free Will," 384 (italics in original in the first instance, added in the second).

Manipulative Human Analogies

Third, as mentioned above, the biblical and common-sense account of the way human beings make decisions contradicts the compatibilist approach. Human analogies of a compatibilist model of free will are repulsive and do not fit the way God has revealed his workings with free persons in Scripture. Searle brings up the notion of posthypnotic suggestion. He gives the illustration of someone who, under hypnosis, is asked to crawl around on the floor. Then, after hypnosis, the individual shows a deep interest in the floor and its floor covering. The person "seems to himself to be behaving freely." His choices are in no way constrained. He is saying "what he wants" to say. "We, on the other hand, have good reasons to believe that his behaviour isn't free at all, that the reasons he gives for his apparent decision to crawl around on the floor are irrelevant, that his behaviour was determined. But it seems empirically very unlikely that all human behaviour is like that."[19]

Michael McKenna and Justin Coates, in their article on compatibilism in the *Stanford Encyclopedia of Philosophy*, refer to being "brainwashed or manipulated . . . say by hypnosis, or by aliens zapping" people into different "psychological preferences" than they would otherwise have, as "manipulation cases." They argue that in these cases, compatibilists "seem committed to the view that such agents act of their own free will and are morally responsible so long as the appropriate psychological mesh is in place, no matter what sort of (merely apparent) freedom and responsibility-undermining history gave way to an agent's having that particular mesh."[20] Steve Lemke is right to surmise that theological compatibilism is as problematic as its secular cousin, bringing to mind what Lemke calls "unpleasant phenomena such as hypnotism or brainwashing. Obviously, these are not pleasant phenomena, and are not appropriate when applied to God."[21]

Influence and Response, Not Cause and Effect

No matter how much Calvinists nuance their presentations of divine determination of human actions, the fact remains that they believe that God causally determines every decision that every human being makes. Yet, as Jeremy Evans states, "Anyone who wants to grant God the type of sovereignty proposed by strong Calvinism, which is a *causal* account of human willing and acting, yet wants to say that the world is not as it should be (sin), is under

19. Searle, *Minds, Brains and Science*, 90.

20. Michael McKenna and D. Justin Coates, "Compatibilism," *The Stanford Encyclopedia of Philosophy* (Summer 2020 Edition), ed. Edward N. Zalta, https://plato.stanford.edu/archives/sum2020/entries/compatibilism, accessed May 31, 2020.

21. Steve W. Lemke, "A Biblical and Theological Critique of Irresistible Grace," in *Whosoever Will: A Biblical-Theological Critique of Five-Point Calvinism*, eds. David L. Allen and Steve W. Lemke (Nashville: B&H Academic, 2010), 150.

a particular burden to explain how they can make these claims in conjunction with one another."[22]

Leroy Forlines accurately describes Calvinism as a cause-and-effect approach to divine-human relationships rather than an influence-and-response approach.[23] Influence and response accords more faithfully with the Bible's picture of how God relates to people. Scripture presents God as a divine person wooing and drawing to himself human persons whom he has created in his image and who are thus capable of knowledge, emotions, and free choice. Arminius used the word "suasion" to describe this interplay between the divine person and human persons: The "Author of grace has determined not to force men by His grace to assent, but by a sweet and gentle suasion to move them; which motion not only does not take away the free consent of a free will, but even strengthens it."[24] Because God designed humanity in his image as thinking, feeling, acting persons, he has designed his plan of salvation to safeguard that *imago Dei*, which involves the personhood of human beings.[25]

An influence-and-response understanding of divine-human relationships means that God does not "get his way" by arranging things so that people think they are making free decisions when he has really absolutely predetermined those decisions. Instead, God deals with human beings as a person relating in a genuine way with other persons, influencing those persons to make rational choices with their intellects, wills, and affections. The category of cause and effect is impersonal and does not rise to the level of Holy Scripture's picture of personal beings made in the image of an infinite-personal God. Instead they are more appropriate when applied to inanimate objects. Yet Calvinism must rely on divine causes having inexorable effects. It cannot function if a divinely intended effect does not follow necessarily, in every human decision, from a divine cause.

Summary

Many Calvinists wish to distance themselves from determinism by advocating that divine causal determinism and human free will are both true. The way they do this is through compatibilism. This requires that they define free will, not as the freedom to make a choice other than the choice one made, but as doing what one desires to do. So as long as individuals get to do what they want, their choices are free, even if they are determined by God. Yet this strikes most Christians, as it does many secular philosophers, as manipulation, and

---

22. Evans, "Reflections on Determinism and Human Freedom," in *Whosevever Will*, 267 (italics added).

23. F. Leroy Forlines, *Classical Arminianism: A Theology of Salvation* (Nashville: Randall House, 2011), 47–59.

24. Jacobus Arminius, *The Works of James Arminius*, 3 vols., trans. James Nichols and William Nichols (Nashville: Randall House, 2007), 3:450. "Examination of Perkins's Pamphlet."

25. Forlines, *Classical Arminianism*, 59–60.

it falls beneath the glory of the Holy God of the Bible, who relates as a person to free creatures he created in his image as personal beings. A causally deterministic system cannot be reconciled with genuine free will, and it cannot be harmonized with Holy Scripture's picture of how God relates to his personal human creatures.

REFLECTION QUESTIONS

1. How do the statements of Calvinists who want to distance themselves from determinism as "external coercion," yet who argue that the Bible teaches that God's drawing power in John 6:44 is an irresistible force that drags people to himself, reveal a tension in Calvinism?

2. What is the difference between compatibilism's definition of free will as the liberty of spontaneity and libertarian free will's definition of free will as the liberty of indifference?

3. What does Robert Picirilli mean when he criticizes compatibilism as an "unfalsifiable position"?

4. What does Robert Kane mean when he says that, if compatibilism is true, human beings are not ultimately responsible for their moral actions?

5. What do you think of Lemke's accusation, reinforced by philosophers such as Searle, McKenna, and Coates, that compatibilism makes God guilty of something akin to manipulation or brainwashing?

Does Arminianism Detract from God's Glory?

One of the most frequent Calvinist critiques of Arminianism is that it is a human-centered theology that detracts from God's glory. Calvinists often argue that Arminianism is anthropocentric and puts the spotlight on man, his innate free will in spiritual matters, his goodness, and God's love for him, while detracting from God's glory as seen in his holiness. Thus, as one Calvinist quips, "the 'god' of Arminianism is not worshippable."[1] It is little wonder that Calvinists say this, because much of what has passed for Arminianism over the past couple of hundred years has done just this. Yet what Calvinists are really criticizing is what one might call "Finneyism"—the approach of Charles Finney that symbolizes the semi-Pelagian theology that has dominated large swaths of evangelicalism.

However, Arminians who embody the Reformation emphases of Jacobus Arminius clash with Finneyism. Carefully reading Arminius and taking a fresh look at him helps one see that his theology focuses on the glory of God. It is anything but human-centered. Instead, it stresses the depravity of humanity and the glory, sovereignty, and holiness of God as Calvinism does. The reason it does is that it shares with Calvinism the sensibilities of pre-Synod of Dort Reformed theology. That broad Reformed theological temperament does not require determinism, absolute predestination, and irresistible grace. Yet it still highlights the glory, justice, rule, and reign of God.

---

1. C. Matthew McMahon, "The 'god' of Arminianism Is Not Worshippable," A Puritan's Mind, https:///www.apuritansmind.com/arminianism/the-%E2%80%9Cgod%E2%80%9D-of-arminianism-is-not-worshippable, accessed 4/5/2020. See Roger E. Olson, "Arminianism is God-Centered Theology," in *Grace for All: The Arminian Dynamics of Salvation*, eds. Clark H. Pinnock and John D. Wagner (Eugene, OR: Resource, 2015).

The Need for Contemporary Arminians to Emphasize God's Glory

Calvinists do not have a corner on God's sovereignty and glory. Non-Calvinist Steve Lemke extols John Piper's emphasis on the sovereignty and glory of God, but he asks, "Which gives God the greater glory—a view that the only persons who can praise God are those whose wills He changes without their permission, or the view that persons respond to the gracious invitation of God and the conviction of the Holy Spirit to praise God truly of their own volition?"[2]

Too many Arminians, however, avoid the themes of the sovereignty and glory of God that we see in preachers like Piper. The reason many Arminians sadly avoid these terms is the unbiblical connotations of statements such as Piper's that God purposefully ordains evil in order to make Christ's glory shine more brightly.[3] Arminians rightly recognize the challenges of that view for answering the New Atheists' arguments about the problem of evil and for making biblical arguments that safeguard the goodness and justice of God.

However, contemporary Arminians need to come to grips with the sovereignty and glory of God and articulate a more robust doctrine of them. Yet they need not go outside the Arminian tradition for the resources with which to do that. Contemporary Arminians could stand to learn from Piper's Edwardsean emphasis on the "God of grace and glory," but they must articulate a more biblical account of those beautiful truths that avoids the determinism of Calvinism.

Arminius and *Soli Deo Gloria*

Arminius's understanding of the Reformation maxim *Soli Deo Gloria* (to God alone be the glory) arises from the other Reformation *solae* at the root of Arminius's theology.[4] Because the Word of God alone is sufficient for the church's doctrine and practice, and because believers are saved by grace alone through faith alone by the mediatorial work of Christ alone, God alone should receive the glory. For Arminius, this meant that there was, as Paul said, "no room for boasting." God alone must be ascribed the glory and perfection and majesty that are due him.

Calvinist critics of Arminianism say that it is man-centered and places more emphasis on human freedom and God's love for man than on God's

---

2. Steve W. Lemke, "A Biblical and Theological Critique of Irresistible Grace," in *Whosoever Will: A Biblical-Theological Critique of Five-Point Calvinism*, eds. David L. Allen and Steve W. Lemke (Nashville: B&H Academic, 2010), 155.

3. John Piper, *Spectacular Sins: And Their Global Purpose in the Glory of Christ* (Wheaton, IL: Crossway, 2008), 54.

4. For a discussion of Arminius and the five *solae* of the Reformation, see J. Matthew Pinson, "Why Arminians Should Celebrate Reformation 500," The Gospel Coalition, October 30, 2017, https://www.thegospelcoalition.org/article/why-arminians-should-celebrate-reformation-500.

glory and holiness. That is no doubt true for many later Arminians, but not for Arminius, and not for all Arminians. For Arminius, God is glorified when his justice and mercy are on full display. God has a "twofold love": He loves his justice and he loves human beings. Because he loves his human creatures, he is merciful to them in offering a way of salvation. Yet that plan always upholds the rigorous demands of divine justice. The only thing God loves more than his creatures, Arminius stresses, is his justice. This twofold love of God gives him ultimate glory.[5]

Arminius believed that God's glory is simply a display of his perfection. God has "always set before Himself as the supreme and ultimate end the manifestation of His own perfection, that is, His own glory." Thus God's glory is rooted in his holiness, his justice. The "manifestation of the Divine perfection, and the illustration of its glory" is the purpose for everything God does. Thus God's glory is simply the "unfolding of the essential properties of God" by his acts, which conform to his perfection. This is why for Arminius God could never foreordain sin, which he believed Calvinism requires. That would rob him of glory because it would not be an unfolding of his essential property of justice.[6]

This manifestation of the divine attributes, this glory, is the entire "end" or purpose of the gospel and the church, Arminius explains. The church's blessedness through union with Christ results in "the glory of God," to whom "the church in her triumphant songs ascribes . . . praise, honour and glory for ever and ever."[7] Arminius's theology is everywhere centered and fixed firmly on the glory of God alone. That alone is the end for which God redeems fallen people. However, as Roger Olson stresses, the end of everything in Arminius's theology is the glory of God, except one thing: evil.[8]

How Calvinism Detracts from God's Glory

Arminians need to emphasize that *Calvinism* is the system that detracts from God's glory, which is rooted in his justice, because the logical outcome of its system makes God the author of evil. No matter how much Calvinists insist that is not so, the Arminian maintains that this *must* be the outcome of a metaphysic that claims that God meticulously and directly ordains every

---

5. Jacobus Arminius, *The Works of James Arminius,* 3 vols., trans. James Nichols and William Nichols (Nashville: Randall House, 2007), 2:221. Public Disputation 14, "On the Offices of Our Lord Jesus Christ." For the best treatment of this concept, see William den Boer, *God's Twofold Love: The Theology of Jacob Arminius* (1559–1609) (Göttingen: Vandenhoeck and Ruprecht, 2010).

6. Arminius, *Works,* 3:276. "Examination of Perkins's Pamphlet."

7. Arminius, *Works,* 2:412. Private Disputation 50, "On the Church of God and of Christ, or On the Church in General after the Fall."

8. Olson, "Arminianism Is God-Centered Theology," 4–6, 9–13.

aspect of reality.[9] If this is true, then every Calvinist has to agree with Piper when he asks, "Has God predetermined every tiny detail in the universe, such as dust particles in the air and all our besetting sins?"[10] and answers, "Yes . . . everything that exists—including evil—is ordained by an infinitely holy and all-wise God to make the glory of Christ shine more brightly."[11] This statement is reminiscent of Jerome Zanchius's comment that "Both the elect and the reprobates were foreordained to sin, as sin, that the glory of God might be declared thereby."[12]

Piper's views reflect those of Calvin, who remarked, "It is not in itself likely that man brought destruction upon himself, by God's mere permission and without any ordaining, as if God did not establish the condition in which he wills the chief of his creatures to be" (*Institutes*, 3.23.8). Calvin also said that "the devil, and the whole train of the ungodly, are, in all directions, held in by the hand of God as with a bridle, so that they can neither conceive any mischief, nor plan what they have conceived, nor how much soever they may have planned, move a single finger to perpetrate, unless in so far as [God] permits, nay, unless in so far as he commands; that they are not only bound by his fetters, but are even forced to do him service" (*Institutes*, 1.17.11). Jonathan Edwards was clear that God wills "to order things so that evil should come to pass."[13] William G. T. Shedd said, "Sin is one of the 'whatsoevers' that have 'come to pass,' all of which are 'ordained.'"[14]

Arminians rightly recoil at statements like this, especially in the face of the New Atheism and more and more young people listing themselves as

---

9. William den Boer argues that defending God's justice against what he saw as Calvinism's making God the author of sin is a central theme in Arminius's writings. See den Boer, *God's Twofold Love*, esp. 92–95, 107–8.

10. John Piper, "Has God Determined Every Tiny Detail In the Universe, Including Sin?" https://www.desiringgod.org/interviews/has-god-predetermined-every-tiny-detail-in-the-universe-including-sin, accessed June 5, 2020.

11. Piper, *Spectacular Sins*, 54.

12. Quoted in R. S. Foster, *Objections to Calvinism As It Is* (Cincinnati: Methodist Book Concern, 1850), 266. See also Cornelius Van Til's statement that "it was God's will that sin should come into the world. He wished to enhance his glory by means of its punishment and removal," *The Defense of the Faith* (Phillipsburg, NJ: Presbyterian and Reformed, 1967), 160.

13. *The Works of President Edwards*, 4 vols. (New York: Robert Carter and Brothers, 1881), 2:163.

14. William G. T. Shedd, *Calvinism: Pure and Mixed* (New York: Charles Scribner's Sons, 1893), 32. See also R. C. Sproul, *What Is Reformed Theology?* (Grand Rapids: Baker, 2016), 141, 172; Lorraine Boettner, *The Reformed Doctrine of Predestination*, 32; Arthur W. Pink, *On the Sovereignty of God*, 42; and J. Gresham Machen, *The Christian View of Man*, 46. These sorts of quotations are ubiquitous in Calvinist literature. For more, see older works by Foster, *Objections to Calvinism*, and John Benson, *The Revival and Rejection of an Old Traditional, Heresy* . . . *or the Doctrine of God Decreeing All Sin Examined and Refuted* (London: T. Ward, 1836).

"nones," having no religious affiliation. The reason they react so negatively is not that determinism bothers their human-centered sensibilities. It is because it impugns the justice of God revealed in Holy Scripture and hence takes away from his glory.

Most Calvinists vigorously deny that their system teaches that God is the author of evil.[15] They often do this by explaining that God does not directly cause an individual to sin but simply withholds the grace necessary for the individual to avoid sinning. This constitutes a Calvinist version of the doctrine of permission. God is not directly causing an individual to sin. He is simply making it so that it is impossible for the individual *not* to sin, and then he is permitting that sin.[16]

As Paul Helm explains, the thing that "determines" a sinful action is not a direct causation on God's part but "a divine withholding. God withholds his goodness or grace, and forthwith the agent forms a morally deficient motive or reason and acts accordingly. So while God ordains and sustains and foreknows the evil action, he does not positively will it."[17] Piper echoes this notion when he argues that "God is able without blameworthy 'tempting' to *see to it* that a person does what God ordains for him to do, even if it involves evil."[18] This seems to the Arminian to amount to God's still being the author of evil because he purposefully withholds his grace from some people, thus making it impossible for them to refrain from doing evil. Calvin himself said, "It is easy to conclude how foolish and frail is the support of divine justice by the suggestion that evils come to be not by His will, but merely by His permission. . . . I admit they are not pleasing to God. But it is quite frivolous refuge to say that God otiosely [nonchalantly] permits them, when Scripture shows Him not only willing but the author of them."[19]

No amount of Calvinists' explaining about God not being the direct determiner or direct cause of sin, but simply withholding his grace on purpose, thus being the indirect determiner or the indirect cause of sin, helps Calvinists in this matter. Arminians believe that libertarian freedom is the only way to remove the culpability of God for sin and evil in the world and thus not rob him of glory.

One thing Arminians must remind Calvinists of, when the latter say that God "sees to it" that people do evil so that greater glory can come to him, is

---

15. When theologians say that God is not the author of evil, they are referring to moral evil, not natural evil.
16. Arminians hold that God permits sinful actions through divine concurrence because they are free choices of the human actor. This is different from the typical Calvinist doctrine of divine concurrence, which holds that God causes or predetermines sinful human actions.
17. Paul Helm, *The Providence of God* (Downers Grove, IL: InterVarsity, 1994), 170.
18. Piper, *Spectacular Sins*, 24 (italics added).
19. John Calvin, *Concerning the Eternal Predestination of God*, trans. J. K. S. Reid (Louisville: Westminster John Knox, 1997), 176.

that glory in itself is not always a good thing. A sovereign can receive glory for doing unjust things. The sovereign God's glory must be rooted in his essential properties, in divine justice as biblically defined and exemplified in the person of Christ. This is what the Arminian seeks to safeguard.

The philosopher Bruce Little has done much to advance our understanding of the problem of evil—why bad things happen in a world created and sustained by a good God. Little discusses two illustrations of gratuitous evil and how Calvinism makes God the author of evil. He refers to Piper's statement after the crash of US Airways flight 1549 in January 2009 that God designed the event and can take down an airplane anytime he pleases and wrong no one because we are all guilty and deserve judgment. Little remarks, "This assertion can only mean that . . . God does not merely *allow* this; God designs and executes it. . . . God is responsible but not morally culpable."[20]

Little also refers to the case of a young Florida girl named Jessica whom a convicted sex offender abducted, tortured, raped, and buried alive. According to the meticulous account of sovereignty and determinism of strong Calvinism advocated by Piper, because this child was a sinner, guilty before God, God did not owe her anything and thus had the right to ordain the state of affairs that led to and entailed her abduction, torture, rape, and burial alive. According to Calvinism, Jessica's torture and death are the only way things could have turned out; they are necessary, ordained by God. This is much different than simply saying that God permitted the state of affairs.[21] This means her murderer's motives and actions are also determined. Still, according to the Calvinist view, her murderer, not God, is fully responsible for the act, even though her murderer could never have done otherwise.[22]

A core component of God's purpose in bringing about evil, according to this view, is to glorify God—"to make the glory of Christ shine more brightly."[23] However, as Little points out, if this is true, "then it seems that people need the ugly in order to appreciate beauty. Adam and Even could not appreciate God's glory, which makes the Fall necessary."[24] Thus supralapsarianism is consistent Calvinism, and this is a common reason why people have left Calvinism—including the first Baptist, Thomas Helwys.[25]

The Scriptures teach that people are solely responsible for their choices (see Question 16). If Jessica's rapist could not help but make the choice he

---

20. Bruce Little, "Evil and God's Sovereignty," in *Whosoever Will*, 279, 288.

21. Little, "Evil and God's Sovereignty," 279.

22. Little, "Evil and God's Sovereignty," 279–80.

23. Piper, *Spectacular Sins*, 54.

24. Little, "Evil and God's Sovereignty," 289.

25. J. Matthew Pinson, "The First Baptist Treatise on Predestination: Thomas Helwys's *Short and Plaine Proofe*," in *Arminian and Baptist: Explorations in a Theological Tradition* (Nashville: Randall House, 2015), chapter 4; Jeremy A. Evans, "Reflections on Determinism and Human Freedom," in *Whosoever Will*, 269.

made, then it was not really a choice; thus he is not responsible for that choice. Yet this presents a problem that cannot be solved simply by appealing to mystery. "The logical end of the Calvinist position on the question of sovereignty leads to a strong form of determinism, which is not the necessary outcome of biblical sovereignty. In addition, moral responsibility for sin must find its final causal agent to be God."[26]

Summary

The logical outcome of God's causing every action is that God is the author of evil, despite Calvinists' protestations to the contrary. This is why Arminians insist that Arminianism is the theological position that is more consistent with the glory of God, and that Calvinism's making God the author of evil detracts from his glory. The consistent, Reformed Arminianism of Arminius is the theology that most coherently extols God's glory, not Calvinism. Arminius's theology of the *duplex amor Dei*, God's twofold love, is the theology of the Bible that provides the answer in a world where the New Atheists question the problem of evil. God's glory is not achieved by his arbitrarily causing sin and misery. Instead, as Arminius stressed, God's glory is a manifestation of his divine perfection and justice.

REFLECTION QUESTIONS

1. Why do many Calvinists believe that Arminianism detracts from God's glory?

2. How does Arminius highlight God's glory, especially in his doctrine of God's twofold love?

3. Why do Arminians believe that Calvinism's teaching that God ordains evil acts detract from his glory?

4. Is the author right when he argues that "glory in itself is not always a good thing. A sovereign can receive glory for doing unjust things." What does he mean by this, and how does it help one understand what it means for God to receive glory, not arbitrarily, but based on his justice?

5. Why do Arminians believe that Calvinism makes God the author of evil, and thus that some Calvinists' insistence that their theology does not do so is incorrect?

---

26. Little, "Evil and God's Sovereignty," 296–97.

Can God Be Sovereign If People Have Free Will?

Calvinists characterize Arminianism as centering on humanity's free will, thus detracting from God's sovereignty. Yet, as this chapter will show, Arminianism not only has a robust doctrine of divine sovereignty but also embodies the biblical understanding of sovereignty as concerning God's rule and reign over his free creatures by means of his laws and his covenants with them. This vision of divine sovereignty coheres more with Holy Scripture than the deterministic view of Calvinism (see Question 16).

Determinism, Not Depravity, the Reason for Calvinism

The doctrine of total depravity is not what causes Calvinists to be Calvinists. In order to affirm the Calvinistic system, Calvinists must in the end add something to total depravity. What they add is *determinism and particular grace*. Human beings are naturally unable to desire God or salvation; they can do so only through divine grace. On this much Calvinists and Arminians agree. Yet Calvinism's doctrine of sovereign grace presupposes a particularistic and deterministic view of divine sovereignty. Thus the real difference between the two systems is that Arminians believe that the grace of God reaches out to everyone, not merely a select portion of humanity. Furthermore, Arminians believe that God has arranged his universe in such a way that his sovereignty allows for the genuine freedom of persons created in his image.

Prior to the Synod of Dort, Reformed theology had room enough for divergent views on divine sovereignty. The confessional theology of the Belgic Confession of Faith and Heidelberg Catechism leaves open the question of how God sovereignly governs his free creatures. The Reformed confessional tradition prior to Dort does not define divine sovereignty *as* divine determinism. Instead, it defines sovereignty as the extension of God's rule over all of life. Those confessional documents emphasized the comfort that comes from knowing that God has "the whole world in his hands," not a hardline doctrine of determinism.

When the Heidelberg Catechism asks how knowing about God's providence helps us, it answers that it helps us "be patient when things go against us, thankful when things go well, and for the future we can have good confidence in our faithful God and Father that nothing in creation will separate us from his love. For all creatures are so completely in God's hand that without his will they can neither move nor be moved."[1] These are the sorts of things with which Arminius, who loved to give out copies of the Heidelberg Catechism, wholeheartedly agreed, and which fully cohere with Arminianism.

This sort of Reformed thought is much more comfortable with the notion of sovereignty exemplified in Abraham Kuyper's statement, "There is not a square inch in the whole domain of our human existence over which Christ, who is Sovereign over all, does not cry, Mine!"[2] This pre-Dort Reformed approach to divine sovereignty does not require the sort of determinism embodied in John Piper's statement, "Everything that exists—including evil—is ordained by an infinitely holy and all-wise God to make the glory of Christ shine more brightly."[3] Calvinism goes beyond these early Reformed confessional documents, and *sovereignty is morphed into determinism*.

Piper's statement above could just as easily have been stated by Calvin, who wrote that "not only heaven and earth and the inanimate creatures, but also the plans and intentions of men, are so governed by his providence that they are borne by it straight to their appointed end. . . . Nothing is more absurd than that anything should happen without God's ordaining it, because it would then happen without any cause" (*Institutes*, 1:21.8). He also said that "men can accomplish nothing except by God's secret command." They "cannot by deliberating accomplish anything except what he has already decreed with himself and determines by his secret direction" (*Institutes*, 1.18.1).

This determinism is the way Calvinists consistently cast divine sovereignty. God foreordains every detail of reality. Every choice is precisely as God was pleased to predestine it. To say that human beings can freely choose a course of action, and could have chosen an alternate course of action, is to make man the measure of all things and detract from the sovereignty of God. That redefinition of divine sovereignty, not total depravity, is what makes Calvinism Calvinism.[4]

---

1. Heidelberg Catechism, Q&A 28, Reformed Church in America website, https://www.rca. org/resources/heidelberg-catechism-god-father, accessed April 7, 2020.
2. James D. Bratt, ed., *Abraham Kuyper: A Centennial Reader* (Grand Rapids: Eerdmans, 1998), 488.
3. John Piper, *Spectacular Sins: And Their Global Purpose in the Glory of Christ* (Wheaton, IL: Crossway, 2008), 54.
4. Most instances of God's foreknowledge of future things in the Bible are of future free contingents: things he does not directly cause. Those passages that Calvinists cite to argue that

A More Biblical Picture of God's Sovereignty

Arminians demur from this approach to divine sovereignty. They believe that it reads deterministic metaphysics into biblical theology. There is nothing in the biblical picture of a sovereign that would lead anyone to think it means meticulous determination of every aspect of reality. In Scripture, a sovereign—even an absolute sovereign—is someone who extends his rule over his subjects and propounds laws for them to obey. If they do not obey those laws, they are subject to punishment or even banishment from the sovereign's realm. Even an absolute sovereign does not determine his subjects' moment-by-moment lives so that they will be guaranteed to carry out his will. The biblical picture of the sovereignty of God fits this biblical understanding.[5] As the Danish Lutheran Hans Martensen said, "God limits His own power by calling into existence . . . a world of created beings to whom He gives in a derivative way to have life in themselves. But precisely in this way above all other—that He is omnipotent over a free world—does He reveal the inner greatness of His power most clearly. That is true power which brings free agents into existence and is notwithstanding able to make itself all in all."[6]

Bruce Little shares this view that meticulous control or determination of every act in reality is not the biblical view of how a sovereign maintains control of that over which he is sovereign. He uses the family as an example: "Another way to understand God's control is that of the man who is in control of his family. He ensures that everybody follows the established rules. This form is called *simple sovereignty* and is the one displayed in Ancient Near Eastern texts referring to the suzerain and his vassal."[7]

Arminianism's view of divine sovereignty emphasizes that God deals with human beings covenantally. As Creator and governor of all, he promulgates laws that he wants to be obeyed. As gracious, redeeming Savior, he strikes covenants with personal beings. The covenantal aspect of God's dealings with his people looms large in the nondeterministic account of sovereignty in traditional Arminian theology. This is one reason why Arminius and Wesley were covenant theologians. They believed that post-Dort Calvinism, with its deterministic view of reality, was at cross-purposes with pre-Dort Reformed

---

God determines human thoughts and decisions (D. A. Carson mentions, e.g., 2 Samuel 24:1; Isaiah 19:13–14; 37:7; Proverbs 21:1; Ezra 1:1; 7:6; 27–28; Nehemiah 2:11–12) must be creatively interpreted to be made to teach that, and even if it could be shown that some of these did establish God's direct foreordination in a certain case, that does not show that he universally works this way. See D. A. Carson, *Divine Sovereignty and Human Responsibility: Biblical Perspectives in Tension* (Atlanta: John Knox, 1981), 27.

5. Steve W. Lemke, "A Biblical and Theological Critique of Irresistible Grace," in *Whosoever Will: A Biblical-Theological Critique of Five-Point Calvinism*, eds. David L. Allen and Steve W. Lemke (Nashville: B&H Academic, 2011), 153.
6. Quoted in Samuel Sprecher, *The Groundwork of a System of Evangelical Lutheran Theology* (Philadelphia: Lutheran Publication Society, 1879), 396.
7. Bruce Little, "Evil and God's Sovereignty," in *Whosoever Will*, 287.

theology, which emphasized God's kingly rule over his free creatures by means of law and covenant.

However, while defining sovereignty to include contingency may rule out a strict Calvinistic determinism, it does not result in the universe being characterized by random chance. Arminians fully agree with Louis Berkhof's definition of divine sovereignty as God's being "clothed with absolute authority over the hosts of heaven and the inhabitants of the earth" so that he "upholds all things with His almighty power, and determines the ends which they are destined to serve." Arminians can even agree with Berkhof that "He rules as King in the most absolute sense of the word, and all things are dependent on Him and subservient to Him."[8] As Arminian theologian Kevin Hester states, "God's sovereignty is such a clear biblical teaching that no biblically conscious Christian would dare assail it. The question is whether, and if so in what way, human freedom (if it exists) coexists with God's sovereign plan and control of the universe."[9]

Arminianism's Robust View of the Sovereignty of God

Thus Calvinism's caricature that Arminianism "denies the sovereignty of God," while commonly repeated in Calvinist circles, is a myth.[10] On the contrary, Arminianism has a robust doctrine of divine sovereignty.[11] Arminians, as Roger Olson argues, advance a strong account of God's general and special providence. They affirm God's "concurring" providence—that if God were to remove his hand from the world, it could not keep going. They also assert that God governs the world to his desired ends while still maintaining creaturely freedom. He permits evil yet does not ordain it.[12] As John Wesley said, if we do not believe that God "governs all things" in the world, "small and great; that fire and hail, snow and vapour, wind and storm, fulfill his word; that he rules kingdoms and cities, fleets and armies, and all the individuals whereof they are composed (and yet without forcing the wills of men or necessitating any of their actions)," we cannot believe that he governs anything.[13]

Olson asks simply, "Does God govern by meticulously determining the entire course of every life, including moral choices and actions? Or does God

---

8. Louis Berkhof, *Systematic Theology* (Grand Rapids: Eerdmans, 1941), 76.

9. Kevin L. Hester, "'Choose You This Day': Free Will and Determinism," Lecture, Annual Session, National Association of Free Will Baptists, July 2019.

10. That quotation is from Edwin H. Palmer, *The Five Points of Calvinism* (Grand Rapids: Baker, 1972), 85.

11. The most compelling succinct account of how Arminians can have a strong view of divine providence while asserting libertarian freedom is found in Robert E. Picirilli, "Toward a Non-Deterministic Theology of Divine Providence," *Journal for Baptist Theology and Ministry* 11 (2014): 38–61.

12. Roger E. Olson, *Arminian Theology: Myths and Realities* (Downers Grove, IL: IVP Academic, 2006), 115–36.

13. John Wesley, "An Estimate of the Manners of the Present Times," quoted in Olson, 127.

allow humans a realm of freedom of choice and then respond by drawing them into his perfect plan for history's consummation?" Arminianism agrees with the mainstream of the Christian tradition in affirming the latter. How can it be otherwise, Olson asks. After all, Jesus taught his disciples to pray, "Thy will be done, on earth as it is in heaven." Yet if God's sovereignty "were already completely exercised de facto, why would anyone need to pray for God's will to be done on earth? In that case, it would always already be done on earth."[14]

In disagreeing with Calvinism's view of God as causally determining every aspect of reality, Arminians affirm the classic distinction between the two modes of God's will—antecedent and consequent. This concept was first popularized by the church father John of Damascus and repeated by Arminius.[15] John distinguished between "God's antecedent will and pleasure," which "springs from Himself," and "God's consequent will and permission," which "has its origin in us." God's antecedent will involves those things that God approvingly wills. His consequent will involves those things that he merely allows. Without God's grace we can do nothing good. Yet our actions are free in the sense of libertarian free will. They depend "neither on His antecedent nor on His consequent will, but are a concession to free-will." Thus it is not God's will "that there should be, nor does He choose to compel virtue."[16]

As William G. Most shows, the mainstream of the Christian tradition affirmed this distinction. It held that one can maintain a strong view of divine providence without the ordination of evil and without the violatation of the view of "freedom from necessity" advocated in the libertarian free will account of human freedom.[17]

---

14. Wesley, "An Estimate of the Manners," 117.
15. See William Most, *Grace, Predestination, and the Salvific Will of God: New Answers to Old Questions* (Front Royal, VA: Christendom, 2004). See, e.g., Arminius, *Works* 3:318; 428–30, "Examination of Perkins's Pamphlet." This was also seen in the mainstream Lutheran dogmaticians of Arminius's day, who disagreed with unconditional election and irresistible grace. Heinrich Schmid, ed., *Doctrinal Theology of the Evangelical Lutheran Church* (Minneapolis: Augsburg, 1961 [1876]), 299–315.
16. John of Damascus, *An Exact Exposition of the Orthodox Faith*, in *A Select Library of Nicene and Post-Nicene Fathers* (Oxford: James Parker and Company, 1899), 9:42. The vast sweep of patristic theology affirmed libertarian free will, conditional election of individuals, resistible grace, and the possibility of apostasy, including Augustine until very late in life. See Most; Thomas C. Oden, *The Transforming Power of Grace* (Nashville: Abingdon, 1993); and Kenneth M. Wilson, *Augustine's Conversion from Traditional Free Choice to "Non-free Free Will,"* Studien und Texte zu Antike und Christentum 111 (Tübingen: Mohr Siebeck, 2018).
17. Most, *Grace, Predestination, and the Salvific Will of God*, passim. For more on free will, see Questions 16–20.

Summary

Arminianism's robust yet indeterministic understanding of God's sovereignty provides a balance between the biblical teaching on God's providential governance of his creation and the biblical teaching that God is not the author of sin—that we are responsible for our sins, not God. In addition to being in harmony with the warp and woof of the Bible, this classic Christian understanding of providence simply gives a more compelling answer to the problem of evil. The causal determinism of Calvinism results in a God who is the author of sin and evil, as discussed in Question 18. Thus, despite the Calvinist criticism that Arminianism obscures the sovereignty of God by focusing on human free will, traditional Arminianism strongly extols the sovereignty of God. Arminians believe that Calvinism took the biblical doctrine of sovereignty as God's kingly rule and reign over his free creatures through law and covenant and transmuted it into determinism. Yet the biblical picture of divine sovereignty is more satisfying than Calvinist determinism because it more carefully mirrors the revealed character of God.

REFLECTION QUESTIONS

1. How does Arminianism claim to affirm God's sovereignty while disagreeing with divine meticulous determination of every human choice?

2. How can one emphasize Reformed teaching on God's sovereignty and kingdom without affirming determinism?

3. Describe how Arminians define the biblical picture of divine sovereignty, and contrast it with Calvinism's definition.

4. What did John of Damascus and Arminius believe about God's antecedent and consequent wills?

5. What do you think of Olson's question about how to interpret the statement, "Thy kingdom come, thy will be done on earth as it is in heaven," if everything is already determined and human free choice cannot change it?

Are People Free If God Knows the Future?

One of the great concerns Arminians have with Classical Calvinism is that it tends to confuse divine foreknowledge with divine foreordination. Calvinists, in other words, believe that, if God *knows* something is going to happen, it will happen and thus it *must* happen. For example, in his classic book *On the Freedom of the Will*, Jonathan Edwards says that "if there be any infallible knowledge of future volitions, the event is necessary; or, in other words . . . it is impossible but the event should come to pass."[1]

Open Theists Agree with Calvinists on This Question

This position is also the view of open theists, who deny the exhaustive foreknowledge of God. They do so because they believe that God's knowledge of a future event renders it necessary, which means that there are no future free events, what scholars call future contingents. This is the same language Edwards used when he argued that "God's certain foreknowledge of the future volitions of moral agents" is not consistent with "a contingence of those volitions."[2] Open theist Richard Rice could not agree more. "If the future is inevitable," he says, "then the apparent experience of free choice is an illusion." He acknowledges his agreement with Edwards on this point: "Edwards, of course, was a staunch predestinarian, but he recognized that absolute foreknowledge by itself excludes free choice, whether one accepts a strong

---

1. Jonathan Edwards, "On the Freedom of the Will," in *The Works of President Edwards* (New York: Robert Carter and Brothers, 1879), 2:73.
2. Edwards, "On the Freedom of the Will," 2:73. For the most perceptive Arminian treatment of Edwards's views on free will, see Robert E. Picirilli, *Free Will Revisited: A Respectful Response to Luther, Calvin, and Edwards* (Eugene, OR: Wipf and Stock, 2017), esp. 60–74.

doctrine of predestination or not."[3] Calvinists and open theists agree on at least one thing: if God knows a future decision, that decision is necessary; it is determined and thus cannot be free.

However, Arminians have historically opposed the idea that God's foreknowledge of future decisions renders them necessary and thus not free. In this way, all traditional Arminians differ from both Calvinists and open theists. They disagree with Calvinism on human freedom and with open theism on divine omniscience. Or, as William Lane Craig argues, Arminians believe that both the Calvinist denial of libertarian freedom and the open theist denial of divine foreknowledge are simply "denials of biblical doctrine."[4]

Open theism argues that it is impossible for God to see the future because it does not exist. God can know only things that exist. This perspective of limited omniscience tries to root itself in Old Testament passages that orthodox Christians have always seen as anthropomorphic (see Gen. 18:20–21; Isa. 38:1–5, Jer. 26:3; Ezek. 12:3; Amos 7:1–6; Jonah 3). Yet taking open theists' literalistic reading of these passages, as Craig has shown, "denies to God, not foreknowledge, but knowledge of what has been and what is presently going on."[5] Furthermore, open theism cannot sidestep the uniform biblical witness of God's exhaustive foreknowledge of the future.[6] Against earlier versions of open theism, Richard Watson exclaimed, "The whole body of prophecy is founded on the certain prescience of contingent actions, or it is not prediction, but guess and conjecture. To such fearful results does the denial of the Divine prescience lead!" Yet against Calvinism he states: "If there be any predictions in the Bible at all, every scheme which denies the prescience of contingencies must compel us into the doctrine of necessity."[7]

An Arminian Understanding of Foreknowledge of Future Contingencies

So how might the traditional Arminian handle the objection that God's foreknowledge rules out human freedom?[8] Question 16 discussed Arminius's

---

3. Richard Rice, "Divine Foreknowledge and Free-Will Theism," in *The Grace of God, the Will of Man: A Case for Arminianism*, ed. Clark H. Pinnock (Grand Rapids: Zondervan, 1989), 127–28.
4. William Lane Craig, *The Only Wise God: The Compatibility of Divine Foreknowledge and Human Freedom* (Grand Rapids: Baker, 1987), 39. See Chapter 2 of Craig's book for excellent arguments for why Calvinism and open theism both veer from the Bible on these points.
5. Craig, *The Only Wise God*, 40.
6. See Picirilli, *Grace, Faith, Free Will*, 60–62. For a detailed Arminian response to open theism, see Picirilli, "An Arminian Response to John Sanders's *The God Who Risks: A Theology of Providence*," *Journal of the Evangelical Theological Society* 44 (2001): 467–91.
7. Richard Watson, *Theological Institutes*, 3rd ed. (London: John Mason, 1829), 1:420–21.
8. Picirilli provides the best treatments of this subject. For a succinct study, see Robert E. Picirilli, *Grace, Faith, Free Will*, esp. 36–41. For a deeper examination, see Picirilli, *Free*

distinction between an event's being certain and its being necessary. He said, "If [God] resolve to use a force that . . . can be resisted by the creature, then that thing is said to be done, *not necessarily* but *contingently*, although its actual occurrence was certainly foreknown by God."[9] There are two sorts of events: contingent events and necessary (predetermined) events. Contingent events are events that could have been otherwise. Necessary events are events that could not have been otherwise. Arminius believed that God designed his universe to contain both sorts of events—some events have to be the way they are because God foreordained them. Other events turn out one way but could have been another way.[10]

How can an event be free if God knows it is going to come to pass? If God's knowledge is true, does it not make the event certain? Therein lies the explanation. A future event can be certain without being necessary. As the old song says, "Que sera, sera, whatever will be will be."[11] No one will deny this. Whatever will be will indeed be. But *why* will it be? What is the cause of its being? Is God's foreknowledge of a future event the cause of its being? No. Knowledge does not cause things. I know, for example, that tomorrow is going to be Tuesday. Yet my knowledge will not cause tomorrow to be Tuesday. Something other than knowledge causes things to happen one way and not another.[12]

If I decide to go crappie fishing at the lake tomorrow morning, God knows that and has always known that. Yet the reason he has always known it is that he knows everything truly and exhaustively. However, if I freely choose instead to go to the donut shop tomorrow rather than the lake, then God instead knows *that* and has always known *it*. So if, in eternity past, God knew that I would go fishing at 7:00 a.m. tomorrow, then it is *certain* that I will do so, but it is not *necessary*. The only reason God knew that I would go is because of my choice to go. My will was the cause of my action, not God's knowledge. Things are caused by other things than knowledge of them, whether divine or human. As Augustine said, "Just as you do not force past things to have happened by your memory, so too God does not force future things to happen by His foreknowledge. And just as you remember some of the things you have done and yet have not done all the things you remember, so too God foreknows all the things of which He is the author and yet is not the author of all the things He foresees."[13]

Will Revisited, 79–87; Picirilli, "Foreknowledge, Freedom, and the Future," *Journal of the Evangelical Theological Society* 43 (2000): 259–71.

9. Arminius, *Works*, 1:753, "Apology against Thirty-One Defamatory Articles," art. 5.
10. See Picirilli, *Free Will Revisited*, 80–82.
11. Picirilli, *Free Will Revisited*, 81.
12. Stephen T. Davis, *Logic and the Nature of God* (London: Macmillan, 1983), 64. Davis's argument remains one of the best critiques of theological determinism.
13. Augustine, *On the Free Choice of the Will, On Grace and Free Choice, and Other Writings*, ed. and trans. Peter King, Cambridge Texts in the History of Philosophy (Cambridge: Cambridge University Press, 2010), 3.4.11.40 (p. 81). Augustine wrote this work before he

Calvinists and open theists object that a thing (God's knowledge) cannot be caused by something that occurs after it (the free act). However, as Stephen T. Davis cogently argues, being contingent on something is not the same thing as being caused by it. The proposition "Matt will go crappie fishing tomorrow" is either true or false. Its truth-value is "contingent upon certain events that will or will not occur in the future."[14] Put simply, "What God knew yesterday is contingent upon what I will freely decide to do tomorrow." If I am free to decide whether to do something or refrain from it, "it is up to me to decide which I shall do; and whichever I decide to do, God will have known yesterday, and indeed, from eternity, that I will do it."[15]

Watson wisely said, "That the subject is incomprehensible as to the *manner* in which the Divine Being foreknows future events of this or of any kind, even the greatest minds, which have applied themselves to such speculations, have felt and acknowledged."[16] The Bible does not conjecture and engage in metaphysical speculation but simply asserts that God sees the future. This has led many theologians through the centuries to see foreknowledge, as Davis does, as "future vision" or what older theologians called "prevision." According to this approach, God does not know the future inferentially. "He simply 'sees' the future, just as we see the present and have seen the past." Davis compares an omniscient computer with a crystal ball. The omniscient computer would "compute" all the facts of the "present" and thus accurately extrapolate what the future would be by inference. This is implausible with regard to people who are making deliberative decisions. However, the crystal ball simply "peers into" the future, thus "seeing" rather than "computing or deducing" future events.[17]

The Question of Molinism

As if the discussion above were not complex and tedious, the highly speculative system of Molinism is much more so (which is probably one of the reasons it has never caught on). One of the things that, lately, has sometimes arisen in a consideration of foreknowledge and free will is whether an Arminian can be a Molinist. Molinism is the speculative theory of the sixteenth-century Jesuit theologian Luis de Molina. He argued that God, via "middle knowledge" (*scientia media* in Latin) knows what people would do

---

embraced unconditional election; see Kenneth M. Wilson's convincing argument that this change did not occur until A.D. 412 in his book *Augustine's Conversion from Traditional Free Choice to "Non-free Free Will,"* Studien und Texte zu Antike und Christentum 111 (Tübingen: Mohr Siebeck, 2018).

14. Davis, *Logic and the Nature of God*, 64.

15. Davis, *Logic and the Nature of God*, 53.

16. Richard Watson, *Theological Institutes* (London: John Mason, 1829), 1:421.

17. Davis, *Logic and the Nature of God*, 65–66. One could be an Arminian and espouse any number of theories about how God knows the future.

if placed in a given set of circumstances. In eternity past, God chose to set into motion one of innumerable "possible worlds" in which God brings about exactly what he wants, or chooses, but people still have libertarian free will.[18]

This includes their receiving or rejecting Christ. Thus, Molina argued, God can foreordain everyone's election or reprobation just as he wants it to occur, but each individual is still free. Thus, as Molina explained in his discussion of Romans 9, "God could have predestined 'any of the elect to have truly been reprobate' and any 'of the reprobate to have truly been elect.'"[19] As Kirk MacGregor cogently argues, Molina was a "firm believer in unconditional election, holding that God elects purely according to his pleasure without regard to any foreseen faith or good works and reprobates without regard to any foreseen unbelief or sins."[20] William Lane Craig explains that in Molina's view, "God knew an infinity of providential orders in which the non-predestined would freely arrive at eternal life and thus would have been predestined . . . [and] an infinity of providential orders in which the predestined would have freely . . . been reprobate." He "chose for the one and for the other the order of providence in which He foresaw that the one would be saved and the other not."[21] Thus Craig argues, there can be a *rapprochement* between Calvinism and Arminianism.[22]

Many contemporary "Arminian-leaning" Molinists such as Kenneth Keathley would differ from Molina's stance on unconditional reprobation while agreeing with him on unconditional election. Keathley, for example, affirms that "simultaneously God's decree of election is unconditional while His rejection of the unbeliever is conditional." He affirmatively quotes Craig that it is "up to God whether we find ourselves in a world in which we are predestined, but it is up to us whether we are predestined in the world in which we find ourselves."[23]

This approach has been rejected by most Arminian theologians over the past four centuries as idiosyncratic and resulting in the sort of unscriptural divine determinism they find problematic in Calvinism. One example of this traditional Arminian approach to Molinism is the early Wesleyan

---

18. In using the phrase "brings about exactly what he wants," I am echoing Craig's statement that God "chose to create the world order he wanted." William Lane Craig, "Middle Knowledge, A Calvinist-Arminian Rapprochement?" in *The Grace of God, the Will of Man*, ed. Clark H. Pinnock (Grand Rapids: Zondervan, 1989), 156.

19. Kirk R. MacGregor, *Luis de Molina: The Life and Theology of the Founder of Middle Knowledge* (Grand Rapids: Zondervan, 2015), 139, citing Molina, *Concordia*, 7.23.4/5.1.2.4.

20. MacGregor, *Luis de Molina*, 140.

21. Craig, "Middle Knowledge," 156–57, quoting the *Dictionnaire de théologie catholique*, s.v., "Molinisme," by E. Vansteenberghe, 10.2., col. 2112.

22. Craig, "Middle Knowledge," 141–64. For full-length but accessible treatments from this perspective, see Kenneth Keathley, *Salvation and Sovereignty: A Molinist Approach* (Nashville: B&H Academic, 2010) and Craig, *The Only Wise God*.

23. Keathley, *Salvation and Sovereignty*, 153–54, quoting Craig, "Middle Knowledge," 157.

theologian Richard Watson. Watson stated that a version of Molinism was followed by some of the Remonstrants, but that they "did not follow their great leader Arminius, who felt no need of this subterfuge, but stood on the plain declarations of Scripture, unembarrassed with metaphysical distinctions."[24]

Recently some scholars have called this traditional understanding into question, arguing that Arminius himself was a Molinist. Arminius's views, however, militate against a Molinist account of predestination. As William G. Witt has masterfully shown, while Arminius showed awareness of Molina's concept of middle knowledge, he did not have a Molinist doctrine of predestination.[25] Robert Picirilli, Roger Olson, F. Stuart Clarke, and Hendrik Frandsen join Witt in this proper interpretation of Arminius on this point, while scholars such as Eef Dekker, Richard Muller, Keith Stanglin, and (to a lesser degree) William den Boer read too much Molinism into Arminius. The most that can be said is that Arminius ambiguously toyed with the concept of middle knowledge but was not a Molinist in his doctrine of predestination.[26]

Olson has asked, "Are Arminian Theology and Middle Knowledge Compatible?" His answer to this question is no. He is right that, "once one believes that God uses middle knowledge to render certain that all creatures do what they do by creating them and placing them in circumstances where he knows they will 'freely' do something, then determinism is at the door if not in the living room, and that is inconsistent with Arminianism's basic impulses. It makes God the author of sin and evil even if only inadvertently." Olson is not saying that Molinists cannot be Arminians; however, he thinks Molinism is an inconsistent form of Arminianism.[27]

Olson offers a helpful illustration that gets to the heart of why Molinism entails determinism: What if he knows a student well enough to know that if he suggests the student read a certain book, the student will misunderstand

---

24. Richard Watson, *Theological Institutes* (London: John Mason, 1829), 1:418.
25. William G. Witt, "Creation, Redemption, and Grace in the Theology of Jacobus Arminius" (Ph.D. diss., University of Notre Dame, 1993), chapter 8.
26. Picirilli, *Grace, Faith, Free Will*; Roger E. Olson, *Arminian Theology: Myths and Realities* (Downers Grove, IL: InterVarsity, 2006); Roger Olson, "Are Arminian Theology and Middle Knowledge Compatible?" https://www.patheos.com/blogs/rogereolson/2013/09/are-arminian-theology-and-middle-knowledge-compatible, accessed April 26, 2020; F. Stuart Clarke, *The Ground of Election: Jacob Arminius' Doctrine of the Work and Person of Christ* (Milton Keynes, UK: Paternoster, 2006); Eef Dekker, "Was Arminius a Molinist?" *Sixteenth Century Journal* 27 (1996): 337–52; Richard Muller, *God, Creation, and Providence in the Thought of Jacob Arminius* (Grand Rapids: Baker, 1991); Keith D. Stanglin and Thomas H. McCall, *Jacob Arminius: Theologian of Grace* (New York: Oxford University Press, 2012); William den Boer, *God's Twofold Love: The Theology of Jacob Arminius (1559–1609)* (Göttingen: Vandenhoeck and Ruprecht, 2010).
27. Olson, "Are Arminian Theology and Middle Knowledge Compatible?"

the subject and fail the course? Olson has grade inflation and needs some students to fail. So he uses his middle knowledge "to bring about infallibly that he fails the course" while maintaining the student's free will. Who would be responsible for the student's failure, Olson or the student, and "can it fairly be said that by rendering his failure certain, using my middle knowledge, I did not make it necessary?"[28] Thus Olson agrees with Eef Dekker (the scholar who first suggested that Arminius was a Molinist) that *if* Arminius used middle knowledge, he "contradicted himself," unwittingly falling "into determinism." However, Olson, correctly, is not prepared to agree that Arminius used middle knowledge.[29]

Summary

Understanding the difference between necessity and contingency helps one understand how God can know the future and his knowledge of the future not cause it to be so. This is also aided by seeing that something's being is not caused by one's knowledge of it. God's knowledge of my future act of going to the hardware store is no more caused by that knowledge than my wife's knowledge of my past act of getting ice cream bars from the grocery store is caused by her knowledge of it.

Another account of divine knowledge and human freedom is Molinism, which Craig puts forth as a "rapprochement" between Calvinism and Arminianism. Molinism tries to make it possible to have one's cake and eat it too—to have the meticulous sovereignty or determism of Calvinism and the libertarian freedom of Arminianism at the same time. Yet this exercise in speculative metaphysics is too deterministic to meet the demands of an Arminian doctrine of divine sovereignty and human freedom.

REFLECTION QUESTIONS

1. What is one thing that Calvinists and open theists agree on regarding the relationship between foreknowledge and foreordination?

2. Why do open theists and Calvinists think that God cannot foreknow anything and that thing still be free?

3. Does knowledge of something cause it?

---

28. Olson, "Are Arminian Theology and Middle Knowledge Compatible?"
29. Olson, "Are Arminian Theology and Middle Knowledge Compatible?" For an insightful discussion of the incompatibility of Arminianism and Molinism, see Robert E. Picirilli, *God in Eternity and Time: A New Case for Human Freedom* (Nashville: B&H Academic, to be published 2022).

4. How do traditional Arminians answer the question that God's knowledge cannot be caused by something that occurs after it?

5. Why does Olson think that Molinism unwittingly results in determinism and is thus inconsistent with Arminianism's basic thrust?

SECTION B

Resistible Prevenient Grace

What Do Arminians Believe About Universal Prevenient Grace?

All Christians believe in prevenient grace except Pelagians and semi-Pelagians. Traditional Arminians have always said that prevenient grace (Latin, *gratia praeveniens*, lit., the grace that goes before) is necessary for salvation. Arminius emphasized this strongly. He was fond of quoting John 6:44, "No one can come to me unless the Father who sent me draws him." Because of this natural inability to come to Christ, the Spirit's prevenient grace must "incline the mind and heart" toward the gospel for one to be converted.[1]

The Remonstrant Confession or Declaration stated that God must "bestow" grace on sinners for them to be "apt and fit to perform all that which is required" of them in the gospel. This bestowal of grace is "not only necessary, but also sufficient for their yielding faith and obedience, when he calleth them by the gospel unto himself." Yet prevenient grace cannot come to fruition *without the Word*. Conversion comes through the "preaching of the gospel," joined with "the virtue or power of the Spirit." God has "a gracious and serious intention to save, and therefore to bring unto faith, all those that are called: whether they really believe and are saved or no, and so obstinately refuse to believe and consequently to be saved." Thus the early Remonstrants affirmed that grace is "the beginning, progress, and complement of all good." Without it no one can "think, will, or perform any thing that is savingly good: much less resist any temptations that do draw and entice unto evil." Therefore, faith and conversion are "wholly to be ascribed to the grace of God in Christ,

---

1. Jacobus Arminius, *The Works of James Arminius* (Nashville: Randall House, 2007), 2:722. "Certain Articles to Be Diligently Examined and Weighed," art. 17.

as their principal and primary cause." Yet human beings can "despise and reject the grace of God, and resist the operation of it."[2]

Thus both Calvinists and Arminians affirm the necessity of *gratia praeveniens*, just differently.[3] The Arminian doctrine of prevenient grace is essentially the outcome of the doctrines of the *gratia universalis* (universal grace) and *gratia resistibilis* (resistible grace). The Calvinist understanding is the outcome of the doctrines of *gratia particularis* (particular grace) and *gratia irresistibilis* (irresistible grace). Thus the argument surrounding prevenient grace—which Arminians and Calvinists affirm—is simply whether it is universal and resisitible or particular and irresistible.

The debate is largely decided based on other beliefs one holds. If one believes that Holy Scripture teaches both the *gratia universalis* and *gratia resistibilis*, then the Arminian doctrine of prevenient grace follows. Arminians believe that one of the most untenable features of Calvinism is its argument against universal grace because of the strong support for the doctrine throughout Scripture (see Questions 12–14). If everyone is enlightened, convicted, and drawn by God's grace—as indicated by John 1:9 (Jesus gives light to everyone), John 12:32 (he draws everyone), John 16:8 (the Spirit convicts everyone), and Titus 2:11 (God brings saving grace to everyone)—and that grace is resistible, therein lies the doctrine of universal, resistible prevenient grace.[4] However, if Scripture plainly teaches that God's grace and Christ's atonement are only for the elect, and it clearly teaches that that grace is irresistible, then the doctrine of universal prevenient grace is implausible.[5]

Things Not Entailed by an Arminian Doctrine of Prevenient Grace

Most Calvinists misunderstand the Arminian doctrine of prevenient grace to entail things that some Arminians teach that are neither biblical nor

---

2. *The Confession or Declaration of the Ministers or Pastors which in the United Provinces are Called Remonstrants* (London: Francis Smith, 1676), 200–5. Cf. Steve W. Lemke, "A Biblical and Theological Critique of Irresistible Grace," in *Whosoever Will: A Biblical-Theological Critique of Five-Point Calvinism*, eds. David L. Allen and Steve W. Lemke (Nashville: B&H Academic, 2010), 109–13.

3. J. V. Fesko, "Arminius on *Facientibus Quod in Se Est* and Likely Medieval Sources," in *Church and School in Early Modern Protestantism: Studies in Honor of Richard A. Muller on the Maturation of a Theological Tradition*, eds. Jordan J. Ballor, et al. (Leiden: Brill, 2013), 353. The term "prevenient grace" was apparently introduced by Augustine. See H. F. Stewart's notes in his translation of *Thirteen Homilies of St. Augustine on St. John XIV* (Cambridge: Cambridge University Press, 1900), 131.

4. For a discussion of exegetical proof for the doctrine of prevenient grace, see W. Brian Shelton, *Prevenient Grace: God's Provision for Fallen Humanity* (Anderson, IN: Francis Asbury, 2015), 13–57. While some Arminians, such as Reformed Arminians, will have differences with Shelton, his work, which is the most extensive book on the doctrine, contains a wealth of insight. See also Lemke, 117–29.

5. On the resistibility of prevenient grace, see Questions 23–26.

required by the Arminian system. There are several things that Reformed Arminians *do not* think prevenient grace means.

Not to Be Confused with Natural Revelation

First, prevenient grace is not to be confused with natural or general revelation. Many Arminians conflate natural revelation and conscience with special grace.[6] John Wesley, for example, sometimes described prevenient grace as the natural moral consciousness that God implants in all human beings. Wesley said that no one "is in a state of mere nature . . . entirely destitute of what is vulgarly called natural conscience." Yet Wesley stressed that natural conscience "is not natural," but instead should be named prevenient grace.[7]

Many Arminians, however, in seeing prevenient grace more as an individualized drawing which, at one time or another, goes out to all people, in God's own timing and manner, do not equate this grace with general revelation.[8] Arminius stated that the "capability of believing is not bestowed on man by virtue of the first creation," but wholly results from special grace.[9] This is one of the reasons why the Reformed Arminian Leroy Forlines prefers the phrase "drawing power of the Holy Spirit."[10] He goes into great detail about how depraved humanity suppresses general revelation—that immediate or innate knowledge of God "preprogrammed" into every human being. He draws a hard line between general revelation as *natural* and the drawing grace of the Holy Spirit as the supernatural, progressive, gracious, relational activity of the Holy Spirit.[11] Wesleyan theologian Thomas Oden agrees: "Grace is not resident in

---

6. Shelton, *Prevenient Grace*, 31–37, 241–42. See M. Elton Hendricks, "John Wesley and Natural Theology," *Wesleyan Theological Journal* 18 (1983): 7–17. William Burt Pope said that while people are in "bondage to sin," that "bondage is not hopeless" because human beings have "a natural capacity of freedom to act as well as to choose and this their very nature is itself grace" (*A Compendium of Christian Theology* [London: Wesleyan Conference Office, 1875], 453).

7. *The Works of the Rev. John Wesley* (New York: J&J Harper, 1826), 7:43, "On Working Out Our Own Salvation." See similar comments by John Goodwin whose works Wesley reprinted in his *Redemption Redeemed*, (London: Thomas Tegg, 1840 [1651]), 91.

8. See the language of the 1660 Standard Confession of the General Baptists: "all men at one time or other are put into such a capacity, as that (through the grace of God) they may be eternally saved" (art. 4). The same statement occurs in the 1812 Abstract (art. 6) of the General Baptists' descendants in the American South, the Free Will Baptists. These confessions are reprinted in J. Matthew Pinson, *A Free Will Baptist Handbook: Heritage, Beliefs, and Ministries* (Nashville: Randall House, 1998), 132, 145.

9. Arminius, *Works*, 2:24, "Apology against Thirty-One Defamatory Articles," art. 19.

10. F. Leroy Forlines, *Classical Arminianism: A Theology of Salvation* (Nashville: Randall House, 2011), 84–88.

11. For more on this, see F. Leroy Forlines and J. Matthew Pinson, *The Apologetics of Leroy Forlines* (Gallatin, TN: Welch College Press, 2019). Forlines believes that there has to be revelation, either general or special, for the Spirit to influence people with drawing grace, but that revelation is not to be equated with that grace.

nature, but a gift to nature. . . . It assists fallen human nature in ways inaccessible to that nature itself. To believe is a work of grace, not of nature."[12]

A Supernatural Drawing, Not a Unilateral Lessening of Depravity
Second, prevenient grace is a supernatural conviction and drawing by the Holy Spirit, not a unilateral lessening of depravity. This is seen numerous times in New Testament texts that show the Holy Spirit working in people's hearts and minds before conversion (Acts 2:37; 10:12; 16:14; 1 Thess. 1:4–5).[13] Wesley sometimes described prevenient grace in terms more like what Forlines calls the drawing power of the Holy Spirit. At other times Wesley conflated it with general revelation or conscience. He sometimes tended to cast prevenient grace as a unilateral lessening of depravity: "Natural free will in the present state of mankind I do not understand: I only assert there is a measure of free will supernaturally restored to every man."[14] In another place he affirmed "that in the moment Adam fell, he had no freedom of will left," but that God, "when of his own free-grace he gave the promise of a Saviour to him and his posterity, graciously restored to mankind a liberty and power to accept of proffered salvation."[15] Because of this ambiguity, some Wesleyans emphasize more the drawing of the Spirit while others stress restored free will. Like William Burt Pope, some Wesleyans stress that the atonement has within it a power that universally mitigates the effects of depravity.[16]

Brian Shelton emphasizes drawing grace more than a lessening of depravity, stating that it is unacceptable "to hold to a partial depravity with a built-in capacity for doing spiritual good of its own accord. Such a position does not do justice to the force of sin's detrimental effects depicted in the New Testament." Yet he also casts doubt on that assertion: "*A new human condition exists, in which all people are not totally depraved* but capable of exercising faith to a greater or lesser degree, depending on the subjective activity of the

---

12. Thomas C. Oden, *The Transforming Power of Grace* (Nashville: Abingdon, 1993), 105.
13. Arminius used Acts 16:14 as evidence of the "internal calling," the Holy Spirit's call to everyone, which is consistent, not at odds, with the external call. Arminius, *Works*, 2:234. Public Disputation 16, "On the Vocation of Men to Salvation." See also Robert E. Picirilli, *Grace, Faith, Free Will: Contrasting Views of Salvation: Calvinism and Arminianism* (Nashville: Randall House, 2002), 154–55, and Matt O'Reilly, "Arminian Essentials: Prevenient Grace," http://evangelicalarminians.org/arminian-essentials-prevenient-grace, accessed July 21, 2020.
14. "Predesination Calmly Considered," *Works*, 10:229–30.
15. "The Scripture Doctrine of Predestination, Election, and Reprobation," in *The Works of the Rev. John Wesley* (New York: J&J Harper, 1827), 9:429. While this was in the 1827 New York edition of his works, it was not written by Wesley, but he published it in his book *A Preservative against Unsettled Notions in Religion* (Bristol: William Pine, 1770), which he "designed for the use of all those who are under my care, but chiefly of the young Preachers" (*Journal*, Dec. 11, 1757, *Works*, 2:432).
16. Pope, *Compendium*, 2:58–59.

Spirit on their individual hearts." Thus Shelton suggests that there are two aspects of prevenient grace: "objective," which "comes to people in an impersonal, unbiased way," and "subjective," which acts "on each human being individually." Regarding the objective aspect of prevenient grace, he remarks, "It is as if, in some mysterious and abstract way, God unilaterally enables people through Christ's work on the cross to respond to the gospel."[17]

Many Wesleyan theologians have tended to speak in terms of prevenient grace in the objective terms Shelton describes—an objective state into which humanity is born. J. Steven Harper, for example, argues that prevenient grace brings about a situation in which "human nature is preserved, including the necessary capacity to recognize and respond to God—or to refuse to do so."[18] Harold B. Kuhn states, "While all were born sinful, they were also born in grace."[19]

This sort of language makes Reformed Arminians extremely nervous. They want to make a starker distinction between *nature* and *supernature*. Thus, the Reformed Arminian Stephen M. Ashby, in wanting to "state emphatically" that the fall "render[s] us unable to respond rightly to God," states that Reformed Arminians

> differ from Wesleyans in our understanding of prevenient grace. It is not like a dense fog settling over a city in which everyone equally shares, hence, canceling out the effects of the Fall for all of humanity. Rather, it is individually directed and brings with it God's enablement as he draws human beings to himself. Though Reformed Arminians insist that God universally provides his salvific grace, they at the same time resist the notion that prevenient grace reverses the effects of the Fall. Rather, such grace, though universal in scope, acts in enablement and drawing on an individual human level.[20]

In another place, Ashby says that according to the Wesleyan view, "God's prevenient grace is scattergun, undoing the effects of the Fall. Given this approach, it does not sound like the Fall at all—rather, a slip. One is not rendered unable to please God, merely infirmed. One is not left blinded by sin—just confused. From this Reformed Arminians respectfully demur."[21] Thus Reformed

---

17. Shelton, *Prevenient Grace*, 2, 7–8, 10 (italics added).
18. J. Steven Harper, "Wesleyan Arminianism," in *Four Views on Eternal Security*, ed. J. Matthew Pinson (Grand Rapids: Zondervan, 2002), 236.
19. Harold B. Kuhn, "Wesleyanism," in the *Beacon Dictionary of Theology*, ed. Richard S. Taylor (Kansas City: Beacon Hill, 1983), 546.
20. Stephen M. Ashby, "A Reformed Arminian Response to J. Steven Harper," in *Four Views on Eternal Security*, 273.
21. Ashby, "A Reformed Arminian Response," 273.

Armininians think the "objective" view of many Wesleyans results in a *de jure* total depravity but not a *de facto* one.

The "individually directed" prevenient grace of which Ashby speaks involves what has traditionally been meant when it is said that someone is "under conviction." There are certain times when unbelievers come under greater conviction than at other times. The Holy Spirit is a person relating to other persons made in his image. Prevenient grace is not a substance one possesses. It is the gracious, enabling influence of the divine person on a human person in a relational dynamic—a back-and-forth, influence-and-response, relational movement. Yet "the Spirit will not always strive with man." This influence, this persuasion, this conviction, this back-and-forth relational experience, is temporary. Like other interpersonal forms of communication and influence, it is something that can come and go.

Some Wesleyans, such as Oden and Vic Reasoner, emphasize this individually directed drawing grace more than others, thus emphasizing the "subjective" aspect of the two poles in Wesley that Shelton describes.[22] Oden says, "Even the first fragile intuition of conviction of sin, the first intimation of our need for God, is the work of preparing, prevening grace." Prevenient grace "draws us gradually, incrementally, in stages. . . . At each stage, we are called to receive and respond to the grace being incrementally given. . . . Prevenient grace is that grace that goes before us to prepare us for more grace, the grace that makes it possible for persons to take the first steps toward saving grace."[23]

One also sees a similar approach in many scholastic Lutheran theologians. August Pfeiffer provides an excellent example when he explains that no one can keep the "motions" of prevenient grace "from arising." Because one cannot "conceal from himself his own thoughts, he must at times permit the good Spirit to create such emotions within his heart. Nevertheless, it is true that a wicked person can forthwith wantonly destroy these good motions, drive them from his heart by sinful thoughts, and thus willfully prevent the Spirit of God from perfecting the good work" and thus "destroy these salutary motions in his soul."[24]

It Does Not Entail Inclusivism

Third, prevenient grace does not mean that people who have never heard the gospel can be saved without the gospel, special revelation, and confessing Christ. Some people state that Wesley held an inclusivist view. Shelton,

---

22. Thomas C. Oden, *John Wesley's Scriptural Christianity: A Plain Exposition of His Teaching on Christian Doctrine* (Grand Rapids: Zondervan, 1994), 246; Vic Reasoner, "John Wesley's Doctrines on the Theology of Grace," in *Grace for All: The Arminian Dynamics of Salvation*, eds. Clark H. Pinnock and John D. Wagner (Eugene, OR: Resource, 2014), 183–89.
23. Oden, *John Wesley's Scriptural Christianity*, 247.
24. August Pfeiffer, *Anti-Calvinism*, trans. Edward Pfeiffer (Columbus, OH: Joint Lutheran Synod of Ohio, 1881 [1699]), 239–40.

however, argues that Wesley never articulated such a doctrine, saying instead that the question must be left to God. Inclusivism does not follow from the Arminian doctrine of prevenient grace.[25]

Most Arminians believe that there are two stages of prevenient grace. People receive some motions of prevenient grace before they receive the gospel or special revelation.[26] However, these can never result in salvation. If individuals do not resist the early motions of prevenient grace, they will be given the gospel. This second stage of prevenient grace, which involves the communication of the gospel-Word, must occur for individuals to be led to conversion.

The Orthodox Creed of the English General Baptists (1678) exemplifies this teaching, saying that in his "general" calling, God "acquaints" humanity with "his gracious good purpose of salvation," thus "inviting and wooing them to come to him." In those who do not resist this calling grace, God "in time worketh unfeigned faith and sincere repentance . . . and by his grace they come to accept" Christ and then are "effectually called" and united by faith to Jesus Christ.[27]

Arminius's detractors accused him of saying that "God undoubtedly converts, without the external preaching of the Gospel, great numbers of persons." He denied this, quoting a common sentiment in his day: "The ordinary means and instrument of conversion is the preaching of the Divine word by mortal men, to which therefore all persons are bound; but the Holy Spirit has not so bound himself to this method, as to be unable to operate in an extraordinary way, without the intervention of human aid, when it seemeth good to Himself."[28]

Arminius believed that God must bring a special revelation of the gospel to people for them to be converted. This might, rarely and extraordinarily, be by "internal revelation of the Holy Spirit or by the ministry of angels." Still, "no one is converted except by this very word, and by the meaning of this word, which God sends by men to those communities or nations whom He hath purposed to unite to himself."[29] Calvinist scholars such as William Shedd, Bruce Demarest, and Timothy George, who articulate a view like Arminius's, have shown that

---

25. Shelton, *Prevenient Grace*, 241, 245.

26. In prevenient grace, the Spirit works with natural revelation in the first stage, and with special revelation in the second.

27. Orthodox Creed, art. 21, http://baptiststudiesonline.com/wp-content/uploads/2007/02/orthodox-creed.pdf. It is worth noting that the Orthodox Creed uses the words "common calling" and "common grace" to indicate a grace that, in God's individually directed timing and manner and measure, goes out to all. One often sees the word "common grace" used in this way in early Arminianism, with "common" meaning "everyone gets some." Thus this is more than the limited meaning given to "common grace" in the Calvinist tradition. An exploration of a full-orbed Arminian definition of "common grace" in conversation with the Calvinian and Kuyperian traditions, while needed, is outside the scope of this book. Cf. Oden, who says, "God promises to offer subsequent grace to one who puts no impediments in the way of the reception of previous grace" (Oden, *Transforming Power of Grace*, 105).

28. Arminius, *Works*, 2:20–21, "Apology against Thirty-One Defamatory Articles," art. 18.

29. Arminius, *Works*, 2:20–21.

it is consistent with Reformed theology as articulated in the Second Helvetic Confession and the Westminster Confession. Christopher Morgan calls this view "special revelation exclusivism."[30] Traditional Arminians are exclusivists who believe that Christ must be preached to individuals for them to be converted.

Summary

Both Arminians and Calvinists believe in prevenient grace. Arminians think it is universal and resistible. Calvinists think it is particular and irresistible. Thus people's views on prevenient grace are simply the result of their views on the universality versus particularity and resistibility versus irresistibility of grace. Many Arminians and Calvinists assume that the Arminian doctrine of prevenient grace entails things it does not necessarily require. They mistakenly believe, for example, that an Arminian doctrine of prevenient grace makes people born free to respond positively to the gospel, or that it is really more like natural revelation, or that it entails inclusivism. However, Reformed Arminians, together with many other Arminians, emphasize that none of these things follows from a biblical, Arminian doctrine of universal prevenient grace.

REFLECTION QUESTIONS

1. What doctrines tend to predispose people to believe or disbelieve the Arminian doctrine of prevenient grace?

2. Does an Arminian have to conflate prevenient grace with natural or general revelation?

3. What does Stephen Ashby mean when he says that many Arminians see prevenient grace as "a dense fog" settling on the human race, or "scattergun," undoing the effects of the fall?

4. What is the difference between the "objective" and "subjective" aspects of prevenient grace that many Wesleyans, such as Brian Shelton, articulate?

5. What did Arminius teach about the salvation of those who have never heard the gospel, and how does this inform an Arminian understanding of the inclusivism/exclusivism debate?

---

30. See Christopher W. Morgan, "Inclusivisms and Exclusivisms," in *Faith Comes by Hearing: A Response to Inclusivism*, eds. Christopher W. Morgan and Robert A. Peterson (Downers Grove, IL: IVP Academic, 2009), 28–30. Many Arminians would affirm the more restrictive view that Morgan calls "gospel exclusivism," which requires a human preacher preaching from the Word and rules out miraculous, extraordinary presentations of the gospel.

How Do Arminians Respond to Objections to Universal Prevenient Grace?

Why do Calvinists object to the Arminian doctrine of prevenient grace, and how do Arminians answer those objections? First, Calvinists tend to misunderstand prevenient grace as the "objective" model some Wesleyans advocate, described in the previous chapter. Thus their primary target is the understanding that prevenient grace is a universal mitigating of the effects of depravity so that everyone is born with an absolute free will in spiritual things. Bruce Demarest encapsulates this response: "Arminians assert that the grace that flows from Christ's cross . . . erases the debilitating effects of sin on minds, restores moral free agency," and "neutralizes inherited sin" and "depravity."[1]

Thomas Schreiner asks, "Does Scripture teach that people are given the ability to choose or to reject God by virtue of the atonement?" Yet that is not what Reformed Arminians are saying. Schreiner says, "Even if the text were suggesting that salvation is potentially available for all people (cf. 1 Tim. 4:10), that is a far cry from saying that through the atonement God has counteracted the effects of Adam's sin so that all people have the opportunity to accept or reject him." Reformed Arminians do believe that Scripture teaches that salvation "is available for all people." Yet they do *not* believe that the atonement has "counteracted the effects of Adam's sin so that all people have the opportunity to accept or reject him." Thus the Arminian model to which most Calvinist objections respond is not what many Arminians teach.[2]

---

1. Bruce A. Demarest, *The Cross and Salvation: The Doctrine of Salvation* (Wheaton, IL: Crossway, 2006), 56, 208, 83.
2. Thomas R. Schreiner, "Does Scripture Teach Prevenient Grace in the Wesleyan Sense?" in *Still Sovereign: Contemporary Perspectives on Election, Foreknowledge, and Grace* (Grand

John 1:9

Some Calvinist objections to the Arminian doctrine of prevenient grace are exegetical. These mainly concern the interpretation of the Gospel of John. Primarily, Calvinists argue that John 1:9 cannot be interpreted to teach universal prevenient grace, that John 6:37, 44 clearly establish irresistible grace, and that Arminians misread John 12:32. Schreiner rests his entire exegetical argument against universal prevenient grace from John's gospel on his assertion that John 6:37, 44 teach irresistible grace.

In dealing with John 1:9, Schreiner says that "the true light, which gives light to everyone" refers "not to inward illumination but to the exposure that comes when light is shed upon something," for example, the fact that someone is already sinful or righteous.[3] Matthew Barrett explains that two other possible interpretations contradict the Arminian doctrine of prevenient grace: The first is that the passage describes general, creational revelation, which Barrett correctly excludes because Christ's enlightening—not creation's—is the focus of the text. The second is that the verse refers to "all without distinction rather than all without exception"—essentially the way five-point Calvinists handle most "all" passages when it relates to universal grace.[4]

As B. F. Westcott said, the words *phōtizei panta anthrōpon* (enlightens every person) "must be taken simply as they stand," to describe "the universal extent of [the Light's] action."[5] Furthermore, the natural context and flow of John 1:9 rule out readings that say Christ's enlightening power has nothing to do with salvation. Such readings must be forced onto the flow of the passage, which is not describing Christ's illumination of everyone just for the purpose of judgment and condemnation, as some Calvinists hold.[6]

Rather, the text in context presents Christ in his totality, the "Light" and the "Life"—or "the Light of Life," as Jesus refers to himself in John 8:12—who is communicating his light and life directly, to everyone, who, as Grant Osborne avers, "illuminates 'every person,' culminating the theme from verses 4 and 7 on the universal convicting power of God."[7] As the Lutheran commentator E. W. Hengstenberg explained, "So here life and light are that

---

Rapids: Baker, 2000), 241. In this chapter I respond mainly to Schreiner's essay because it is the most significant modern critique of the Arminian doctrine of prevenient grace, and other scholars such as Matthew Barrett and William Combs rely heavily on it. See Matthew Barrett, *Salvation by Grace: The Case for Effectual Calling and Regeneration* (Phillipsburg, NJ: P&R, 2013).

3.   Schreiner, "Does Scripture Teach Prevenient Grace," 240.

4.   Barrett states that he relies on Schreiner's chapter and agrees with his interpretations of John 1:9 and 12:32 (*Salvation by Grace*, 253).

5.   Brooke Foss Westcott, *The Gospel according to St. John* (London: John Murray, 1908), 1:13–14.

6.   See G. R. Beasley-Murray, *John*, Word Biblical Commentary (Waco, TX: Word, 1987), 12, who supports this assertion.

7.   Grant R. Osborne, *John Verse by Verse* (Bellingham, WA: Lexham, 2017), 30; Westcott, 14.

which exists in the Logos for the whole human race." The Light is "the designation of salvation and the Saviour."[8]

Westcott stressed that John 1:9 is the description of a relationship that is not merely "collective, corporate," but "personal, and universal while personal." This is the eternal Word as "the spiritual Sun" enlightening everyone with his spiritual grace. It is a "special personal manifestation of the Light" to everyone. It is Christ's own light and life and the personal, spiritual possibilities that come with them.[9] Hengstenberg correctly averred that "Light" in John 1 is "according to the common *usus loquendi* of Scripture, a figurative designation of *salvation*."[10] This beautiful gospel metaphor cannot be reduced to mere exposure of everyone's current spiritual state. That is a horribly forced reading of the text.

Quite simply, verses 4–5 say that Christ is the life and light of men. Verses 6–8 explain that John the Baptist came to bear witness to that light *so that everyone might believe*. Then verse 9 says that this light of men, to whom John bore witness so that everyone might believe, *gives everyone his light*. Verses 10–11 continue this idea that Jesus *really is* giving everyone his light so that everyone might believe: Neither the world nor his own people tended to believe and receive him, but everyone who does can be God's child. This whole line of thought implores the reader to understand that Jesus is the Light that draws people to his Life—to salvation, to belief, to receiving Jesus—and his light goes out to everyone. Interpretations that claim that when Jesus gives his light to everyone, it is only general revelation or only shining a light on people's sinfulness but is not in any way a *saving* light, the light *of life*, place a strain on the text that it cannot bear.[11]

In contrast, F. F. Bruce states that

> the illumination that the Evangelist has primarily in mind is that spiritual illumination which dispels the darkness of sin and unbelief; and it was by coming into the world that the true light provided this supreme illumination—and provided it for all mankind. He is the light "which enlightens every human being" in the sense that the illumination which he has brought is for all without distinction. True, there are those who refuse to come to the light (cf. John 3:19f.). If they remain in darkness, it is not because there is no illumination

---

8. E. W. Hengstenberg, *Commentary on the Gospel of St. John* (Edinburgh: T&T Clark, 1865), 1:30.

9. Westcott, *The Gospel according to St. John*, 14.

10. Hengstenberg, *Commentary on the Gospel of St. John*, 1:28.

11. One of the best descriptions of what is going on in John 1:9 and its immediate context is Frederick Dale Bruner, *The Gospel of John: A Commentary* (Grand Rapids: Eerdmans, 2012), 16–33. See also Osborne, *John Verse by Verse*, 27–32.

for them, but because they deliberately prefer the darkness. Here, then, we have an anticipation of the theme which is elaborated more than once throughout the Gospel—that Jesus is "the light of the world" (8:12; 9:5).[12]

It is not John 1:9 that leads Calvinists to discount universal prevenient grace. It is their doctrine of irresistible grace read into John 1:9. If one has already established that Calvinism is true, there is a need to explain this text in a way that teaches something other than its obvious meaning, but to do so is to engage in eisegesis, to import an alien meaning into the natural drift of the Apostle John's thought.

The consensual exegesis of the Christian tradition is preferable. That interpretation is seen in Chrysostom's beautiful reflection on John 1:9, which epitomizes the consensus reading of the church fathers and nearly every other commentator prior to Calvin:

> If He "lighteth every man that cometh into the world," how is it that so many continue unenlightened? For not all have known the majesty of Christ. How then doth He "light every man"? He lighteth all as far as in Him lies. But if some, wilfully closing the eyes of their mind, would not receive the rays of that Light, their darkness arises not from the nature of the Light, but from their own wickedness, who willfully deprive themselves of the gift. For the grace is shed forth upon all. . . . And those who are not willing to enjoy this gift, ought in justice to impute their blindness to themselves; for if when the gate is opened to all, and there is none to hinder, any being willfully evil remain without, they perish through none other, but only through their own wickedness.[13]

John 12:32

Regarding John 12:32, "And I, when I am lifted up from the earth, will draw all people to myself," as Brian Shelton observes, this passage's canonical context situates it squarely in redemptive history. As Moses "lifted up" the bronze serpent in the wilderness so that "*everyone*" who looked on it would be healed (Num. 21:8), so Jesus will be "lifted up" on the cross (John 3:14). In that lifting up, he will draw "*everyone*" to himself (John 12:32).[14] It is natural

---

12. F. F. Bruce, *The Gospel of John* (Grand Rapids: Eerdmans, 1983), 36.
13. John Chrysostom, *Homilies on the Gospel of St. John* in *A Select Library of the Nicene and Post-Nicene Fathers*, ed. Philip Schaff (New York: Charles Scribner's Sons, 1906), 14:29.
14. W. Brian Shelton, *Prevenient Grace: God's Provision for Fallen Humanity* (Anderson, IN: Francis Asbury, 2015), 39.

to infer a universal drawing from John, based on what he has already quoted Jesus as saying about his being lifted up like the serpent so everyone can be healed, and then saying that he, the one lifted up like that serpent, will draw everyone.

Barrett's main argument regarding John 12:32 is that the passage cannot have that straightforward meaning, because it "would contradict what Jesus said earlier in John 6:37" and other texts he has already stated teach irresistible grace. Like other Calvinists, he says that 12:32 is talking about ethnic (Jew-Gentile) diversity, so that it is all *kinds* of people that are being drawn to Jesus, rather than everyone.[15] Calvinists argue that evidence for this assertion exists in the fact that, as Demarest argues, "Jesus' audience included not only Jews but 'some Greeks' (v. 20) or non-proselyte Gentiles."[16]

However, Westcott rightly states that "all men" "must not be limited in any way. It cannot mean merely 'Gentiles as well as Jews,' or 'the elect,' or 'all who believe.' We must receive it as it stands: Rom. 5:18 (8:32); 2 Cor. 5:15; (Eph. 1:10); 1 Tim. 2:6; Hebr. 2:9; 1 John 2:2."[17] As Frederick Dale Bruner argues, "all people," the "Greek masculine-plural single-word *pantas*," is most naturally translated in modern English by the word "everyone." He correctly states, "Jesus' *universal* drawing, we notice all too well, continues to be widely resisted in many places to this day. Nevertheless, Jesus' drawing '*all*' must be allowed to be a real all (not, e.g., an 'all *kinds* but not all *persons*' all. . . .)."[18]

Hengstenberg was right when he said that "the drawing power" in John 12:32 "exists for *all*: unbelief is the only thing which can exclude from this glorious benefit, John 3:15–16." He explained that "the main point" of verse 32 is "the drawing of the Holy Spirit, who was to be obtained by the atoning death of our Lord, and who reveals to the heart the meaning of that death (cf. 7:39). John 6:44 alludes to an internal attractive power, and in 16:8 Christ says that He would exercise, through the Holy Ghost, the power here described."[19]

Albrecht Oepke explains that John 12:32 refers, not to an irresistible, particular "force or magic," but to the "supernatural power of the love of God or Christ which goes out to all (12:32) but without which no one can come (6:44). The apparent contradiction shows that both the election and

15. Barrett, *Salvation by Grace*, 255. See also Robert A. Peterson and Michael D. Williams, *Why I Am Not An Arminian* (Downers Grove, IL: InterVarsity, 2004), 166–67.

16. Demarest, *The Cross and Salvation*, 83. See Shelton's helpful rebuttal to this in *Prevenient Grace*, 41–44.

17. B. F. Westcott, *The Gospel according to St. John* (London: John Murray, 1889), 183. Lenski agrees, stating that "all are alike drawn, but by their perverse obduracy many nullify all the power of grace and harden themselves in unbelief." *The Interpretation of St. John's Gospel* (Minneapolis: Augsburg, 1961), 876.

18. Bruner, *The Gospel of John*, 719; James M. Leonard, "The Universality of Jesus' Drawing All to Him (John 12:32)," http://evangelicalarminians.org/the-universality-of-jesus-drawing-all-to-him-john-12-32, accessed May 7, 2020.

19. Hengstenberg, *Commentary on the Gospel of St. John*, 2:118 (italics in the original).

the universality of grace must be taken seriously; the compulsion is not automatic."[20] This brings to mind Hosea 11:4, which says that God drew Israel "with gentle cords and bands of love," with many modern translations rendering the Hebrew word *mashak* ("drew") as "led," indicating a loving, gentle leading of a personal being.

Leroy Forlines is correct when he says that, to interpret John 12:32 as Calvinism does, one "must first find a passage elsewhere that irrefutably teaches that there is such an irresistible drawing" and import it into the text.[21] In essence, Schreiner's exegetical critique of the Arminian doctrine of prevenient grace, in the primary Calvinist response to the doctrine in modern times, does just that. He simply asserts that irresistible grace is true and reinterprets two texts from the Gospel of John—1:9 and 12:32—to wrest them into the service of the doctrine of irresistible grace. While Calvinists sometimes ridicule the lack of exegesis Arminians use to establish the Arminian doctrine of universal prevenient grace, they do not refute it by exegesis of John 1:9 and 12:32. Instead, they essentially assert that these texts cannot be interpreted as Arminians interpret them because the doctrine of irresistible grace is true, and that doctrine contradicts the natural reading. One sees this in the next response Calvinists make to universal prevenient grace.

Calvinism's Performative Contradiction

Schreiner's third response is to the Arminian's contention that God would be unjust in commanding people to repent and damning them for not doing so, if he did not give them grace to repent and believe.[22] Schreiner responds to what he sees as the "most powerful" Arminian argument for prevenient grace: "Why would God give commands unless people were given some ability to obey them? Romans 2:4 says that his kindness is intended to lead people to repentance. Does this not imply that people have the ability to repent if they would only choose to do so?" Schreiner's answer is no.[23]

Arminians think Calvinists make God guilty of a "performative contradiction," which philosophers say occurs when a person's actions defy his or her words (e.g., a young man saying, "I want you to marry me" to a young

---

20. Albrecht Oepke, "*Hélkō*," in *Theological Dictionary of the New Testament*, abridged in one volume, eds. Gerhard Kittel and Gerhard Friedrich (Grand Rapids: Eerdmans, 1985), 227.

21. F. Leroy Forlines, *Classical Arminianism: A Theology of Salvation* (Nashville: Randall House, 2011), 160.

22. Schreiner deals with this under two topics: (1) God commanding people to repent and believe without giving them the grace to do so and (2) God's "justice, wisdom, mercy, and love." I am collapsing these two into one category here.

23. Schreiner, "Does Scripture Teach Prevenient Grace," 242. See Shelton's incisive comments on Romans 2:4 as evidence for the Arminian doctrine of prevenient grace (47–51).

woman he knows he will never marry).[24] Schreiner's answer to this is simply to say that "even though their logic is impeccable, it does not necessarily follow that their conclusion is true." He boldly says that Arminians "are incorrect in deducing that God would give commands without giving the moral ability to obey them." Schreiner gets right to the heart of the matter here.[25]

What is his response? He argues that human beings are "physically" capable of fulfilling God's command to repent and believe but not morally capable. Human beings should "keep his commandments because they are right and good and are not physically impossible to keep." Schreiner acknowledges that "all people are summoned to believe in Jesus and are censured for not believing. Nonetheless, the Scriptures also teach that they have no moral ability to believe, and the only way they will believe is if they are given by the father to the son." He concludes that the Arminian doctrine of prevenient grace is "guided by human logic and rationality rather than the Scriptures." The doctrine is "attractive because it neatly solves, to some extent, issues such as the problem of evil and why human beings are held responsible for their sin. But the Scriptures do not yield such neat solutions."[26]

Echoing Schreiner, Barrett states: "The gospel call is seriously meant regardless of the fact that man cannot fulfill it. It is objected that since sinners do not have the ability to believe (due to depravity), a gospel call cannot be genuinely offered."[27] That is not technically accurate. The objection should have been stated like this: "It is objected that since depraved sinners do not have the ability to believe *because God is withholding the grace necessary for them to do so*, a gospel call cannot be genuinely offered." Either way, Barrett's assertion entails a performative contradiction.

What if a teenage child had been born unable to walk and his or her parent refused to provide a wheelchair but said, "Come over here and take this pen from me. If you don't, I'll punish you for refusing, and the more I call and plead and command you to, and the more you resist my repeated calls and pleadings and commands, the more severely I'll punish you." Then what if the next day the parent went up to the child, begged again, then tenderly wept and lamented that the child would not fulfill the command, knowing full well that he or she was purposefully withholding the ability for the child to do so? This would be as unjust as it would be if God did it, based on the divine standard of justice outlined in Holy Scripture.

Still, Schreiner cites Romans 2:4, "God's kindness is meant to lead you to repentance," and remarks that "God's kindness is not a charade but is

---

24. Dermot Moran, ed., *The Routledge Companion to Twentieth Century Philosophy* (London: Routledge, 2008), 98. I have enjoyed my conversations with my colleague Richard E. Clark on this issue.
25. Schreiner, "Does Scripture Teach Prevenient Grace," 243.
26. Schreiner, "Does Scripture Teach Prevenient Grace," 245.
27. Barrett, *Salvation by Grace*, 77.

profoundly present." The Arminian wonders, how is God's kindness to those for whom he has purposefully set it up so that they will be unredeemable not a charade when he is holding out his hand pleading for them to repent? He gives us the answer: "God's kindness is not a charade but is profoundly present *in that he spares people and does not immediately destroy them for their sin. . . .* God is merciful and loving in not destroying [the reprobate] immediately and offering them salvation."[28]

That kindness, as Schreiner defines it, however, is precisely *not* intended to lead the reprobate to repentance. If the kindness's only purpose is to stave off one's destruction, which God's plan for that individual guarantees, how can it be said to be intended to *lead* the individual to *repent*? It is interesting that Schreiner is not disagreeing with Arminians that God's kindness and mercy are seen in the fact that he *offers salvation to reprobates.* But how is it *not* a charade, if God is holding out the hope of salvation to people whom he, by his careful design, is purposefully depriving of his grace?

The Arminian argument regarding this performative contradiction in Calvinism is not a matter of logic over Scripture. The plainest thrust of the Bible, the very heart of God's revelation, is the pleading God is doing in his sincere, free offer of salvation to everyone, elect and reprobate alike. So Calvinism's performative contradiction is not just a logical problem. It is a theological problem, a biblical problem. It requires that Calvinists unintentionally go against the heart of the good news Christ is freely holding out as the only hope for sinners.[29]

Summary

In the end, what Schreiner's argument against the Arminian doctrine of universal prevenient grace amounts to is this: he asserts that the plain reading of texts like John 1:9 and 12:32—the consensual reading of the universal church prior to Calvin—cannot be true because he has already argued that the doctrine of irresistible grace is true. (I am not criticizing his motives. Everyone has to make sense of Scripture the best way he or she can.) Then he simply asserts that the doctrine of universal prevenient grace is logically compelling but unscriptural because the Bible clearly teaches the doctrine of irresistible grace or effectual calling, which will be taken up in the following chapters.

---

28. Schreiner, "Does Scripture Teach Prevenient Grace," 244 (italics added).

29. I say "unintentionally" here because I do not mean to impugn the motives of many of my dear brothers and sisters who are Calvinists whose evangelistic and missionary heart is unmistakable (although I have other dear Primitive Baptist brothers and sisters who are Hyper-Calvinists and do not affirm the free offer of the gospel).

REFLECTION QUESTIONS

1. How do some Calvinists misunderstand the Arminian doctrine of prevenient grace?

2. Read John 1:1–11. Is Jesus's discussion of being the Light and Life who brings people salvation also being talked about in John 1:9 when he says he is giving that Light to everyone, or is it a different kind of light?

3. Why does Chrysostom think many people remain in darkness despite Jesus's light shining on them?

4. Read John 3:14 and 12:32. How do these verses relate, and what does the illustration of the bronze serpent being lifted up say about Jesus's being lifted up on the cross and how that provides spiritual healing to anyone who "looks"?

5. What is meant by the term "performative contradiction," and why do Arminians think Calvinism commits this fallacy?

What Do Arminians Believe About the Doctrine of Irresistible Grace?

This question lies at the heart of the disagreement between Calvinists and the rest of the Christian tradition. It boils down to a few basic dilemmas about God's salvific will as revealed in Holy Scripture. How individuals deal with these basic dilemmas colors the way they interpret the rest of Scripture. One might call the ways people deal with these dilemmas "controlling beliefs." This chapter will begin with a discussion of two of the most basic controlling beliefs regarding whether salvific grace is resistible or irresistible.

"Controlling Beliefs"

For most Christians, the controlling belief about God's salvific intent has been that God is holding out his hand to people, beckoning them to come to him, indeed commanding them to come, and he is weeping over them because they are digging in their heels and refusing his repeated entreaties and wooings. He is saying that he has done all he can to draw them to himself, but they will not come, and thus he will laugh at their calamity because of their resistance, and their punishment will be enlarged.[1]

Most Christians have historically seen this common-sense, phenomenal call from the Spirit as the basic gospel thrust of Scripture. Believing what the Bible teaches about the sincerity and truthfulness of God, they cannot believe that he would look people in the eye with an outstretched hand and beckon them to come and enlarge their punishment for refusing to do so, when he

---

1. The exegetical evidence for this argument will be discussed in the next chapter. See the Anglican Daniel Whitby's book *A Discourse Concerning the True Import of the Words Election and Reprobation* (London: John Wyat, 1710), 231–67. See also Steve W. Lemke, "A Biblical and Theological Critique of Irresistible Grace," in *Whosoever Will: A Biblical-Theological Critique of Five-Point Calvinism*, eds. David L. Allen and Steve W. Lemke (Nashville: B&H Academic, 2010), 117–29.

has meticulously arranged the universe in such a way that they never can because he has refused to give them the grace to do so. Thus when this picture is painted for most Christians, they recoil at it. It seems to them to go against the most basic teachings of Scripture about God's will and justice and character and good news.

However, when this same picture is painted for Calvinists, it does not seem to bother them. So what is their most basic "controlling belief" regarding the irresistibility of grace? For most, it seems to be that for God to give his enabling grace to two people—one who will resist it and the other who will not—presents a conundrum: Why does one person resist and the other person not resist? The only answer for Calvinists seems to be that the one who does not resist has something inherently good about himself or herself that the one who resists does not. This, they argue, contradicts the clear teaching of Scripture that we have nothing to boast about in our salvation. This is one of the main issues that drive Calvinists to be Calvinists.

As I once explained to my seventeen-year-old son who was asking about this, "You have to 'pick your poison,' because either system has mysteries that cannot be solved by the rational mind." So I told him, "You have to decide which mystery the Bible and its gospel thrust will let you live with:

> (Mystery 1) Would God be unjust and inglorious and hypocritical in stretching out his hand, beckoning people to come to him, when he has carefully arranged their personal universe to see to it that they never will?
>
> or
>
> (Mystery 2) Would one person's resisting God's grace and the other person's not, if both were given grace, make the latter 'better' or more meritorious than the former, giving the individual something to boast about salvifically?[2]

These are mysteries that you will not solve this side of eternity." Calvinists have chosen to live with the first mystery, Arminians with the second.[3]

---

2. Many non-Calvinists argue that Calvinism gives the elect the right to boast because they are one of the chosen few, as opposed to the mass of humanity, whom God did not deign to give an opportunity. See Leighton Flowers, "Answering Calvinism's Most Popular Argument," https://soteriology101.com/2016/08/11/answering-calvinists-1-argument/#_ftn6, accessed May 13, 2020.

3. Still, Arminius represents most Arminians who do not really believe this is a mystery, since, as he argues, most people would not see a starving beggar's passively receiving bread from a rich man as meritorious in any way (Jacobus Arminius, *The Works of James Arminius*,

I went on to tell him: "There are two kinds of people. Ask people, based on their reading of the Bible, what they would think about a God who says he is doing everything he can to get the reprobate to come to him, lamenting their refusal, and making hell hotter for them because of it, when he painstakingly designed it all this way so that they would refuse. The first kind of person reacts in horror. The second kind says, 'Sure. I can see that.'" Based on the overwhelming thrust in Scripture of the free offer of the gospel and its consistency with the secret-and-revealed gracious desire of God to save every individual, I cast my lot with the Arminians (and Lutherans and all other non-Calvinist Christians).

Arminians, with Arminius, have soundly denied the semi-Pelagian maxim *Facientibus quod in se est Deus non denegat gratiam*—God will not deny his grace to those who do what is in them.[4] Arminianism believes that divine grace is necessary at every step of the way to enable anyone to be saved, but this grace can be resisted by people to whom God gives it. Yet Arminians *do not go beyond Scripture and speculate about why some who receive this grace resist and others do not.*

They simply say: "Holy Scripture is *very clear* that God is sincerely calling and commanding everyone to repent and believe the gospel by his grace. *What is not clear* is why some people resist and others do not, and we will not go beyond the Bible and speculate about why that is. We cannot allow our speculations about this to overthrow the gospel thrust of redemptive history writ large across the pages of Scripture."

Of course, most Calvinists, who are infralapsarians, encounter the same mystery regarding why Adam and Eve chose to sin or why sin entered into the world. Their answer is simply, "I don't know. Nor have I found anyone yet who does know" (Sproul) or "the Bible does not tell us" (Piper). That is, they are appealing to mystery on a very similar question.[5]

Irresistible Grace in Calvinism

The dilemma of why some resist and others do not is perhaps the central controlling question for the Calvinist approach to Scripture, not the dilemma of why God calls people whom he has every intention of leaving outside the

---

3 vols. Trans. James Nichols and William Nichols [Nashville: Randall House, 2007], 2:52, "Apology against Thirty-One Defamatory Articles," art. 27).

4. Heiko A. Oberman, "*Facientibus quod in se est Deus non denegat Gratiam*: Robert Holcot, O.P. and the Beginnings of Luther's Theology," *The Harvard Theological Review* 55 (1962): 317–42. Arminius decisively responds to the allegation that he is teaching that "God will not deny his grace to any one who does what is in him" in his "Apology against Thirty-One Defamatory Articles," *Works*, 2:19.

5. R. C. Sproul, *Chosen by God* (Wheaton, IL: Tyndale, 2005), 31; John Piper, "The Hardening of Pharaoh and the Hope of the World," https://www.desiringgod.org/messages/the-hardening-of-pharaoh-and-the-hope-of-the-world, accessed May 13, 2020.

reach of his grace and damning for eternity. Thus Calvinism has taught that the grace of God that draws people toward salvation is irresistible. This most fully accords with a deterministic understanding (whether hard determinist or soft determinist/compatibilist) of the sovereignty of God, in which God's sovereignty infallibly causes all effects. Thus there can be no human element of resistance to God's omnipotence. In this view God calls all people externally, yet internally he calls only the elect. This secret calling cannot be resisted.

Calvin explained the reason: "Good takes its origin from God alone. And only in the elect does one find a will inclined to good." Since humanity is "by nature inclined to evil with our whole heart," the only way we can "begin to will good" is "out of mere grace." Good cannot arise from the human will "until it has been reformed; and after its reformation, in so far as it is good, it is so from God, not from ourselves" (*Institutes*, 2.3.8).

Calvin acknowledged that "God's loving-kindness is set forth to all who seek it, without exception." However, the only ones who seek it are "those on whom heavenly grace has breathed." In this way they cannot "claim for themselves the slightest part of his praise." When God regenerates the elect, their wills are "moved and governed" irresistibly by him. God "does not move the will in such a manner, as has been taught and believed for many ages—that it is afterward in our choice either to obey or resist the motion—but by disposing it efficaciously" (*Institutes*, 2.3.10).

Cause and Effect, Influence and Response

What Arminians have found striking about statements like these is what seems to them to be Calvin's mechanical view of the way God operates. This mechanical approach predisposes Calvin to downplay, almost to ignore, the scriptural motifs that portray God's grace as persuasive. Thus Calvin sidesteps the way Scripture has led most Christians to think of grace as God's entering into relational interactions with persons he has created in his image as people who think, feel, and make free choices. Thus, as Arminians such as Leroy Forlines have taught, Calvin skirts the side of Scripture that portrays grace as what Forlines calls "influence and response." Instead, Calvin approaches the divine relationship mechanistically, in a wooden, "cause and effect" manner. As Forlines says,

> A person is one who thinks with his mind, feels with his heart, and acts with his will. In the simple sense of the terms cause and effect, one person cannot cause another person to do anything. This does not depend upon the lack of ability that one person has to influence another. Rather, the inability of one person to cause another person to do something grows out of the nature of what it means to be a person. . . . Calvinism's approach to irresistible grace (or effectual call)

sounds more like cause and effect than influence and response. When the appropriate time comes with regard to the
elect, God regenerates him or her. As a regenerated person,
he or she is *caused* by God to have faith in Jesus Christ as Lord
and Savior. . . . The possibility of a negative response does not
exist. It was a guaranteed response. The fact that it was guaranteed makes the terms cause and effect appropriate.[6]

The Lutheran theologian Samuel Sprecher agreed with the influence-and-
response model. Irresistible grace, he argued, "reduces the divine power to
a mere physical force—an omnipotence in the negative sense of being un-
controlled by any other force." This robs God of "his personality," making his
power "like a blind nature-force, which must go out into all the effects for
which it is cause." Sprecher argued that this is inconsistent with the biblical
portrait of God as interpreted by the Reformation, with its emphasis on personal communion with God through justifying faith. Instead, the Bible presents a "personal" God, "self-controlling and self-limiting in the creation and
government of his creatures." His power "operates on its creatures" as "peculiar personal beings," accommodating itself to "the receptivity of the human
spirit; and whose glory, as Luther says, is in condescending love."[7]

In C. S. Lewis's *The Screwtape Letters*, the head devil Wormwood decries
the way God relates to human beings: "The Irresistible and Indisputable are
two weapons which the very nature of [God's] scheme forbids Him to use.
Merely to override a human will . . . would be for Him useless. He cannot
ravish. He can only woo. For his ignoble idea is to eat the cake and have it; the
creatures are to be one with Him, but yet themselves; merely to cancel them,
or assimilate them, will not serve."[8]

In the language Calvin used above, however, the cause-and-effect dynamics
obscure those personal, relational dynamics that pervade Holy Scripture and
the Christian tradition. Calvin is very wooden and matter-of-fact. He defines
grace as simply that which takes evil people and makes them good—by fiat. It
is plain common sense to Calvin: Evil people cannot make themselves good.
A good person has to make them good. Only God is good. So God must
simply make them good by sheer omnipotence. God must determine by fiat
that their wills *will be made* good. It is as simple as that.

---

6. F. Leroy Forlines, *Classical Arminianism: A Theology of Salvation* (Nashville: Randall
House, 2011), 50 (italics added).
7. Samuel Sprecher, *The Groundwork of a System of Evangelical Lutheran Theology*
(Philadelphia: Lutheran Publication Society, 1879), 395–96. Pages 390–410 of Sprecher's
book are must-reading for those wanting to understand the influence-and-response model
of grace.
8. C. S. Lewis, *The Screwtape Letters* (New York: Macmillan, 1961), 128.

One can imagine how wooden that seems to Christians outside the Calvinist orbit. Christians throughout the ages were unaccustomed to speaking of grace so unabashedly in this cause-and-effect way, whatever their view of the mystery of election might have been. Calvin strikes out and does something new in the history of Christianity (with the exception of a few like Gottschalk of Orbais, Thomas Bradwardine, and Gregory of Rimini).[9] He is brazen in what strikes non-Calvinists as a profoundly impersonal approach to grace and how it simply *causes* persons to be changed into something—with little attention to the personal and relational categories that pervade the pages of Scripture. Grace, in this view, must be omnipotent, irresistible. It simply cannot involve a relational dynamic between God and persons he has created who think, feel, and make genuine choices.

Arminius on Influence and Response

One clearly sees in the theology of Arminius what Forlines calls the influence-and-response model of divine grace. Questions 16 and 20 considered Arminius's distinction between necessity (things that must occur) and contingency (things that could go more than one way). He said that Calvinism entails that things that, from the human side, are "done contingently" are, from the divine side, "done necessarily." However, he said. "No contingent thing—that is, nothing which is done or has been done CONTINGENTLY—can be said to be or have been done NECESSARILY."[10]

Arminius stressed that an event's necessity belongs to God's "omnipotent and irresistible action." Salvation in the Bible is not by necessity. Rather, God "has determined to save believers by grace, that is, by gentle and sweet persuasion, fitting or congruous to their own free will; not by almighty action or motion, which they neither will nor can resist, nor can will to resist."[11] Arminius often used the language of "suasion" or "persuasion" to describe the operation of divine grace. God's "special grace," which is necessary for individuals to come to faith and "moves, excites, impels and urges to obey" operates by "the mode of suasion." It "concurs" with the "the will of man" and "is not denied to him to whom exciting grace is applied, unless the man offers resistance to the grace exciting."[12]

God works with sinners as persons created in his image, who have intellect, emotions, and will, not as impersonal things that can be moved about by omnipotent and irresistible action. "For a large mass is moved naturally and necessarily by the application of force exceeding its gravity; but we men

---

9. Augustine sometimes sounds like this but on the whole is more mysterious in his presentation of prevenient grace, even in his later years.
10. Arminius, *Works*, 1:755. "Apology against Thirty-One Defamatory Articles" (italics added).
11. Arminius, *Works*, 3:443. "Examination of Perkins's Pamphlet."
12. Arminius, *Works*, 2:451, Private Disputation 70, "On Obedience to the Commands of God in General."

are moved according to the mode of liberty, with which God has endued the will, whence it is called 'free will.'"[13] Again, Arminius did not believe that humanity's will is free in the sense that it can naturally counteract depravity. Divine grace is necessary to do this. However, the Calvinist view of grace that requires God to draw someone irresistibly to himself, as occurs with physical objects, violates the picture the Bible paints of divine-human relations as influence and response.

No one can come to the Father unless the Spirit draws him (John 6:44), but that drawing of the Spirit is not infallible, inflexible, or irresistible. These are concepts that would apply to inanimate matter—a hammer to a nail—not to a personal being God has created in his image who thinks, feels, and makes meaningful choices, whom God has created for a relationship with himself.[14] With this concept, Arminius says, he "by no means" does

> injustice to grace, by attributing, as it is reported of me, too much to man's free-will. For the whole controversy reduces itself to the solution of this question, "is the grace of God a certain irresistible force?" That is, the controversy does not relate to those actions or operations which may be ascribed to grace, (for I acknowledge and inculcate as many of these actions or operations as any man ever did,) but it relates solely to the mode of operation, whether it be irresistible or not. With respect to which, I believe, according to the scriptures, that many persons resist the Holy Spirit and reject the grace that is offered.[15]

Summary

Scripture does not reveal the mystery of why some whom God draws with his grace resist and others do not. Yet it consistently presents a God who is genuinely reaching out for people to come to him and lamenting that they resist and reject his gracious calling. Scripture throughout paints a picture of a personal God who has created personal beings who think, feel, and make authentic choices. Grace is a personal dynamic between two personal beings, not a cause-and-effect relationship between a personal being and a physical object. The Bible does not portray grace woodenly as a thing, a force. Rather, it is a "sweet persuasion" aimed at people created in the image of a personal God.

---

13. Arminius, *Works*, 3:473, "Examination of Perkins's Pamphlet."
14. Arminius, *Works*, 3:473.
15. Arminius, *Works*, 3:473.

REFLECTION QUESTIONS

1. How do the two main "controlling beliefs" of Calvinism and Arminianism, and the mysteries to which they appeal, influence the respective groups' doctrines of the resistibility or irresistibility of grace?

2. Why do you think Arminians think of Calvin's view of irresistible grace as "wooden" or "mechanical"?

3. Compare and contrast the cause-and-effect and influence-and-response models of grace. Toward which of these do you think God's gospel invitations in Scripture tend?

4. How does one's concept of whether there is any contingency in the universe (whether things could have gone a different way based on individual human decisions) affect the question of the resistibility versus irresistibility of grace?

5. How does what people believe about being a person created in the image of a personal God affect what they believe about the question of cause-and-effect and influence-and-response?

Does the Bible Teach That People Can Resist God's Grace?

Arminians rely on host of passage throughout Scripture to support the doctrine of the resistibility of divine grace. They appeal to texts throughout the Old and New Testaments that teach that God reaches out to people with his grace again and again and that the only reason people do not come to him is solely their resistance to his gracious overtures, not his eternal plan for them.

Jesus's Desire Expressed in Matthew 23:37

Matthew 23:37 (cf. Luke 13:34) is one of the primary proof texts for the Arminian doctrine of resistible grace. Jesus says, "O Jerusalem, Jerusalem, the city that kills the prophets and stones those who are sent to it! How often would I have gathered your children together as a hen gathers her brood under her wings, and you were not willing!" This text shows that Jesus was sincerely and graciously calling people to be his own, and the sole reason they did not become his own is that they were not willing, and he is lamenting, weeping over it. That is what God is doing in prevenient grace: calling, convicting, wooing, persuading, enabling people to be his own, but maintaining their freedom to resist his grace. As Steve Lemke correctly argues, the Greek verb *thelō* (to will) is used twice in the verse: "I willed . . . but you were not willing." Jesus is not referring only to the elect within Jerusalem but for all Jerusalem over many generations. Thus Jesus's will (*thelōs*) is for all the children of Jerusalem to come to him, yet they frustrate his will and do not come for one reason: their will (*thelōs*). Thus the reason they do not come is not the divine will but their own.[1]

---

1. Steve W. Lemke, "A Biblical and Theological Critique of Irresistible Grace," in *Whosoever Will: A Biblical-Theological Critique of Five-Point Calvinism*, eds. David L. Allen and Steve W. Lemke (Nashville: B&H Academic, 2010), 119–20.

This is a difficult passage for advocates of irresistible grace. Jesus is putting on display his fervent love for these unbelieving Jews, which is as deep as that of a mother hen who earnestly desires what is best for her chicks. He uses this image, says Theophylact, "to show his affection."[2] When an animal comes to prey on them, she gathers them under her wings to protect them. Likewise, Jesus wants to gather these unbelieving Jews under his wings in the same way, to protect them, as Luther said, from the "devil in the air" who wishes to prey on them.[3]

Jesus is *willing* for them to be under his wings, to be his own children. It is they who are *unwilling*. So there is nothing he can do about it, based on his plan of redemption for his free creatures. His weeping "represents a true lament," as Keener argues. "Jesus' love for Jerusalem here gives way to the broken-hearted pain of their rejection."[4] The fact that they are not under his wings is to blame, not on his unwillingness, but on their unwillingness. He comes to them again and again, as is seen in the phrase "how often." And they, again and again, are unwilling to be gathered under his wings to be sheltered from the evil one. The Scottish preacher William Barclay encapsulated the plain meaning of these verses when he said, "Nothing hurts so much as to go to someone and offer love and have that offer spurned. It is life's bitterest tragedy to give one's heart to someone only to have it broken. That is what happened to Jesus in Jerusalem; and still he comes to men, and still men reject him."[5]

Most Christians, Arminians among them, believe that the concept of irresistible grace makes God blameworthy for the reprobate's not being under Jesus's wings.[6] It is thus "disparaging to the glory of God."[7] Yet Arminians

---

2.   Theophylact of Ochrid, *The Explanation of the Holy Gospel According to St. Matthew* http://www.holytrinitymission.org/books/english/matthew_theophilactos.htm#_Toc67666099. Cf. Chryostom, *Homilies of S. John Chrysostom on the Gospel of St. Matthew* (Oxford: John Henry Parker, 1851), 3:987.

3.   *Luther's Explanatory Notes on the Gospels*, ed. E. Mueller, trans. P. Anstadt (York, PA: P. Anstadt and Sons, 1899), 134.

4.   Craig S. Keener, *Matthew*, IVP New Testament Commentary (Downers Grove, IL: InterVarsity, 1997), 341; idem, *The Historical Jesus of the Gospels* (Grand Rapids: Eerdmans, 2009), 237.

5.   William Barclay, *The Gospel of Luke* (Philadelphia: Westminster, 1975), 186.

6.   This is indicated by the confessional standards of most of the world's Christian denominations, such as Lutheran, Wesleyan, Arminian, Catholic, Orthodox, Anabaptist, and Stone-Campbell Restorationist. Conservative Presbyterian and Reformed denominations explicitly affirm irresistible grace, while the Anglican Communion and most Baptist denominations have advocates of both resistible and irresistible grace within their membership. See Roger E. Olson, Frank S. Mead, et al., *Handbook of Denominations in the United States*, 14th ed. (Nashville: Abingdon, 2018).

7.   August Pfeiffer, *Anti-Calvinism*, trans. Edward Pfeiffer (Columbus, OH: Joint Lutheran Synod of Ohio, 1881), 244.

insist that human beings, in their resistance to the grace Jesus is offering, are solely to blame for their not being under his wings.

The Lutheran dogmatician August Pfeiffer was right when he asked, "If Christ should explain His meaning to be that He had often made mere verbal pretenses and commanded them to repent, but that His hearty will and decree was not to have this actually accomplished in them, who could imagine it to be the true and faithful Saviour speaking thus?" This leads one to "consider the attested commiseration hypocrisy, and the tears to be feigned, since in this case the Saviour's words and heart would not agree, as His mouth would be speaking of love and truth, while His heart would be harboring hatred and destruction." How could the incarnate God say he wanted to gather people together but could not do so because they were not willing, but at the same time, "according to the true purpose of His heart He should have said, You would not come when I called you outwardly, for it was never my earnest will truly to gather you together, to work faith and conversion in you, or to prosper you in every good work?"[8]

Thus Thomas Helwys exclaimed: "What impiety is this to account these words feigned, and if any shall say they do not account them feigned, then must they be forced to confess that God would have had all Israel and all their posterity [saved]. . . . And yet they that hold this fearful opinion hold that God would not have some men, yea the most men, to believe, but hath decreed their condemnation."[9]

Calvinists have dealt with this objection in a few ways, engaging in what Pfeiffer called a "number of wonderful and absurd distinctions."[10] One of these is between the revealed and secret wills of God.[11] Thus Jesus is portrayed as both (1) sincerely desiring that the reprobate be his and begging them to be and weeping because they are unwilling to be and (2) being pleased, calculatedly and purposefully, to deprive them of his grace so that they cannot, of necessity, be his.

This casts doubt on God's justice and hence his glory. It makes his plea look like a pretense, as if Christ is pretending to call and command everyone to repent (Acts 17:30) while in reality it actually pleases him to pass over most

---

8. Pfeiffer, *Anti-Calvinism*, 246–47. Cf. Thomas Oden: "It is contrary to divine sincerity to make an offer that cannot under any circumstances be accepted." Thomas C. Oden, *The Transforming Power of Grace* (Nashville: Abingdon, 1993), 153.

9. Thomas Helwys, *A Short and Plaine Proofe by the Word and Workes of God that Gods decree is not the cause of anye Mans sinne or Condemnation* (London, 1611), sig. B2r; repr. in Joe Early, Jr., *The Life and Writings of Thomas Helwys*. Early English Baptist Texts (Macon, GA: Mercer University Press, 2009). For more on Helwys's soteriology, see J. Matthew Pinson, *Arminian and Baptist: Explorations in a Theological Tradition* (Nashville: Randall House, 2016), chapters 3–4.

10. Pfeiffer, *Anti-Calvinism*, 244.

11. See Arminius, *Works*, 3:478–79, "Examination of Perkins's Pamphlet." For more on the secret and revealed wills of God, see Question 12.

of them and deprive them of the grace he knows they need to repent, believe, and be his. Then, when people try to find out why Calvinists believe God is outwardly imploring them to come, and weeping because they will not, they read from Calvin, Jonathan Edwards, John Piper, and other Calvinists that it is so that Christ will be glorified by their damnation, hell will be hotter for them, and their condemnation will be enlarged, all to bring him glory. They believe, as Calvin said, that "since the disposition of all things is in God's hand, since the decision of salvation or of death rests in his power, he so ordains by his plan and will that among men some are born destined for certain death from the womb, who glorify his name by their own destruction" (*Institutes*, 3.23.6). Incidentally, it is curious to note the lack of hymnody in historic hymnals of Calvinistic denominations that would give the elect a way to sing praise to God for the damnation of the reprobate, according to God's good pleasure, in withholding his grace from them.[12]

Calvinist readers need to understand the force this has on non-Calvinists: The Calvinist system has God giving out his gracious invitation and call, his beckoning, to people, but it is not really his grace. Despite what it looks like he is doing in reaching out to them and imploring them to come to him, it is actually his design to damn them and deprive them of the grace necessary for them to cease their resistance. And for this very resistance to his call, he will enlarge their condemnation, he will laugh at their calamity, which he has arranged, for his greater glory, to befall them.[13]

Some Calvinists, such as Theodore Beza, have attempted to handle Matthew 23:37 and Luke 31:34 by distinguishing between Christ's divine and human will: Jesus *in his humanity* desired everyone to whom he preached to come to him. Yet this has Jesus having more compassion in his human nature than he does in his divine nature. Christ would not will something in his human nature that his divine nature had decreed against. That would contradict Jesus's statement, "My doctrine is not mine, but His that sent me" (John 7:16), which he indicated when Philip said, "Lord, show us the father," and he replied, "Have I been with you so long, and you still do not know me, Philip? Whoever has seen me has seen the Father." Arminius called this distinction between the intentions of Jesus and the Father "absurd, and not a fit one for solving the objection. We see, truly, on what weak foundations that opinion rests."[14]

---

12. A study of Hymnary.org shows that Arminians and Lutherans are the ones who write hymns that refer to reprobation (criticizing the Calvinistic doctrine), but, historically, Calvinists do not tend as much to publish hymns praising God for withholding his grace from the nonelect.

13. Because he purposefully foreordains every aspect of their reality, intentionally withholding grace from the reprobate, the effect is the same whether a Calvinist holds single or double predestination.

14. Arminius, *Works*, 3:479–80, "Examination of Perkins's Pamphlet." Beza is discussed by Pfeiffer, 247; for more detail on this, see Pfeiffer, *Anti-Calvinism*, 245–52.

A very few Calvinists, such as John Gill and James White, argue that Jesus is referring only to the Jewish leaders.[15] However, Calvin was right when he said that, while Jesus "principally charges the leaders," he did not "spare the rest, who were all guilty in knowledge and approval and action."[16] After all, the Old Testament prophets did not just prophesy to the leaders, but to "all the people" (Jer. 19:14; Dan. 9:6).

Jesus's desire as expressed in his saying in Matthew 23:37 and Luke 13:34 is simply a continuation of the prophetic witness attested to throughout Holy Scripture. Many passages demonstrate God's genuinely giving his grace to people, knowing that they will resist and reject it and that their resistance and rejection will result in their condemnation. Other authors discuss these passages at length.[17] The remainder of this chapter will consider only a few of the biblical texts that have God lamenting people's resistance to his salvific grace.

Resistible Grace in Redemptive History

Redemptive history is a history of the resistibility of divine grace. One sees this in the Old Testament. From the Pentateuch to the Prophets, God is calling and wooing people who will finally resist him, but text after text make clear that the reason they will not be saved is not his design for them that requires his withholding his grace from them, but their wanton resistance to the grace he has given them.

"My Spirit Will Not Always Strive with Man"

This principle is borne out in Genesis 6:3. The Holy Spirit had been graciously striving with the individuals who vainly knocked on the door of Noah's ark, but the Lord said, "My spirit shall not always strive with man" (KJV). It was too late for them. As seen in Question 14, Jonathan Edwards preached a great deal on this passage to implore people that "there will be last knocks and last calls," that God would not always be knocking at the unbeliever's heart's door but would cease his overtures of grace to the reprobate.[18] Historically, Arminians have often appealed to this text as evidence of the doctrine of resistible, prevenient grace.[19] One can see why: it indicates that

---

15. John Gill, *The Cause of God and Truth* (Philadelphia: William S. Young, 1842), 61; the quotation is from James R. White, *The Potter's Freedom* (Amityville, NY: Calvary, 2000), 238–39.

16. John Calvin, *Commentaries: A Harmony of the Gospels* (Grand Rapids: Eerdmans, 1972), 67.

17. For extensive discussion of these passages, see especially the Anglican theologian Daniel Whitby, *A Discourse Concerning the True Import of the Words Election and Reprobation* (London: John Wyat, 1710), 231–67. See also Pfeiffer, *Anti-Calvinism*, 252–56.

18. Jonathan Edwards, "The Manner in Which the Salvation of the Soul, Is to Be Sought," *The Works of President Edwards*, 4 vols. (New York: Robert Carter and Brothers, 1879), 4:373.

19. Arminius, *Works*, 2:232; Public Disputation 16. The "Articles of Faith" section of the Free Will Baptist Treatise of Faith and Practices alludes to this text when it says, "God desires the salvation of all, the Gospel invites all, the Holy Spirit strives with all, and whosoever

grace is not a "thing given," but a personal interplay between the Spirit and the human person. That gracious influence, however, can be resisted to the point that the Spirit will no longer graciously call the individual.

The hymn "My Spirit Shall Not Always Strive" by Abigail Bradley Hyde, well-known in the nineteenth century and printed in more than two hundred hymnals, artfully summarizes this teaching:

> Say, sinner, hath a voice within
> Oft whisper'd to thy secret soul,
> Urg'd thee to leave the ways of sin,
> And yield thy heart to God's control?
>
> Hath something met thee in the path
> Of worldliness and vanity,
> And pointed to the coming wrath,
> And warn'd thee from that wrath to flee?
>
> Sinner, it was a heavenly voice—
> It was the Spirit's gracious call;
> It bade thee make the better choice,
> And haste to seek in Christ thine all.
>
> Spurn not the call to life and light;
> Regard in time the warning kind;
> That call thou may'st not always slight,
> And yet the gate of mercy find.
>
> God's Spirit will not always strive
> With harden'd, self-destroying man;
> Ye, who persist his love to grieve,
> May never hear his voice again.
>
> Sinner—perhaps this very day
> Thy last accepted time may be;
> O shouldst thou grieve him now away,
> Then hope may never beam on thee.[20]

---

will may come and take of the water of life freely." This is reprinted in J. Matthew Pinson, *A Free Will Baptist Handbook: Heritage, Beliefs, and Ministries* (Nashville: Randall House, 1998), 176.

20. *Hymns, Selected and Original, for Public and Private Worship* (Philadelphia: General Synod of the Evangelical Lutheran Church in the United States, 1828), hymn 229. This was at a time when all Christians sang their doctrine. It is likely that "life and light" in the fourth stanza is an allusion to John 1.

God Stretches Out His Hand to Receive People, but They Refuse Him

The entire Old Testament is a story of God's reaching out to unrepentant, unbelieving people with an outstretched hand, pleading with them to listen to him, only to lament that the unbelievers are resisting his overtures of grace. Because through his prophets he compassionately and persistently gives Israel opportunities to repent, and they mock and despise and scoff at his words, he unleashes his wrath without remedy (2 Chron. 36:15–16). Ezekiel indicates that the reason the people will not be cleansed is not God's will and design, but their resistance: "I would have cleansed you and you were not cleansed" (24:13). God's wrath will come upon them, not because he designed that they would be outside the scope of his grace but "because when I called, no one answered, when I spoke, they did not listen" (Isa. 66:4). Despite his persistent calls and attempts to get them to listen and repent and come to him, they refuse to do so; thus he will bring disaster on them (Jer. 7:13; 25:4–5; 35:15–17).

Lady Wisdom, which Bruce Waltke describes as the personification of God's wisdom, not the "wisdom of creation" or "natural theology," calls out to sinners in Proverbs 1:24–33.[21] Historically, Calvinist and Arminian authors alike have, like Calvin, Wesley, and Edwards, treated this passage as describing God's overtures toward people, not simply wisdom as abstracted from God. Divine wisdom has reached out to sinners with her hand extended, sweetly calling them to herself, but they have refused to listen, paying her no attention. She has patiently given them counsel and admonished them, but they have ignored and despised her and her reproof. She has given them knowledge, for which they have shown nothing but hatred, turning away from divine wisdom in their foolish complacency. Their resistance is the reason she will no longer call out to them and will laugh at their calamity. This image of God's reaching out to sinners with hands held out to them as if to receive them, pleading with them to come to him, and lamenting their refusal to do so (e.g., Isa. 65:2, quoted in Rom. 10:21) is a tangible symbol that his calling and drawing are sincere.

God Has Done All He Can to Bring People to Himself

Perhaps more riveting is the picture Isaiah (5:1–4) paints of God's doing everything he can for his vineyard, the inhabitants of Jerusalem and Judah, who resist his grace:

> My beloved had a vineyard
>   on a very fertile hill.
> He dug it and cleared it of stones,
>   and planted it with choice vines;

---

21. Bruce K. Waltke, *The Book of Proverbs: Chapters 1–15* (Grand Rapids: Eerdmans, 2004), 54–55.

he built a watchtower in the midst of it,
　　and hewed out a wine vat in it;
and he looked for it to yield grapes,
　　but it yielded wild grapes.
And now, O inhabitants of Jerusalem
　　and men of Judah,
judge between me and my vineyard.
What more was there to do for my vineyard,
　　that I have not done in it?
When I looked for it to yield grapes,
　　why did it yield wild grapes?

There was nothing more God could have done in his vineyard for it to yield good grapes. The reason it yielded wild grapes was not because he willed it, but because of the resistance of the vineyard. As Arminius argued, if God had not given the vineyard "all things necessary" to produce good grapes, then "it would be absurd" for him to expect good grapes and to be angry with the vineyard and punish it for producing wild grapes.[22]

Arminius correctly explained that God provided sufficient grace for the vineyard to bring forth good grapes—"What more was there to do for my vineyard, that I have not done in it?"—but it produced wild grapes instead. This means the grace was sufficient but not effectual.[23] One sees this all throughout the Old Testament: God's doing all he can to give people grace to receive him, only for them to resist it (cf. Isa. 65:2; Jer. 13:11; Ezek. 24:13).[24] Scripture bears out, again and again, Arminius's principle that if God requires something of people, he is "bound" by his own justice to give them the grace "without which the act cannot be performed."[25]

The Only Reason People Do Not Come to the Great Banquet Is Their Resistance

This same reasoning carries over into the New Testament, in addition to Jesus's weeping over Jerusalem in Luke 13:34 and Matthew 23:37. One sees it in the parable of the great banquet in Luke 14:16–24 (paralleled in Matt. 22:1–14). The host who has spread the feast has no part in the fact that people he has invited refuse to come. The fault is wholly their own. Thus they deserve his anger. The Calvinist account would have it that the host has, in advance, arranged things so that certain invited guests will refuse his invitation, yet he

---

22. Arminius, *Works*, 3:475, "Examination of Perkins's Pamphlet."
23. As Kevin Hester has noted in conversation, it was effectual in achieving its end, but not efficacious in leading to "good grapes."
24. Romans 10:21 quotes Isaiah 65:2.
25. Arminius, *Works*, 3:317, 475, 478.

still invites them and is angry with them for not coming. However, this understanding is the opposite of this parable, and of the entire biblical witness to God's sincere, earnest invitation to people to come to him. When he invites them, he knows that they have a real opportunity to come to him, not that he has fixed their circumstances such that they of necessity cannot come to him, refusing to give them the grace to do so.

This, Arminians say, would violate the scriptural principle that "God is no respecter of persons" (Acts 10:34 KJV). What if a host invited everyone to a party indiscriminately but had worked it out in advance, managing people's circumstances, so that they would not be able to come, yet he had hypnotized others so that they could not help but want to come? That would make that host a respecter of persons, showing partiality to one invited guest over another. That is what Calvinism has God doing.[26]

Summary

This idea that God is repeatedly giving people an opportunity to come to him, giving them the grace to do so, and that the reason they do not is not his design but simply that they are resisting the grace he has given them, is the thrust of the Bible.[27] It is seen clearly in St. Stephen's famous speech in Acts 7:51, which is reminiscent of what Jesus said to the Jewish leaders in Matthew and Luke: "You stiff-necked people, uncircumcised in heart and ears, you always resist the Holy Spirit. As your fathers did, so do you."[28] How could texts like this mean anything else? How can one be said to "resist" something that has not been given?

The reason people are not converted is because they resist genuine grace from God that is sufficient for their conversion. That is the consistent witness of the whole of Scripture: It is possible for people "to receive the grace of God in vain" (2 Cor. 6:1), to rebel against and grieve the Holy Spirit when he has lovingly reached out with his grace (Isa. 63:10). People have the freedom, like the Pharisees in Luke 7:30, to reject God's counsel or purpose for them.[29] That is precisely what the reprobates do. God reaches out to them with genuine grace. He has done all he can for them. He has given them sufficient grace to receive him. They, however, are not willing. They resist him. They refuse him. Thus, he is just in his condemnation of them.

---

26. See Question D, which discusses the philosopher John Searle's use of the illustration of hypnosis in his critique of secular psychological and philosophical versions of compatibilist determinism. See also Lemke, 150.
27. For more discussion of this, see Lemke, "A Biblical and Theological Critique of Irresistible Grace," 117–29.
28. See Lemke, "A Biblical and Theological Critique of Irresistible Grace," 118–19.
29. Robert E. Picirilli, *Grace, Faith, Free Will: Contrasting Views of Salvation: Calvinism and Arminianism* (Nashville: Randall House, 2002), 81, 112.

REFLECTION QUESTIONS

1. What does Jesus's statement, "I willed . . . but you were not willing" in Matthew 23:37 say about the resistibility or irresistibility of his grace?

2. What would be Jesus's motivation for pleading with his Jewish audience to come to him and lamenting, "I willed . . . but you were not willing," if he purposefully was withholding his grace from them?

3. What does Proverbs 1:24–33 say about God's heart for people to whom he is reaching out?

4. Why does God say in Isaiah 5:1–4 that he has done all he can in his vineyard to get good grapes, only to get wild ones? What does he mean by this, and why does the context say they were wild?

5. Luke 14:16–24 says that some of the people the host invited to the great banquet did not come. What was the reason they did not come? Could it be that secretly the host did not want them to, and had secretly arranged it so that they could not? What would this say about the host's character?

How Do Arminians Interpret the Argument for Irresistible Grace from John 6?

To answer this question, this chapter will consider the passages and principles to which Calvinists appeal most frequently. In defending the doctrine of irresistible grace, Calvinists cite texts such as Romans 1:7; 1 Corinthians 1:9; Galatians 1:15; and 2 Thessalonians 2:14. They argue that these texts, which speak of God's calling people, "assert the sovereign efficacy of God's calling," which "accomplishes his goal of saving the elect."[1] This chapter will not spend time on this argument. These texts say that God calls the elect, but they do not establish whether the calling is resistible or irresistible.

The text to which Calvinists appeal most in their discussions of this doctrine is John 6.[2] Bruce Ware begins his discussion of that chapter by saying that people too quickly assume, based on verses 35, 37, 40, 47, and 51, that "ought" implies "can." This is the idea that, if Jesus is saying people ought to do something, then surely he would provide them with sufficient grace to do it. Ware replies that John 6 "devastates the logic of this position." However, what he goes on to establish is not that the concept of "ought implies can" is devastated, but that "our text never explicitly makes this logical inference . . . nor is it implied."[3]

1. Shawn D. Wright, *40 Questions About Calvinism* (Grand Rapids: Kregel Academic, 2019), 207.
2. Wright, *40 Questions About Calvinism*, 213.
3. Bruce A. Ware, "Effectual Calling and Grace," in *Still Sovereign: Contemporary Perspectives on Election, Foreknowledge, and Grace,* eds. Thomas R. Schreiner and Bruce A. Ware (Grand Rapids: Baker, 2000), 212–13.

Ware paraphrases Jesus's statement in his conversation with his Jewish audience, "All that the Father gives me will come to me" (6:37, cf. vv. 39, 65), as follows: "Because all the Father gives me come, and because of your refusal to come even though you have been shown the sign, it is evident that you have not been given to me by the Father." He explains that "the multitudes' disbelief is evidence that they are not among those given to Christ by the Father. They do not believe *because* they are not given to the Son." Ware believes that this dovetails with what Jesus says in 10:26 and 8:47, that people do not believe because they are not his sheep. "Coming to Christ is causally linked by Jesus to having been given by the Father."[4]

The Condition of Faith in John 5–6

Can it be established from these texts that God's giving or granting (*didōmi*) the elect to Jesus is an unconditional, irresistible act, not conditioned on faith? The answer is no. In John 5–6 Jesus clearly teaches that the Father's giving of the elect to the son is *conditioned on their belief* in him.[5] This is borne out over and again in this discourse. Jesus has already excoriated the unbelieving Jews with whom he has been dialoguing in John 5: "[The Father's] voice you have never heard . . . and you do not have his word abiding in you, for you do not believe the one whom he has sent. You search the Scriptures because you think that in them you have eternal life; and it is they that bear witness about me, yet you refuse to come to me that you may have life. . . . I have come in my Father's name, and you do not receive me" (John 5:37–40, 43).

Here Jesus tells his Jewish interlocutors that they have never heard the Father's voice and do not have his word abiding in them (vv. 37–38). Yet then he immediately tells them *why* they are in this condition: "*because* [*hoti*: since, because] you *do not believe* the one whom he sent" (v. 38, NRSV, NET), because "you *refuse* to come to me that you may have life" (v. 40), "you *do not receive* me" (v. 43, italics added).

Thus the context of John 6:37 explains its meaning: Who is it that the Father gives Jesus? Those who do not refuse him (5:40), those who believe him (5:38), those who receive him (5:43). "He came to his own, and his own people did not receive him. But to all who did receive him, who believed in his name, he gave the right to become children of God" (John 1:11–12). It is clear that Jesus is holding out hope to these people that they can come to him if they stop refusing, if they believe him and receive him: "I say these things so that you may be saved" (6:34). Why would he say he was telling them these things so they could be saved if his design for them, not their refusal (5:40), was what was keeping them from salvation?

---

4. Ware, "Effectual Calling and Grace," 214 (italics added).
5. F. Leroy Forlines, *Classical Arminianism: A Theology of Salvation* (Nashville: Randall House, 2011), 161.

The Arminian emphatically believes that sinners cannot come to Jesus unless the Father draws them (6:44), that the Father will give believers—those who do not refuse him—to his Son, and that God must draw sinners and enable them with his grace for them to be saved. That is what John 6 is teaching, not irresistible grace. Just before John 6:37, Jesus says this:

> "Do not work for the food that perishes." . . . Then they said to him, "What must we do, to be doing the works of God?" Jesus answered them, "This is the work of God, that you believe in him whom he has sent." So they said to him, "Then what sign do you do, that we may see and believe you? What work do you perform? Our fathers ate the manna in the wilderness; as it is written, 'He gave them bread from heaven to eat.'" Jesus then said to them, "Truly, truly, I say to you, it was not Moses who gave you the bread from heaven, but my Father gives you the true bread from heaven. For the bread of God is he who comes down from heaven and gives life to the world." They said to him, "Sir, give us this bread always." Jesus said to them, "I am the bread of life; whoever comes to me shall not hunger, and whoever believes in me shall never thirst. But I said to you that you have seen me and yet do not believe." (John 6:27–36)

This is a give-and-take conversation between Jesus and his Jewish interlocuters. He is giving them the impression that they can partake of salvation—the eternal food which he "*will give*" to them (6:27). They ask him what they have to do to partake of it, and he replies: believe in me (6:29). Then they ask him what he would do to persuade them to believe, noting that their forefathers ate manna, heavenly bread, in the wilderness. He replies to them that it was not Moses, but the Father, who gives the "true bread from heaven." So far, all these things indicate that he is having a normal conversation with these people to whom he is perfectly willing to give his heavenly bread, his eternal food. He is directly offering it to them. Why is he talking to them as if he wants to give them his heavenly bread if they have been purposefully excluded from grace?

Then in verse 34, they come right out and say, "Sir, give us this bread always." Jesus replies that he is that bread, and if they come to him in faith, they will neither hunger nor thirst. Yet in verse 36 he laments their unbelief. This is a give-and-take, influence-and-response conversation. Jesus is offering himself to them. He is willing to give them his eternal food. Yet he laments that they "do not believe." This ties to the previous chapter, in which he clearly states the reason some people do not hear the Father's voice and have his word abiding in them: They do not believe (John 5:38). These repeated offerings and statements lamenting their unbelief would make no sense if he was excluding them from the scope of his grace. Then comes 6:37, and that verse simply does not state *why* the Father gives people to Jesus, but all around that verse, Jesus makes it plain: *The Father gives Jesus those who believe in him.* Calvinists are reading irresistible grace into the word *didōmi* (give or grant) in this chapter.

The Process of Conversion in John 6

The basic question, then, is this: Is *didōmi*, the Father's giving of people to the Son, unconditional, or is it conditioned on belief? That it is the latter is demonstrated by understanding that, as part of *drawing* everyone to himself, without which no one can or will come to him (John 6:44; 12:32), God *teaches* everyone (6:45). Those who do not *resist* that teaching (5:39–40) and believe (1:12; 6:35, 39–40, 47; 7:38) are the ones whom the Father *gives* to the Son (1:12; 6:37, 39; 17:12) and who *come* to the Son (6:37, 65).[6]

Listening to the Divine Teaching

John 6 states that the divine *teaching* is how God draws (6:44) people to himself, not impersonally and irresistibly, but as personal beings made in his image who not only feel and make meaningful choices but also think and reason and can, through his grace, be taught. John 6:45, quoting Isaiah 54:13, explains how the drawing is accomplished: "they will all be taught by God." As Westcott said, "The promise of direct divine teaching" emphasizes the "twofold aspect" of the divine drawing: "the divine and human elements are combined. The 'hearing' brings out the external communication, the learning the internal understanding of it."[7] Thus central to the drawing process is God's graciously influencing unbelievers with information about their lost state and about the fact that there is a Savior for them.

This brings to mind the 1812 Abstract, the Free Will Baptist confession of faith that states: "We believe that sinners are drawn to God, the Father, by the Holy Ghost, through Christ His Son, and that the Holy Ghost offers His divine aid to all the human family so that they all might be happy, would they give place to His *divine teaching*; whereas such who do not receive the divine impressions of the Holy Spirit, shall, at a future day, own their condemnation just, and charge themselves with their own damnation, for willfully rejecting the offers of sovereign grace."[8]

---

6. This section on the process of conversion loosely follows Jack Cottrell, "John 6:65 and Calvinism," https://jackcottrell.com/uncategorized/john-665-and-calvinism, accessed May 3, 2020.

7. Brooke Foss Westcott, *The Gospel According to St. John* (London: John Murray, 1908), 1:235.

8. Art. 9; reprinted in J. Matthew Pinson, *A Free Will Baptist Handbook: Heritage, Beliefs, and Ministries* (Nashville: Randall House, 1998), 145 (italics added).

This connection of drawing to teaching in John 6 is common in the church fathers. Cyril of Alexandria, for example, equated divine drawing grace in the passage with being "God-taught," with the knowledge of Christ taught by God being "a work of the grace from above" such that sinners cannot "attain unto Him, save *drawn by the teaching* of the Father." The drawing Jesus speaks of in 6:44, Cyril asserted, "is not a compulsory nor forcible drawing" precisely because it involves the divine teaching mentioned in verse 45: "For where there is hearing and learning and the benefit of instruction, there is faith, to wit by persuasion and not of necessity." The knowledge of Christ, he said, is given by "love rather than constraining. For the word of doctrine requires that free will and free choice be preserved to the soul of man."[9]

Chrysostom also tied divine drawing and giving to divine teaching, saying, "Whether we will be taught is a matter of choice, and also whether we will believe. And in this place, by the 'which the Father gives Me,' He declares nothing else than that 'the believing on Me is no ordinary thing, nor one that comes of human reasonings, but needs a revelation from above.'"[10]

Ceasing Resistance to Jesus and Believing in Him

John 6:45 continues, "Everyone who has heard and learned from the Father comes to me." Divine grace brings to Jesus everyone who does not reject the divine teaching. Clearly, Jesus stressed this element in 5:39–40, where he chided the Jewish leaders for hearing the divine teaching ("You search the Scriptures," v. 39) but still resisting ("yet you refuse to come to me," v. 40). When sinners do not reject the divine teaching, they are given the gift of faith. It is the Father's will, as John 6:40 says, that everyone who believes in the Son "will have eternal life" (cf. 6:35, 47; 7:38). As Steve Witzki points out, verse 40 explains who "all he has given me" in verse 39 refers to: "everyone who looks on the Son and believes in him." The literary structure of these verses, and John's use of the word "for" at the beginning of verse 40, which logically connects it to verse 39, makes this interpretation unmistakable:

> A raise them up at the last day
>   B that I shall lose none of all that he has given me
>   C this is the will of him who sent me
>   C' For this is the will of my Father
>   B' that everyone who looks to the Son and believes in him shall have eternal life
> A' raise him up at the last day

---

9. Cyril of Alexandria, *Commentary on the Gospel According to S. John* (Oxford: James Parker and Co., 1874), 1:399–401 (italics added).

10. John Chrysostom, *Homilies on the Gospel of St. John* in *A Select Library of the Nicene and Post-Nicene Fathers*, ed. Philip Schaff (New York: Charles Scribner's Sons, 1906), 14:162.

Those who look on the Son and believe in him (v. 40) are those the Father gives the Son (v. 39).[11]

Giving and Coming

This is the juncture at which the divine "giving" comes in. Once the believing sinner has not rejected the gift of faith, thus receiving Christ (1:12), the Father now gives or grants (*didōmi*) the believer to Jesus to be his own. They now have the "right" to become children of God (1:12). As Jack Cottrell explains, "those who have been given the right to become children of God are now actually *given to Jesus* by the Father, so that we are now able to *come to Jesus* in order to receive eternal life. That is, because we have been foreknown and wanted and drawn and taught, and because we have heard and willed and learned and believed, the Father now *gives us to Jesus* (John 6:37, 39; 17:2)."[12] It is worth noting that it is far from an established principle in the Gospel of John that the Father's giving someone to the Son means that the gift is unconditional. After all, Jesus told the Father in 17:12 that he had kept those the Father had given him *except Judas*.[13]

Thus believers, whom the father gives to Jesus, now come to him, thus culminating the process of conversion. Thus, when John 6:65 says that "no one can come to me unless it is granted him by the Father," Arminians readily agree. They simply note that everything in the gospel of John suggests that the grace that gives or grants the believer to Jesus is conditional and resistible. The doctrine of unconditional, irresistible grace has to be imported into the text from elsewhere.

It is important to underscore that many Arminians, like Arminius, believe that *faith is a gift* (though this is an open question among Arminians). For example, the Free Will Baptist Treatise of Faith and Practice states that "the power to believe is the gift of God," citing Ephesians 2:8 as a proof text. This is one thing that Arminius had in common with his Lutheran scholastic contemporaries such as Niels Hemmingsen.[14]

One seventeenth-century Lutheran theologian, August Pfeiffer, is representative of this way of thinking. He explained that "man is merely passive in his conversion which is not his own, but only and solely God's work; so that man does not assist in the work, but merely does not hinder God's power from working with him. Therefore the prophet says, Jer. 31:18: 'Turn Thou me, and I shall be turned' . . . and in Lam. 5:21: 'Turn Thou us unto Thee, O Lord, and we shall be turned.'" He explains that Calvinists wrongly accuse his

---

11. Steve Witzki, "Calvinism and John 6: An Exegetical Response, Part One," *The Arminian Magazine* 23 (2005): http://www.fwponline.cc/v23n1/johnsixPt1_witzki.html, accessed May 5, 2020.

12. Jack Cottrell, "John 6:65 and Calvinism."

13. Chrysostom, *Homilies on the Gospel of St. John*, 14:29.

14. Arminius, *Works*, 2:51, "Apology against Thirty-One Defamatory Articles."

position of implying that, since "man can hinder his conversion and resist the divine operation," conversion must be dependent on human will and effort. However, asserting that "man is able to hinder his conversion" does not entail that "he can assist in the work. For it is most assuredly in man's power to despise and wantonly to reject the proffered grace; nevertheless, he can not on that account co-operate in his conversion."[15]

Summary

To interpret the account in John 6 of the Father's gift to Jesus of believers who have not resisted the divine teaching as a proof of unconditional election and irresistible grace, as Calvinists must do, is unsound. Such an understanding must be imposed on the text from outside it. The consistent teaching of the Gospel of John, as of the entire New Testament, is that sinners will never respond positively to the gospel unless they receive a special, gracious drawing from God (6:44). Yet this drawing goes out to everyone (12:32). God gives the gift of faith (1:12; 6:35, 39–40, 47; 7:38) to those who do not resist the divine drawing and teaching (6:45; 5:39–40). These are the individuals whom the Father gives to the Son.

REFLECTION QUESTIONS

1. What is the Calvinist argument for why John 6:37 teaches irresistible grace?

2. What does Jesus's Jewish interlocutors not listening to the Father because they refuse to believe in the Son in John 5:37–40 say about the resistibility of grace?

3. What does John's statement in 6:45 about people needing to learn from the divine teaching say about the resistibility of grace?

4. Does the way Jesus talks with his audience in John 5–6 indicate a cause-and-effect approach to grace or one of influence-and-response?

5. How does the literary structure of John 6:39–40 that Steve Witzki explains help one understand the nature of the meaning of "given" in John 6?

---

15. August Pfeiffer, *Anti-Calvinism*, trans. Edward Pfeiffer (Columbus, OH: Joint Lutheran Synod of Ohio, 1881), 257–58.

How Do Arminians Interpret Other Proof Texts for Irresistible Grace?

Arminians and Calvinists disagree on two other kinds of Scripture texts. Calvinists argue that passages that teach that God's drawing people to himself with his grace entail the doctrine of irresistible grace. They also argue that biblical images that compare human sinfulness to death and conversion to birth and creation entail the doctrine of irresistible grace.

The Drawing (*Helkuō*) of People to Jesus

The other important image in John's Gospel that Calvinists use to argue for irresistible grace is divine drawing. Ware asserts that Arminians misinterpret John 6:44 as being a resistible drawing. Instead, he says, "this text teaches that the drawing of the Father is both effectual (i.e., people not only are made able to believe, but also are drawn unfailingly and irresistibly to such belief) and selective (i.e., he draws those whom he chooses to give to the Son)." Ware argues that the drawing ineluctably results in final, not just possible, salvation, because Jesus says, "I will raise him up at the last day." Yet this does not follow. Jesus is saying that no individual can come to him unless the Father draws that individual, and if that individual *comes* to him, he will raise him or her up at the last day, *not* that everyone who is *drawn* will be raised up at the last day. This would result in universalism, since later in 12:32, Jesus makes it plain that everyone is being drawn.[1]

Calvinists employ John's use of *helkuō* (draw) in his gospel as an argument for irresistible grace. Robert Yarbrough, for example, points to a few others places outside the gospel of John where the word occurs—for example,

---

1. Bruce A. Ware, "Effectual Calling and Grace," in *Still Sovereign: Contemporary Perspectives on Election, Foreknowledge, and Grace*, eds. Thomas R. Schreiner and Bruce A. Ware (Grand Rapids: Baker, 2000), 216.

in Acts 16:19 and 21:30, where Paul and Silas are dragged (*heilkysan*) into the marketplace and Paul is dragged (*heilkon*) out of the temple (cf. James 2:6, which refers to the rich oppressing and "dragging" the poor into court against their will). Yarbrough thinks John 6:44 is speaking of a *"forceful attraction"* that brings sinners to Christ.[2]

But is this what the text means? As Leroy Forlines suggests, interpreting *helkuō* as a "forceful attraction" is to impose an alien concept on the text.[3] The word is sometimes used in mechanical, physical contexts. However, when used in connection with interpersonal relationships, or "influence-and-response" relationships, as Forlines stresses, imposing a mechanical, cause-and-effect meaning on the term is mistaken. This is the way gracious drawing is seen elsewhere in Scripture. It is the divine person who is relating to human persons created in his image as thinking, feeling persons who make meaningful choices. God draws feeling persons, not with force, but with gentleness and love: "I have drawn you with lovingkindness" (Jer. 31:3); "I drew them with gentle cords, with bands of love" (Hos. 11:4, NKJV, same Heb. word for "draw"). God draws thinking persons, not by force, but by teaching them and urging them to listen to that teaching: "Everyone who has heard and learned from the Father comes to me" (John 6:45).

BDAG supports this understanding of *helkuō*, noting that the more forceful meaning of the word applies to "objects" or persons "unwilling to do so voluntarily."[4] This flies in the face of most Calvinists' compatibilistic interpretation of effectual calling, which interprets those myriad scriptural passages that talk about the regenerate as those who are willing and the unregenerate as those who are unwilling, having the elect "made willing" by effectual calling, not being compelled against their wills. If God is really able to get people to do "most freely" what he wants them to do, as the Westminster Confession says, this would contradict the definition of drawing as forcibly dragging people.

Furthermore, as Forlines points out, to define the word as "forceful attraction," universalism would have to follow, because of John 12:32. Here Jesus would be made to say: "I, when I am lifted up from the earth, will forcefully attract all people to myself." Of course, if "all people" is interpreted as "all sorts of people, not just Jews but Gentiles," which is what Schreiner argues, then the Calvinist thinks this objection vanishes. But John 12:32, interpreted using the lexical meaning of *pantas* ("everyone"), determines John's meaning

---

2. Yarbrough, "Divine Election in the Gospel of John," in *Still Sovereign*, 50 n. 10 (italics added).

3. F. Leroy Forlines, *Classical Arminianism: A Theology of Salvation* (Nashville: Randall House, 2011), 159.

4. Walter Bauer, *A Greek-English Lexicon of the New Testament and Other Early Christian Literature*, rev. and ed. Frederick W. Danker, 3rd ed. (Chicago: University of Chicago Press, 2000), 318.

in 6:44: *Helkuō*, in these spiritual, interpersonal, relational terms, refers to a wooing, a persuasion, an influence, not a forceful attraction.[5]

Richard Chenevix Trench concurred in his discussion of *helkuō* and *surō*. The latter is used in several New Testament contexts to mean forcefully drag. Yet, as Trench argues, the two words "differ, and with differences not theologically unimportant. . . . How does a crucified, and thus an exalted, Saviour draw all men unto Him? Not by force, for the will is incapable of force, but by the divine attractions of his love." He goes on to cite John 6:44, then say: "Now as many as feel bound to deny any '*gratia irresistibilis*,' which turns man into a mere machine, and by which, willing or unwilling, he is dragged to God, must at once allow, must indeed assert, that this ἑλκύσῃ [*helkysē*] can mean no more than the potent allurements, the allective force of love, the attracting of men by the Father to the Son." Trench explained that, in these interpersonal contexts in the New Testament, the Septuagint, and other Ancient Greek literature, interpreting *helkuō* as forceful is untenable.[6]

Interestingly, based on the secular philosopher John Searle's likening of nontheological forms of compatibilism to hypnosis as seen in Question 17, one of the meanings Liddell and Scott mention in classical Greek could apply: "draw to oneself or attract . . . as by a spell."[7] This is an image that comes to many people's minds when they learn about compatibilism, as it does to Searle—something like God casting a spell or hypnotizing people to *make* them willing.[8]

In short, the word *helkuō* would not lead the reader to impose such an interpretation, in these clearly interpersonal contexts, unless one had already decided that the doctrine of irresistible grace were true. Furthermore, compatibilism contradicts this. R. C. Sproul, in making an argument for compatibilism, states that God does not coerce the human will. Yet several pages later he argues that *helkuō* means to drag by force.[9]

The Calvinist interpretation of divine drawing as a "forceful attraction" is reminiscent of a verse from Isaac Watts's classic hymn, "How Sweet and Awful is the Place."

5. Forlines, *Classical Arminianism*, 157–60. For more discussion of John 12:32, see Question 22.
6. Richard Chenevix Trench, *Synonyms of the New Testament* (London: Macmillan, 1865), 69–71.
7. Henry George Liddell and Robert Scott, *A Greek-English Lexicon*, 6th ed. (Oxford: Clarendon, 1869), 471.
8. John Searle, *Minds, Brains and Science* (Cambridge, MA: Harvard University Press, 1984), 89–90; Michael McKenna and D. Justin Coates, "Compatibilism," *The Stanford Encyclopedia of Philosophy* (Summer 2020 Edition), ed. Edward N. Zalta, https://plato.stanford.edu/archives/sum2020/entries/compatibilism, accessed May 31, 2020; Steve W. Lemke, "A Biblical and Theological Critique of Irresistible Grace," in *Whosoever Will*, eds. David L. Allen and and Steve W. Lemke, 150.
9. R. C. Sproul, *Chosen by God* (Wheaton, IL: Tyndale, 1986), 59, 69.

'Twas the same love that spread the feast
That sweetly drew us in,
Else we had still refused to taste
And perished in our sin.

Modern Calvinist hymnals say God's love "sweetly drew us in," but Isaac Watts's original words, which were retained in Calvinist hymnals for a century and a half, were "sweetly *forced* us in."[10] Calvinist exegetes obviously did not get a vote on the later editions. As Carl Bangs stated, "Grace is *not a force*; *it is a person*, the Holy Spirit, and in personal relationships there cannot be sheer overpowering of one person by another."[11]

Images Like Death, Creation, and Birth

Calvinists also argue for irresistible grace from texts saying that sinners are dead in trespasses and sins (e.g., Eph. 2:1, 5; Col. 2:13) and using images such as creation and birth to describe regeneration (e.g., 2 Cor. 5:10; Eph. 2:10; 4:24; John 1:13; 3:3–8; 1 Peter 1:3, 23; 1 John 3:9; 5:4, 18). How can a dead person resist being brought to life; how can an uncreated being resist being created; and how can an unborn person resist being born?

Dead in Trespasses and Sins

Arminians agree with Calvinists that sinners are "dead in trespasses and sins" and can do nothing to move toward God without the intervention of divine grace. However, to jump from this biblical assertion to the notion of irresistible grace, that God has a cause-and-effect relationship with the one who comes to faith, militates against the influence-and-response way in which the Bible describes how God's grace acts in those who are dead in sin to bring them to new life. Passages like Ephesians 5:14 show that God calls out to spiritually dead people: "Awake, O sleeper, and arise from the dead, and Christ will shine on you." Obviously, they can awaken from their spiritually dead state only through his grace; they cannot do it themselves. Yet the Bible indicates throughout that the way people awaken from their dead state is through an influence-and-response dynamic with the Spirit who is drawing them out of it, not through a cause-and-effect "making" them to do it.

As Forlines argues, Christians are "dead to sin" and "alive to God" and thus cannot live any longer in the practice of sin (Rom. 6:2). Statements that believers are dead to sin or dead to the law or dead to the world indicate

---

10. Isaac Watts, *The Psalms, Hymns and Spiritual Songs of the Old and New Testament, faithfully translated into English metre: being the New England Psalm Book* (1758), https://hymnary.org/text/how_sweet_and_aweful_is_the_place/fulltexts, accessed May 3, 2020 (italics added).
11. Carl O. Bangs, *Arminius: A Study in the Dutch Reformation* (Nashville: Abingdon, 1971), 343 (italics added).

what the Bible means by "dead" when used of spiritual realities. Interpreting the "dead" motif the way Calvinism does renders this basic biblical principle unintelligible.[12]

Calvinists also cite Ephesians 1:19–20, emphasizing that God is raising people from the dead like he raised Jesus from the dead. However, this passage is talking about the power of God toward those who already believe, and it is "resurrection life." As Robert Picirilli notes, Colossians 2:12, John 5:24, and John 12:46 teach that "resurrection from spiritual life is 'by faith.'"[13] Just as importantly, though, omnipotent, irresistible power is not consistent with how the Bible actually describes the process of people coming to Christ. Otherwise, the Bible would describe them not as "turning to Christ" but "being turned to Christ."[14]

What is needed is an explanation of the process of conversion that protects *both* (1) the utter graciousness of God in salvation and the utter helplessness of people without that grace *and* (2) the straightforwardness with which the Bible, throughout, describes the process of people turning to Christ in faith and actually ceasing to resist him, rather than simply being "turned by" God. Semi-Pelagians and some who refer to themselves as Arminians underemphasize the first truth, whereas Calvinists underemphasize the second. Both groups are no doubt trying to be as consistent as possible and "tie up the loose ends," but Holy Scripture does not do so. It emphasizes both.

Images Like Creation and Birth

As Shawn Wright explains, Calvinists emphasize a "parallel between God's sovereign work in creation and his sovereign work in new creation."[15] Just as people cannot resist their physical birth, Calvinists argue, they cannot resist the new birth. Again, the trouble is that this is not the way the Bible describes grace. The Bible discusses new birth, new life in Christ, as something that comes about *through faith.*[16]

The Lutheran scholastic August Pfeiffer discussed two reasons Scripture and the majority of the Christian tradition have not interpreted these images woodenly. First, similes should not be "stretched beyond their proper limit and the purpose for which they were used." That is not the way the Bible is using them. When the Bible compares conversion to creation or birth or resurrection, its "only purpose is to show that man can help himself in conversion as little

---

12. Forlines, *Classical Arminianism*, 23–24.

13. Picirilli, *Grace, Faith, Free Will: Contrasting Views of Salvation: Calvinism and Arminianism* (Nashville: Randall House, 2002), 172–73.

14. Daniel Whitby, *A Discourse Concerning the True Import of the Words Election and Reprobation* (London: John Wyat, 1710), 235.

15. Shawn D. Wright, *40 Questions About Calvinism* (Grand Rapids: Kregel Academic, 2019), 212.

16. See Question 32 on faith preceding regeneration.

as one can create himself, or a dead man restore himself to life." Scripture uses similes in ways that accord with the influence-and-response manner in which it describes the gracious relationship between God and sinners.[17]

Second, the *body* and the *spirit* are two different things. This gets back to the whole question of cause-and-effect (a hammer making a nail go into a board) versus influence-and-response (one person who thinks, feels, and makes free choices persuading another person who thinks, feels, and makes free choices to do something). It gets back to the question of seeing grace as a force or a thing rather than one person relating to another. Scripture is clearly on the side of the influence-and-response approach. Thus, Pfeiffer says, "although God in the *bodily* creation uses the free and unlimited power of His omnipotence, this need not on that account take place in the *spiritual* creation of a new spirit, for which He Himself ordained a certain measure and order, according to which He will act."[18]

Summary

To view divine drawing as forcibly dragging, as the Calvinist does, not only contradicts the compatibilism of most Calvinists but also defies the influence-and-response motif in Scripture regarding the way the Spirit interacts with personal beings he has created in his image. The crux of the matter is this: The Bible consistently sounds as if "whosoever will may come." Yet it also consistently sounds as if God's grace has to draw totally depraved people who are dead in trespasses and sins and who, without that grace, would never come. These two scriptural poles must be held in tension, and a traditional, Reformed-oriented Arminianism is able to maintain this delicate biblical balance.

REFLECTION QUESTIONS

1. How do Arminians respond to the Calvinist argument that divine drawing is a forcible dragging?

2. Is there a contradiction between compatibilism, freedom defined as doing what one wants and not being compelled against one's will, and the interpretation of drawing as forcible dragging?

3. How do Arminians explain the concept of the sinner being dead in trespasses and sins?

---

17. August Pfeiffer, *Anti-Calvinism*, trans. Edward Pfeiffer (Columbus, OH: Joint Lutheran Synod of Ohio, 1881 [1699]), 262–63.
18. Pfeiffer, *Anti-Calvinism*, 262–63 (italics added).

4. How do Arminians respond to Calvinists' use of images like birth and creation to argue that God's grace is irresistible?

5. Does the way the gospel invitations of the Bible read seem naturally to cohere with God forcibly dragging people to himself?

PART 4

Questions About
Election and Regeneration

Does Ephesians 1:4–11 Teach Unconditional or Conditional Election?

When Arminians read passages like Ephesians 1:4–11 about God's choice of individuals for eternal salvation, they do so with the revealed gospel clearly in view. They take Romans 9:15 very seriously: "I will have mercy on whom I have mercy, and I will have compassion on whom I have compassion." They want to know the answer to the question: On whom does God, from eternity, desire to have mercy and compassion? In answering that question, they believe that Holy Scripture points to the gospel. That is why Arminius argued that God's decree to elect people for eternal salvation is "not legal" but "evangelical." When Christians speak of election, they should use the revealed language of the gospel.[1] Here Arminius echoed Luther, who said that "we dare not begin to dispute God's predestination from the Law or from reason, but from the grace of God and the Gospel which is proclaimed to all men."[2]

Thus among the first verses Arminius cites in his public disputation "On Predestination" are gospel verses, John 6:40 and Romans 10:9, which get to the heart of what election is all about: "For this is the will of my Father, that everyone who looks on the Son and believes in him should have eternal life"

---

1. Jacobus Arminius, *The Works of James Arminius*, trans. James Nichols and William Nichols, 3 vols. (Nashville: Randall House, 2007), Public Disputation 15, "On Divine Predestination."
2. George H. Schodde, ed., *The Error of Modern Missouri: Its Inception, Development, and Refutation* (Columbus, OH: Lutheran Book Concern, 1897), 361; *Concordia Triglotta: The Symbolical Books of the Evangelical Lutheran Church* (St. Louis: Concordia, 1921), 221. Melanchthon emphasized the same thing, as J. K. S. Reid points out in his classic article, "The Office of Christ in Predestination," *Scottish Journal of Theology* 1 (1948): 167 (this is in part two of a two-part article). Reid's two-part article is the best place to go to learn more about the role of Christ in election in early Reformed and Lutheran theology.

(John 6:40). "If you confess with your mouth that Jesus is Lord and believe in your heart that God raised him from the dead, you will be saved" (Rom. 10:9). These gospel declarations get to the heart of God's eternal purpose, his eternal counsel, his decree of whom to choose for eternal salvation. Arminians believe that these gospel texts loudly and plainly answer the question, on whom does God, from eternity, desire to have mercy and compassion?

For Arminius, God's decree to elect is simply the administration, *in eternity*, of what he does *in time* when he justifies believers who come into union with Christ through faith. Thus, Arminius argued, to find out why God elects people, one must look to his will that he has clearly revealed in the gospel, not to an alleged secret will that he has hidden from everyone.

This reading of the predestination and election texts through the lens of the gospel is what drives Arminians. God's will revealed in the gospel answers the question on whom God, from eternity, wants to have mercy and compassion: believers. He gives sufficient grace for anyone to be converted yet maintains everyone's freedom to resist that grace. Thus from eternity he decided to make it possible, through the gospel of his grace in Christ, for everyone to believe. His consistent will, from eternity, is for everyone who looks on the Son and believes to have eternal life, so that anyone who confesses and believes in Jesus will be saved (John 6:40; Rom. 10:9). In his own manner and timing, he gives anyone and everyone the grace to do this, though unbelievers could never do it of their own ability. It is from this clear vantage point that Arminians interpret the passages that speak of the eternal counsel of God in election.

The remainder of this chapter will argue from Ephesians 1:4–11, with special reference to verse 4, that God's decree to elect individuals to eternal salvation is based on his consideration of the merit of Christ imputed to an individual through faith. Or as many non-Calvinistic scholastic theologians said, God elects individuals for eternal salvation *intuitu Christi meriti fide apprehendi*, that is, in consideration of the merit of Christ apprehended by faith.[3]

intuitu Christi meriti fide apprehendi:
in consideration of the merit of Christ apprehended by faith

As William Most and Thomas Oden have shown, the doctrine of individual, conditional election through divine foreknowledge is the classic doctrine of election common to all the church fathers up to and beyond Augustine, and it was the latter's doctrine until his older years. Even after Augustine, with the exception of only a very few, such as Gottschalk of Orbais, Thomas Bradwardine, and Gregory of Rimini, the doctrine held sway in both the eastern and western branches of Christendom. The Lutheran, Anabaptist,

---

3. This phrase was made popular by the sixteenth-century Lutheran dogmatician Aegidius Hunnius. See *The Error of Modern Missouri*, 25.

and Arminian branches of the Reformation-era church continued to confess variations of election in consideration of the merit of Christ apprehended by faith. A historical survey is beyond the scope of this chapter. Yet it is important to understand how deeply rooted this doctrine is in the consensual teaching of the fathers and the medieval period, as well as the majority of Reformation-era Protestantism.[4]

Elect in Christ

Ephesians 4:1–11 praises God for his salvific blessings in Christ (v. 3), one of which is that he chose or elected (*exelexato*) individuals in Christ before creation (v. 4) so that they might be holy and blameless. These chosen individuals have been predestined (*proorisas*) to adoption as God's children (v. 5). His choice of individuals in Christ to be his for eternity accords with his good pleasure (*eudokian*) and will (*thelēmatos*) (v. 5). In other words, it pleases him—he desires—to choose, to foreordain certain people to be his for eternity. It is important to note here, as Picirilli stresses, that "when God acts in a manner that is in accord with His sovereign good pleasure or will, He may act unconditionally or on the basis of conditions He sovereignly establishes. The words themselves do not tell us which applies in any given instance. Indeed all God's acts are 'according to the good pleasure of his will.'"[5]

The salvific blessings described in verses 3–6, initiated in eternity past, motivate believers to praise God's glorious grace (v. 6). Verse 7 transitions to a consideration of God's salvific blessings in time (vv. 7–10). He lavishes the riches of his grace—redemption through his blood and forgiveness—on believers and makes known the mystery of his eternal salvific will, purpose, and plan. Thus verses 9–10 connect God's blessings in time with his blessings in eternity. Verse 11 continues this theme, reasserting that God predestined those he chose and gave an inheritance. This predestination accords with his purpose (*prothesin*), counsel (*boulēn*), and will (*thelēmatos*)—synonyms meaning what God desires.[6] The key phrases in these verses that deal with the doctrine of predestination and election are "chose us in him" (v. 4), "predestined us for adoption to himself as sons" (v. 5), and "predestined according to the purpose of him who works all things according to the counsel of his will" (v. 11).

These verses say nothing of unconditional election. Many Calvinists, like Charles Hodge and Sam Storms, stress that the phrase "in him" is ambiguous and refers to Christ as the "federal head" of the elect: "It was in Christ as their

---

4. William G. Most, *Grace, Predestination, and the Salvific Will of God: New Answers to Old Questions* (Port Royal, VA: Christendom, 2004); Thomas C. Oden, *The Transforming Power of Grace* (Nashville: Abingdon, 2000).
5. Robert E. Picirilli, *Grace, Faith, Free Will: Contrasting Views of Salvation: Calvinism and Arminianism* (Nashville: Randall House, 2002), 68.
6. Picirilli, *Grace, Faith, Free Will*, 70.

head and representative [that] they were chosen to holiness and eternal life, and therefore in virtue of what he was to do in their behalf."[7] Yet this oddly seems closer to the traditional Arminian argument that election is in consideration of the merit of Christ apprehended by faith—far from a cogent argument that the election spoken of is unconditional.

There is also no indication that "in him" in verse 4 refers to "Christ's participation in God's act of choosing," as some Calvinists suggest.[8] This unnatural construction flies in the face of the way Paul discusses the concept of believers being "in Christ," a phrase Paul uses eleven times in the first thirteen verses of Ephesians 1. When speaking of individuals being "in Christ," Paul uniformly means salvific connection with Christ, union with Christ.[9]

The question at issue is this: Are the election and predestination in and through Christ in Ephesians 1:4, 5, and 11 conditional or unconditional? At best, Calvinists must insert unconditional election into these verses because it is not there. Arminians, however, argue that to say God "chose us in Christ" *entails the doctrine of conditional election*, because once God's consideration of Christ comes into the picture, a condition is introduced. As Picirilli notes, Paul universally teaches that the only way people are "in Christ" is through faith. Paul teaches in this passage that God chose us "in saving union with Christ."[10] Thus conditional election—election in consideration of the merit of Christ apprehended by faith—is logically entailed.

Arminius's Interpretation

Commenting on Ephesians 1:4, Arminius argued that the Calvinist view of election is not Christ-centered enough, not gospel-centered enough. In that view, he said, "Christ does not seem to me to obtain that place which He merits and which the Apostle assigns to Him." Calvinism unintentionally reduces Christ and his merit to the *mere means* by which salvation occurs, since it makes salvation's *cause* unconditional election. Thus Calvinism cannot really say that God elected us *in Christ*; it must say that God elected us *to be* in Christ.[11]

---

7. Charles Hodge, *Commentary on the Epistle to the Ephesians* (Old Tappan, NJ: Revell, n.d.), 31; quoted in Sam Storms, *Chosen for Life: The Case for Divine Election* (Wheaton, IL: Crossway, 2007), 110.

8. Clinton E. Arnold, *Ephesians*, Zondervan Exegetical Commentary on the New Testament (Grand Rapids: Zondervan, 2010), 80.

9. Mark Seifrid, "In Christ," in *Dictionary of Paul and His Letters*, eds. Gerald F. Hawthorne and Ralph P. Martin (Downers Grove, IL: InterVarsity, 1993), 436.

10. Robert E. Picirilli, *Ephesians*, Randall House Bible Commentary, ed. Robert E. Picirilli (Nashville: Randall House, 1988), 134; Picirilli, *Grace, Faith, Free Will*, 66. Jack Cottrell uses the same language in his *What the Bible Says about God the Ruler* (Joplin, MO: College Press, 1984), 344.

11. Arminius, *Works*, 3:293, "Examination of Perkins's Pamphlet."

On the contrary, Arminius argued, in Ephesians 1, Christ is "not merely the medium by which the salvation already prepared by election is obtained, but, as it were, the *meritorious cause* in respect of which that election took place, and on account of which that grace has been prepared."[12] J. K. S. Reid agreed, characterizing the Calvinist view as being that "Christ is merely the exhibitor of a decision already made in an eternity in which He has Himself been, even if existent, at least inoperative."[13] Arminius was here articulating the concept spoken of earlier, *intuitu Christi meriti fide apprehendi*. Christ's work is the meritorious cause of election. For Arminius, with his Christocentric view of election, Calvinism gets it backward, emphasizing God's absolute choice of individual sinners out of the mass of humanity, then treating Christ and his merit almost as an afterthought.[14]

Instead, Ephesians 1:4 presents Christ as "the Mediator by whose blood salvation and life have been gained for us, and as in the Head from whom those benefits flow down to us." God cannot choose anyone for eternal salvation except in Christ. Yet no one "can be considered in Christ by God, unless he be grafted upon Him by faith." Christ is "in reality a Saviour to no one, except He be apprehended by faith."[15]

An Arminian Proof Text

Thus, far from being a Calvinist proof text, Arminians see Ephesians 1:4 as providing grave difficulty for Calvinism. If Paul had wished to say that we are chosen *to be* in Christ, he simply would have said that. As Jack Cottrell states, "The elect are chosen *in* (*en*) Christ, that is, because they are in Christ; they are not chosen *into* (*eis*) Christ, that is, in order that they may be in Christ. They are in Christ before the foundation of the world not in reality but in the foreknowledge of God."[16] The only way the language of "in Christ" in Ephesians 1:4 has any meaning is if Christ's merit and all his salvific benefits are ours, but those cannot be experienced outside of union with Christ. In short, the only way election "in Christ" makes sense is if it is election in union with Christ, in the merit of Christ, in the salvific work of Christ. And if God regards this, if he "considers" it, then conditional election is the logical result: election *intuitu Christi meriti fide apprehendi*.

Calvinists struggle to explain how people can be elect in Christ without God's taking their in-Christ status into account in his decree of election. Most Calvinist books on election do not discuss what it specifically means to be elect "in Christ." They simply quote from Ephesians 1 and assert, but not

---

12. Arminius, *Works*, 3:293 (italics added).
13. Reid, "The Office of Christ," 16.
14. Arminius, *Works*, 3:293.
15. Arminius, *Works*, 3:293.
16. Cottrell, *God the Ruler*, 344.

argue, that it teaches that election is not conditioned on the merit of Christ apprehended by faith.[17]

Examples of this tendency are John Lafayette Girardeau, the great nineteenth-century Southern Presbyterian theologian, and John Piper. Girardeau stated that when Paul says the elect were chosen in Christ, "he must mean that they were elected *to be* redeemed by Christ, appointed as their mediator and federal head."[18] Piper explains: "It is true that all election is in relation to Christ. Christ was in the mind of God crucified before the foundation of the world (Revelation 13:8). There would be no election of sinners unto salvation if Christ were not appointed to die for their sins. So in that sense they are elect in Christ. But it is they who are chosen out of the world to be in Christ."[19]

The Arminian response to this sort of argument is twofold: First, how does an omniscient God who makes his decree of election with Christ crucified in his mind, electing individuals in that crucified Christ, not actually consider Christ's merit? Second, Piper's doctrine necessitates that he insert the words "to be" as he does in the last sentence of the above quotation: "they who are chosen out of the world *to be* in Christ." Yet the text does not say they are chosen *to be* in Christ. It says they were chosen *in Christ*. Piper must add the words "to be" to the passage for it to cohere with the doctrine of unconditional election.[20]

Michael Horton comes closer than most in his open acknowledgment that election in Ephesians 1:4–5 is connected to "the theme of union with Christ." Horton states, "In the mind of the eternal Father, the Lamb without blemish had already been sacrificed when he chose the heirs of redemption and placed them in Christ for eternity." Horton's order is noteworthy: God (1) "chose the heirs of redemption" then (2) "placed them in Christ for eternity." Yet Horton never addresses the pressing question: If election takes into account *union* with Christ, if election is *in* union with Christ, how can it be unconditional? Why does Paul insist that we are elect in Christ when, if he had meant to, he could simply have said we are elect *into* Christ or *to be* in Christ?[21]

The early Reformed predestinarian theologian Amandus Polanus exemplifies the tension between the desire to present election as Christocentric while at the same time insisting that the merit of Christ has no effect on election: "God the Father elected us IN CHRIST. The work was accomplished,

---

17. A survey of the most popular Calvinist books on election reveals this. See, e.g., Lorraine Boettner, *The Reformed Doctrine of Predestination*; R. C. Sproul, *Chosen by God* and *What Is Reformed Theology?*; Thomas R. Schreiner and Bruce A. Ware, eds., *Still Sovereign*.

18. John L. Girardeau, *Calvinism and Evangelical Arminianism* (New York: Baker and Taylor, 1890), 37 (italics added).

19. John Piper, "What We Believe about the Five Points of Calvinism," https://www.desiringgod.org/articles/what-we-believe-about-the-five-points-of-calvinism, accessed July 3, 2020.

20. Piper, "What We Believe about the Five Points of Calvinism" (italics added).

21. Michael Horton, *Putting Amazing Back into Grace* (Grand Rapids: Baker, 2002), 108, 147.

indeed, by this means in which we are elect: since without that means union between electing God and elect men would not have been possible. Therefore Christ is the bond by which God and the elect shall be conjoined."[22] Arminians do not see how it is possible to posit side-by-side that Christ is necessary to "conjoin" God and the elect, though his meritorious work on the elect's behalf is not considered in the absolute, unconditional decree to elect.

The Lutheran dogmatician August Pfeiffer's reading of the text is much more natural: "The election that was made *in Christ* and *in the Beloved* took place not by the mere will and good pleasure of God absolutely, but in consideration of *faith* in Christ Jesus." The phrase "in Christ" has clear reference, Pfeiffer said, "through, or on account of, His merit, which He acquired as the propitiation for all men." Paul "makes it plainer still by the preposition *dia* (by, through) in the fifth verse; *so that the passage can be interpreted to mean nothing else than that God elected us in consideration of the merit of Christ and its appropriation by true faith.*"[23]

Election Cannot Be Outside of the *Merit* of Christ

As Leroy Forlines says, Ephesians 1:4 "puts Calvinism in serious contradiction with Paul" by saying that "the elect were chosen by God as His very own before the decree to provide atonement."[24] Yet it is also in serious contradiction with the Reformed doctrine of atonement.

> It is not the prerogative of sovereign grace to enter into a personal relationship with a person apart from the application of the death and righteousness of Christ to his account. If that is the case, it was not the prerogative of sovereign grace in eternity past efficaciously and affectively to know or elect a member of the human race apart from foreknowing him or her to be in Christ. Calvinism is harmed rather than helped by Ephesians 1:4.[25]

The Lutheran scholastic theologian Johann Gerhard agreed when he said that because of the "rigor of divine justice, Christ had to intercede," not only in

---

22. Quoted in Richard A. Muller, *Christ and the Decree: Christology and Predestination in Reformed Theology from Calvin to Perkins* (Grand Rapids: Baker Academic, 2008), 58 (capitalization in the original).

23. August Pfeiffer, *Anti-Calvinism*, trans. Edward Pfeiffer (Columbus, OH: Joint Lutheran Synod of Ohio, 1881 [1699]), 174–75, 178. Italics added in the first instance, in the original in the second. See also Oliver Crisp, *God Incarnate: Explorations in Christology* (London: T&T Clark, 2009), chapter 2, "The Election of Jesus Christ," 36–39.

24. F. Leroy Forlines, *Classical Arminianism: A Theology of Salvation* (Nashville: Randall House, 2011), 184.

25. Forlines, *Classical Arminianism*, 184.

time (justification), but in God's eternal decree (election). Thus Christ's merit "placated" divine wrath *even in eternity.* "For this reason we say that Christ is the cause of election, or, what is the same, we say that God made His decree of election in view of the satisfaction to be made by Christ and to be received by faith." Gerhard explained that since Ephesians 1:7, 11 state that there is no redemption through Christ's blood or remission of sins outside of Christ, "neither did election happen outside of Christ."[26]

Arminians (and Lutherans like Pfeiffer and Gerhard) see a contradiction between two concepts in Calvin's *Institutes.* Calvin said that "God, who is the highest righteousness, cannot love the unrighteousness that he sees in us all" (*Institutes,* 2.16.3). Thus Christ's expiation has to intervene for God to be "pleased with and kindly disposed toward us" (2.16.3).[27] Calvin criticized those who avoided the discussion of Christ's merit in their discussions of election (2.17.1). However, a few lines down, Calvin insisted that, when referring to Christ's merit, "we do not consider the beginning of merit to be in him, but we go back to God's ordinance, the first cause. For God solely of his own good pleasure appointed him Mediator to obtain salvation for us. . . . For this reason nothing hinders us from asserting that men are freely justified by God's mercy alone, and at the same time that Christ's merit, subordinate to God's mercy, also intervenes on our behalf" (2.17.1). Thus J. K. S. Reid rightly concludes: "'We shall find no assurance of our election' says Calvin (3.24.5), '. . . even in God the Father, considered alone, abstractedly from the Son.' But in the last resort, it is that of a God into whose counsels Christ has not been admitted, and the inmost recesses of whose wisdom Christ has not illuminated."[28]

Arminians believe that Calvinists cannot simply leave these loose ends untied between Calvin's affirmation that Christ's merit must intervene because "God, who is perfect righteousness, cannot love the iniquity which he sees in all" and his affirmation that God can set his elective love on people before there is satisfaction for their sins. This represents not a mystery but a contradiction. As Arminius averred, "He who is not in Christ, cannot be loved in Christ. But no one is in Christ except by faith. . . . God acknowledges for His own, and loves to life eternal, no sinner, except as He regards him as a believer in Christ, and by faith made one with Him." Arminius's doctrine of the twofold love of God, wherein the only thing he loves more than human beings is his justice, requires the decree of election to comprehend the merit of Christ in an individual apprehended by faith.[29]

---

26. Johann Gerhard, *Theological Commonplaces: On Creation and Predestination,* trans. Richard J. Dinda, eds. Benjamin T. G. Mayes and Joshua Hayes (St. Louis: Concordia, 2013 [1611]), 197, 201.
27. Henry Beveridge translates it "placable and propitious to us."
28. J. K. S. Reid, "The Office of Christ," 12. This quotation is from part one of a two-part article.
29. Arminius, 3:296–97. See William den Boer, *God's Twofold Love: The Theology of Jacob Arminius (1559–1609)* (Göttingen: Vandenhoeck and Ruprecht, 2010), passim.

Thus in Calvinism, God not only has two wills and two callings, but he also has two graces: one is the grace of election given in eternity; the other is the grace of Christ's merit given in time. Indeed, as Calvin stated, "election precedes grace." Reid says that the weakness in Calvin's view "is evident in a chance phrase which Calvin is at least once betrayed into using (3.22.1): '*gratiam istam Dei praecedit election*': thus, election precedes grace. If this is true, then one's worst forebodings are fulfilled. The God and Father of Jesus Christ is a God of grace. Who, then, is this God who determines men's election before grace becomes operative?"[30] Arminians argue that the divine will, calling, and grace are all consistent with each other. Just as there is no contradiction between God's secret will and his revealed will, or between God's internal calling and his external calling, there is also no contradiction between God's electing grace and his justifying grace in the merit of Christ.

Christ the Cause of Salvific Blessings in Both Time and Eternity

Thus there is also no contradiction between God's saving action in time and his saving action in eternity. As Gerhard explained, God "includes Christ" as the cause of both "that blessing by which God blesses us with spiritual blessings in time" and "the act of election by which God elected us to eternal life before the foundation of the world."[31] This is why the text so frequently and fluidly uses the phrase "in him" or "in Christ" or "in the beloved"—eleven times in Ephesians 1:1–13—to refer to God's salvific blessings in time (adoption, justification, etc.) and eternity (election, predestination). It is artificial, in view of this fluid use of "in Christ" for God's salvific blessings in both time and eternity, to suggest that God considers the merit of Christ with regard to one but not the other.

God's immutability entails that one cannot say that he "has decided one thing from eternity in one way and then acts in a different way in time."[32] Ephesians 1:3–4 states that God "blessed us [in time] in Christ with every spiritual blessing . . . *even as* he chose us in him [in eternity]." God's salvific purpose, counsel, and decrees *in eternity* are consistent with what he announces *in time* he will do, and what he executes *in time*.

Thus, again, there is no secret will, no secret decree in eternity. God's decrees in eternity are fully consonant with his publicly announced gospel purpose in time. This is clear from Ephesians 1:9, which says that God has not hidden his eternal salvific purpose from us, but has "ma[de] known to us the mystery of his will, according to his purpose, which he set forth in Christ."

---

30. Reid, "The Office of Christ," 12.
31. Gerhard, *Theological Commonplaces*, 198. See also Picirilli, *Ephesians*, 138, and R. C. H. Lenski, *The Interpretation of St. Paul's Epistles to the Galatians, to the Ephesians, and to the Philippians* (Minneapolis: Augsburg, 1961), 355.
32. Gerhard, *Theological Commonplaces*, 199.

As Paul says elsewhere in Ephesians, the reason he preaches the gospel is "to bring to light for everyone" the "plan of the mystery hidden for ages in God" (3:8–9). In Romans 16:25–26 Paul describes the "gospel and preaching of Jesus Christ" as announcing the "revelation of the mystery that was kept secret for long ages but has now been disclosed and through the prophetic writings has been made known to all nations."

Christ the Cause of Election

Another argument many Calvinists make is that Christ and his merit are the *effect* of election. Beza said, "Christ is not the cause of our election," and Peter Martyr Vermigli stated, "We deny that Christ is the cause of our predestination, as far as His humanity or death is concerned."[33] As Richard Muller persuasively argues, early Reformed predestinarian theologians such as Gulielmus Bucanus, Amandus Polanus, Theodore Beza, Jerome Zanchi, William Perkins, John Sharp, and Bartholomäus Keckermann included the entire Trinity in the decree to elect. Thus election is clearly in Christ in this sense. However, Muller correctly states that the involvement of Christ in the decree of election in Calvinist thought "in no way predicates election upon the temporal activity of Son and Spirit: the cause of election is in God alone and is in him from eternity." In that system, nothing temporal can cause election, he explains, "for election rests entirely upon the grace of God; thus neither the foreknowledge of faith or of good works is the cause of our election to life eternal. God first decrees the end and then the means so that faith and works, as means, depend on the decree."[34]

As Arminius said, however, Christ's merit is the *cause* of election. It is incoherent to say, with Ephesians 1:4, that we are elect *in Christ* if being in Christ is merely an effect of our election. Again, if the text stated that we are elect *into Christ* or elect *to be* in Christ, it could be said that the merit of Christ is the effect of election. Yet being *in* Christ cannot be an effect of election.

Summary

The following words from Johann Gerhard summarize the view of Arminians and other non-Calvinists that to be elect in Christ, as Ephesians 1:4 states, requires the view that God's election of individuals for eternal salvation was in consideration of the merit of Christ apprehended by faith:

> Either God foreknew the satisfaction of Christ or He did not foreknew it. To say the latter is blasphemy. If He foreknew it, either He was satisfied by the foreknowledge of it or He was

---

33. Gerhard, *Theological Commonplaces*, 202.
34. Muller, *Christ and the Decree*, 157–58. Thus for Beza, Muller argues, one's being elect in Christ "implies some subordination of Christ to the eternal counsel of God" (87).

not. We cannot say the latter, because the sacrificial victim offered in time was propitiatory for the sins of the world. Thus foreknowledge and consideration of it were of the same efficacy from eternity. Therefore it follows that God was placated by the consideration of the satisfaction of Christ which was to be offered in time. Therefore that consideration cannot be excluded from the decree of election.[35]

REFLECTION QUESTIONS

1. What does Arminius mean when he says that God's decree to elect is simply the administration, *in eternity*, of what he does *in time* when he justifies believers who come into union with Christ through faith?

2. What does Arminius mean when he says that, to find out why God elects people, one must look to his will that he has clearly revealed in the gospel, not to an alleged secret will that he has hidden from everyone?

3. What do non-Calvinists mean when they say that election was "in consideration of the merit of Christ apprehended by faith"?

4. Why do Arminians think that to say that the elect were chosen "*in* Christ" means that God could not have done anything but consider the merit of Christ apprehended by faith?

5. What does Leroy Forlines mean when he says that it is incoherent to affirm that God embraces people with his elective love without regard to whether or not their sins have been covered by the atonement through their union with Christ by faith?

---

35. Muller, 203.

Does Romans 8:28–30 Teach Unconditional or Conditional Election?

Romans 8:28 reinforces the entire thrust of this section of Paul's letter: No matter how severe the sufferings are that believers endure, as they remain in union with Christ through faith, they will never be separated from God's love. Paul says in verse 28 that, for those who love God, who have not spurned his loving call, all things work together for their good. What is the "purpose" (*prothesin*) Paul refers to in this verse? The word is a synonym for terms Paul uses such as "counsel" and "will," indicating his eternal salvific plan, which is revealed in the gospel.

Romans 8:28 and the Purpose of God in Salvation

Calvinists point to a secret purpose, counsel, or will of God for the salvation of those who are unconditionally chosen from the mass of humanity, the rest of whom God excludes from his grace. Arminians point to the only purpose or plan of God for salvation, his revealed will: that everyone come to the knowledge of the truth (1 Tim. 2:4) and that everyone who looks on the Son and believes in him should be saved (John 6:40). They argue that God has clearly revealed what his eternal plan, counsel, will, and purpose are. When one looks at *God's openly revealed purpose—to provide a way of salvation for everyone through his son's death and to provide grace for everyone to believe and save those who do so*—one sees the purpose according to which he calls people to himself. God's election is "according to the purpose of him who works all things according to the counsel of his will" (Eph. 1:11). And one discovers God's eternal purpose, counsel, good pleasure, will, and plan by looking to his revealed will in Scripture.

So who are "the called according to his purpose"? Paul states very clearly that they are those who love God. In other words, they are believers, people who did not spurn the loving call of God in the gospel, of which the church father Chrysostom says in his comments on this verse, "the calling was not forced upon them, nor compulsory. All then were called, but all did not obey the call."[1] As I. Howard Marshall has said, "God has a purpose of salvation for men, in accordance with which He calls them by the Gospel, and the persons described in this verse are those who have answered this call, as is plain from the fact that they now love God. Salvation thus depends upon God's purpose and call and upon human response to that call."[2]

One does not have to be a Calvinist to glory in the eternal salvific purpose, will, and counsel of God. The perennial question is, what is that purpose? Is it conditional or unconditional? It is the same question that Romans 9:15 presses: On whom does God desire, from eternity, to show mercy and compassion? The answer is found by looking at that eternal purpose, counsel, will, and plan of God as clearly and openly revealed in Holy Scripture, which Paul "did not shrink from declaring" to everyone (Acts 20:27). The whole reason Paul said he preached the gospel was "to bring to light for everyone" the "plan of the mystery hidden for ages in God" (Eph. 3:8–9), publicly announcing the "revelation of the mystery that was kept secret for long ages but has now been disclosed and through the prophetic writings has been made known to all nations" (Rom. 16:25–26). There is nothing secretive in these texts. God has openly made known in his Word his *only* eternal salvific purpose, counsel, and will.

Romans 8:29, Foreknowledge, and Predestination

Verse 29 goes on to say that God predestined those he foreknew to be conformed to his son's image. The Calvinist is forced to say that foreknowledge is a synonym for foreordination. Yet this would mean that the Greek word *proginōskō* has no relationship to its use elsewhere in the New Testament or in extrabiblical Greek as "to know beforehand." Yet, as Johann Gerhard averred, there would be a "tautology in the words of the apostle unless the word 'foreknow' denotes the foresight of future things."[3] Leroy Forlines is correct when he notes, "When *proginōskō* is translated as 'foreordination' or some word that is equivalent, the translator has become an exegete."[4] Another reason for

1. *Homilies of S. John Chrysostom . . . on the Epistle of S. Paul the Apostle to the Romans*, trans. J. B. Morris (Oxford: James Parker and Co., 1877), 264.
2. I. Howard Marshall, *Kept by the Power of God: A Study of Perseverance and Falling Away* (Eugene, OR: Wipf and Stock, 2008), 101–2.
3. Johann Gerhard, *Theological Commonplaces: On Creation and Predestination*, trans. Richard J. Dinda, eds. Benjamin T. G. Mayes and Joshua Hayes (St. Louis: Concordia, 2013 [1611]), 202. See Robert E. Picirilli, *Grace, Faith, Free Will: Contrasting Views of Salvation: Calvinism and Arminianism* (Nashville: Randall House, 2002), 77.
4. F. Leroy Forlines, *Classical Arminianism: A Theology of Salvation* (Nashville: Randall House, 2011), 179. See Jack W. Cottrell, "Conditional Election," in *Grace for All: The Arminian Dynamics of Salvation*, eds. Clark H. Pinnock and John D. Wagner (Eugene, OR: Resource, 2014), 79–80.

seeing foreknowledge and predestination in this text as two different divine actions is that, as Grant Osborne argues, "none of the other [of the] five stages in verses 29–30 are synonymous, but each one leads to the next. This means that for Paul foreknowledge *leads to* predestination."[5]

Calvinists often say that "foreknown" here is used to indicate God's "foreloving" his people.[6] This was the position of William Perkins, to whom Arminius responded. Arminius said Perkins was mistaken to say that foreknowledge in this verse should be taken to mean *only* affectionate knowledge, to the exclusion of prescience, God's omniscience applied to future events. Arminius agreed that God's foreknowledge of believers in Romans 8:29 is an affectionate foreknowledge. However, he insisted that this very thing makes it necessary to affirm that the word also means God's simple foreknowledge of what is going to take place in the future. These two senses of the word "agree perfectly," he said. The "former sense cannot be true without this latter."[7]

As Arminius perceptively argued, "God can regard no sinner with affection beforehand and love him as His own, unless He has foreknown Him in Christ, and has regarded him as believing upon Christ. . . . God acknowledges no one from amongst sinners as His own, and loves no one to life eternal, except in Christ and on account of Christ." Thus the word "foreknowledge" also means that God foreknows in the simple sense of prescience, because the only way he can affectionately foreknow people is if he knows them as believers, and to know them as believers, he has to know *the fact* that they are believers—a fact that he cannot help but know because he is omniscient.[8]

---

5. Grant R. Osborne, *Romans Verse by Verse*, Osborne New Testament Commentaries (Bellingham, WA: Lexham, 2017), 252.
6. See, e.g., S. M. Baugh, "The Meaning of Foreknowledge," in *Still Sovereign: Contemporary Perspectives on Election, Foreknowledge, and Grace*, eds. Thomas R. Schreiner and Bruce A. Ware (Grand Rapids: Baker, 2000), 183–200, passim; Wayne Grudem, *Systematic Theology* (Grand Rapids: Zondervan, 1994), 676. They cite 2 Timothy 2:19; Matthew 11:27; Romans 11:2; and 1 Corinthians 8:3, which Arminius agreed taught affectionate foreknowledge but *also* prescience.
7. Jacobus Arminius, *The Works of James Arminius*, trans. James Nichols and William Nichols (Nashville: Randall House, 2007), 3:296, "Examination of Perkins's Pamphlet."
8. Arminius, *Works*, 3:296–97. It is interesting that, while many Arminians wish to limit foreknowledge simply to prescience, Reformed Arminians (following Arminius), as well as Lutherans, tend to argue that it consists of both affectionate knowledge and prescience. See, e.g., Forlines, *Classical Arminianism*, 181–82; Picirilli, *Grace, Faith, Free Will*, 77; R. C. H. Lenski, *The Interpretation of St. Paul's Epistle to the Romans* (Minneapolis: Augsburg, 1961 [1936]), 557–58; and George H. Schodde, ed., *The Error of Modern Missouri: Its Inception, Development, and Refutation* (Columbus, OH: Lutheran Book Concern, 1897), 720. The Lutheran exegete R. C. H. Lenski states that the usage of "to know" in this "pregnant sense" is adopted by the orthodox Lutheran dogmaticians (557). I. Howard Marshall and Grant Osborne also articulate this position. See Marshall, *Kept by the Power of God*, 102; Grant R. Osborne, *Romans*, IVP New Testament Commentary (Downers Grove, IL: IVP Academic, 2010), 220–21.

No one can become conformed to the image of God's son unless he is a believer. The text does not say that God predestined people to belief. It says he predestined those he foreknew as believers to conformity to Christ's image. The only way someone can be conformed to Christ's image is by being in Christ through faith, and since God is consistent in his salvific plan in both time and eternity, he had to have taken individuals' faith into consideration in eternity. Otherwise, how could he have predestined them to be conformed to Christ's image?[9]

This rules out the view that people are predestined to believe. Nowhere are election or predestination said to be *to belief*. As Forlines says, the "terminus" of election and predestination in the New Testament is always either (1) eternal salvation or (2) things that can occur only by means of union with Christ through faith, such as conformity to Christ's image (Rom. 8:29) or adoption (Eph. 1:5).[10] The terminus of election and predestination is never belief. Thus Arminius said,

> If adoption and righteousness be received by faith, then those who are predestinated to become righteous and sons of God, must necessarily be considered as believers. For what is destined for any one by predestination, that he will certainly receive. And, indeed, such as he is when receiving it, just such was he considered when predestinated to receive it. The believer receives it, and no one else: therefore the believer only was predestinated to receive it. Whence again I conclude, that no one is loved by God to adoption and the bestowal of the gift of righteousness, unless he has been considered by Him as a believer.[11]

Paul's teaching that God predestines those he foreknows as believers who love him makes even more sense when seen against the backdrop of Peter's statement that election is "according to the foreknowledge of God the Father" (1 Peter 1:2). That is the only place in the Bible other than Romans 8:28 that discusses foreknowledge with direct connection to God's salvific plan.[12] If foreknowledge in 1 Peter is simply another way of saying predestination, it is more than the tautology that would have been achieved if Romans 8 meant that those whom God foreordained, he foreordained. As Osborne notes, in 1 Peter 1:2, "the choosing is *based on* the foreknowledge."[13]

---

9. Arminius, *Works*, 3:297.
10. Forlines, *Classical Arminianism*, 171, 174.
11. Arminius, *Works*, 3:298.
12. Picirilli, *Grace, Faith, Free Will*, 77.
13. Osborne, *Romans*, IVP New Testament Commentary, 221.

Calvinism's only argument is simply to affirm that, since foreknowledge can denote "knowledge of" and not only "knowledge that," it must mean only the former in Romans 8:29 and 1 Peter 1:20.[14] Yet the most compelling reading of these texts is that God knows these people in Christ. This affectionate knowledge entails his knowing *that* they are in Christ. Based on this foreknowledge, he elects them *intuitu Christi meriti fide apprehendi*, in consideration of the merit of Christ apprehended by faith.

Romans 8:30 and the "Golden Chain"

Romans 8:30 goes on to say that the ones God foreknew and hence predestined are called, justified, and glorified. Two key questions arise from this verse. First, is it describing an inviolable order of salvation (*ordo salutis*), a "logical chain of individual participation" in salvation, as Calvinists assert?[15] Or is it simply describing what happens to the elect? Second, does this mean that no one else was called, other than those whom God foreknew as believers, whom he predestined?

It is important to understand that most Arminians and other non-Calvinists who teach that believers can fall from grace affirm that God elects for eternal salvation only those people whom he foreknows will persevere in faith to the end of life. If God's conditional election of individuals is in consideration of their persevering in union with Christ through faith, then verse 30 makes perfect sense: all those God foreknew in persevering faith, he predestined. That they did not spurn his call is obvious in the fact that they were justified, which occurs only through faith. The elect will also be glorified.

One cannot infer from this verse, however, that everyone who is justified will be glorified. That is simply not what the verse states. It says that those whom God foreknew (v. 29) as those who love God (v. 28), he predestined, justified, and glorified. Yet this coheres perfectly with an election in consideration of the merit of Christ apprehended by faith. As the Anglican exegete Henry Alford stated, those who apostatize, while they were once regenerate, were never elect. This text is "one among many passages where in the Scripture, as ever from the teaching of the Church, we learn that 'elect' and 'regenerate' are not convertible terms. All elect are regenerate: but all regenerate are not elect."[16] Thus, as Lenski said, because "in eternity, before the mind of God, all time and all that occurs in time were finished and complete," God's elective decree "excludes all those who believe only for a time and become apostate before their death."[17]

14. See, e.g., Baugh, "The Meaning of Foreknowledge," 195–96.
15. Michael Horton, *The Christian Faith: A Systematic Theology for Pilgrims on the Way* (Grand Rapids: Zondervan, 2011), 561.
16. Henry Alford, *The Greek Testament* (London: Rivingtons, 1859), 4:113.
17. Lenski, *Romans*, 557.

John Wesley stressed that St. Paul does not say that "precisely the same number are called, justified, and glorified." Nor does he say that a believer cannot apostatize between justification and glorification. Nor does he "deny that many are called who are never justified. He only affirms that this is the method whereby God leads step by step toward heaven."[18] At each stage in salvation, there is conditionality. God has unconditionally decreed that election, like salvation, is conditional, and in his foreknowledge he knows those who are in Christ, that is, who meet the condition of faith, which includes perseverance in faith.[19]

What about the second question above? Does this verse prove that there is a secret calling that goes out only to the elect that is effectual and irresistible, as distinguished from the general call that goes out to everyone? Neither this nor any other text indicates that. As Jesus said, "many are called, but few are chosen" (Matt. 22:14).[20] As Forlines argues, "Paul likes to use the word 'called' in referring to believers to stress that our personal redemption owes its existence to God, who took the first initiative." Referring to believers as having been called "does not mean that the call has not been extended to anyone else." Paul is only stating that "those who are present have been invited. They are not intruders. It does not mean that no one else was invited."[21]

God's call to the elect is the same as his call to everyone. It is the same divine beckoning Paul refers to when he says in Acts 17:30 that God is commanding everyone to repent, and when he says in Romans 10:13 that everyone who calls on the Lord's name will be saved. "No one is justified who was not first called. There can be no question that Paul is referring to those cases where the call has had its desired effect. That is not the same as saying that the call is irresistible, nor that it has succeeded in every case. This simply cannot be read out of the language."[22]

Summary

Romans 8:28 teaches that all things will work together for the good of believers: those who love God, who have not resisted his loving call, which flows out of his eternal salvific purpose and plan. Paul states in several places what that purpose is, and that it is not hidden in secrecy but has been openly and plainly revealed in the gospel. Verse 29 teaches that those whom God affectionately foreknew in Christ (which means he had to foreknow *that* they were

---

18. John Wesley, *Explanatory Notes Upon the New Testament*, vol. 2 (Grand Rapids: Baker, 1981), quoted in Forlines, 149–50.
19. See the Wesleyan exegete Daniel D. Whedon, *Commentary on the New Testament* (New York: Eaton and Mains, 1871), 3:334. Forlines illustrates this with Mark 4:28 (*Classical Arminianism*, 150).
20. Chrysostom, *Romans*, 264.
21. Forlines, *Classical Arminianism*, 147–48.
22. Forlines, *Classical Arminianism*, 148.

in Christ by faith) are predestined to conformity to Christ's image. Verse 30 states that these people were also called, justified, and glorified, but it does not deal with two questions: first, whether the nonelect received the same call but resisted it; or second, whether everyone who is justified will also be glorified. The text simply states that those whom God foreknew in Christ from eternity received a call that they did not ultimately reject; thus they will eventually be glorified. Nothing in the text suggests that God's choice of individuals for eternal salvation is unconditional.

REFLECTION QUESTIONS

1. What do Arminians believe is God's eternal purpose in salvation mentioned in Romans 8:28?

2. Is there anything is verses 28–29 that requires one to think that the call Paul speaks of went only to the elect and not to others?

3. How do Arminians believe Romans 8:29 is connected to Peter's statement that election is according to God's foreknowledge, and what do they think that means?

4. What did Arminius mean when he said that, to foreknow someone affectionately in Christ (knowledge *of*), God had to foreknow the *fact* that they were in Christ by faith (knowledge *that*)?

5. When the author says that Romans 8:28–30 does not clearly state that everyone who is justified will be glorified, but it does clearly state that the elect will be glorified, is he right?

Does Romans 9:6–23 Teach Unconditional or Conditional Election?

The interpretation of Romans 9 in this chapter goes against the grain of some of the recent Arminian interpretation of Romans 9, which relies on the doctrine of corporate election. Leroy Forlines is correct in arguing, like Calvinists, that Paul's emphases are against corporate election in this chapter.[1] The Jewish theology of Paul's day had emphasized corporate election and works righteousness. Paul's emphasis in Romans 9, however, is on conditional, individual election, an election conditioned on union with Christ, which occurs through faith alone, not by either works or Jewish descent.[2]

Forlines's exegesis of Romans 9 dovetails with Arminius's own interpretation four centuries earlier. Arminius taught that Paul's intent in Romans 9 was to show that believers are saved by faith alone, not to teach unconditional

---

1. F. Leroy Forlines, *Classical Arminianism: A Theology of Salvation* (Nashville: Randall House, 2011), 99–149; Forlines, *Romans*, Randall House Bible Commentary (Nashville: Randall House, 1987), 248–82. My interpretation here relies heavily on Forlines's individual-election understanding of Romans 9. The best treatment of Romans 9 from a corporate-election perspective is Brian J. Abasciano, *Paul's Use of the Old Testament in Romans 9.1–9: An Intertextual and Theological Exegesis* (London: T&T Clark, 2005) and idem, *Paul's Use of the Old Testament in Romans 9.10–18: An Intertextual and Theological Exegesis* (London: T&T Clark, 2011).

2. Robert E. Picirilli supports Forlines's basic approach. See his *Grace, Faith, Free Will: Contrasting Views of Salvation: Calvinism and Arminianism* (Nashville: Randall House, 2002), 71–76, and his *The Book of Romans* (Nashville: Randall House, 1975), 172–88. Forlines's and Picirilli's approach to Romans 9 bears similarities to scholastic Lutheran interpreters, as discussed in George H. Schodde, ed., *The Error of Modern Missouri: Its Inception, Development, and Refutation* (Columbus, OH: Lutheran Book Concern, 1897). This perspective is represented by R. C. H. Lenski, *The Interpretation of St. Paul's Epistle to the Romans* (Minneapolis: Augsburg, 1961 [1936]), 579–627.

election or reprobation.[3] As Stephen Ashby says, "Arminius felt constrained by the text to address the redemptive-historical dilemma facing the Apostle Paul."[4] Paul had been preaching that salvation comes through faith in Christ alone, which entailed that most Jews were not part of the covenant. The Jewish response that Paul anticipated was that if God had rejected most of the Jews, God's word or covenant with Abraham was of no effect.

According to Arminius, Paul's burden is to show that God's word still stands even if Jews who do not have faith in Christ are excluded from God's promise and blessings, just as some descendants of Abraham have always been excluded. Thus the question of the text is not whether people are elected unconditionally but whether God's Word fails if Jews who seek righteousness by the law instead of faith are excluded from the covenant. This is Paul's real question in Romans 9.[5]

The Jewish Objection

Calvinists believe that Romans 9 teaches unconditional election. They take as the starting point of their discussion their belief that 9:14—"What shall we say then? Is there injustice on God's part? By no means!"—is Paul's response to an objection against God's choice of Jacob and not Esau. However, a closer look at the context shows that Paul is defending divine justice against the objection that God would be unjust in *rejecting unbelieving Jews*.[6]

The first thirteen verses of the chapter deal with Paul's intense concern for his kinspeople, the Jews, who, by and large, had failed to respond to his gospel and recognize Jesus as Messiah. After ending chapter 8 with the triumphant blessedness of the gospel, Paul begins chapter 9 with sadness because of those of his Jewish kinspeople who have rejected the gospel. He then deals with their failure to respond to the gospel. Romans 10–11 emphasizes the faith of the individual as the condition for God's loving choice. Romans 8–11 forms a unified argument, from which the Calvinist interpretation abstracts chapter 9.[7]

To grasp the meaning of Romans 9, one must understand the belief in second temple Judaism in the corporate election of Jews as the covenant descendants of Abraham. Jesus and John the Baptist dealt with this mentality (Matt. 3:8–9; John 8). As Forlines argues, there was a tension in the Jewish thought of the second temple period between salvation by corporate election

---

3. Some of the material on Arminius in this chapter is adapted from J. Matthew Pinson, *Arminian and Baptist: Explorations in a Theological Tradition* (Nashville: Randall House, 2015), 15–17.

4. Ashby, "Introduction" to *The Works of Arminius*, 3 vols., trans. James Nichols and William Nichols (Nashville: Randall House, 1999), xix.

5. Ashby, "Introduction," xix–xx.

6. Forlines, *Classical Arminianism*, 100–2.

7. Jerry L. Walls and Joseph R. Dongell, *Why I Am Not a Calvinist* (Downers Grove, IL: InterVarsity Press, 2004), 85.

and salvation by works of the law. Some emphasized one over the other, while others held the two concepts in tension.[8]

In verse 6a, Paul says, "It is not as though the word of God had failed." Most Jews thought the word of God guaranteed their salvation by virtue of their being Israelites. If Paul is right and they must come to God by faith in the Messiah, then, in their minds, the word of God has failed. Therefore, Paul must show them how it has not, that the Old Testament never taught the corporate election of all Israelites. So he proceeds to argue that God never promised to save all who descended from Abraham or Jacob (Israel). Paul's strategy in verses 6–13 is to demonstrate that the Jewish people themselves do not truly believe in the corporate election of all of Abraham's or Isaac's descendants.

Thus Paul says in verse 7 that "not all Abraham's children are his true descendants; but 'It is through Isaac that descendants shall be named for you'" (NRSV). Jews would readily grant this. They were well aware that the covenant descendants came not through Ishmael nor through the children Abraham had with Keturah. The offspring of these children were not the covenant descendants of Abraham. Paul then argues that the promise God made to Abraham did not guarantee salvation to all his descendants. Salvation does not come from mere natural descent. Jews would argue that this is beside the point, since the Israelites are descendants of Isaac and not Ishmael. So Paul says that not even all of Isaac's descendants are the covenant descendants of Abraham (verses 10–13).

Ishmael and Isaac, Esau and Jacob

Calvin and his modern adherents such as John Piper have argued that the choice of Jacob over Esau is a case of the unconditional election of individuals to salvation. They say that Paul was attempting to convince his Jewish readers that they were not corporately elected just because they were Jews, but that God would unconditionally elect certain individual Jews (and Gentiles) but not others.[9]

---

8. Walls and Dongell, *Why I Am Not a Calvinist*, 103–4. Forlines formulated his ideas, first published in his 1987 Romans Commentary and expanded on in his 2001 book *The Quest for Truth*, prior to the widespread use of the term *variegated nomism*, but he agrees with the concept. See D. A. Carson, Peter T. O'Brien, and Mark A. Seifrid, eds., *Justification and Variegated Nomism*, 2 vols. (Grand Rapids: Baker, 2001, 2004).

9. John Calvin, *Commentaries on the Epistle of Paul the Apostle to the Romans*, trans. John Owen (Edinburgh: Calvin Translation Society, 1849), 350; John Piper, *The Justification of God: An Exegetical and Theological Study of Romans 9:1–23* (Grand Rapids: Baker, 1983), 44. Piper believes that Romans 9 teaches double predestination, that both election and reprobation are unconditional. See also Thomas R. Schreiner, "Does Romans 9 Teach Individual Election unto Salvation?" in *Still Sovereign: Contemporary Perspectives on Election, Foreknowledge, and Grace*, eds. Thomas R. Schreiner and Bruce A. Ware (Grand Rapids: Baker, 2000), 89–106.

However, as Arminius argued, Ishmael and Isaac, and Esau and Jacob, are types. The former in each pair represent children of the flesh, the latter children of the promise. Arminius quoted Galatians 4:21–31 to show that Paul himself sees these pairs as types.[10] In that passage, Paul had contrasted Hagar and Sarah and Ishmael and Isaac and then expressly stated that they were allegorical (v. 24): "Now you, brothers, like Isaac, are children of promise" (v. 28). Thus Arminius concludes: "Isaac is reckoned in the seed: Isaac is the type of all the children of the promise: Therefore, all the children of the promise are reckoned in the seed. . . . Ishmael is not reckoned in the seed: Ishmael is the type of all the children of the flesh: Therefore none of the children of the flesh are reckoned in the seed."[11]

Ashby correctly states that, according to Arminius, "when man had failed in performing the demands of the Creation covenant, and indeed had 'by the fall incurred inability to perform it,' God transferred the condition of this covenant to faith in Christ."[12] God was, Arminius averred, "at liberty to fix in that covenant whatever conditions He might have thought fit. . . . It is free to Him to make a decree according to election, by which He may ordain to have mercy on the children of promise, but to harden and punish the children of the flesh."[13]

Verses 6–13 are not dealing with individual election and reprobation but with Israel's redemptive history. Paul is demonstrating that not all of Abraham's descendants were the covenant descendants of Abraham, and he uses God's choice of Isaac and Jacob and rejection of Ishmael and Esau in the history of redemption to illustrate that fact. This meant that the Jewish people could not claim to be saved based simply on the fact that they were descendants of Abraham.[14] Furthermore, God's choice of Jacob over Esau emphasizes God's not basing his choice on anything "good or bad" that they "had done" (9:11). Paul's point here is that salvation is by faith alone, "not because of works" (9:11). Paul reinforces this idea in verse 32, which indicates that the reason for God's rejection of Israelites is "because they did not pursue it by faith, but as if it were based on works." The church fathers emphasized that God's "loving" of Jacob and "hating" of Esau are conditional, based on divine foreknowledge, which he obviously had before they were born.[15]

Paul's primary aim in verses 6–13, then, is to establish that the Jewish concept of the corporate election of all Jews is incorrect. Conditional election to salvation is not corporate, but individual (see Question 31). No one can be

---

10. Arminius, *Works*, 3:490, "Analysis of the Ninth Chapter of St. Paul's Epistle to the Romans."
11. Arminius, *Works*, 3:491.
12. Ashby, "Introduction," xxi, quoting Arminius, 3:497.
13. Arminius, *Works*, 3:502.
14. Picirilli, *The Book of Romans*, 178.
15. See, e.g., Jerome, *Commentaries on the Twelve Prophets*, ed. Thomas P. Scheck. Ancient Christian Texts (Downers Grove, IL: IVP Academic, 2017), 2:120.

saved based on mere birth or descent. So the Jew must reexamine the belief
that birth or descent guarantees salvation.

The Jewish Question in 9:14

This brings the reader of Romans back to the linchpin of chapter 9: verse
14. Paul continues in that verse with the question, "What then are we to say? Is
there injustice on God's part?" John Piper is representative of how Calvinism
gets Paul's thrust in this verse wrong: "When Paul said that God chose to bless
Jacob over Esau apart from any basis in their actions but simply on the basis
of his choice (*ek tou kalountos*, Rom. 9:12), his opponent objected that this
would call God's righteousness into question (9:14)."[16]

This misunderstanding gets the whole conversation off of Paul's line of
argument and onto the question of unconditional versus conditional election. Yet the question Paul asks in 9:14 is *not* a response to an objection to
the seeming injustice of God in arbitrarily selecting Jacob and rejecting Esau.
That does not fit the context. "The Calvinistic interpretation of verse 14 is
based on a Jewish concern that the Jews did not have."[17] Jews would have no
problem with the rejection of Esau. Far from trying to convince Jews of the
doctrine of unconditional election, Paul's task here was to get them to see that
the only way for them to be saved was through faith in Jesus as Messiah.[18] So,
contra the Calvinist interpretation, the primary objection of the Jews of Paul's
day to his teaching would never have been unconditional election, had he
been teaching that. Their objection would be that if God had failed to make
good on (what they thought was) his promise of the absolute election of all
Jews, it would mean that he had failed to keep his word, that he was unjust.[19]

So the interpretation that best fits the context is that the objection against
which Paul is defending God's justice is that God would be unjust if he did not
save all Jews, since that would compromise the covenant he had made with
Abraham to save his descendants. Paul says that God cannot be unjust and
then argues that God's rejection of unbelieving Jews is just, because of the sovereignty of God in salvation. In the next few verses, Paul provides illustrations
from Israel's history of God's sovereignty in the plan of salvation to show that
God's plan has always been, not a matter of natural descent, nor of the works
of the law, but of faith. Paul wants to illustrate two principles: First, God is just

---

16. Piper, *The Justification of God*, 100.
17. Forlines, *Classical Arminianism*, 127.
18. Forlines, *Classical Arminianism*, 127–28.
19. Forlines, *Classical Arminianism*, 128. As Jerry Walls and Joseph Dongell correctly note,
"Paradoxically . . . God's selection of Isaac and Jacob over Ishmael and Esau ultimately
served to broaden the flow of mercy" because salvation is not simply through "genetic connection to Abraham" but is provided for all, a fact Paul confirms in Romans 11:32 (Walls
and Dongell, 91).

in choosing some, but not all, from Israel for salvation. Second, the Jews are not in a position to argue with God.

On Whom Does God Desire to Show Mercy?

Paul's first illustration is from Moses in Exodus 33:19: "For God says to Moses, 'I will have mercy on whom I have mercy, and I will have compassion on whom I have compassion'" (9:15). To see this as teaching divine determinism in salvation misses Paul's point. The simple question one must ask is: On whom does God desire to show mercy? Paul clearly answers this question in 9:30–33 and the entirety of chapter 10, especially verses 10–21, which detail that he desires to show mercy to Jew and Gentile alike if they will have faith in Jesus the Messiah (10:8–13). Indeed he is stretching out his hand to beckon Israel to this faith, but they are resisting his gracious call (10:21). To understand the first twenty-three verses of Romans 9, one needs to read the rest of the chapter, as well as chapters 10–11. Here one finds the answer to the question on whom God chooses to show mercy: those who receive the Messiah through faith.

Romans 9–11 highlight the revealed will of God throughout Holy Scripture. In 9:15, Paul is driving home the point that God is the one who decides what salvation consists of, not finite human beings, and he is establishing that salvation is not by works, "human will and exertion," but by God's grace, "God who has mercy" (9:16). Piper believes that in verse 16 Paul is going against conditional election, but one cannot extrude that from the passage. It is clearly opposing faith to works, not unconditional election to conditional election. Verses 15–16 do not require readers of Scripture to affirm that God's election of individuals to eternal salvation is unconditional.[20]

The Hardening of Pharaoh

Paul shares a second illustration from redemptive history to emphasize God's sovereignty in the plan of salvation and to show that salvation has always been through faith. This illustration is from God's hardening of Pharaoh after Pharaoh hardened his heart. Paul states, "So then He has mercy on whom He desires, and He hardens whom He desires" (9:18 NASB). Again, the natural question arises: On whom does God desire to have mercy, and whom does he desire to harden?

The answer has been clearly revealed in Holy Scripture: God's desire from eternity is to show mercy to everyone by giving them all an opportunity to be saved, and his desire is to show the mercy of redemption and eternal salvation to those in union with the Messiah through faith. Yet he will further harden the hearts of those who obstinately resist him and harden their hearts to him, as Paul's Jewish kinspeople had done. As Matthew McAffee

---

20. Forlines, *Classical Arminianism*, 131.

has shown, the clear import of the Old Testament context is that God's hardening of Pharaoh was in response to Pharaoh's consistent hardening of his own heart against God.[21]

However, as Romans 11 goes on to argue, there is still hope for hardened Jews who respond in faith to the Messiah. The hardening spoken of in this text is not an unconditional hardening, nor is it irreversible. As Lenski stated, "Even the hardening by God's agency is not complete at once; it follows these stages, permissive, desertive, and judicial, only the last being final and hopeless." Likening mercy to a door, Lenski correctly says that it is "not shut at once upon the self-hardened so that they crash into the locked door with a bang. WE might close it thus. God's mercy closes it gradually and is ready to open it wide again at the least show of repentance in answer to his mercy; and, not until the warnings of the gradually closing door are utterly in vain does the door sink regretfully into its lock."[22]

The Potter and the Clay

Paul then uses a third illustration from the Old Testament in 9:19–24, apparently referring to Jeremiah 18:1–10: mere human beings do not answer back to the sovereign God and determine for themselves what the terms of salvation are. That is God's prerogative and his alone. Paul is intimating that many Jews' attitude toward God is like this. It is like the clay pot who says to the potter, "Why have you done this?"

However, to read unconditional election into a simple passage that is challenging Jewish people not to talk back to God for making faith in Jesus the Messiah the condition of salvation is to read more into the passage than is there. Paul is simply saying that God decides the conditions for salvation. In the passage Paul cites, Jeremiah is clearly discussing conditions that the Potter considers before he decides what to do with the clay (Jer. 18:7–10). God decides who is saved and who is condemned, not Paul's Jewish interlocutors, who are finite human beings. God has set the terms of salvation as faith in the Messiah, not works of the law or Jewish descent. The interpretation that this text is teaching unconditional election is not compelling.[23]

---

21. Matthew McAffee, "The Heart of Pharaoh in Exodus 4–15," *Bulletin for Biblical Research* 20 (2010): 331–53. See also Lenski, *Romans*, 616–17. Cf. Thomas R. Schreiner, who says God's hardening "precedes" Pharaoh's, indicating that Paul is teaching "double predestination," in Romans 9. Schreiner, *Romans*, Baker Exegetical Commentary on the New Testament, 2nd ed. (Grand Rapids: Baker Academic, 2018), 483.

22. Lenski, *Romans*, 617. See also I. Howard Marshall, *Kept by the Power of God* (Minneapolis: Bethany House, 1974), 104. John Piper agrees that God "is free to step in at any time he pleases with anyone he pleases to free them from that hardness," https://www.desiringgod.org/interviews/does-god-ever-soften-a-heart-he-has-hardened, accessed July 27, 2020.

23. Picirilli, *The Book of Romans*, 186–88.

Vessels of Wrath, Vessels of Mercy

Calvinists such as Piper interpret the "vessels of wrath" and "vessels of mercy" in 9:22–23 as teaching unconditional double predestination.[24] Yet Arminius was right when he affirmed that Romans 9 teaches *conditional* double predestination. God determined to make people vessels of mercy "who should perform the condition [of the covenant]." Those "who should transgress it, and should not desist from transgressing" he determined to make vessels of wrath. In essence, Arminius remarked, "God makes man a vessel: man makes himself a bad vessel, or sinner: God decrees to make man, according to conditions pleasing to Himself, a vessel of wrath or of mercy; which in fact He does, when the condition has been either fulfilled, or wilfully neglected."[25]

Arminius stated that God has the power to make a decree regarding people "by the mere judgment and pleasure of his will," but that it is "ratified by certain conditions, according to which He makes some men vessels to dishonor, others vessels to honor." Therefore, people cannot find fault with God, claiming that he has hardened them "by His irresistible will," because "obstinacy in sins intervenes between the determination of His will and the hardening itself." To say that God arbitrarily makes someone a "vessel to dishonor and wrath," Arminius argues, is to "do the greatest injustice to God" and "contradict clear Scripture."[26]

This gets back to the question: Whom does God will to harden? As Arminius taught, God wills to harden those whom he foreknows will not meet the faith-condition of the covenant: the children of the flesh. On whom does God will to have mercy? The answer is, those whom he foreknows will meet the faith-condition of the covenant: the children of the promise.

Summary

Paul's purpose in Romans 9, as it is in chapters 10–11, is to establish that salvation is not by corporate election because of Jewish descent, nor by law-keeping, but by faith alone. Conditional election to salvation is not corporate but individual, because it is conditioned on one's faith in Jesus the Messiah. For the same reason, salvation cannot be by the works of the law. Paul knows that his recentering of election and salvation on faith in the Messiah, rather than the mistaken Jewish concept that the Jewish people are elect as a group because they are physical descendants of Abraham, will be met by resistance from Jews. They will respond that his doctrine would render God unjust and his Word a failure. Paul's response is to show his Jewish kinspeople that their theology was a misunderstanding of the way God dealt with people (on the

---

24. Piper, *The Justification of God*, 194.
25. Arminius, *Works*, 3:513.
26. Arminius, *Works*, 3:514.

basis of their faith). Thus he brings up Jacob and Esau to demonstrate that God has never saved people merely because they are Abraham's descendants.

Paul uses three illustrations from the history of redemption to argue that the sovereign God alone has the right to set the terms of communion with himself, including his rejection of unbelieving Jews. These illustrations—the hardening of Pharaoh, the potter and the clay, and the vessels of wrath and mercy—do not establish the unconditionality of election but rather underscore Paul's message that it is God, not human beings, who sets the terms of salvation, and this is by faith in the Messiah, not by Jewish descent or law keeping. Most Jews have hardened themselves against God and his anointed one, and God is hardening and blinding them in response, but they still have an opportunity to repent and be saved if they will not resist his loving overtures.

REFLECTION QUESTIONS

1. Why would the Jews of Paul's time think his position made God unjust and his Word a failure?

2. What do Arminians like Leroy Forlines mean when they say the reason Paul introduces Jacob and Esau is to show Jews that God had never automatically saved people merely because they are descendants of Abraham?

3. What do Arminians mean when they respond to Romans 9:15 and 18 by saying that God has chosen to have mercy on believers and to harden those who resist his grace and harden their hearts against him?

4. Was God's hardening of Pharaoh's heart arbitrary, or did Pharaoh already have a hardened heart against God?

5. Does Paul's illustration about the divine potter who molds vessels of mercy and wrath according to his plan of salvation clearly establish that his molding is unconditional, thus ruling out the possibility that God takes into consideration a person's belief or unbelief?

What Does the Rest of the New Testament Teach About Election?

Several other texts are debated between Calvinists and Arminians regarding the doctrine of election. The most important of these are Matthew 22:14, Acts 13:48, and 2 Thessalonians 2:13. However, both groups also cite other, less crucial passages such as 1 Thessalonians 1:4; 5:9; Titus 1:1; 1 Peter 2:9; and Revelation 13:8.

Matthew 22:14

Calvinists point to Matthew 22:14 ("For many are called, but few are chosen") as evidence of unconditional election. They argue that the invitation to the wedding feast spoken of in this parable represents a general or external call that is different from God's internal, irresistible call to only the elect, and that is why the text says that "few are chosen." Michael Horton exemplifies this approach when he says, "The gospel is proclaimed publicly to all people, but only the elect receive it (Mt 22:14)."[1]

This text, at the least, is not a Calvinist prooftext because it says nothing about God's choice being unconditional. In reality, it favors the Arminian account. Jesus is comparing the kingdom to a wedding feast a king gives for his son. The king repeatedly invites people to the feast, and they repeatedly refuse his invitation and even kill his servants who are extending the invitation. The king is angry, kills the murderers, and lays waste to their city. Then his servants go out and gather everyone they can find to come to the feast, but some, who arrive without wedding garments, are cast out into "outer darkness. In

---

1. Michael Horton, *The Christian Faith: A Systematic Theology for Pilgrims on the Way* (Grand Rapids: Zondervan, 2011), 682–83. See also, e.g., Charles H. Spurgeon, *Spurgeon's Sermons on the Cross of Christ* (Grand Rapids: Kregel, 1993), 65.

that place there will be weeping and gnashing of teeth." Then Jesus says, "For many are called, but few are chosen."

This story refers to God the Father and his Son. The Father is inviting the Jewish people to salvation, to "the messianic feast," as George Eldon Ladd says, but they refuse his invitation and even "kill the prophets" (Matt. 23:37) whom he has sent with his invitation. So he invites the Gentiles, some of whom want to accept the divine invitation, but on their own self-righteous terms, not the gospel terms he has given. Because of their refusal of his gracious invitation, God will cast those who refuse him or his terms into outer darkness, where there will be weeping and gnashing of teeth, a repeated reference in Matthew's gospel to eschatological judgment, or exclusion from the "messianic feast of the Kingdom of God."[2]

It is hard for the Arminian to see how—after reading this parable, with its intentional reference to the resistance and refusal of the invitees, which results in the king's wrath—one could come away arguing that everyone is invited externally, but only those who receive a secret, irresistible invitation are chosen. As Gottlob Schrenk stated, "Nowhere do we read that those invited are *forced* to refuse. The whole point of the parable is that one does not *have to* decline or to appear in an unsuitable garment."[3] Yet if God purposefully sets up the universe in such a way that some will not receive the secret invitation and thus will refuse the public one, and he enlarges their punishment for doing so, what Shrenk describes is exactly the situation with which one is left.

Luther rightly said, "Some conceive other thoughts, explaining the words thus: 'Many are called' i.e., God *offers* His grace to many, 'but few are chosen,' i.e., He *imparts* such grace to only a few; for only a few are saved. This is an altogether wicked explanation. For how is it possible for one who holds and believes nothing else of God not to be an enemy of God, whose will alone must be blamed for the fact that not all of us are saved?"[4] The Arminian could not agree more. Interpreting this parable as teaching unconditional election not only reads into the passage but also flies in the face of its plain meaning.

---

2. George Eldon Ladd, "Matthew" in *The Biblical Expositor*, ed. Carl F. H. Henry (Grand Rapids: Baker, 1985), 3:61; Jeffrey Crabtree, *Matthew*, Randall House Bible Commentary (Nashville: Randall House, 2015), 365. For similar perspectives see, e.g., R. T. France, *The Gospel of Matthew*, New International Commentary on the New Testament (Grand Rapids: Eerdmans, 2007), 827; Herschel Hobbs, *An Exposition of the Gospel of Matthew* (Grand Rapids: Baker, 1965), 304–5; R. C. H. Lenski, *The Interpretation of St. Matthew's Gospel* (Minneapolis: Augsburg, 1964), 859–60; John Nolland, *The Gospel of Matthew*, New International Greek Text Commentary (Grand Rapids: 2005), 892.

3. Gottlob Schrenk, "ἐκλέγομαι, ἐκλογή, ἐκλεκτός," *Theological Dictionary of the New Testament*, ed. Gerhard Kittel, trans. Geoffrey W. Bromiley (Grand Rapids: Eerdmans, 1967), 4:186 (italics added).

4. Quoted in *Concordia Triglotta: The Symbolical Books of the Evangelical Lutheran Church* (St. Louis: Concordia, 1921), 222 (italics added). In his older years, Luther modified his earlier predestinarianism.

Acts 13:48

Calvinists also argue that Acts 13:48 teaches unconditional election. Calvin stated that "it is a ridiculous cavil to refer this unto the affection of those which believed, as if those received the gospel whose minds were well-disposed. For this ordaining must be understood of the eternal counsel of God alone."[5] Shawn Wright agrees: "There is no way around the order of thought to arrive at Arminian conclusions."[6]

The context of this text is Paul's and Barnabas's ministry in Pisidian Antioch. In verses 46–47 they address unbelieving Jews who are part of their audience: "It was necessary that the word of God be spoken first to you. Since you thrust it aside and judge yourselves unworthy of eternal life, behold, we are turning to the Gentiles." They quote Isaiah about the Messiah being a light to the Gentiles. Then verse 48 says, "And when the Gentiles heard this, they began rejoicing and glorifying the word of the Lord, and as many as were appointed to eternal life believed."

Those who were "appointed to eternal life" (v. 48) were Gentiles, who had not "thrust aside" the Word of God as the Jews in their audience had, thus making themselves "unworthy of eternal life." As Robert Picirilli explains, this reference to the Gentiles, coupled with an examination of the grammar of the passage, makes it even clearer. The verb form of "appointed" "is a participle of the Greek *tetagmai*," not the usual New Testament word used for "ordained" (*orizō*, as in *proorizō*, the word used for foreordained). *Tetagmai* can be either middle or passive voice. "The verb itself (Greek *tassō*) means basically to put in place or place in a position and can have a broad range of meanings that grow out of that."[7] Interpreting this verb as a middle voice in Acts 13:48 would mean, "as many as had inclined themselves to eternal life believed." Picirilli explains that the parallel with "judge yourselves unworthy of eternal life" in verse 46 offers contextual support for the middle interpretation of *tassō* in verse 48. The Gentiles in Paul's and Barnabas's audience "who had put themselves in a position for eternal life (in contrast to the Jews who judged themselves unworthy of eternal life) put their faith in Jesus as their Savior."[8]

5.   John Calvin, *Commentary upon the Acts of the Apostles*, ed. Henry Beveridge (Edinburgh: T&T Clark, 1859), 440.

6.   Shawn D. Wright, *40 Questions about Calvinism* (Grand Rapids: Kregel Academic, 2019), 163; Horton, *The Christian Faith*, 681; Bruce A. Ware, "Divine Election to Salvation: Unconditional, Individual, and Infralapsarian," in *Perspectives on Election: Five Views*, ed. Chad Owen Brand (Nashville: B&H, 2006), 7.

7.   Robert E. Picirilli, *Free Will Revisited: A Respectful Response to Luther, Calvin, and Edwards* (Eugene, OR: Wipf and Stock, 2017), 116. See Walter Bauer, *A Greek-English Lexicon of the New Testament and Other Early Christian Literature*, rev. and ed. Frederick W. Danker, 3rd ed. (Chicago: University of Chicago Press, 2000), 991.

8.   Picirilli, *Free Will Revisited*, 116.

The seventeenth-century General Baptist biblical scholar Charles du Veil interpreted *tassō* as "sincerely and honestly disposed . . . not of destination or appointment."[9] Thus the verb is being used in the same way as when someone today would say, "I was predisposed to enroll in this course" or "I was inclined to go to that seminary." Picirilli is right when he concludes that there is "no convincing reason, then, to think that Acts 13:48 means that God had already ordained or appointed to eternal life those who were saved by faith in Antioch."[10]

2 Thessalonians 2:13

Calvinists argue that 2 Thessalonians 2:13, which says that God "chose" (*haireō*) the Thessalonians "from the beginning for salvation [*eis sōtērian*] through sanctification by the Spirit and faith in the truth" (NASB), teaches unconditional election.[11] Like Calvin, most Calvinist interpreters assert but do not argue that the election spoken of here is unconditional.[12]

This is a very difficult passage to interpret. It is, frankly, not a solid text with which to lead, whether one is a Calvinist or Arminian. Several variations occur in the translation of this verse. Textual variants could make the verse read either that God chose the elect "from the beginning" for salvation or "as first fruits" for salvation. Furthermore, some translations, following an early tradition from the Geneva Bible, curiously translate *eis sōtērian* not as "for salvation," as the KJV and most subsequent translations rendered it, but as "to be saved."

Some Arminians identify 2 Thessalonians 2:13 with eternal election to salvation, while others argue that the choice was made only at the beginning of the preaching of the gospel in Thessalonica. No matter where one falls on the questions above, this verse does not challenge the Arminian approach to conditional election. As Leroy Forlines explains, either way, "the salvation spoken of was experienced by 'belief of the truth.'"[13]

At most, however, it is an Arminian passage. Many Arminians have interpreted it as a conditional election passage. Brian Abasciano makes a compelling case for seeing conditional election in the grammar of this text. He

---

9. C. M. Du Veil, *A Commentary on the Acts of the Apostles* (London: The Hanserd Knollys Society, 1851 [1685]), 303.

10. Picirilli, *Free Will Revisited*, 116. I appreciate Matthew McAffee's insights that informed this section on Acts 13:48.

11. Sam Storms, *Chosen for Life: The Case for Divine Election* (Wheaton, IL: Crossway, 2007), 110–13; Michael Horton, *Putting Amazing Back into Grace: Embracing the Heart of the Gospel* (Grand Rapids: Baker, 2002), 81.

12. John Calvin, *Commentaries on the Epistles of Paul the Apostle to the Philippians, Colossians, and Thessalonians*, trans. and ed. John Pringle (Edinburgh: Calvin Translation Society, 1851), 341–43.

13. Forlines, *Classical Arminianism: A Theology of Salvation* (Nashville: Randall House, 2011) 185.

challenges the notion that "through faith" modifies "salvation" and not "has chosen," arguing that prepositional phrases in both the New Testament and Septuagint rarely modify anything but a verb.[14]

The passage does not present a problem for the Arminian doctrine of conditional election, whether or not the election was in eternity past and whether the election is "of first fruits" or "from the beginning." The text says that God chose the elect in faith, which presents a problem for Calvinism, not Arminianism. However, even if one tries to force "in faith" to modify the noun "salvation" rather than the verb form "has chosen," as Calvinists must do, the passage still does not state whether election is unconditional or conditional.

John 15:16

Some Calvinists quote this passage about the election of the apostles as evidence for unconditional election.[15] Calvin said, "True, the subject now in hand is not the ordinary *election* of believers, by which they are adopted to be the children of God, but that special *election*, by which he set apart his disciples to the office of preaching the Gospel." However, Calvin explains, the fact that this election was a gift from God makes it "certain that the *election*, by which, from being the children of wrath and an accursed seed, we become the children of God, is of free grace."[16]

Robert Yarbrough's chapter "Divine Election in the Gospel of John" does not spend much time on this text, though he does say that God's choice of the disciples is "of a piece with their election to salvation." Still, one senses that even Yarbrough sees the difficulty in asserting that John 15:16 and 6:70 can be used to support unconditional election to salvation, because Judas, one of the chosen, fell away; "in his case the 'choice' of which Jesus speaks is a step removed from sovereign election to actual salvation in the full sense. . . . Is Judas possibly among those of whom Jesus speaks in the difficult saying, 'For many are invited but few are chosen' (Matt. 22:14)?" The Arminian, who sees John 15:16 as not dealing with election to salvation, immediately asks, does not the admission that Judas was chosen, yet fell, seriously challenge the notion that his election to apostleship was "of a piece" with election to salvation? This opacity leads back to the whole question of the coherence of the concept

---

14. Brian Abasciano, "2 Thessalonians 2:13, Greek Grammar, and Conditional Election," Society of Evangelical Arminians, http://evangelicalarminians.org/2-thessalonians-213-greek-grammar-and-conditional-election, accessed July 13, 2020. Abasciano goes into much greater detail.

15. Lorraine Boettner, *The Reformed Doctrine of Predestination* (Woodstock, ON: Devoted, 2017), 40–45; Charles H. Spurgeon, *Spurgeon's Sermons*, vol. 45: 1899, https://ccel.org/ccel/spurgeon/sermons45/sermons45.xxv.html, accessed July 14, 2020.

16. John Calvin, *Commentary on the Gospel according to John*, trans. John Pringle (Edinburgh: Calvin Translation Society, 1847), 2:119.

of unconditional election with the straightforward way salvation is presented in the gospels.

Other Texts

Several texts (e.g., 1 Thess. 1:4; Titus 1:1; 1 Peter 2:9) refer to the elect but say nothing about whether their election is unconditional or conditional. While many contemporary Calvinists do not appeal to 1 Thessalonians 5:9 ("God has not destined us to wrath"), some, especially double predestinationists, argue that the text supports unconditional election.[17] Yet Arminians believe that those who resist the calling and grace of the Holy Spirit have been destined to wrath in the eternal counsel of God. Arminians who affirm both conditional election and conditional reprobation have no objection to saying that God has not destined believers to wrath.

Some Calvinists cite Revelation 13:8 as support for unconditional election. That text says that the elect have their names written in the book of life. It says nothing, however, about how or why one's name is added, whether the addition is unconditional or conditional.

Summary

The texts this chapter has considered either do not address the question of whether election is conditional or unconditional, or they privilege the doctrine of conditional election. The parable of the wedding feast, with its emphasis on the reason for the king's wrath being people's refusal of his invitation, makes the importation of a secret, irresistible invitation seem forced. The case for unconditional election in Acts 13:48 simply does not reckon with the Jew-Gentile dynamic that is explicit in the text, nor with the interpretation of *tassō* in verse 48, as being disposed or inclined toward something. This interpretation fits with the emphasis on conditionality in verse 46, in which the Jews thrust the gospel-word aside and "judge [them]selves unworthy of eternal life." The verse gives conditional election no problem. Second Thessalonians 2:13 provides too many interpretive difficulties to be a text on which to hang either side's hat. However, it certainly does not rule out conditional election, but actually one can argue from the grammar that belief conditions God's choice. Far from suggesting unconditional election, Jesus's election of his disciples, which included Judas, does not deal with the question of election to eternal salvation and in fact contains an implicit argument against Calvinism. Various other prooftexts Calvinists cite are simply indecisive in demonstrating that election is unconditional.

---

17. This passage is not dealt with in *Still Sovereign*, Grudem, or Horton.

REFLECTION QUESTIONS

1. Does Matthew 22:1–14 discuss either a secret, irresistible call to the elect, or that God's gracious election is unconditional or rests in his secret will and not his revealed will in the gospel?

2. What are the basic arguments by Calvinists and Arminians on what the Greek word for "appointed" means in Acts 13:48?

3. What do scholars say about whether "in faith" in 2 Thessalonians 2:13 modifies the noun "salvation" or the verb "has chosen"? Is either argument decisive in your opinion?

4. Who is being elected in John 15:16, and for what purpose, and how do you think this relates to the debate between Arminianism and Calvinism?

5. Does 1 Thessalonians discuss how and why God chooses individuals for salvation?

Do Arminians Believe That God Elects Individuals to Salvation?

Most traditional Arminians would say that conditional election to eternal salvation is individual, whereas many contemporary Arminians would say that it is primarily corporate. I will never forget my first interchanges with Calvinists after I became interested in theology as a young adult. My Arminian pastor and Sunday school teachers had given me a basic Arminian understanding of conditional election by means of God's foreknowledge. So I recoiled when I told Calvinist friends that I was an Arminian, and they would always immediately say, "Oh, you're one of those people who doesn't believe in predestination."

It seemed odd to me that there would be people who would think the *sine qua non* of Arminianism is that they do not believe in predestination. "Arminians believe in predestination, just differently than Calvinists," I always replied. I began to read Leroy Forlines and Robert Picirilli and eventually Arminius.[1] They, like my pastor and Sunday school teachers, taught a clear doctrine of the conditional election of individuals according to divine foreknowledge, though with greater precision and detail. I later read Wesley saying the same thing.

So I was surprised when I discovered that some Arminians believe that "election" in the ordinary way most people tend to use the word—individuals being chosen in eternity past for salvation—is not the teaching of the New Testament. I first encountered this in books by Robert Shank and Roger Forster and Paul Marston.[2] I thought, "Here are entire books saying basically

---

1. F. Leroy Forlines, *Classical Arminianism: A Theology of Salvation* (Nashville: Randall House, 2011), 121–28, 181; Robert E. Picirilli, *Grace, Faith, Free Will* (Nashville: Randall House, 2002), 51–52.
2. Robert Shank, *Elect in the Son: A Study of the Doctrine of Election* (Springfield, MO: Westcott, 1970); Paul Marston and Roger Forster, *God's Strategy in Human History* (Eugene, OR: Wipf and Stock, 2001 [1973]). The most perceptive of the recent treatments

what Calvinists accused me of in high school: "We don't believe in predestination." It seemed they had switched the definition of election to say that, in essence, it is of the church, the people of God, embracing individuals only indirectly, insofar as they participate in the church.

Recently more Arminians have been downplaying or even denying the election of individuals. This movement is fueled somewhat by N. T. Wright and the New Perspective on Paul, which tries to correct the overly individualized gospel of modern evangelicalism. This is obviously a needed corrective. However, many traditional Arminians believe that Wright and the New Perspective have overcorrected, making the gospel too much about collective categories and eclipsing the individual categories that are intrinsic to the New Testament doctrine of salvation in Christ.[3]

The classic Arminian doctrine of predestination, however, is that God does indeed choose individuals. He elects believers for eternal salvation and reprobates unbelievers to eternal damnation. Hence the traditional Arminian doctrine is the *conditional election of individuals*. As Roger Olson explains, according to this doctrine, the election of individuals is conditional, but the election of the church is unconditional.[4] Conditional election is necessarily individual election. The corporate election of the body of Christ, the church, is, after all, unconditional by definition. Conditional election can be spoken of only with respect to individuals. All Christians, of course—Calvinists and Arminians alike—believe the church is unconditionally, corporately elect.

Before delving into Arminius's doctrine of individual election, it is important to establish that not only Reformed Arminians but also classic Wesleyans emphasize individual election. Wesley defined election as "a divine appointment of some men to eternal happiness. But I believe this election to be conditional, as well as the reprobation opposite thereto."[5] Likewise, one of the foremost modern Wesleyan theologians, Thomas Oden, affirmed that God's elective decree was in respect to individuals, approvingly quoting the Lutheran scholastics, what Oden called "centrist Protestant orthodoxy" regarding:

from a corporate election perspective are from Brian J. Abasciano. See his *Paul's Use of the Old Testament in Romans 9.1–9: An Intertextual and Theological Exegesis* (London: T&T Clark, 2005); *Paul's Use of the Old Testament in Romans 9.10–18: An Intertextual and Theological Exegesis* (London: T&T Clark, 2011). See also his "Clearing Up Misconceptions about Corporate Election," *Ashland Theological Journal* 41 (2009): 59–90.

3. See, e.g., N. T. Wright, "Yet the Sun Will Rise Again: Reflections on the Exile and Restoration in Second Temple Judaism, Jesus, Paul, and the Church Today," in *Exile: A Conversation with N. T. Wright*, ed. James M. Scott (Downers Grove, IL: InterVarsity, 2017), 72–80.

4. Roger E. Olson, *Arminian Theology: Myths and Realities* (Downers Grove, IL: IVP Academic, 2006), 181.

5. From "Predestination Calmly Considered," in *The Works of the Reverend John Wesley, A.M.* (New York: Methodist Episcopal Church, 1831), 6:28.

the eternal, divine decree, by which God, from His im-
mense mercy, determined to give His Son as Mediator, and,
through universal preaching, to offer Him for reception to
all men who from eternity He foresaw would fall into sin;
also through the Word and Sacraments to confer faith upon
all who would not resist; to justify all believers, and besides
to renew those using the means of grace; to preserve faith
in them until the end of life, and in a word, to save those
believing to the end.[6]

Numerous other contemporary Arminian scholars affirm that conditional
election is individual. Examples, in addition to Roger Olson, include Grant
Osborne and Jack Cottrell. Osborne states: "Several have taken this corporately of the choosing of the church rather than individuals . . . but it is hard to
see why such a distinction should be maintained. God has chosen individuals
who form the church."[7] Cottrell argues, among other things, that one biblical
image of individual election is the elect's very *names* being written in the book
of Life: "What can this be but individual predestination?"[8]

Arminius's Understanding

A fresh look at Arminius will help us understand the traditional Arminian
view of election, which is the view of almost all non-Calvinists throughout history. As Oden and William Most have shown, almost no orthodox Christian
from before the seventeenth century affirmed what is today called corporate
election.[9] An examination of Arminius gets us back in touch with this tradition of Christian teaching, and with the thought forms of the New Testament,
which Arminius breathed like fresh air.

Arminius discussed only individuals in connection with the New Testament
doctrine of predestination and election. Of course, he discussed individuals in
both the singular and the plural. This is necessary to say, because some theologians who advocate corporate election use the New Testament's plural language as evidence of corporate election, as though when Paul says in Ephesians
1:5 "having predestined us to adoption as sons by Jesus Christ to Himself, according to the good pleasure of His will," this entails corporate election because

---

6. Thomas C. Oden, *The Transforming Power of Grace* (Nashville: Abingdon, 1993), 140–41.
7. Grant R. Osborne, *Romans*, IVP New Testament Commentary (Downers Grove, IL: IVP
Academic, 2010), 222, citing Shank and William W. Klein, *The New Chosen People: A
Corporate View of Election* (Eugene, OR: Wipf and Stock, 2015).
8. Jack Cottrell, *What the Bible Says about God the Ruler* (Joplin, MO: College Press, 1984),
340–41.
9. William G. Most, *Grace, Predestination, and the Salvific Will of God* (Front Royal, VA:
Christendom, 1997); Oden, passim.

the language is plural.[10] However, this is a flawed premise, since it would entail that I, as an individual Christian, have not been adopted as a son.

Arminius's writings on election are permeated with individual language.[11] He believed that God is always *relating* to people in his predestining decrees, whether elective or reprobative, as individual *persons*. Thus, for example, he averred that, though Christ died for the reprobate, he did not "hold" them "as his own," and "them He does not know as His own, or acknowledge as His own," but he did acknowledge the elect as his own.[12]

The most direct language in Arminius on individual versus corporate election is found in his *Examination of the Treatise of Perkins on the Mode and Order of Predestination*. Arminius criticized William Perkins's view that "all" in the universal atonement passages means "'not single individuals of classes, but classes of single individuals'; as if the apostle had said 'God wills that some of all classes, states, and conditions of men should be saved.'" Arminius explained that Perkins appealed to "the diverse use of the word *all,* which is taken, at one time distinctively, at another collectively." Yet he believed that Perkins had "interchanged the distributive and collective use of the word." Arminius used Noah's ark to illustrate what he meant about the distinctive or distributive and collective senses of "all": All the animals were on Noah's ark in a distinctive or distributive sense. All people were on Noah's ark in a collective sense.[13]

Arminius then argued that "all" is used "not for classes of single individuals, but for single individuals of classes; for the will of God goes out toward single individuals of classes, or to single human beings." It is in his explanation of this concept that Arminius, indirectly but forcefully, propounded a doctrine of individual election:

> As the knowledge of the truth and salvation belong to single human beings, and is, in fact, prepared, by predestination, for the salvation of single individuals, not for classes, and is denied, by reprobation, to single individuals, not to classes, so, also, in the more general providence of God, antecedent, in the order of nature, to the decree of predestination and reprobation, the divine will has reference to single individuals of classes, not to classes of single individuals.[14]

---

10. Klein, *The New Chosen People*, 153.
11. Arminius, *Works*, 3:333, "Examination of Perkins's Pamphlet," Bagnall edition; *The Works of James Arminius, D.D.*, vol. 3, trans. William R. Bangall (Auburn, ME: Derby and Miller, 1853); cf. 361–62.
12. Arminius, *Works*, 3:423, London ed.
13. Arminius, *Works*, 3:461, Bagnall ed.
14. Arminius, *Works*, 3:461. Arminius's Latin wording is *singulis hominibus* (individual men) and *non generibus singulorum* (not classes of individuals). Jacobus Arminius, *Opera*

He went on to explain that the "providence which ministers salvation and the means necessary for salvation, pertains to the preservation and salvation of individuals."[15] It is instructive to see that, not only did Arminius believe that election and reprobation are of individuals, but he also took great pains to emphasize that election does *not* refer to classes of individuals.

The passage just quoted provides two clues as to why Arminius affirmed the concept of individual election, which will be touched on later. First, God *desires* to save individuals and *decrees* predestination for individuals. This tethers election to the rest of the components of salvation, rather than seeing it as merely a preamble to or preparation for salvation. In other words, adoption, justification, and sanctification represent the administration of redemption *in time*; election represents its administration *in eternity*.[16] Second, if God desires the salvation of every individual and not just classes of individuals, then his decree of election to save sinners will be an extension of his salvific will and hence comprehend individuals, not just classes of individuals.

As discussed in Question 28, Arminius argued that foreknowledge in the New Testament is not mere prescience of belief or unbelief, but also an affectionate foreknowledge of the believer in union with Christ.[17] Thus divine foreknowledge of believers is more than God's "knowledge *that*." It is also God's personal "knowledge *of*" an individual.[18]

Also, the above quotation from Arminius underscores his primary concern about Calvinism: it does not root God's elective decree in the mediatorial work of Christ. God's decreeing first which individuals would be elected and reprobated, and only then decreeing to appoint Christ as mediator for the salvation of the elect, "inverts the order of the gospel." Yet Holy Scripture "puts Christ as the foundation, not of the execution only, but also of the making of election itself."[19]

Theologica (Leiden: Godefridus Basson, 1629), 740. The London edition maintains the same meaning, translating "single individuals" as "each": "The will of God tends to each one of classes, or to each separate man" (3:428).

15. Arminius, *Works*, 3:461, Bagnall ed.

16. When I use the language of "time and eternity" in this passage, I am using it popularly, not taking a position on various views on the relationship of time and eternity, whether timeless eternity, or a temporal everlasting approach. What I am saying could be affirmed by advocates of either view. See Gregory Ganssle, ed., *God and Time: Four Views* (Downers Grove, IL: InterVarsity Academic, 2001).

17. "Mere prescience" is from Robert E. Picirilli, *Grace, Faith, Free Will* (Nashville: Randall House, 2002), 56.

18. Arminius, *Works*, 3:296, "Examination Perkins's Pamphlet." Leroy Forlines and Robert Picirilli are unusual among modern Arminian theologians in arguing similarly to Arminius on foreknowledge as not mere prescience but also an affectionate knowledge of the individual. See Forlines, *Classical Arminianism*, 181; Picirilli, *Grace, Faith, Free Will*, 56.

19. Gunter, *Arminius and His Declaration of Sentiments: An Annotated Translation with Introduction and Theological Commentary* (Waco, TX: Baylor University Press, 2012), 122; cf. Arminius, *Works*, 1:632; Arminius, *Works*, 3:296, 303. "Examination of Perkins's Pamphlet."

In his *Declaration of Sentiments*, Arminius stated that God decrees "to save and to damn *certain particular persons*" according to his foreknowledge "through which God has known from all eternity *those individuals who through the established means of his prevenient grace would come to faith and believe, and through his subsequent sustaining grace would persevere in the faith*. Likewise, in divine foreknowledge, God knew who would not believe and persevere."[20] Thus Arminius taught *conditional, individual election* and *conditional, individual reprobation*. Those individuals whom God lovingly foreknew as believers, he elected as his own. Those individuals whom he foreknew to be unbelievers, he reprobated.[21]

Influence and Response

One of the most important implications of individual election for Arminianism is how it dovetails with what Leroy Forlines calls the "influence-and-response" model of God's redemptive dealings with humanity. This model privileges conditional, individual election. In it, God, the divine personality, vitally engages the human personality in a personal, relational, influence-and-response dynamic (see Questions 17 and 23).

Seeing election as a corporate category that has individual implications only by virtue of the individual's participation in the blessings of the *corpus*, the church, does damage to this concept, in which the divine person exercises his total personality—intellect, will, and affections—to engage the total personality of the human person—intellect, will, and affections—in an influence-and-response dynamic rather than the cause-and-effect dynamic that Calvinism necessitates. This dynamic, at least as it relates to election, is unintentionally undermined in corporate-election theology.

Conditional Salvation Entails Conditional Election

Arminians affirm that, because salvation is conditioned on belief, election is conditioned on belief. Predestination is an eternal administration of what is taking place in the lives of the elect in time. Thus, if salvation and damnation are conditional, then election and reprobation are conditional. This accords with the gospel revealed in Holy Scripture.

It seems, however, that corporate electionists are forced by their approach to *abstract* the way God works salvifically with people in time from what his plan is in eternity. Their theology forces them to say that regeneration,

---

20. Gunter, *Declaration of Sentiments*, 135; cf. Arminius, *Works*, 1:653–54 (italics added). Portions of this and the previous paragraph have been adapted from J. Matthew Pinson, "Will the Real Arminius Please Stand Up? A Study of the Theology of Jacobus Arminius in Light of His Interpreters" *Integrity* 2 (2003): 121–39, reprinted in Pinson, *Arminian and Baptist: Explorations in a Theological Tradition* (Nashville: Randall House, 2015), chapter 1.
21. Arminius also spoke of "the particular election of believers and the particular reprobation of unbelievers" (*Works*, 3:441).

justification, sanctification, and glorification of believers are primarily about individuals, but election is primarily about the group. This is what most corporate-election Arminians appear to be saying. All but the strictest adherents to N. T. Wright and the New Perspective do not seem to be going to the extreme of saying that *salvation* is primarily corporate.

When most corporate electionists preach on Galatians 2:20, for example, they would not say, "Brothers and sisters, the church has been crucified with Christ. It is no longer it that lives, but Christ who lives in its midst. And the life the church now lives in the flesh it lives by its corporate faith in the Son of God, who loved it and gave himself for it. And by virtue of your faith, brothers, and sisters, you have been incorporated into the church and thus share the blessings of Christ on this body." Now of course all this is true, because there is a balance in the New Testament between individual and communal aspects of salvation. Yet Paul in Galatians 2:20 is discussing his individual salvation, not the salvation of the church as a corporate body.

Some strict adherents of the New Perspective might frame things this way in a sermon, but most corporate-election Arminians would preach this passage the same way a traditional Arminian or Calvinist would. Preaching like this is not individual*istic*. For example, in Ephesians, Paul uses some of this same language to speak of the church as a whole: "Husbands, love your wives, as Christ loved the church and gave himself up for her, that he might sanctify her, having cleansed her by the washing of water with the word" (5:25–26).

Almost everyone would preach these passages alike. They would point out how all these blessings are not only for individuals but also for the aggregate of individuals in the church, and that this communal aspect has profound significance for what it means to be saved and to work out *one's own* salvation with fear and trembling (Phil. 2:12). In fact, strong Calvinists camp out on the corporate aspect of the above passage from Ephesians—Christ died for the church so that he could have a people for his name. They celebrate that to the extreme that they believe he died *only* for the church. All but the most committed New Perspective advocates would preach that the church is justified by faith only insofar as it is a community of individuals who have been justified by their own faith (not the collective faith of the group) and are working out their own salvation (not the collective salvation of the group) with fear and trembling.

Election should not be abstracted from the rest of salvation and its collective implications artificially pressed and overemphasized in a way that strains New Testament texts. A natural reading of the election texts makes election salvific as much as the other aspects of salvation. Still, there is a need to avoid overemphasizing the individual facet of these blessings in Christ to the neglect of their communal, ecclesial aspects. It is unfair to say that the traditional Arminian approach is "individual*istic*," that it does not do justice to the communal or corporate or ecclesial aspects of God's salvation of sinners.

Thus election is not an abstraction but rather an integral part of the *ordo salutis*. Arminius accused his Calvinist interlocutor Perkins of abstracting election from the rest of salvation. Arminius believed that Calvinism makes election a *mechanism* whereby the benefits of Christ are procured for God's elect, whom he has unconditionally chosen for purposes known only to him, without respect to Christ as mediator. Thus, he argued, unconditional election is not itself an intrinsic element or component of redemption. Rather it is a mechanism or vehicle by which redemption is obtained. For Arminius, however, election is the first intrinsic component in the *ordo salutis*, which includes adoption, justification, sanctification, and glorification. Christ, in the administration of his mediatorial office, is at the center of the salvation that occurs not only in the life (and afterlife, via glorification) of the believer, but also prior to the life of the believer in the eternal counsel of God.

Election and Spirituality

The doctrine of corporate election also risks making election and predestination into abstract concepts, bifurcated from individual spirituality. In meditating on, or praying through, or even writing a hymn on Ephesians 1:3–6, as an advocate of individual election, one can pray—to the "praise of God's glorious grace"—"Father, I praise you for blessing me with *every* spiritual blessing, for choosing me in Christ before the foundation of the world so that I will be holy before you in love. I thank you for predestining me to adoption as your child, according to the good pleasure of your will. For these blessings, I praise your glorious, electing grace, which I am so thankful made me accepted in the beloved." While holding firmly to the conditionality of election, Arminius would have prayed in just this way. He would have heartily prayed such a prayer individually. The same can be said of the church fathers and medieval teachers, as well as later traditional Arminians and Lutherans.

One sees an example of this dynamic in a devotional book of the Lutheran theologian Johann Gerhard, who taught individual, conditional predestination in a way very similar to that of Arminius. In his 1606 work *Sacred Meditations*, Meditation 24 on "Predestination" reads: "O devout soul, as long as thou wouldst meditate upon thy predestination, look up to Christ hanging on the cross. . . . Take good heed then that thou seekest not to solve the mystery of thy predestination from the law."[22] Most writers in the Christian tradition spoke like this because they saw election and every other component of salvation spoken of in Ephesians 1 as a spiritual blessing Christ communicates to each persevering believer.

---

22. Johann Gerhard, *Sacred Meditations*, trans. C. W. Heisler (Philadelphia: Lutheran Publication Society, 1896), 130.

Summary

The move away from the classic Arminian doctrine of individual election is born of good motives to protect Arminianism and refute Calvinism. However, Arminius would warn us not to throw out the baby with the bathwater. He would urge Arminians not to throw out a natural reading of a New Testament concept (individual election) to try to sidestep a poor interpretation of it (*unconditional* individual election). Arminius would say that corporate election is a bad tactical move for Arminians. It risks making them look as though they are trying to sidestep the clear teaching of Scripture to buttress their theological system. More than that, however, Arminius would simply say that corporate election is just not what the New Testament writers mean when they talk about election. Instead, they are referring to God's affectionate foreknowledge and loving choice in Christ of individual believers, for which election we can praise God for his glorious salvific grace toward us in Christ.

REFLECTION QUESTIONS

1. What does Roger Olson mean when he says that, when Arminians speak of conditional election, they are referring to individual election, but that the church is unconditionally elected?

2. What did Arminius mean when he said that God elected single individuals of classes, not single classes of individuals?

3. Why do some Arminians believe that the condition of election being the mediatorial work of Christ applied to the individual by faith makes conditional election primarily individual rather than corporate?

4. What are some ways the chapter outlines that a doctrine of corporate election abstracts election, as one of the blessings of salvation discussed in Ephesians 1, from the rest of a believer's salvation?

5. If Arminius is right that God's decree to elect is simply the administration, *in eternity*, of what he does *in time* when he justifies believers who come into union with Christ through faith, does that not entail that election is primarily individual?

Do Arminians Believe That Faith Precedes Regeneration?

The primary question regarding the *ordo salutis* (order of salvation) in the dispute between Arminianism and Calvinism is whether regeneration precedes faith. If God unconditionally elects certain people from eternity and reprobates the rest, sending Christ to die only for the elect and bringing them effectually to himself, leaving no freedom to resist, then this would have to be a complete changing of the will. God would change the human will to *make it* desire him (compatibilism). Regeneration's preceding faith fits logically within this schema.

Still, some Calvinists, such as Millard Erickson and Bruce Demarest, though they affirm the doctrines of unconditional election and irresistible grace, reject the notion that regeneration precedes faith.[1] In this, Erickson and Demarest are in the company of earlier Calvinists such as Stephen Charnock and John Leadley Dagg.[2] It needs to be noted briefly at this juncture that most Calvinists (as well as Arminians), when they consider the relationship of regeneration and faith in the *ordo salutis*, are speaking of a logical order, not a chronological order. However, some Calvinists believe regeneration chronologically precedes faith, whether by seconds (Wayne Grudem) or years (James P. Boyce).[3]

Erickson gives the basic reason why many Calvinists have not affirmed that regeneration precedes faith: It is not biblical, and one ought not teach as doctrine a speculative concept just because it seems logically entailed by one's doctrinal system. "The biblical evidence favors the position that conversion

---

1. Millard J. Erickson, *Christian Theology* (Grand Rapids: Baker, 1986), 933; Bruce A. Demarest, *The Cross and Salvation* (Wheaton, IL: Crossway, 2006); 264–65.
2. David L. Allen, "Does Regeneration Precede Faith?" *Journal for Baptist Theology and Ministry* 11 (2014): 50–51.
3. Wayne Grudem, *Systematic Theology* (Grand Rapids: Zondervan, 1994), 702; James Petigru Boyce, *Abstract of Systematic Theology* (Louisville: SBTS Press, 2013 [1882]), 341.

is prior to regeneration. Various appeals to respond to the gospel imply that conversion results in regeneration." The New Testament yields the idea that repentance and faith (conversion) results in the new birth (regeneration): One becomes a "born-again Christian" only as a result of repentance and faith.[4]

Some examples of the gospel appeals to which Erickson refers are as follows: When the Philippian jailor in Acts 16:31 asked, "What must I do to be saved?" Paul responded, "Believe on the Lord Jesus Christ, and you will be saved." Likewise, Peter says in Acts 2:38, "Repent, and be baptized every one of you in the name of Jesus Christ for the forgiveness of your sins, and you shall receive the gift of the Holy Spirit." These and other texts of Holy Scripture prompt the idea that regeneration is part of salvation, and that one has to have faith to have salvation (Acts 16:30–31; Rom. 10:9–10, 13, 17; Eph. 1:13).

A doctrine must have exegetical support, which is very thin for the notion that regeneration precedes faith. From the vantage point of New Testament theology, modern Calvinism seems to wrench the question of regeneration, the new birth, from its biblical-theology moorings. It would work better for Calvinism if there were another sort of regeneration in the New Testament than being born again. The new birth is too gospel-centered, too Christ-centered, to be abstracted from union with Christ, which results from faith in him. This becomes clearer as one considers the texts under discussion regarding this doctrine.

"You Must Be Born Again"

Obviously the most basic issue one must consider in this discussion is Jesus's teaching on the new birth in John 3:1–15. When most Christians read this text, it seems obvious that Jesus is talking about a vital relationship into which Nicodemus needs to enter by placing his faith in Jesus and being born again. This is an evangelistic encounter. Jesus is trying to get Nicodemus to believe in him. This is what one sees throughout the New Testament, what Christians do today when they share the gospel with an unbeliever.

The natural reading of this text—with Jesus urgently pressing on Nicodemus, "You *must* be born again!"—does not convey the idea that Jesus is talking theology with Nicodemus, discussing with him a work that the Spirit must do in him if he is ever to be able to have faith and come to Jesus, a work abstracted both from faith and from Jesus. Instead, what the passage presents here is vital, relational evangelizing. Jesus is simply exhorting Nicodemus *to be* born again. The fact that the passage says that individuals must be born again to "see" (v. 3) and "enter" (v. 5) the kingdom cannot be wrested into the service of the doctrine of the precedence of regeneration before faith. Nothing in the text suggests that the new birth in Christ takes place without faith in Christ.

---

4. Erickson, *Christian Theology*, 932.

Spiritual Life Before Faith and Hence Without Christ

The Calvinist Anthony Hoekema argues, "Regeneration is a radical change from spiritual death to spiritual life, brought about in us by the Holy Spirit—a change in which we are completely passive. This change involves an inner renewal of our nature, is a fruit of God's sovereign grace, and takes place in union with Christ."[5] This quotation gets to the heart of the problems this teaching has with regard to biblical theology.

How can one be brought to "spiritual life" without faith, and hence outside of Christ? This is the same problem (in time) that Arminians see in the doctrine of unconditional election (in eternity). Just as Calvinism's doctrine of election posits God's embracing individuals with his elective love without consideration of faith in Christ, its doctrine of regeneration posits spiritual life itself without consideration of faith in Christ. This teaching simply is not Christ-centered or gospel-centered enough to be biblical. How can people experience an "inner renewal of our nature" without being justified in union with Christ, which cannot occur without faith?

As Henry Clarence Thiessen observed, regeneration is "the communication of divine life to the soul (John 3:5; 10:10, 28; 1 John 5:11, 12), the impartation of a new nature (2 Peter 1:4) or heart (Jer. 24:7; Ezek. 11:19; 36:26), and the production of a new creation (2 Cor. 5:17; Eph. 2:10; 4:24)."[6] These things cannot be experienced apart from faith. John 20:31 summarizes the Johannine and New Testament understanding of regeneration and faith: "But these are written so that you may believe that Jesus is the Christ, the Son of God, and that by believing you may have *life* in his name" (John 20:21; italics added). In short, faith is necessary for spiritual life. It is by believing that we have life in Christ. Without faith it is impossible to please God (Heb. 11:6). It is impossible to be in Christ. Thus it is impossible to have spiritual *life*. Arguing that regeneration precedes faith only logically, not chronologically, does nothing to alleviate this problem.

Sanctification Before Justification

Leroy Forlines discusses the conundrum into which this doctrine tangles Calvinists because it places sanctification before justification. As the great Calvinist theologian Louis Berkhof stated, "Regeneration is the beginning of sanctification."[7] If regeneration is the beginning of sanctification, and if

---

5. Anthony A. Hoekema, *Saved by Grace* (Grand Rapids: Eerdmans, 1989), 101.
6. Henry Clarence Thiessen, *Introductory Lectures in Systematic Theology* (Grand Rapids: Eerdmans, 1949), 367. It must be noted that some time after the seventh edition of Thiessen's book, and after his death, the book was revised to teach four-point Calvinism. This original edition taught total depravity and a traditional doctrine of the certain perseverance of the saints yet held to conditional election and resistible grace.
7. F. Leroy Forlines, *Classical Arminianism: A Theology of Salvation* (Nashville: Randall House, 2011), 262.

justification results from faith, then logically Calvinism is placing sanctification prior to justification. This same dynamic led Lorraine Boettner to argue, "A man is not saved because he believes in Christ; he believes in Christ because he is saved."[8] Steve Lemke responds to this argument by asking a related question; "When does the Spirit come into a believer's life? . . . What do the Scriptures say about the order of believing and receiving the Spirit?" (Acts 2:38).[9]

Forlines zeroes in on why this is a theological difficulty for the Calvinist system:

> God cannot perform the act of regeneration (an act of sanc-tification) in a person before he or she is justified. God can move in with His sanctifying grace only after the guilt problem is satisfied by justification. To think otherwise is to violate the law of non-contradiction. I realize that when we talk about the *ordo salutis* (order of salvation) we are talking about logical order instead of chronological order. But that logical order is inviolable![10]

Since Berkhof and Boettner are correct that regeneration is the beginning of salvation and sanctification, the Calvinist *ordo salutis*, which places regeneration prior to faith, and thus prior to justification and the gift of the Spirit, is at cross-purposes not only with its own theology but also with that of the New Testament.

As Robert Picirilli has shown, the New Testament uniformly assumes that the whole of salvation, not just justification, is by faith (Acts 16:31; 1 Cor. 1:9, 21, 30; Eph. 2:8–9; Luke 8:12): Receiving the Holy Spirit (Gal. 3:2, 5, 14; John 7:39; Eph. 1:13; Acts 11:17; 15:7–9), becoming children of God (Gal. 3:26; John 1:12; 1 John 5:1); being resurrected from the dead (Col. 2:12; John 5:24; John 12:46), and possessing eternal life (John 3:36; 6:40, 47; 1 Tim. 1:16) are all *by faith*.[11]

Other Calvinist Proof Texts

Calvinists argue that various other Scripture passages teach that regen-eration precedes faith. John 1:12–13 states: "But to all who did receive him, who believed in his name, he gave the right to become children of God, who were born, not of blood nor of the will of the flesh nor of the will of man, but

---

8. Loraine Boettner, *The Reformed Doctrine of Predestination* (Philadelphia: P&R, 1965), 101.

9. Steve W. Lemke, "A Biblical and Theological Critique of Irresistible Grace," in *Whosoever Will: A Biblical-Theological Critique of Five-Point Calvinism*, eds. David L. Allen and Steve W. Lemke (Nashville: B&H Academic, 2010), 137.

10. Forlines, *Classical Arminianism*, 86.

11. Robert E. Picirilli, *Grace, Faith, Free Will: Contrasting Views of Salvation: Calvinism and Arminianism* (Nashville: Randall House, 2002), 170–77.

of God." Many Calvinists infer from the fact that "were born" is in the aorist tense that the passage means the individual is "born" before "believing in his name." Yet, as David Allen rightly argues, "nothing in the grammar and syntax mandates such an interpretation."[12] Even Calvinists such as D. A. Carson and Andreas Köstenberger say that this text does not speak to the issue of the *ordo salutis*.[13] As Brian Abasciano persuasively argues, this text "is determinative in establishing faith as prior to regeneration in John's theology." Believing in Christ is what gives one the right to become a child of God.[14]

Another verse Calvinists often cite in this connection is 1 John 5:1, which John Piper says is "the clearest text in the New Testament on the relationship between faith and the new birth."[15] The text reads: "Everyone who believes that Jesus is the Christ has been born of God, and everyone who loves the Father loves whoever has been born of him."

Some Calvinists interpret the perfect tense "has been born" to indicate an ongoing state (being a born-again person) that resulted from a prior action (the new birth). So they see the text as teaching that everyone who is believing has *first* been born of God. For them, this means that being born again precedes and leads to faith. Most will agree that the perfect tense focuses on the state of being rather than a prior action that produced the state.[16] What John is stating is, "Everyone who is believing . . . is in a having-been-born-again state." To take this to mean that the new birth came before faith stretches the perfect tense beyond what it will bear. Based on grammar and tenses alone, the sentence states only that the two conditions coincide: believing and having been born again. Yet it does not say anything about which condition precedes

---

12. Allen, "Does Regeneration Precede Faith?" 39.

13. D. A. Carson, *The Gospel according to John* (Grand Rapids: Eerdmans, 1991), 126; Andreas Köstenberger, *John*, Baker Exegetical Commentary on the New Testament (Grand Rapids: Baker, 2004), 39; see Allen, 39.

14. Brian J. Abasciano, "Does Regeneration Precede Faith? The Use of 1 John 5:1 as a Proof Text," *Evangelical Quarterly* 84 (2012): 318–20.

15. Quoted in Abasciano, "Does Regeneration Precede Faith?" 307. In addition to Piper, other notable examples of Calvinist arguments based on 1 John 5:1 include Bruce A. Ware, "Divine Election to Salvation: Unconditional, Individual, and Infralapsarian," in *Perspectives on Election: Five Views*, ed. Chad Owen Brand (Nashville: B&H Academic, 2006), 19–20; and Matthew Barrett, "Does Regeneration Precede Faith in 1 John?" *Mid-America Journal of Theology* 23 (2012): 5–18.

16. This is true whether or not one agrees with contemporary verbal aspect theory about the Greek tenses. This formulation does not deny the fact that lexical factors must also be considered when interpreting tenses. As Köstenberger, Merkle, and Plummer note, "in some cases the author's choice of tense-form is determined by the verb itself" (*Going Deeper with New Testament Greek: An Intermediate Study of the Grammar and Syntax of the New Testament* [Nashville: B&H Academic, 2016], 236). The lexical meaning of some verbs may be described as telic (focused on the goal or end of the action) rather than atelic. That said, the author's choice of the perfect tense for a given verb is done "to focus on the state of being that results from a previous action" (p. 297).

the other. However, the entire context of First John and John's Gospel indicates that faith is the condition for the new birth.[17]

As David Allen points out, John uses the same grammatical construction in v. 10: "Whoever does not believe God has made him a liar." John 3:18 does as well. Yet these verses clearly cannot be interpreted the way some Calvinists interpret 1 John 5:1. There is simply no warrant for interpreting 1 John 5:1 in that way.[18]

Calvinists also point to Ephesians 2:1–10 to argue that regeneration precedes faith. They usually argue that the spiritually dead being "made alive" (v. 5) entails that regeneration precedes faith because otherwise the dead would be making themselves alive, or the dead would be exercising faith, which dead people cannot do.[19] Both Arminians and Calvinists believe that people are spiritually dead before conversion and have no ability to be converted apart from the radical grace of God. However, this text does not discuss the order of regeneration as it relates to faith and does not entail Calvinist conclusions. Paul's statement in verse 5 that God "made us alive together with Christ" is theologically incoherent without union with Christ, which Calvinists agree comes about by faith. One who is not in union with Christ cannot be made alive together with him.[20]

Calvinists also often quote Ezekiel 36:26 to argue that regeneration precedes faith: "And I will give you a new heart, and a new spirit I will put within you. And I will remove the heart of stone from your flesh and give you a heart of flesh." All Christians agree with this. There is no indication in this passage, however, about the mechanics of how God does this or of the order of regeneration and faith. It is simply a leap from this universally preached gospel text to the view that one does not need to have faith to be born again.

Summary

The Arminian argument that faith precedes regeneration is simply this: in the Bible, being born again requires faith. Being born again is the beginning of spiritual life in Christ, and without believing in him, one cannot see life. Without faith it is impossible to please God, and God will not enter into a saving relationship with anyone, giving them new spiritual birth from above, without faith and hence union with Christ and the application of atonement for sin.

---

17. This argument originated with Robert Picirilli, who discussed it with me in email correspondence on August 8–11, 2020.
18. See Abasciano, "Does Regeneration Precede Faith?" and Allen, "Does Regeneration Precede Faith" for more detailed argumentation of this point.
19. Peter Van Mastricht, *Treatise on Regeneration* (New Haven, CT: Thomas and Samuel Green, 1750), 13–15.
20. For more on how spiritual death relates to regeneration, see Question 26.

REFLECTION QUESTIONS

1. Do all Calvinists always insist that regeneration precedes faith, as most contemporary Calvinists do? Who are some of the Calvinists who diverge from this perspective?

2. How do straightforward gospel appeals in the New Testament, in texts such as Acts 2:38 and 16:31, affect one's understanding of the order of faith and regeneration?

3. What do Arminians mean when they appeal to texts such as Acts 16:30–31; Romans 10:9–10, 13, 17; and Ephesians 1:13, saying that, since regeneration is part of salvation, and salvation is by faith, regeneration has to be by faith?

4. Is it coherent to say that spiritual life and sanctification can come before faith, and does this mean that spiritual life and sanctification come to someone outside of Christ?

5. What does the author mean when he says that Paul's statement in Ephesians 2:5 that God "made us alive together with Christ" is theologically incoherent without union with Christ by faith?

PART 5

Questions About Perseverance and Apostasy

Calvinist Arguments
for Perseverance

What Do Calvinists Believe About Perseverance?

Calvinists believe in the certain perseverance of those who have been re-generated.[1] The term "Calvinist" needs to be defined for the purposes of these chapters on perseverance. Many evangelicals demur from unconditional election, limited atonement, and irresistible grace but still affirm total depravity and unconditional perseverance. Most of them come from a confessional background that was once Calvinistic, but they have moderated their Calvinism and abandoned most of it.

Thus it is difficult to know what to call them. Norman Geisler, for example, called himself a moderate Calvinist. However, there are members of the Society of Evangelical Arminians who have begun referring to themselves as Arminians though they still hold to certain perseverance. Others refer to themselves as "Calminians."[2] Among Southern Baptists, a common designation for this is "Traditional Baptist"—with the slogan "Neither Calvinist nor Arminian, but Baptist."[3] Leroy Forlines, following J. Oliver Buswell, calls them

---

1. I have elected to use the term "certain perseverance" rather than "unconditional perseverance" because it is the most widely used traditional term that both Calvinist and Arminian authors employ. Furthermore, technically, classical Calvinists believe that perseverance is conditioned on continued belief but that God will certainly ensure that the elect meet that condition.
2. Roger E. Olson, *Arminian Theology: Myths and Realities* (Downers Grove, IL: IVP Academic, 2009), 61, 67–69.
3. See David Allen, Steve Lemke, Malcolm Yarnell, et al., "Neither Calvinists nor Arminians, but Baptists," https://v7.swbts.edu/tasks/render/file/?fileID=E626C670-D3E5-136B-BD2A516CB0D788AB; Eric Hankins, et al., "A Statement of the Traditional Southern Baptist Understanding of God's Plan of Salvation," https://soteriology101.com/about-2/statement-of-faith; David L. Allen, Eric Hankins, and Adam Harwood, eds., *Anyone Can be Saved: A Defense of "Traditional" Southern Baptist Soteriology* (Eugene, OR: Wipf and Stock, 2016).

"pseudo-Calvinists," while Robert Picirilli dubs them "sub-Calvinists." I have sometimes referred to them as "post-Calvinists."[4] "Non-Calvinist," another label, seems to be the weakest of all because it is more about what the position is not than what it is.[5]

It is important to be sensitive to this large group of evangelicals. For the purposes of this chapter, when I refer to the "Calvinist" doctrine of unconditional perseverance, it will encompass both classical Calvinists and these eternal securitists who disagree with Calvinism more broadly. Yet when distinguishing between the two groups, I will call them "classical Calvinists" and "eternal securitists."

Certain Perseverance Logically Entailed by the Classical Calvinist System

If one is a classical Calvinist who affirms unconditional election and irresistible grace, the certain perseverance of the regenerate follows logically and theologically. If divine sovereignty entails a cause-and-effect relationship, not an influence-and-response one, it makes sense that God's salvific grace would be irresistible.[6]

If God's grace is irresistible before conversion, it is perfectly coherent, both logically and theologically, to think that God's grace is irresistible after conversion as well.[7] In other words, if God's cause-and-effect relationship with human beings whom he has elected results in their automatically being converted with no power to resist, it will result in their automatically persevering with no power to resist. Stephen Ashby explains it this way:

> If *sovereignty* can only be sovereign when God acts in a cause-and-effect relationship with his creation,
>
> and if *grace* can only be gracious when it is applied in a manner than cannot be resisted,

---

4. See J. Matthew Pinson, "Dissent from Calvinism in the Baptist Tradition," in *Calvinism: A Biblical and Theological Critique*, eds. David L. Allen and Steve W. Lemke (Nashville: B&H Academic, forthcoming).

5. F. Leroy Forlines, *Classical Arminianism: A Theology of Salvation* (Nashville: Randall House, 2011), 280; Robert E. Picirilli, *Grace, Faith, Free Will: Contrasting Views of Salvation: Calvinism and Arminianism* (Nashville: Randall House, 2002), 194–95. I use the phrase "eternal securitist" here as shorthand for people who believe that the regenerate always persevere but who are non-Calvinistic in the rest of their soteriology.

6. In discussing "salvific grace" or "saving grace," we can distinguish between prevenient grace, regenerating grace, justifying grace, sanctifying grace, and so forth. However, these are all forms of saving grace, the grace that brings initial and final salvation. Both classical Calvinists and eternal securitists believe that saving grace after conversion is irresistible.

7. Stephen M. Ashby, "A Reformed Arminian View," in *Four Views on Eternal Security*, ed. J. Matthew Pinson (Grand Rapids: Zondervan, 2002), 155.

and if *election* can only be of God when it is unconditional
and particularistic,

then Calvinism is obviously correct.[8]

However, as Ashby cogently argues, these are theological assumptions that
Calvinists bring to the texts in Scripture that concern perseverance and apostasy, whether the warning passages or those that deal with promise, assurance, or security.

Candidly, the only two consistent soteriological systems are classical
Calvinism and Arminianism. Affirmation of the "U" and the "I" in the TULIP
(and of course the "L," which many Calvinists do not affirm—again, I think
inconsistently) require, both logically and theologically, affirmation of the "P."
However, denial of the "U" and "I" in the TULIP require, both logically and
theologically, denial of the "P."[9]

A Logical and Theological Dilemma for Eternal Securitists

Thus eternal securitists who have jettisoned classical Calvinism are in a
logical and theological quandary. They are caught in a dilemma of arguing
strenuously for a libertarian understanding of the human will and against
irresistible grace when they are discussing what happens *before* conversion.
Yet when they begin discussing what happens *after* conversion, they must
dial back their strong libertarian arguments and their vigorous (and correct)
protestations against irresistible grace.

After all, in the view of eternal securitists, grace *is* indeed irresistible
for the believer (though they might not prefer that terminology). It is only
for unbelievers that grace is resistible. When they become believers, they
can no longer resist divine grace. This presents both a logical and theological dilemma for eternal securitists. They strongly agree with Arminian
arguments that God works with his human creatures whom he created
in his image as persons who think, feel, and make free choices. Thus, he
does not relate to these persons in a cause-and-effect relationship but in an
influence-and-response relationship. This influence-and-response dynamic

---

8. Ashby, "A Reformed Arminian View," 155.
9. William Lane Craig presents another option (I think highly speculative and untenable).
   While he affirms the possibility of apostasy, he says that it is coherent for a Molinist to
   affirm that, while apostasy is possible, it will not occur because God has chosen a possible world in which the warnings will have their intended effect of keeping all believers
   from apostatizing. See his "'Lest Anyone Should Fall': A Middle Knowledge Perspective on
   Perseverance and Apostolic Warnings," *International Journal for Philosophy of Religion* 29
   (1991): 65–74.

makes it possible for these divine image-bearers, in their personhood, to resist God's gracious influence.[10]

However, turning from this argument *against* absolute predestination prior to conversion to an argument *for* absolute perseverance after conversion puts eternal securitists on the horns of a dilemma. They must argue that when an unbeliever becomes a believer through conversion, God shifts from an influence-and-response relationship, which he had with unbelieving persons whom he had created in his image, to a cause-and-effect relationship, which he now has with those who are not only his image-bearers but also his children.

Thus eternal securitists are stuck with both a logical and theological problem. Logically, they believe in both irresistible and resistible grace in the same person, and thus both libertarian freedom and determinism in the same person. Theologically, in one discussion eternal securitists are extolling the virtues of God's relational dynamic with his free, personal creatures whom he created in his image to think, feel, and make free choices and thus are not *absolutely destined* for salvation and *irresistibly drawn* to it. Yet in another discussion, they are forced to argue that God no longer relates to people, after their conversion, in a relational, influence-and-response relationship. Instead, it is now a cause-and-effect relationship. Believers no longer have the freedom to resist divine grace. Now, they are *absolutely destined* for salvation and *irresistibly drawn* to it. If one really believes that the doctrines of unconditional election and irresistible grace depersonalize the human person, that for God to relate to *persons* means he relates in an influence-and-response way, not a cause-and-effect way, then to remain consistent anthropologically, one must maintain resistible grace after conversion as well as before it.

Thus Arminianism and classical Calvinism are the only two logically and theologically coherent systems. This is why in the past I have often said that the "once saved, always saved" or "eternal security" teaching is a "doctrine in search of a theology." Eternal securitists in the twentieth and twenty-first centuries have no strong confessional tradition. They assert what they believe to be a biblical doctrine—eternal security—while denying what they cannot fathom to be a biblical doctrine—irresistible grace. This, however, ties them in a logical and theological knot from which they cannot extricate themselves.

One cannot have it both ways. If people are *absolutely destined* and *irresistibly drawn* to salvation, then all of Calvinism, including unconditional election and irresistible grace (and I would add limited atonement) is true. If, however, no one is *absolutely destined* and *irresistibly drawn* to salvation, then all of Arminianism, including the possibility of apostasy, is true. One cannot have it both ways.

---

10. This concept of cause and effect and influence and response and how they apply to human beings made in the divine image as persons is dependent on Forlines, *Classical Arminianism*. 12, 47–51, 78–82, 338–40.

Beyond the Battle of the Proof Texts

The debate about perseverance should not devolve, as it so often does, into a "battle of the proof texts," in which Arminian warning texts are pitted against Calvinist assurance texts. As Thomas Schreiner and Ardel Caneday explain, the two basic types of texts in the perseverance and apostasy discussion are "warning" passages and "promise" passages.[11] Other words for "promise" passages could be "assurance" or "security" passages.

The debate needs to be reframed into how one can do justice to both sorts of texts. Arminians believe that the warning passages teach the possibility of apostasy and that Calvinists are reading their interpretation of the assurance passages into the warning passages. Calvinists believe that the assurance passages teach certain perseverance and that Arminians are reading their interpretation of the warning passages into the assurance passages. Both groups, however, often fail to respond to the other group's criticism and thus fail to do justice to both kinds of texts.

Reformed Arminianism allows for one to affirm both the "eternal security of believers" (if they remain believers) and still take the texts warning against apostasy at face value. This is accomplished by refocusing on the New Testament's emphasis on *sola fide*, "faith alone," as an enduring, continuing action, not merely a past event. Thus believers, as long as they remain in union with Christ through faith, are righteous in him. The active and passive obedience of Christ are imputed to them. They are "dressed in his righteousness alone, faultless to stand before the throne."[12] That theological component upholds the integrity of the promise/assurance/security teaching of the New Testament: God promises and assures the believer security in Christ, but that security, and thus that promise and assurance, come only to the one in union with Christ through faith.

Here is how the integrity of the warning passages is upheld: this promise and assurance of security in union with Christ goes hand in hand with the if-clauses spread throughout the Scriptures—*if* you continue, *if* you endure, *if* you overcome. The warning passages deal with stern warnings to the believer about what happens if one does not endure, if one ceases believing.

> **Promise:** *If you continue* in union with Christ through faith, you are promised, assured, secure in Christ: "He has now reconciled [you] in his body of flesh by his death, in order

---

11. Thomas R. Schreiner and Ardel B. Caneday, *The Race Set before Us: A Biblical Theology of Perseverance and Assurance* (Downers Grove, IL: IVP Academic, 2001), 40–43.
12. Edward Mote, "My Hope Is Built on Nothing Less," *Rejoice: The Free Will Baptist Hymn Book* (Nashville: Executive Office, National Association of Free Will Baptists, 1988), no. 419.

to present you holy and blameless and above reproach before him, *if indeed you continue in the faith*, stable and steadfast, not shifting from the hope of the gospel that you heard" (Col. 1:21–23).

Warning: *If you fall away*, you will be lost without hope of salvation: "*If you fall away*, it is impossible to renew you again to repentance, since you crucify again for yourself the Son of God, and put him to an open shame" (Heb. 6:4, 6).[13]

Assurance, promise, and security texts like John 10:27–29 are assuring the believer, "If you believe, you will be saved." Yet Calvinists read *preservation in* belief into these texts, or they read into them the idea that the belief is a *past act*—that they came to believe. However, these texts do not refer to one who believed in Christ at some point in the past but to one who is believing and will continue to believe in Christ. This is indicated by the use of the present active indicative in passages like John 10:27: "My sheep *are hearing* my voice, and they *are following* me." The warning passages, however, do explicitly address the question of continuance in belief. They explicitly warn believers, "If you do not *continue* in belief, you will apostatize."

"Works-oriented" Arminians have to dodge the promise passages and say, in essence, "We know they cannot mean what they seem to say because we have learned elsewhere in Scripture that when believers drift into sin, they fall from grace." Calvinists and eternal securitists have to dodge the warning passages and say, in essence, "We know they cannot mean what they seem to say because we have learned elsewhere in Scripture that regenerate believers will certainly persevere." Yet a Reformed Arminian can heartily affirm the plain meaning of both kinds of texts: "God promises that if believers continue to believe, they will continue in union with Christ and thus will certainly persevere but warns that believers can resist his grace, cease to believe, and thus apostatize."

Important Practical Questions

This leads to a very practical question both Arminians and Calvinists need to ask, and this regards the doxological and liturgical import of Christian doctrine: *If a warning or promise passage is read as a responsive reading, without comment, in a church service, which theological approach allows the congregation to say a hearty "Amen"?* Reformed Arminians believe that their approach allows believers to say "Amen" to both warning texts and assurance texts, without having to engage in a great deal of theological wrangling and

---

13. The "they" words have been changed to "you," and the "it is impossible" has been moved from verse 4 and inserted here for ease of reading.

explanation. They believe that some Arminians, who have a more works-oriented view of perseverance, must dodge the assurance passages, and they believe that Calvinists must dodge the warning passages.

How many times does one hear a public reading (or singing)—without comment—of a warning passage in a typical Calvinist church, or of an assurance/security passage in a typical Arminian church? The optimal approach to perseverance and apostasy is the approach that allows wholehearted affirmation of both the warnings to believers to continue in belief lest they apostatize, and the assurances to believers that if they continue as believers, they will ultimately be saved.

This practical question is especially problematic for the Calvinist position, which holds that the warning passages are means God uses to ensure believers' perseverance. Does any Calvinist minister actually preach and teach these texts this way in the pulpit? It would seem that, to be consistent with that viewpoint, for a preacher to tell people that they cannot apostatize robs the warning passages of the effect the preacher thinks God intended them to have.

Summary

Classical Calvinism is logically and theologically consistent. Yet its doctrine of perseverance is a logical deduction from its other doctrines and cannot be exegetically derived from the text of Holy Scripture. It imposes its theological system on the straightforward warning passages in the New Testament.

Conversely, the post-Calvinist once-saved, always-saved approach that jettisons the "U," "L," and "I" but keeps the "P" is logically and theologically inconsistent. In its understanding of depraved human persons before conversion, it posits an influence-and-response understanding of the way God relates to his free creatures whom he created in his image as persons who think, feel, and make free choices. Yet in its understanding of redeemed human persons after conversion, it is forced unintentionally to depersonalize them, transitioning to Calvinism's cause-and-effect understanding of the salvific divine-human dynamic.

The best way to get beyond the divide between Calvinists and Arminians on perseverance and apostasy is to emphasize *continuing in the righteousness of Christ alone through faith alone*. This Reformed Arminian posture is preferable to an Arminian approach that emphasizes *continuing intermittently in faith-plus-lawkeeping* or an eternal securitist posture that emphasizes *relying on a past decision that cannot be reversed*. That Reformed Arminian approach alone does justice to the warning passages, which warn believers to continue in faith lest they fall from grace, as well as the promise passages, which assure believers of their security in Christ alone *if they continue* in faith alone.

REFLECTION QUESTIONS

1. Who do you think is most consistent theologically and logically: Arminians, classical Calvinists, or eternal securitists?

2. Is the standard once-saved, always-saved view consistent in jetissoning unconditional election and irresistible grace but holding to certain perseverance?

3. How does one's theological understanding of human personhood as being consistent with "influence and response" rather than "cause and effect" affect one's view of perseverance?

4. How do classical Calvinists and eternal securitists differ from Reformed Arminians and other Arminians on how they interpret the warning passages and promise passages?

5. What do you think about the author's consideration of the doxological or liturgical response to public readings of warning passages and promise passages in church?

How Do Arminians Respond to Calvinist Theological and Logical Arguments?

The previous chapter dealt with the fact that classical Calvinism logically and theologically entails the certain perseverance of those who have once believed: if people accept the "U" and "I" of the TULIP, they must accept the "P," and this colors the way they interpret the New Testament texts about perseverance and apostasy. Thus many of the Calvinist theological arguments for certain perseverance assume the answer of Calvinism in the question about whether Calvinism is correct on perseverance. This chapter will also consider common theological and logical arguments of eternal securitists who do not accept the rest of classical Calvinism.

The Other Points of Calvinism Imply Certain Perseverance

Consistent Calvinists often make arguments that assume that the rest of the points of the TULIP are true. For example, they argue that unconditional election, the covenant of redemption in which God gave a certain number of elect to his son, or Christ's atonement that redeemed the elect alone require that the regenerate will persevere necessarily to the end and be saved.[1] These arguments basically assert that because God unconditionally predetermined to save certain people, he will see to it that they persevere. Salvation-by-unconditional-election is assumed in the argument. Consistent Arminians, who affirm the possibility of apostasy, will of course agree with classical Calvinists on this, insisting that it is incoherent to affirm Arminianism yet be Calvinistic on the fifth point. Eternal securitists, as discussed in the previous chapter, disagree. In the end, these arguments should not be repeated in a

---

1. Louis Berkhof, *Systematic Theology* (Grand Rapids: Eerdmans, 1996), 547.

discussion of perseverance, because they will already have been settled, one way or another, in a discussion of the other four points of Calvinism.

Another question classical Calvinists ask is, If saving faith is a gift of grace (*charis*, gift), how can it be renounced?[2] Yet this argument assumes a Calvinist definition of grace as unconditional. If someone gives a gift with conditions (e.g., a spouse's saying, "I give you the gift of this wedding ring, but if you desert me, you have to give it back"), does that make it not a gift? This question assumes that the only way salvation can be gracious is by a Calvinistic, unconditional definition of grace.

The Work of the Father, Son, and Spirit in the Believer's Life Will Not Fail

The arguments in this and the next section are employed by both classical Calvinists and eternal securitists. They do not assume unconditional election or irresistible grace prior to conversion. Instead, they *do assume* the certainty of final salvation after conversion, thus begging the question. Essentially, they argue that (1) God has made unconditional promises to the believer, and that (2) Christ's atonement, justification, and mediation, and (3) the Holy Spirit's work in the believer's life are unconditional and will inexorably achieve their ends.[3] Again, for these arguments to have any force, the answer to the question under discussion must be assumed at the outset. That is, God will ensure that believers will infallibly meet the condition of salvation, continued faith, but this is the very question under consideration. Yet if one assumes, based on other biblical-theological, redemptive-historical considerations, that salvation is inherently conditional and that believers can fail to meet the condition of continued faith, then God's promises and Christ's and the Spirit's work do not automatically entail the certainty of perseverance.

Nothing in the doctrines of the promises of God and the work of Christ and the Holy Spirit is inconsistent with the idea that believers can resist divine grace after conversion. Nothing keeps one from believing these doctrines and also affirming that a regenerate person can cease to believe, thereby failing to meet the condition of salvation, *sola fide*, and thus being taken out of union with Christ.

Regarding the argument about God's keeping his promises, just as was stated above about there being nothing untoward about an individual giving a gift of a wedding ring conditionally to his or her spouse, there is nothing problematic about a conditional promise. The Bible is replete with conditional promises. Furthermore, a promise stated without an explicit condition

---

2. Lorraine Boettner, *The Reformed Doctrine of Predestination* (Grand Rapids: Eerdmans, 1954), 183.

3. A. W. Pink, *Eternal Security* (Lafayette, IN: Sovereign Grace, 2001), 43–44; Berkhof, *Systematic Theology*, 547–48.

one place in Scripture does not contradict there being a condition for that promise stated elsewhere.[4]

The doctrine of eternal security must be imported into the doctrines of Christ's intercession, union with Christ, and the work of the Holy Spirit. As Robert Picirilli states, if salvation is conditional, "then final salvation is for those who persevere in the believing. Therefore the intercessory prayers of Jesus are prayers for persons viewed as believers and requiring persistence in faith for the answer to the prayers to be consistent with the efficacy of [Christ's] prayers."[5] The prayer has to allow for conditionality and human response. Otherwise, when Jesus prayed for his disciples in John 17, which included Judas, the "son of perdition," he was praying in vain.

The arguments about the work of Christ and the Holy Spirit guaranteeing perseverance also interpolate into the discussion the assumption that believers will infallibly meet the condition of salvation: perseverance in belief. However, if the Bible teaches the conditionality of salvation, that believers must meet the condition of *continuing* in belief to be saved, then there is nothing irregular in saying that one who is in union with Christ will cease to be in union with Christ if he or she ceases meeting the condition for that union: continued faith in Christ. That is exactly what John 15 says happens (see Question 39).

Furthermore, it seems fitting to say that those who treat the Spirit contemptuously (*enubrizō*), which is what Hebrews 10:29 says apostates do, would frustrate the Spirit's work in their lives. There is nothing theologically odd about suggesting that the Holy Spirit would not continue unconditionally to be united to an individual who by contumacious apostasy had done despite to him by refusing to meet the condition of salvation—continuance in faith. Again, these arguments simply beg the question, which is whether or not a believer can fail to meet the condition of continued belief.

Other Arguments

Classical Calvinists and eternal securitists employ various other theological and logical arguments to defend the Calvinist doctrine of certain perseverance. Five of them appear below. Eternal securitists tend to use the last two more than classical Calvinists.

---

4. An excellent discussion of this question of conditional promises in Scripture is found in Albert N. Nash, *Perseverance and Apostasy: Being an Argument in Proof of the Arminian Doctrine on That Subject* (New York: N. Tibbals and Son, 1871), 112–18.
5. Robert E. Picirilli, *Grace, Faith, Free Will: Contrasting Views of Salvation: Calvinism and Arminianism* (Nashville: Randall House, 2002), 190.

The possession of "eternal" life implies certain perseverance because it would not be eternal if it could end.[6]

In answer to this argument, Arminians note that, in Scripture, eternal life refers to the quality of life in Christ, not its mere endurance. Otherwise, Scripture would speak of unbelievers as having eternal life, since their life after death is as everlasting as that of the believer. Ashby is correct when he explains, "Eternal life is not merely perpetual existence; it is the very life of God. I participate in that life because I am forensically *in Christ*. No one who is outside of Christ has eternal life. The life of God was eternal before I got it, and it will continue to be eternal, even if I were to forfeit it by rejecting Christ."[7]

The possibility of apostasy takes away assurance of salvation.

This argument is tricky, because it causes many Calvinists to make the doctrine of eternal security their doctrine of assurance of salvation. Yet the assurance of salvation is not the same thing as the doctrine of eternal security. Whether or not one can forfeit saving faith in the future is not tied to whether one can be assured that he or she is regenerate. That is what assurance is, and Calvinists and Arminians both believe that professing Christians can have assurance of salvation because they have faith in Christ, have the internal testimony of the Holy Spirit, have good works that evidence that faith, and bear the fruit of the Holy Spirit.

If I am an eternal securitist or Classical Calvinist, there is no guarantee in my theology that I will not stop being a professing Christian in the future, thus proving (according to my once-saved, always-saved doctrine) that I was never regenerate but simply mistakenly thought I was. Thus, the doctrine of eternal security does not give even Classical Calvinists and eternal securitists assurance of final salvation. Whether one can, at some point in the future, fall from grace is not the measure of whether or not one can have assurance that he or she is a genuine Christian in union with Christ through faith, which is what assurance is about.

Removing someone from the body of Christ would damage that body.

This argument has no scriptural support. It stretches the analogy too much. As Ashby says, "Scripture does not teach that he is complete in us . . . rather, Paul says that we are complete *in him* (Col. 2:10)."[8]

---

6. Charles H. Spurgeon, "Free Will—A Slave," in *The New Park Street Pulpit* (Carlisle, PA: Banner of Truth Trust, 1963), 1:399.
7. Stephen M. Ashby, "A Reformed Arminian View," in *Four Views on Eternal Security*, ed. J. Matthew Pinson (Grand Rapids: Zondervan, 2002), 169.
8. Ashby, "A Reformed Arminian View," 169.

"Once a child, always a child."[9]

The problem with this argument is that the Bible contradicts it, saying that before conversion all people are children of the devil. If "once a child, always a child" were valid, no one could become a child of God, because he or she was once a child of the devil and so must always be a child of the devil.

One cannot become unborn once one is born.[10]

This argument is invalid. In the Arminian view, the Bible does not teach that apostates "become unborn." It teaches that apostates *die*. As Jude 12 says, they are "twice dead" trees, "uprooted."[11] As Ashby points out, before conversion, we are spiritually dead (Eph. 2:1). If we apostatize, we "return to that spiritually dead state. As John 3:36 says: 'Whoever believes [present participle, is believing] in the Son has eternal life, but whoever rejects [is not believing] the Son will not see life, for God's wrath remains on him.'"[12]

Summary

When responding to theological and logical arguments by Calvinists, Arminians readily grant that if Calvinists can prove that God absolutely destines people for salvation unconditionally and draws them irresistibly to it, then certain perseverance logically follows and theologically fits. Thus the argument between classical Calvinists and Arminians is always going to go back to the other points of Calvinism. Most of the theological and logical arguments for eternal security beg the question and assume Calvinism in the answer to the question regarding perseverance and apostasy. Most of the rest of their arguments fail to reckon with the notion of the continued *conditionality* of salvation after conversion. However, the New Testament presents a continuing faith, not just faith at the moment of conversion, as the condition for salvation. Understanding this concept shifts the emphasis to the conditional nature of the divine salvific gifts and promises.

---

9. See Charles F. Stanley, *Eternal Security: Can You Be Sure?* (Nashville: Oliver-Nelson, 1990), ch. 5.
10. Charles F. Stanley, *Understanding Eternal Security* (Nashville: Oliver-Nelson, 1998), 46.
11. John Wesley believed that Jude 12 referred to a total and final apostasy that was irremediable: "*twice dead*—In sin, first by nature, and afterwards by apostasy, *plucked up by the roots*—And so incapable of ever reviving." *Explanatory Notes upon the New Testament* (Peabody, MA: Hendrickson, 1986), note on Jude 12. See also Thomas Grantham, *Christianismus Primitivus* (London: Francis Smith, 1678), book 2, part 2, 155.
12. Ashby, "A Reformed Arminian View," 168, quoting the NIV. Brackets in original.

REFLECTION QUESTIONS

1. How does one's doctrines of election and grace affect how one views perseverance and the possibility of apostasy?

2. How does an understanding of the conditionality of post-conversion salvation, that it is conditioned on continuing faith, affect the theological arguments that Calvinists make for certain perseverance?

3. How does an understanding of the conditionality of salvation affect the arguments Calvinists make based on salvation as God's gift and promise? Is it coherent to argue that one can give a free gift that is conditional (like a wedding ring)?

4. Explain what the author means when he says that assurance and eternal security are not the same thing, that even if one affirms eternal security it still does not give that person assurance that he will, in fact, be saved in the future.

5. Is "eternal life" more about the extension of existence after death or about the quality of life in Christ? Or, do the unregenerate, who exist after this life, have what Jesus calls "eternal life"?

How Do Arminians Respond to Calvinist Scriptural Arguments?

The five most important texts Calvinists cite for certain perseverance are John 10:28–29; Romans 8:35, 38–39; Romans 11:29; Philippians 1:6; and Ephesians 4:30. These represent the "promise" side of the promise-warning tension in the New Testament writings. Obviously, in answering Calvinist scriptural objections to the possibility of apostasy, it is not necessary to show that these texts teach the possibility of apostasy, but only that they are consistent with that doctrine. This chapter will consider each of these passages.

John 10:28–29

John 10:28–29 reads: "I give them eternal life, and they will never perish, and no one will snatch them out of my hand. My Father, who has given them to me, is greater than all, and no one is able to snatch them out of the Father's hand." Calvinists argue that this text proves certain perseverance. Millard Erickson, for example, argues that Jesus "is categorically excluding the slightest chance of an apostasy by his sheep. A literal translation would be something like, 'They shall not, repeat, shall not ever perish in the slightest.'" He states that this statement is followed by ones saying that no one can snatch believers from God's hand: "All in all, this passage is as definitive a rejection of the idea that a true believer can fall away as could be given."[1]

This passage, however, is about God's protection of his sheep from external enemies. Furthermore, verses 28 and 29 are in the context of verse 27, which explains who it is that will never perish and whom no one will be able to pluck from God's hand: "My sheep hear my voice, and I know them, and they follow me." When they read, "no one is able to snatch them out of the Father's hand," Arminians wholeheartedly agree. Yet the question must be

---

1. Millard J. Erickson, *Christian Theology*, 2nd ed. (Grand Rapids: Baker, 1998), 1003.

answered: Who are these who hear his voice and follow him and whom no one can pluck from his hand? The answer is, believers—Christ's sheep who are hearing his voice and whom he is knowing and who are following him.

The present indicative verbs in this text present faith as being in progress: "My sheep *are hearing* my voice, and I *am knowing* them, and they *are following* me," not "My sheep *heard* my voice at some point in the past, and they *came to know* me in the past, and they *decided to follow me* in the past." The New Testament everywhere stresses that justifying faith is an enduring faith, not simply a past decision on which the individual can rely. Thus believers have not merely "been saved." They "are being saved," and they "will be saved." Justifying faith is a continuing faith, not a past experience.

No one can snatch this kind of person—one who meets the condition of faith by continuing, by enduring, in belief—from God's hand. Thus this passage teaches that believers, those *believing* Jesus and *following* Jesus, will never perish nor be snatched from God's hand. However, it does not discuss what befalls those who cease believing Jesus and cease hearing Jesus's voice and cease following him. The Bible teaches that saving faith must endure; it must persevere; and this endurance and perseverance are not guaranteed. This is the universal teaching of the New Testament, as the chapters that follow will show.

John 5:24

John 5:24 reads: "Truly, truly, I say to you, whoever hears my word and believes him who sent me has eternal life. He does not come into judgment, but has passed from death to life." Calvinists use this text to argue that those who have once believed have passed from death to life and that this is an irreversible condition. Norman Geisler said that this means that "those who truly believe *now* can be certain now that they will be in heaven *later*."[2] But is this what the text entails?

Robert Picirilli is correct when he states that this argument "proves too much." The eternal security argument from John 5:24, as well as other texts that say that "believers" will not come into judgment, and other similar images, asserts that the promises in these texts "require the impossibility of a changed situation." This argument, however, "places too great a burden on the syntax of these statements." This can be seen by a simple comparison of two promises of Jesus about salvation used in John's gospel: John 5:24 says that those who believe in Jesus will not come into judgment, but John 3:36 says that those who reject Jesus will not see life.[3]

---

2. Norman L. Geisler, "A Moderate Calvinist View," in *Four Views on Eternal Security*, ed. J. Matthew Pinson (Grand Rapids: Zondervan), 71. Michael Horton cites this same text in his chapter on "Classical Calvinism," 25.
3. Robert E. Picirilli, *Grace, Faith, Free Will: Contrasting Views of Salvation: Calvinism and Arminianism* (Nashville: Randall House, 2002), 200.

As Picirilli argues, "Grammatically, if the first means that the condition of the believer cannot be changed, then the second means that the condition of the unbeliever likewise cannot be changed. In fact, neither passage is even speaking to that issue." Both texts speak of God's promise of what will occur if individuals believe in Christ or reject him. If individuals do not believe and persist in that unbelief, they will not see life. If individuals do believe and persist in that belief, they will meet the condition of election.[4]

Leroy Forlines avers that if the words "shall not see life" in John 3:36, "which describe the unbeliever, are not contradicted when the unbeliever becomes a believer and sees life, where is the contradiction when it is said that a believer 'shall not perish,' but that if he becomes an unbeliever he will perish? The fact is that a believer, as long as he remains a believer, 'shall not perish.'"[5] When we read these promises to the believer, we must remember that these are not promises to one who has believed in the past, but to one who is currently believing. The definition of belief in these texts from John's gospel is the same as it is throughout the New Testament: saving faith is an enduring faith, not a past experience.

Romans 8:35, 38–39

Romans 8:35, 38–39 reads: "Who shall separate us from the love of Christ? Shall tribulation, or distress, or persecution, or famine, or nakedness, or danger, or sword? . . . neither death nor life, nor angels nor rulers, nor things present nor things to come, nor powers, nor height nor depth, nor anything else in all creation, will be able to separate us from the love of God in Christ Jesus our Lord." Advocates of certain perseverance say that this text, as well as other verses in Romans 8 (vv. 1, 5, 16–17), teach that doctrine.[6]

Paul does not mean for these texts to address the question of endurance in the faith or the security of the believer. Rather, they concern the benefits that come to the believer through union with Christ. An Arminian can preach these texts strongly, yet the passages have nothing to do with justifying faith or continuance in that faith. Rather, they are encouraging believers by reminding them of the blessings they have by virtue of their union with Christ. As Ashby argues, these blessings "are not abstract entities that I possess. They result from my *union with Christ*. If that union is broken by unbelief, then the benefits are gone."[7] Romans 8:35–39 is not considering the question whether a regenerate person can be lost again. It states that one who is in union with

---

4. Picirilli, *Grace, Faith, Free Will*, 201.
5. F. Leroy Forlines, *Classical Arminianism: A Theology of Salvation* (Nashville: Randall House, 2011), 315. See also Stephen M. Ashby, "A Reformed Arminian View," in *Four Views on Eternal Security*, ed. J. Matthew Pinson (Grand Rapids: Zondervan, 2002), 165–66.
6. James Petigru Boyce, *Abstract of Systematic Theology* (Louisville, KY: SBTS Press, 2013 [1882]), 384.
7. Ashby, "A Reformed Arminian View," 167.

Christ cannot be separated from God's love. Yet it simply does not discuss what occurs when one ceases to endure in that vital union.

However, Forlines explains that, even if the text were referring to the security of the believer, it would be interpreted the same way as Jesus's statement that no one can snatch those who are following Jesus out of God's hand (John 10:27–28). "Paul would be saying as emphatically as human language can make it that our personal salvation is a matter between the individual believer and God." None of the things or persons mentioned in Romans 8:35 and 38 "can take a believer away from Christ." Paul's teaching here "in no way contradicts the viewpoint that if a believer turns away from God in defiant, arrogant unbelief, God will take him out of Christ (Jn. 15:2, 6)."[8]

Romans 11:29

Romans 11:29 reads: "For the gifts and the calling of God are irrevocable." As A. T. Robertson demonstrates, the word *ametameleta*, translated as "irrevocable" by some translations, means "to be sorry afterwards," or, as all English translations rendered it before the mid-twentieth century, "without repentance."[9] Calvinists argue that this passage proves that because God can neither change nor break his promises, he will not take back his salvific gifts. As the Calvinist Puritan John Owen, attempting to refute the Arminian Puritan John Goodwin, stated: "The 'gifts and calling of God' are said to be 'without repentance.' The gifts of his effectual calling . . . shall never be repented of. They are from Him with whom there is no change."[10]

However, Goodwin's original response to this argument is difficult to refute. In one sense the text simply means, as Robertson would later say, that "God is not sorry for his gifts to and calling of the Jews."[11] Yet Goodwin explained that the meaning of Romans 11:29 could not be "that what God once gives he never takes away" because there are too many plain examples in Holy Scripture of things God gives that he takes away, based on conditions not met by individuals. Thus, Goodwin concludes, "the gifts and calling of God are not in this sense without repentance."[12]

Goodwin further remarked that if believers disregard all the scriptural warnings against apostasy and reject Christ, God still does not repent of having given them the gift of salvation to begin with, simply because they did not continue to believe. If they "divest and despoil themselves of that very

---

8. Forlines, *Classical Arminianism*, 316.

9. E.g., Wycliffe, Tyndale, Bishops', Geneva, KJV, Douay-Rheims, ASV. See A. T. Robertson, *Word Pictures in the New Testament* (Nashville: Broadman, 1931), 4:339.

10. John Owen, *The Doctrine of the Saints' Perseverance Explained and Confirmed* [1654] in *The Works of John Owen*, ed. William H. Goold (London: Johnstone and Hunter, 1853), 11:122.

11. A. T. Robertson, *Word Pictures in the New Testament*, (New York: Harper, 1930), 4:339.

12. John Goodwin, *Redemption Redeemed* (London: Thomas Tegg, 1840 [1651]), 224.

qualification on which God, as it were, grafted his benefit or gift vouchsafed to them; in this case, though he recalls and takes away his gift, he cannot be said to repent of the giving it, because the terms upon which he gave it please him still; only the persons to whom he gave it, and who pleased him when he gave it unto them, have now rendered themselves, by their unworthiness, displeasing unto him."[13]

This is another way of saying that salvation is, from beginning to end, conditional, and its being conditional in no way changes God's faithfulness to make good on his promises. He will faithfully fulfill the terms of his covenant. If we apostatize it is we, not he, who have repented or regretted that God gave us his salvific gift.

Philippians 1:6

Philippians 1:6 reads: "And I am sure of this, that he who began a good work in you will bring it to completion at the day of Jesus Christ." Calvinists argue that this verse proves that the believer's perseverance "is guaranteed by God's perseverance."[14] This text presents no difficulties for those who believe that true believers must endure in the faith lest they fall away and be lost. As with the texts above, Philippians 1:6 does not discuss the issue of conversion or continuance in the faith. It is an expression of Paul's confidence in the Philippian believers that they will remain faithful. The text promises that Christ will "perform the work of salvation until the day of Jesus Christ in those who continue in faith."[15] However, this promise is not made to unbelievers, but to believers, and as Forlines states, there is "no contradiction if one who is a believer becomes an unbeliever and the promise no longer applies."[16]

This passage, like similar expressions in 2 Thessalonians 3:3; 2 Timothy 1:12, 4:18; and Jude 24–25, is simply, as Ashby explains, an expression "of thanksgiving and confidence that God will remain faithful in doing his part. But the paranetic sections of Scripture show that he demands that his free creatures continue in the faith in order to partake in his blessings fully and finally."[17] These texts encourage "confidence in what God will do, *from His side*, assuming that the persons spoken about continue in faith."[18]

---

13. Goodwin, *Redemption Redeemed*, 225; see also Thomas C. Oden, *The Transforming Power of Grace* (Nashville: Abingdon, 1993), 197.

14. Michael Horton, *The Christian Faith: A Systematic Theology for Pilgrims on the Way* (Grand Rapids: Zondervan, 2011), 681.

15. Forlines, *Classical Arminianism*, 317.

16. Forlines, *Classical Arminianism*, 317.

17. Ashby, "A Reformed Arminian View," 167.

18. Picirilli, *Grace, Faith, Free Will*, 203.

Ephesians 4:30

Ephesians 4:30 reads: "And do not grieve the Holy Spirit of God, by whom you were sealed for the day of redemption." Calvinists argue that this passage, and similar ones like Ephesians 1:13–14 and 2 Corinthians 1:22, automatically "guarantee" (Eph. 1:14) that the believer's perseverance will be certain, and any possibility of apostasy suggests that "God's guarantee . . . is not good!"[19]

Arminians respond by saying that this sealing (*esphragisthēte*—"you were sealed") and "down payment" (*arrabón*, also used in 2 Cor. 1:22; other translations use "pledge" or "earnest") do not produce an automatic result. "Seal" does not mean to "seal up" something, as in our modern usage. It means "to mark with a seal as a means of identification."[20] Such a seal identifies what it is on as belonging to, or being from, the one who seals it. Picirilli indicates that this word is used in modern Greek to refer to an engagement to be married. Seals can be broken, stamps can be effaced, and down payments often do not result in a deal's closing. The same verse (4:30) teaches that believers can grieve the Spirit by whom they are sealed.[21] This verse is likely based on Isaiah 63:10, which clarifies the meaning of "grieved": "But they rebelled and grieved his Holy Spirit; therefore he turned to be their enemy, and himself fought against them." Far from teaching that the seal of the Holy Spirit automatically results in final salvation, it teaches that believers can grieve the Holy Spirit and make the Spirit their enemy.[22]

Summary

Again, all of this hangs on whether or not salvation is conditional from beginning to end. If final salvation is conditioned on "continuing in the faith" (Col. 1:23) or "enduring in the faith" (Heb. 10:36), as Arminians believe it is, and if the Bible consistently warns people not to apostatize, as Arminians believe it does, then there is nothing in the above texts that *contradicts* this. The problem, for either Arminians or Calvinists, is how to interpret warning passages and assurance or promise passages. Arminians believe Calvinists must dodge the warning passages, but Reformed Arminians, who affirm that perseverance is by *sola fide* and not by confession of sin and penitence, believe that they do not have to dodge the assurance passages like those above, which assure believers that if they *are* believers—not if they *were once* believers—they *will be* saved.

---

19. Geisler, "A Moderate Calvinist View," 74–75.
20. *A Greek-English Lexicon of the New Testament and other Early Christian Literature*, 3rd ed., rev. and ed. Frederick William Danker (Chicago: University of Chicago Press, 2000), 980.
21. Robert E. Picirilli, "Ephesians," *Randall House Bible Commentary: Galatians through Colossians* (Nashville: Randall House, 1988), 141.
22. Cf. I. Howard Marshall, *Kept by the Power of God: A Study of Perseverance and Falling Away* (Minneapolis: Bethany House, 1969), 108.

REFLECTION QUESTIONS

1. How might the verb tense used in John 10:27, which indicates Christ's sheep "are hearing" his voice, and they "are following" him, lead an Arminian to believe that John 10:28–29 does not contradict the possibility of a believer ceasing to believe?

2. Does it make sense to say that, if arguing that a believer "will not come into condemnation" (John 5:24) proves that a believer cannot become an unbeliever, saying an unbeliever "will not see life" (John 3:36) would have to mean that an unbeliever cannot become a believer? Why or why not?

3. Does saying that Romans 8 teaches that nothing can separate from Christ's love those who are believers in union with Christ contradict the teaching of John 15 that God the Father can take "branches" out of union with Christ "the vine" when they cease to abide in him?

4. In verses like Ephesians 1:13–14; 4:30; and 2 Corinthians 1:22, if the Greek word for "sealed" means "a king's stamp" and "guarantee" means "down payment," does this weaken the argument that these images clearly prove that God will ensure that all believers will infallibly persevere?

5. How might an Arminian understanding that emphasizes faith alone—that believers can apostatize only through ceasing to believe and not by committing sins—change the way one might read these texts?

How Do Calvinists Interpret the Warnings Against Apostasy in Scripture?

One of the greatest exegetical challenges facing Calvinism is the ubiquity of warning passages throughout Holy Scripture. How do Calvinists respond to the myriad passages in the New Testament that seem to teach that true believers can fall from grace? The Arminian wonders: "If Jesus expressly tells his followers, 'I have said all these things to you to keep you from falling away' (John 16:1), how is it that Calvinists can escape the import of all the passages that seem to indicate that a regenerate individual can fall away?" This chapter will consider four interpretations of the New Testament warning passages that disagree with the Arminian contention that genuine believers can turn from Christ and apostatize.

The Tests of Genuineness View

The first position is that the people described in the warning passages as having fallen away "were never regenerate. They merely tasted of the truth and the life, were exposed to the word of God; they did not fully experience these heavenly gifts. They do in fact apostatize, but from the vicinity of spiritual truth, not from its center."[1]

Calvin affirmed this position. In his commentary on Hebrews 6:4–6, he suggested that God grants the reprobate "some taste of his grace" and "irradiate[s] their minds with some sparks of his light," giving them "some perception of his goodness," and writing "his word on their hearts." He believed that the passage was speaking of the "temporary faith" spoken of in the parable of the soils in Mark 4:17. There is "some knowledge even in the reprobate,

---

1. Millard J. Erickson, *Christian Theology* (Grand Rapids: Baker, 1991), 992–93. For a modern presentation of this interpretation, see Michael S. Horton, "A Classical Calvinist View," in *Four Views on Eternal Security*, ed. J. Matthew Pinson (Grand Rapids: Zondervan, 2002), 21–42.

which afterwards vanishes away, either because it did not strike roots sufficiently deep, or because it withers, being choked up."[2] Thomas Schreiner and Ardel Caneday call this position, which John Owen also held, the "tests of genuineness" view. This view holds that the purpose of the warning passages is to cause believers to test the genuineness of their profession of faith, to examine themselves to see whether they are in the faith.[3]

Schreiner and Caneday explain that Owen, the scholar who has exerted the greatest influence on contemporary "tests of genuineness" advocates, was arguing against the notion that the individuals spoken of in the warning passages are "real and true believers." Owen argued "that a person may be 'enlightened,' yet this light does not 'renew, change, or transform' the person 'as a gracious saving light' does." Similarly, someone can "taste the heavenly gift," the Holy Spirit, while not experiencing his "saving work." These people "only taste the gift for an 'experiment' or 'trial' but do not eat or drink. So also, some may receive a 'share of the Holy Spirit,' which refers to spiritual gifts, and fail to receive salvation, just as Simon Magus did (Acts 8:21)." Owen said the same thing about the tasting of the goodness of the Word of God and the powers of the coming age. Thus he concluded that Hebrews 6:4–6 is aimed at individuals who "are not true and sincere believers," and he believed that this is confirmed by "the absence of any reference to faith or believing in their description." This chapter will not respond to the "tests of genuineness" view. The Arminian interpretation of the warning passages in Questions 37–39 will serve as a response to that interpretation.[4]

The Hypothetical View

The second position is often termed the hypothetical view. Millard Erickson takes this position. He says the "never regenerate" (tests of genuineness) view "is difficult to accept" because the "vividness of the description and particularly the statement '[those who] have become partakers of the Holy Spirit,' argues forcefully against denying that the people in view are (at least for a time) regenerate." Erickson argues that, while Hebrews 6:4–6 affirms that people *can* fall away, Hebrews 6:9 and John 10 affirm that they *will not* fall away. In a footnote, he says that the "distinction appears to elude [the Arminian I. Howard] Marshall, who regards the 'hypothetical theory' as 'a thoroughly sophistical theory which evades the plain meaning of the passage. There is no evidence whatsoever that the writer was describing an imaginary danger which could not possibly threaten his readers.'" However,

---

2. John Calvin, *Commentaries on the Epistle of Paul the Apostle to the Hebrews*, trans. John Owen (Edinburgh: Calvin Translation Society, 1853), 138.

3. Thomas R. Schreiner and Ardel B. Caneday, *The Race Set before Us: A Biblical Theology of Perseverance and Assurance* (Downers Grove, IL: IVP Academic, 2001), 195–96.

4. Schreiner and Caneday, *The Race Set before Us*, 196.

Marshall's brief statement suffices for explaining why most interpreters, whether Calvinist or not, do not accept the hypothetical interpretation.[5]

The Means of Perseverance View

Another Calvinistic interpretation of the warning passages, which Schreiner and Caneday have articulated, could be called the "means of perseverance" or "means of salvation" view. This view has recently grown in popularity. Its adherents argue that "the Scriptures assure us who believe that God secures all who are in Jesus Christ (Rom 8:29–39). But at the same time the Scriptures also admonish and warn us that we must persevere in obeying Jesus Christ or else die eternally (Rom 8:12–13)." They believe that, while God "promises salvation to all who believe in Christ," he also "uses means to secure his promise to save everyone who believes." Those means are "warnings framed in the same contingent or conditional form as the initial call of the gospel."[6]

Schreiner and Caneday explain that the warnings are real and "crucial." God "warns us by calling on us to use our imaginations to conceive or envision the dreadful and inviolable consequence of failing to persevere in faithfulness to Christ. He does not frighten us by threatening that we may fall away or that it is likely that we will fail to persevere." By means of these warnings, God strengthens the believer's faith "by assuring us that he will preserve us safely to the end and by warning us lest we perish by failing to persevere in steadfast loyalty to Jesus Christ."[7]

Why does this view seem "absurd," as Richard Watson characterized it, to the vast majority of interpreters of Scripture, even most Calvinists? It is because, as Watson averred, if the writers of the New Testament had taught their readers "that they never could fall away, and so perish, this was no warning at all to them."[8] Or, as Albert Nash quipped, this view, in essence, has the Bible saying to the believer, "*If you do what you cannot, God will do what he will not.*"[9]

However, if one thinks about it, this is really the most consistent position for a rigorous Calvinist to take. One would expect no less from Edwards.[10] After all, that is what is involved in the Calvinist doctrine of the call of the gospel, as discussed in Questions 12 and 14. It has God requiring people to do something that he has determined in advance they cannot and will not do

---

5. Erickson, *Christian Theology*, 993–94.
6. Schreiner and Caneday, *The Race Set before Us*, 200.
7. Schreiner and Caneday, *The Race Set before Us*, 213.
8. Richard Watson, *Theological Institutes* (Bellingham, WA: Lexham, 2018), 2:366.
9. Albert Nash, *Perseverance and Apostasy: Being an Argument in Proof of the Arminian Doctrine on That Subject* (New York: N. Tibbals and Son, 1871), 38 (italics added).
10. For an insightful treatment of Edwards's doctrine of perseverance from a Reformed Arminian perspective, see Matthew McAffee, "Jonathan Edwards on Perseverance: A Reformed Arminian Interaction," paper presented at the Free Will Baptist Theological Symposium, October 2011.

because he has arranged the universe in such a way that they will necessarily and infallibly be reprobate. This is what philosophers call a performative contradiction, as if a young man proposes and tells a young woman, "I wish you would marry me. I want you to marry me. I would love it if you would marry me. Will you please marry me?" Yet all the while he knows he never had any intention of marrying her and never will do so.[11]

Consider another example. If a teacher warns students, "If you don't do well in my course, you'll get an F," is this (to use Schreiner and Canedays's language above) "calling on" students to use their "imagination[s] to conceive or envision the dreadful and inviolable consequence" (an F) of failing to do well in the course, or "frightening" them by "threatening" that they may make an F if they fail to do well in the course? It would seem to be both. Yet it would be absurd for the teacher to tell students on the second day of class, "if you don't do well in my course, you'll get an F" if on the first day of class the teacher said, "I have determined ahead of time that there is no way you will get less than an A in this course."[12]

To repeat Watson's concern, is the teacher really giving a warning that if students do not do well they will get an F, if it is not possible to make less than an A? Is the teacher really giving a warning if it does not "frighten" students by "threatening" that they will fail the course if they do not do well in it, if indeed they have been informed that the teacher has determined ahead of time that they cannot fail?[13]

If the warning passages in the New Testament are simply a means to ensure the perseverance of believers who, of necessity, by God's eternal decree, can never do anything *except* persevere, this puts God in the position of saying something like the following to believers:[14]

---

11. Dermot Moran, ed., *The Routledge Companion to Twentieth Century Philosophy* (London: Routledge, 2008), 986. I have enjoyed gleaning from the insights of Richard E. Clark on this topic.

12. Schreiner and Caneday appeal to the story of the shipwreck in Acts 27 to prove their point that God warns people of consequences he says are impossible (*The Race Set before Us*, 209–12). Yet there are too many unanswered questions and details that any interpreter would have to assume, in that brief summary narrative, to base doctrine on it. For more on this, see Brian Abasciano, "Acts 27 and the Possibility of Apostasy," Society of Evangelical Arminians, February 9, 2012, http://evangelicalarminians.org/brian-abasciano-acts-27-and-the-possibility-of-apostasy, accessed February 12, 2021. See also Daniel D. Whedon, *Commentary on the New Testament* (New York: Eaton and Mains, 1899), 3:271.

13. A side issue is Schreiner and Canedays's statement that God does not "frighten" believers by "threatening" that "it is likely that we will fail to persevere." This seems irrelevant to the discussion, because the Arminian argument does not entail that it is "likely" that Christians will fail to persevere.

14. All biblical references in the following three paragraphs are from Hebrews.

Dear believer, I have chosen you from eternity and made you a believer in my Son, bringing the light of redemption to you, giving you the heavenly gift of salvation, making you a partaker of the Holy Spirit (6:4), and giving you a saving experience of the goodness of my Word and the powers of the age to come (6:5). I have sanctified you with the blood of the covenant I have made with you (10:29), and you have received the benefit of my Son's sacrifice for your sins (10:26), from which you have repented (6:6). Therefore, I promise you that you can never fall. Falling from grace, because you have believed, is impossible for you. I have from eternity decreed that you will infallibly persevere to the end of your life and be saved. It is impossible for you to apostatize. I assure you of this.

Still, I must solemnly and urgently warn you: be very careful lest you allow an evil heart of unbelief to develop within you, leading you to fall away from me (3:12) because your heart has become hardened by sin's deceitfulness (3:13). Strive to hold your original confidence firm to the end (3:14), because if you do not—if you fall away—you cannot be restored to repentance (6:6). Indeed, if you fall away, you will have recrucified my Son and held him up to contempt. And this will be to your own harm (6:6). Be cautious lest you commit apostasy (6:6, RSV), thus trampling underfoot my Son and making his blood, which sanctified you, common and unholy, and spitefully outraging the Holy Spirit (10:29), because if you do, you can never be renewed to the repentance you once had (6:6). That would not be possible, because my Son's sacrifice for your sin, which you once appropriated through repentance and faith, will no longer be available for you (10:26). Please understand, *if* you do not throw away your confidence (10:35)—*if* you endure to the end, which you *need* to do (10:36)—you will receive what I have promised you (10:36), *but* if you draw back from me, my soul will have no pleasure in you (10:38).

Now, do not forget: I have made an unconditional promise to you that *you can never fall.* But please, I warn and caution you, endure in the faith to the end of your life, because, *if you do fall*, you will be eternally lost with no opportunity to be renewed to the repentance in which you once stood. Yet, please understand, because of my solemn promise to you, dear believer, you *can never fall.*

The Arminian agrees with the Calvinist Philip Edgcumbe Hughes, who said that, according to the "means of perseverance" view, Hebrews' "warning about the impossibility of restoration for the apostate is unrelated to reality and little better than the invention of a bogey for the purpose of frightening them into being better Christians." Hughes was right when he said that "the end does not justify the means, and to resort to subterfuge and deception, and that too within so solemn a context, would be sub-Christian and incompatible with the whole tenor of the epistle."[15]

The Loss of Rewards View

One final perspective is probably the most widespread popular-level interpretation of the warning passages by those who believe in certain perseverance: the loss of rewards view. In brief, this position holds that those spoken of in the warning passages are genuine believers but that what can be forfeited by them is not salvation, which is by faith, but eternal rewards, which are earned by works.[16]

Stephen Ashby encapsulates the Arminian response to this perspective. He explains that, while the Bible teaches the loss of heavenly rewards to believers, advocates of this position are wrong to create a "one-size-fits-all" category of loss of rewards and impose it on the warning passages. The great difficulty with this position is the severity of the warnings themselves, which can hardly be seen as merely depriving the glorified believer of heavenly rewards.[17]

Ashby discusses Hebrews 10:38–39 to refute the loss of rewards theory, which he sees as a bald attempt to dodge the issue. "The just," Ashby points out, live by faith (v. 38), are encouraged to hold fast to their confession of hope (v. 23), are of those who believe (v. 39), and if they continue to believe they will receive salvation (v. 39). This is contrasted with "those who shrink back." These individuals throw away their confidence (v. 35); thus God has no pleasure in them (v. 38). They do not continue to believe. However, the text does not say that they are thus deprived of rewards. Rather, it clearly states that "their end is destruction."[18]

Summary

Either the individuals spoken of in the warning passages are not believers, as Calvin's and Owen's view holds, or they are believers who can fall away. The means-of-perseverance and loss-of-rewards views attempt to maintain exegetical integrity by acknowledging that the people spoken of are believers.

---

15. Philip Edgcumbe Hughes, "Hebrews 6:4–6 and the Peril of Apostasy," *Westminster Theological Journal* 35 (1973): 144.

16. Schreiner and Caneday, *The Race Set before Us*, 24–29. Recent scholarly advocates of this approach include Norman L. Geisler, "A Moderate Calvinist View," in *Four Views on Eternal Security*, ed. J. Matthew Pinson (Grand Rapids: Zondervan, 2002), 61–112; David L. Allen, *Hebrews*, New American Commentary (Nashville: B&H, 2010); and Randall C. Gleason, "A Moderate Reformed View," in *Four Views on the Warning Passages in Hebrews*, ed. Herbert W. Bateman IV (Grand Rapids: Kregel Academic, 2007), 336–77.

17. Stephen M. Ashby, "A Reformed Arminian View," in *Four Views on Eternal Security*, 177. For more on this, see the discussion of Hebrews 10:27 in Question 38.

18. Ashby, "A Reformed Arminian View," 177.

Yet their adherents have to reckon either with God's being disingenuous in warning against a destruction (Heb. 10:38) that he knows cannot and will not occur, or with the fact that what believers are being warned of in these passages is clearly something much more severe than the mere loss of rewards. These include things like being destroyed (Heb. 10:38); not being able to be restored to repentance (Heb. 6:6); being consumed as an enemy of God (Heb. 10:27); not being able to enter God's rest (Heb. 3:11); and their last state being worse than their preconversion state (2 Peter 2:20). The tests of genuineness view reckons with the reality of the warning about apostasy and its irremediability. However, this approach has a difficult time explaining away the clear picture of these individuals as genuine believers in Christ.

REFLECTION QUESTIONS

1. Which of the four views of certain perseverance believe that the warning passages are aimed at, or describe, genuine believers, and which believe they are aimed at unregenerate individuals?

2. If God knows believers cannot fall from grace, is it disingenuous for him to use warnings against falling away to keep them from doing so?

3. What problems do Arminians point out with interpreting the people referred to in the warning passages as unregenerate people rather than true believers?

4. What do you think about the interpretation that says that apostates cannot be restored to repentance, even though, according to that perspective, they never repented to begin with?

5. How do critics of the "loss of rewards" view statements in the warning passages that warn the people against apostasy lest they be destroyed cast doubt on that view?

The Possibility of Apostasy

Does the Letter to the Hebrews Teach the Possibility of Apostasy? (Part 1)

The possibility of regenerate believers apostatizing from Christ is a major theme in the letter to the Hebrews. This chapter will consider the three main warning passages in Hebrews: 3:12–14; 6:4–6; and 10:26–29. Numerous other texts from Hebrews teach that regenerate believers can apostatize. Chapter 12, for example, is directed at the Hebrew believers, God's sons (v. 7), of whose faith Jesus is the founder and perfecter (v. 2), and whom the writer exhorts to run the Christian race with endurance (v. 1). Yet verse 25 warns them twice not to refuse or turn from (*paraiteomai*) God. The theme of defection from Christ also figures prominently in texts such as 2:1–4; 4:1–11; and 10:35–39. We could spend an entire chapter on each warning passage in Hebrews, but in this chapter and the next, these three texts—3:12–14; 6:4–6; and 10:26–29—will be the primary objects of our consideration.

The three texts that follow teach four truths about perseverance and apostasy: First, the people referred to are regenerate believers. Second, believers need to be concerned about enduring in faith, because final salvation is conditioned on doing so. Third, it is possible for a believer to fall away through unbelief. Fourth, apostasy cannot be remedied.

> [12] Take care, brothers, lest there be in any of you an evil, unbelieving heart, leading you to fall away from the living God. [13] But exhort one another every day, as long as it is called "today," that none of you may be hardened by the deceitfulness of sin. [14] For we have come to share in Christ, if indeed we hold our original confidence firm to the end.
>
> *Hebrews 3:12–14*

[4] For it is impossible, in the case of those who have once been enlightened, who have tasted the heavenly gift, and have shared in the Holy Spirit, [5] and have tasted the goodness of the word of God and the powers of the age to come, [6] and then have fallen away, to restore them again to repentance, since they are crucifying once again the Son of God to their own harm and holding him up to contempt.

Hebrews 6:4–6

[26] For if we go on sinning deliberately after receiving the knowledge of the truth, there no longer remains a sacrifice for sins, [27] but a fearful expectation of judgment, and a fury of fire that will consume the adversaries. [28] Anyone who has set aside the law of Moses dies without mercy on the evidence of two or three witnesses. [29] How much worse punishment, do you think, will be deserved by the one who has trampled underfoot the Son of God, and has profaned the blood of the covenant by which he was sanctified, and has outraged the Spirit of grace?

Hebrews 10:26–29

Regenerate Believers

As will be argued below, the people referred to in each of these passages are regenerate believers. If one were to give anyone the characteristics described in these texts, outside the context of the perseverance debate, and ask if they refer to a regenerate or unregenerate person, almost everyone would say they refer to a regenerate person. It is hard to imagine a better description of a regenerate believer in Christ than the one given in these texts.

They share in/are partakers of Christ (3:14) and the Spirit (6:6).

These people are said to have shared in or been partakers of Christ and the Holy Spirit. The word *metochoi*, used in both 3:14 and 6:6, means someone who shares with or partakes of something.[1] Because of the way the author of Hebrews uses this term elsewhere in the letter, it refers to a profound, saving sense of sharing in or partaking of Christ and the Spirit. Hebrews 3:1 refers to the readers as "holy brothers" who "*share in* a heavenly calling." Hebrews 12:8 refers to sons of God who *partake* (*metochoi*) in the discipline of their Father. Hebrews 5:13 refers to believers who "live on

---

1.   Walter Bauer, *A Greek-English Lexicon of the New Testament and Other Early Christian Literature*, rev. and ed. Frederick W. Danker, 3rd ed. (Chicago: University of Chicago Press, 2000), 643.

milk" rather than meat. "Live on" is the ESV's translation of *metechōn*. The text does not describe these believers as having a superficial acquaintance with milk, but rather *living on* it.

As Thomas Schreiner says, the "gift of the Holy Spirit is the clearest indication in the NT that one is a Christian, so for the author to say that the readers were sharers of the Holy Spirit demonstrates that he is saying they were Christians."[2] This is very different from the way some Calvinists such as Wayne Grudem interpret this sharing and partaking as a slight, superficial experience of Christ and the Spirit by being a mere professing Christian.[3]

They "have once been enlightened" (6:4).

The text also says they were "once for all enlightened" (from *phōtizomai*, to give light or bring into the light).[4] The same Greek word is used in 10:32, "recall the former days when, after you were enlightened, you endured a hard struggle with sufferings," leaving no doubt that it refers to conversion.[5] Some Calvinist interpreters argue that "enlightened" in 6:6 and 10:32 does not *have to mean* believing the gospel, but could mean only learning about the gospel.[6] Yet 10:32 is directed at "brothers," who "have confidence to enter the holy places by the blood of Jesus." Saying these could be "people who had only learned the gospel but did not believe" seems like an exercise in grasping at straws.

They have "tasted" the "heavenly gift, the "goodness of the Word," and "the powers of the age to come" (6:4–5).

The same goes for the "tasted" statements. If the doctrine of certain perseverance did not have to be protected, no one would question that these statements refer to conversion. The author of Hebrews uses the Greek word for "taste," *geuomai*, to mean a full experience of something in 2:9, which states that Jesus tasted death for everyone. As Schreiner argues, "Certainly Jesus did not just sip death or dabble with it a bit. He died! He fully experienced all the horrors of death. So, when the author says the readers 'tasted the heavenly gift,' the expression most naturally means they experienced the

---

2. Thomas R. Schreiner, *Commentary on Hebrews*, Biblical Theology for Christian Proclamation (Nashville: Holman, 2015), 186. Schreiner is a Calvinist who believes the warnings are given to genuine believers as a means to help them persevere, though their perseverance is certain because God has ensured that they *will* heed the warning.
3. Wayne Grudem, "Perseverance of the Saints: A Case Study from the Warning Passages in Hebrews," in *Still Sovereign: Contemporary Perspectives on Election, Foreknowledge, and Grace*, eds. Thomas R. Schreiner and Bruce A. Ware (Grand Rapids: Baker, 2000), 147.
4. Robert E. Picirilli, *Grace, Faith Free Will: Contrasting Views of Salvation: Calvinism and Arminianism* (Nashville: Randall House, 2002), 217.
5. Picirilli, *Grace, Faith Free Will*, 217. See also I. Howard Marshall, *Kept by the Power of God: A Study of Perseverance and Falling Away* (Minneapolis: Bethany House, 1975), 142.
6. Grudem, "Perseverance of the Saints," 141.

salvation that comes from above."[7] This argument from 2:9 would seem to settle the issue.

However, that is not enough for some Calvinists. Grudem, for example, does not deny that *taste* means having a "genuine experience" of something, as in Jesus having a genuine experience of death. Yet the question, he says, is not whether these people had a genuine experience of the heavenly gift, the goodness of the Word of God, or the powers of the age to come. "The question is whether they had a *saving* experience of these things," which Grudem says the text does not *have to* mean.[8] So what this interpretation leaves the reader with is that these people had experienced the heavenly gift, the goodness of the Word of God, and the powers (a word which in itself implies a profound experience) of the eschatological kingdom just as Jesus had experienced death on the cross, but that is no proof that theirs was a "saving" experience.

The Arminian sees this as a stretch too far. The natural reading of the text is that these individuals had a full and deep experience of God's gift of "new life or salvation"[9]—God's good Word, which, as Matthew McAffee has demonstrated, is saying they genuinely experienced the divinely promised blessing of the covenant promise and the powers of the coming age.[10]

They had been in a state of repentance (6:6).

These people were believers who had repented of their sin. Otherwise, the statement that they cannot be restored to repentance is meaningless. It is inconceivable that one could ever be restored to something one had never experienced. Still, the Calvinist "hypocrite" argument of Grudem and others. simply says that *repent* here does not mean repentance from sin in the normal New Testament sense. Instead, it means a superficial "sorrow for sin and a decision to forsake that sin," but it is not saving repentance.[11] David Allen is correct when he avers that if Grudem's approach were correct, we would expect these texts to be calling these people to repentance and faith rather than exhorting them to maturity and endurance in faith.[12]

---

7. Schreiner, *Commentary on Hebrews*, 184.
8. Grudem, "Perseverance of the Saints," 146.
9. Schreiner, *Commentary on Hebrews*, 184. See also Scot McKnight, *A Long Faithfulness: The Case for Christian Perseverance* (Colorado Springs: Patheos, 2013), Kindle loc. 815–26.
10. Matthew McAffee, "Covenant and the Warnings of Hebrews: The Blessing and the Curse," *Journal of the Evangelical Theological Society* 57 (2014): 537–53.
11. Grudem, "Perseverance of the Saints," 150.
12. David L. Allen, *Hebrews*, New American Commentary (Nashville: B&H, 2010), 358. Allen is an eternal securitist who believes the warnings are given to genuine believers to keep them from losing divine rewards.

They were sanctified by Christ's blood (10:29).

Those who argue that the individuals in Hebrews 6 were mere professed, not true, believers make a similar argument about Hebrews 10. The writer of Hebrews states that these people had been sanctified by the "blood of the covenant," that same blood that, according to 10:19, gives these believers confidence to enter the Holy of Holies.[13] Like Grudem does with Hebrews 6, John Owen, almost with a wave of the hand, dismissed the idea that these people were sanctified by Christ's blood in the ordinary biblical sense of that phrase. He states, "It is not real or internal sanctification that is here intended, but it is a separation and dedication unto God." He believes the passage speaks of merely professing Christians "who by baptism, and confession of faith in the church of Christ, were separated from all others, were peculiarly dedicated to God thereby," but were never truly sanctified.[14] However, this is simply a bald assertion, with nothing near an indication in the text that someone who is sanctified by the blood of Christ is actually a professed believer who was never genuinely converted.[15]

The Need to Be Concerned About Enduring

These warning passages from Hebrews also teach that believers *need to be concerned* about enduring in faith, because their final salvation is conditioned on doing so. These believers are exhorted and warned, over and over again, to be vitally concerned about persevering, enduring in faith. The writer repeatedly warns them that *only if* they endure will they be finally saved. They need to "take care" lest they develop an evil heart of unbelief (3:12). Why is this condition, this "if," given if they cannot help but meet it? The author says that they frequently need to exhort each other so that their hearts will not be hardened by sin's deceitfulness (3:13). Final salvation occurs only if believers "hold their confidence firm to the end" (3:14). They need to "hold fast the confession of [their] faith without wavering" (10:23). They "have need of endurance" (10:36).

The Possibility of Falling Away in Hebrews 3 and 6

The remainder of this chapter and the next one will turn to a consideration of what Hebrews warns these believers can happen to them: it is possible for a believer to fall away—to apostatize or defect from Christian belief. The reason the letter to the Hebrews exhorts its readers to be concerned about enduring in faith to be finally saved is its consistent teaching that falling away is

---

13. W. Stanley Outlaw, *Hebrews*, Randall House Bible Commentary (Nashville: Randall House, 2005), 256.

14. John Owen, *Exposition of the Epistle to the Hebrews*, in *The Works of John Owen*, ed. William H. Goold (London: Johnstone and Hunter, 1855), 23:545.

15. Other indicators in chapter 10 that these were regenerate people are seen in verses 19, 22, 26, 35, 36, and 38.

indeed possible for believers. The above texts provide four axioms concerning the possibility of genuine, regenerate believers committing apostasy. Believers can (1) become spiritually hardened by sin, which will lead to unbelief (3:12, 14); (2) "turn away" (3:12) or "fall away" (6:6) into a state of unbelief; (3) become "adversaries" of God again (10:27); and (4) trample Christ underfoot, profane his blood, and outrage the Holy Spirit (10:29). This chapter will consider the possibility of falling away in 3:12, 14 and 6:6, and the next chapter will consider it in 10:27–29.

Spiritual Hardening and Unbelief

The writer warns his readers, whom he acknowledges as brothers, that they can develop an "evil, unbelieving heart" that causes them to "fall away from the living God" (3:12). The text connects this unbelief with a spiritual hardness of heart that results from "the deceitfulness of sin" (3:13). The more believers allow themselves to be deceived into what Leroy Forlines calls "tampering with sin," the more their hearts will be hardened to the conviction of the Spirit. This spiritual hardening, if left unchecked, will lead to the believer's becoming an unbeliever again and thus falling away from God.[16]

Turning Away and Falling Away

In 3:12, the author of Hebrews says that believers can develop an "evil heart of unbelief," thus "departing from the living God." The Greek word here for falling away is *apostēnai*, the root of the English word "apostasy." It means to desert, forsake, depart from, or turn away from something.[17] In 3:12, "*in leading you* to fall away" does not appear in the Greek text as it does in the RSV and ESV. As with most translations, a better rendering is "*in* departing from the living God" (e.g., KJV, NKJV) or "*that* turns [or falls] away from the living God" (e.g., NRSV, NASB, HCSB, NIV).

In 6:6 another word, *parapiptō* is used. It is usually translated "fall away" and means to fall beside, slip aside, or deviate from.[18] Picirilli says it means "defection from the experience described in the four positive clauses that precede."[19] The use of this construction intrinsically demonstrates the nature of the case for, as Daniel Whedon said, "Of course they could not fall if they did not once stand." In this connection he cites another warning passage: "Therefore let anyone who thinks that he stands take heed lest he fall" (1 Cor. 10:12). "*Away* means from the previous state of renewal in which the warning requires them to stand. It was not a fall from a state of condemnation, but

---

16. F. Leroy Forlines, *Classical Arminianism: A Theology of Salvation* (Nashville: Randall House, 2011), 351–52.
17. James A. Swanson, *Dictionary of Biblical Languages with Semantic Domains: Greek (New Testament)*, 2nd ed. (Bellingham, WA: Lexham, 2001), 923.
18. Swanson, *Dictionary of Biblical Languages*, 4178.
19. Picirilli, *Grace, Faith, Free Will*, 221.

from a state of salvation. And this *fall away* is the central thought of the whole epistle."[20]

Philip Edgcumbe Hughes is correct when he remarks that the "peril" or "danger" of apostasy in these texts is "real, not imaginary, and the situation called for the gravest possible warning; for loss of confidence and the slackening of the will to contend in the Christian race . . . pointed alarmingly to the ultimate possibility of their dropping out of the contest altogether, and in doing so of placing themselves beyond all hope of restoration."[21]

Summary

While this consideration of the Hebrews warning passages will continue in the next chapter, this chapter has shown that these texts are aimed at genuine, regenerate believers in Christ who have authentically shared in and been partakers of Christ and the Spirit, having been "enlightened" and in a state of repentance. These "brothers" who "have confidence to enter the holy places by the blood of Jesus" have been sanctified by that blood and have the ability to "draw near with a true heart in full assurance of faith," with their hearts "sprinkled clean from an evil conscience and [their] bodies washed with pure water." These "righteous" individuals, living by faith, have done the will of God and are due to receive what he promised.

Yet these individuals are in danger of apostatizing, and the author is impressing on them their need to endure in faith, because their final salvation is conditioned on doing so. The letter stresses that sin can harden believers, and this can lead to unbelief, causing them to "turn away" or "fall away" from Christ, becoming God's adversaries, trampling Christ underfoot, profaning his blood, and outraging his Spirit.

REFLECTION QUESTIONS

1. When the author of Hebrews says these individuals shared/were partakers in Christ and the Spirit and were enlightened, what does that indicate about their spiritual condition?

2. What does comparing Hebrews 6:4–5 with Hebrews 2:9 indicate about the nature of what it means to "taste" of a spiritual reality?

---

20. Daniel D. Whedon, *Commentary on the New Testament: Titus to Revelation* (New York: Phillips and Hunt, 1880), 5:81.
21. Philip Edgcumbe Hughes, "Hebrews 6:4–6 and the Peril of Apostasy," *Westminster Theological Journal* 35 (1973): 138.

3. Does the use of the word "power" in "tasting of the powers of the age to come" (Heb. 6:5) indicate a superficial experience?

4. Is David Allen's comment valid—that if the repentance these individuals had experienced was not saving repentance, we would expect the texts to be calling these people to repentance and faith rather than exhorting them to maturity and endurance in faith?

5. Is the Arminian argument fair that the text would not warn people about falling or turning from something if they had never had it—Whedon's comment, "Of course they could not fall if they did not once stand"?

Does the Letter to the Hebrews Teach the Possibility of Apostasy? (Part 2)

Hebrews 10 underscores the possibility of apostasy the letter dealt with earlier. As noted before, the people to whom chapter 10 refers are clearly regenerate believers. Hebrews 10:26 states that such believers can get into a state in which there is no more sacrifice for their sins. As Hughes noted, the "very real dangers of apostasy and its dire consequences, against which the most solemn warnings have already been given (2:1ff.; 3:12; 4:1ff.; and especially 6:4ff.), is now stressed once more. Persons who lapse into the irremediable state of apostasy are precisely those members of the Christian fellowship who *sin deliberately after receiving the knowledge of the truth.*"[1]

High-handed Sin

Forlines, Hughes, and many others agree that the "sin" described here is no ordinary sin but refers to the "high-handed sin" of Numbers 15, which is unforgivable.[2] This is the same thing as the unforgivable sin or the sin against the Holy Spirit to which Jesus refers in the Gospels. Thus apostasy does not result from ordinary, forgivable sins. Rather, high-handed sins, which are unforgivable because there is no more atoning sacrifice for them, result from turning one's back on Christ, returning to unbelief, and thus renouncing the only, once-for-all sacrifice for one's sin.

This is the majority position among traditional Calvinists, who follow Calvin and John Owen, though they believe the apostates were not genuine

---

1. Philip Edgcumbe Hughes, *A Commentary on the Epistle to the Hebrews* (Grand Rapids: Eerdmans, 1977), 418–19 (emphasis in original).

2. Forlines has an entire appendix on this question in *The Quest for Truth* (Nashville: Randall House, 2000). See also Forlines's former student Matthew McAffee, "Covenant and the Warnings of Hebrews: The Blessing and the Curse," *Journal of the Evangelical Theological Society* 57 (2014): 537–53. Cf. Hughes, *A Commentary on the Epistle to the Hebrews*, 419.

believers but only professed believers and members of the visible church. Calvin averred, "Now this is wholly to renounce God. We now see whom he excluded from the hope of pardon, even the apostates who alienated themselves from the Gospel of Christ, which they had previously embraced, and from the grace of God; and this happens to no one but to him who sins against the Holy Spirit."[3]

Hughes is correct when he states that this question "involves considerably more than the question of the irremissibility of a particular sin." He emphasizes that apostasy is not "so much an act as an attitude of which he is speaking—an attitude, to be sure, which will disclose itself in disgraceful acts inconsistent with a profession of Christian faith. . . . A life that once professed obedience to Christ but now openly blasphemes his name and denies his gospel is the mark of the apostate."[4] Notice that the Calvinist Hughes says these high-handed sins are inconsistent with a *profession* of Christian faith. While he shows that irremediable apostasy is spoken of in this text, he asserts that the apostate was only a professing believer, not a genuine one. Yet this belies the fact that the high-handed sin in Numbers is obviously referring to apostasy from a spiritual state that is not just professed, but actual.

Adversaries of God

In 10:27, the text says that these "brothers" who "have confidence to enter the holy places by the blood of Jesus," having been sanctified by that blood, can again become "adversaries" of God (10:27). This is a salient image of an unregenerate state used frequently in the New Testament. The people referred to here as God's adversaries are those who were formerly believers for whom there is no longer a sacrifice for sin (10:26), but only "a fearful expectation of judgment, and a fury of fire that will consume the adversaries" (10:27). Thus, if believers turn away from Christ, the only sacrifice for their sin, and if they can no longer avail themselves of his sacrifice, then the only thing that awaits them is judgment and fire that will consume them as adversaries of God.

Amazingly, Gleason, who thinks the punishment described here is only "severe physical punishment leading to loss of life but not eternal judgment," says there is a "conspicuous absence" in verses 26–27 of the "'damnation' terminology" that is found elsewhere in the New Testament. He mentions

---

3. John Calvin, *Commentaries on the Epistle of Paul to the Hebrews*, trans. John Owen (Edinburgh: Calvin Translation Society, 1853), 136. Sometimes it sounds as if Calvin believes that apostasy can happen to true believers but not to the elect. Yet he states in his commentary on this passage that "God indeed favors none but the elect alone with the Spirit of regeneration."

4. Hughes, *A Commentary on the Epistle to the Hebrews*, 215. Calvin remarks: "But the Apostle speaks not here of theft, or perjury, or murder, or drunkenness, or adultery; but he refers to a total defection or falling away from the Gospel, when a sinner offends not God in some one thing, but entirely renounces his grace." Calvin, *Commentaries*, 136.

phrases such as "eternal fire," "eternal punishment," and "eternal destruction," suggesting that if Hebrews were talking about apostasy, the word "eternal" would be used with "judgment," "punishment," and so forth.[5]

However, this is to wiggle feverishly out of the obvious import of these images. The text clearly states that these people for whose sins there will never be any more sacrifice have nothing but fear in their future—an expectation of divine judgment and a "fury of fire" that will consume (*esthiein*—"devour") the enemies of God. How is that not a description of eternal judgment and only a mere description of chastisement? Besides, that reading flatly contradicts the text, which clearly states that the punishment of apostates is "much worse" than physical death (10:28–29), and the only thing that is worse than temporal, physical death is eternal, spiritual death.

Trampling, Profaning, and Outraging

The passage also affirms that believers can "trample under foot" or "spurn" the Son of God, profane his blood, and outrage (earlier translations, following Wycliffe, have "do despite to") the Spirit of grace (10:29). In the context, which says there is no more sacrifice for these people's sins, it is obvious that these images denote apostasy, a turning away from the only sacrifice that can atone for their sin, which they are profaning. They are spurning and trampling under foot the individual who made this sacrifice for them, and they are doing despite to the Holy Spirit who brought them salvific grace.

John Owen, commenting on 10:29, describes these three images as clear examples of apostasy: "There are no such cursed, pernicious enemies unto religion as apostates. Hence are they said to 'do despite unto the Spirit of grace,' . . . injure him so far as they are able. The word includes *wrong with contempt*. . . . All these great and terrible aggravations are inseparable from this sin of apostasy from the gospel, above those of any sin against the law of Moses whatever."[6]

No Remedy for Apostasy

Hebrews clearly teaches that apostasy is irremediable. Scot McKnight states plainly of the phrase "cannot be restored to repentance" in 6:6: "This is a singular comment; it is grave and sad beyond comprehension. They have reached the point of no return."[7] When believers turn from Christ, as I. Howard Marshall remarked, "it is impossible to bring them back to repentance, and all

---

5. Randall C. Gleason, "A Moderate Reformed View," in *Four Views on the Warning Passages in Hebrews*, ed. Herbert W. Bateman IV (Grand Rapids: Kregel Academic, 2007), 360–61.

6. John Owen, *Exposition of the Epistle to the Hebrews*, in *The Works of John Owen*, ed. William H. Goold (London: Johnstone and Hunter, 1855), 23:547.

7. Scot McKnight, *A Long Faithfulness: The Case for Christian Perseverance* (Denver: Patheos, 2013), Kindle loc. 809.

that awaits them is judgment. . . . Thus to the possibility of falling away there is added the impossibility of restoration to faith and salvation."[8]

Why is this so? First, Hebrews 6:4, 6 states explicitly that it is impossible to restore or renew to repentance those who have fallen away. Thomas Schreiner is right when he says that the "language of renewing to repentance makes clear that the sin is apostasy." He explains that "repentance" and "faith" are concepts the New Testament often uses "to describe the human response necessary to enter the people of God." Thus, "by saying that they couldn't repent again, the author indicates that they would be outside the people of God if they fall away, that there would be no room for coming back in through repentance and faith."[9]

Interpreters have often asked if the impossibility is an impossibility for God or for people. While McKnight does not agree that it is "metaphysically" impossible for God to restore the apostate to repentance, he believes it is practically impossible: "God will not work in them any longer so it is impossible for them to be restored."[10] The Spirit who brings grace (10:29) will no longer bring grace to the apostate. Thus, in this unregenerate state, and without divine enabling grace, it is impossible for the apostate to be regenerated again. One can see this principle of the necessity of enabling grace in point four of Stephen Ashby's incisive statement:

1. Prior to being *drawn and enabled,*
   one is *unable to believe . . . able only to resist.*

2. *Having been drawn and enabled,* but prior to regeneration,
   one is *able to believe . . . able also to resist.*

3. After one *believes,* God then *regenerates;*
   one is *able to continue believing . . . able also to resist.*

4. Upon *resisting* to the point of *unbelief,*
   one is *unable again to believe . . . able only to resist.*

   The reason persons 1 and 4 are unable to believe and are able only to resist God is that God is not drawing or enabling them. And "apart from [him] you can do nothing" (John 15:5).[11]

---

8. I. Howard Marshall, *New Testament Theology: Many Witnesses, One Gospel* (Downers Grove, IL: InterVarsity, 2004), 619.

9. Thomas R. Schreiner, *Commentary on Hebrews,* Biblical Theology for Christian Proclamation (Nashville: Holman, 2015), 181.

10. Scot McKnight, "The Warning Passages in Hebrews: A Formal Analysis and Theological Conclusions," *Trinity Journal* 13 (1992): 33 n. 39.

11. Stephen M. Ashby, "A Reformed Arminian View," in *Four Views on Eternal Security,* ed. J. Matthew Pinson (Grand Rapids: Zondervan, 2002), 159.

Verse 6 gives the most obvious reason why restoration to repentance is impossible: They are crucifying Jesus all over again *to themselves* (*heautois*). Forlines insightfully notes that "this is a crucifixion in relationship, that is, to themselves." He gives Galatians 6:14 as an example of crucifixion to oneself: "The world has been crucified to me, and I to the world." Forlines explains, "So far as reality was concerned, both Paul and the world were living and active; but so far as relationship was concerned, they were dead to each other. . . . The relationship of Christ to the unsaved is that of a dead Christ; but to the saved, He is a living Christ." This leads Forlines to the conclusion that someone "could not crucify to himself the Son of God afresh unless he were in a living relationship to Him; therefore, such could be committed only by a saved person."[12]

Very few interpreters, whether Arminian or Calvinists, take the position that the apostasy described here is remediable. This is true even of some Arminians who believe there is another kind of apostasy in the New Testament that is remediable. However, a small minority of Arminians, like Robert Shank, affirm that the apostasy Hebrews 6 and 10 discuss is remediable, but even he thinks that rare cases of apostasy are irremediable (Matt. 12:31; Mark 3:29; Luke 12:10).[13]

No More Sacrifice for Sin after Apostasy

Hebrews 10:27 gets to the heart of the reason why it is impossible to renew the apostate to repentance: There is no sacrifice for the sins of apostates (10:27). The author of Hebrews goes into great detail about the unrepeatability of Christ's once-for-all sacrifice. Christ did not sacrifice himself "repeatedly" like the high priest who entered the Holy of Holies every year "with blood not his own." Instead, Christ "has appeared once for all at the end of the ages to put away sin by the sacrifice of himself" (9:25–26; see v. 28). In the immediate context, the writer explains that, "since the law has but a shadow of the good things to come instead of the true form of these realities, it can never, by the same sacrifices that are continually offered every year, make perfect those who draw near." Then the author asks, "Otherwise, would they not have ceased to be offered, since the worshipers, having once been cleansed, would no longer have any consciousness of sins?" (10:1–2).

Yet in the old-covenant sacrifices, "there is a reminder of sins every year. For it is impossible for the blood of bulls and goats to take away sins" (10:4). The epistle goes on to explain, in 10:11–12, that "every priest stands daily at his service, offering repeatedly the same sacrifices, which can never take away

12. F. Leroy Forlines, *Classical Arminianism: A Theology of Salvation* (Nashville: Randall House, 2011), , 322.
13. Robert Shank, *Life in the Son: A Study of the Doctrine of Perseverance* (Springfield, MO: Westcott, 1961), 318, 322. See Question 40.

sins. But when Christ had offered for all time a single sacrifice for sins, he sat down at the right hand of God." This background explains why the writer in 10:29 states emphatically that, for the apostate, "there no longer remains a sacrifice for sins." The death of Christ is a once-for-all event. It cannot be repeated. Christ "offered for all time a single sacrifice for sins" (10:12).

As Hughes explains, if this is true of the old-covenant person in Numbers 15 whose sins can no longer be forgiven, it is "even more obviously true of the apostate under the new covenant, since, as our author has so carefully explained, the multiplicity of priests and sacrifices of the levitical system has now been superseded by the one priest and the one sacrifice by whose virtue alone we are sanctified and perfected forevermore (vv. 10–14 above). Clearly, then, to reject this sacrifice is to be left with no sacrifice at all." Hughes explains that the individuals described here have "repudiate[d] Christ's once-for-all sacrifice." Thus there is no more sacrifice for their sins. They have "willfully cut themselves off from the sole means of forgiveness and reconciliation."[14]

As if this were not enough, the author proceeds to state that there is *no mercy* for apostates, but *only judgment*. The text states that, since apostates can no longer avail themselves of Christ's once-for-all sacrifice for sin, there is no mercy for them, just as there was no mercy for the old-covenant believer "who set aside the law of Moses" (10:28). The only thing that awaits these individuals is a "fearful expectation of judgment," a "fury of fire that will consume" them, and "much worse punishment" than the death penalty that was given the one who set aside Moses's law.

Advocates of the "loss of rewards" interpretation wish to minimize the severity of this description of the apostates' condition by viewing it as mere temporal punishment. Yet, as Owen observed, the consequence described in this passage "shall be a sorer punishment than that which was appointed for willful transgressors of the law, which was death without mercy." Owen asks how the punishment described here can be worse than that. He answers, "Because that was a temporal death only; for though such sinners under the law might and did many of them perish eternally, yet they did not so by virtue of the constitution of the law of Moses, which reached only unto temporal punishments: but this punishment is eternal."[15]

Summary

The sin of apostasy is unlike any other sin. Instead it is the "high-handed sin," the unforgivable sin of Numbers 15, the sin against the Holy Spirit.

---

14. Hughes, *A Commentary on the Epistle to the Hebrews*, 418. See McKnight, "The Warning Passages in Hebrews," 34. Sometimes as a pastor I encountered Christians struggling with sin who were worried that they had committed apostasy. As McKnight notes, those who are concerned that they may have committed apostasy "show thereby that they have not" (42).
15. Owen, *Exposition of the Epistle to the Hebrews*, 23:548.

Apostates once again become adversaries of God, having spurned and trampled on Jesus, profaning his sacrifice, and doing despite to the Holy Spirit who brought them salvific grace. Thus apostasy is irremediable. It is impossible to restore to repentance those who have fallen away, because there is no more sacrifice for their sin: they can no longer avail themselves of the unrepeatable "single sacrifice for sins." There is no mercy for them, only judgment, and this merciless judgment is not just a loss of rewards, but "a fury of fire" that will "consume" them.

REFLECTION QUESTIONS

1. How does the high-handed sin of Numbers 15 inform one's understanding of the nature of apostasy or falling away, and whether one can recover from it?

2. Were the old-covenant believers in Numbers 15 apostatizing from merely professing to be members of the covenant community, or were they apostatizing from actual membership in the covenant community? How does this affect one's interpretation of whether the apostates in Hebrews had been genuine believers or not?

3. Is it possible for a regenerate believer to become an adversary of God again without apostatizing from Christ?

4. Can one recover from the apostasy described in the letter to the Hebrews, given that it causes there to be no more sacrifice for one's sins?

5. If the punishment for apostasy is worse than the death penalty for breaking Moses's law, is it tenable to say that the punishment is merely loss of heavenly rewards?

What Does the Rest of the New Testament Teach About Apostasy?

The New Testament, outside the letter to the Hebrews, is replete with texts warning believers about the possibility of their apostasy or fall from grace. While the majority of this chapter will consider two of the most important such texts, John 15:1–6 and 2 Peter 2:21–22, it will begin with a simple mention of representative warning passages outside Hebrews that fall into various categories.[1]

The New Testament throughout makes continuing in faith a necessary condition of final salvation. No text exemplifies this better than Colossians 1:21–23, in which Paul tells the Colossian believers that Christ desires to present them "holy and blameless and above reproach before him, if indeed you continue in the faith."

First Timothy 1:19–20 is an example of a text that refers to believers who have actually renounced their faith in Christ. Paul warns his readers to hold "faith and a good conscience," saying that "by rejecting this, some have made shipwreck of their faith." Then he mentions their names: Hymenaeus and Alexander.

In Galatians 4:9–11, Paul tells the Galatians, whom he says "have come to know God": "I am afraid I may have labored over you in vain." In 1 Corinthians 9:27, Paul is concerned about the possibility that he himself might become

---

1. A number of works consider these sorts of texts in detail. See, e.g., John Goodwin, *Redemption Redeemed* (London: Thomas Tegg, 1840 [1651]); I. Howard Marshall, *Kept by the Power of God: A Study of Perseverance and Falling Away* (Minneapolis: Bethany House, 1968); Albert Nash, *Perseverance and Apostasy: Being an Argument in Proof of the Arminian Doctrine on that Subject* (New York: N. Tibbals and Son, 1871); Robert L. Shank, *Life in the Son: A Study of the Doctrine of Perseverance* (Springfield, MO: Westcott, 1961).

adokimos (unapproved, failing the test, disqualified, reprobate).[2] He tells the Galatians that some among them "are severed from Christ, you who would be justified by the law; you have fallen away from grace" (5:4).

John 15:1–6

John 15:1–6 reads:

> I am the true vine, and my Father is the vinedresser. Every branch in me that does not bear fruit he takes away, and every branch that does bear fruit he prunes, that it may bear more fruit. Already you are clean because of the word that I have spoken to you. Abide in me, and I in you. As the branch cannot bear fruit by itself, unless it abides in the vine, neither can you, unless you abide in me. I am the vine; you are the branches. Whoever abides in me and I in him, he it is that bears much fruit, for apart from me you can do nothing. If anyone does not abide in me he is thrown away like a branch and withers; and the branches are gathered, thrown into the fire, and burned.

The Arminian Interpretation

Arminians see the warning in this passage similarly to those in other warning passages. John portrays believers as branches who are growing out of a vine, the image for Jesus. The Father is pictured as the vinedresser who tends and cultivates the vine. As branches in the vine, believers are, as Cyril of Alexandria said, in vital union with Christ, having been "united with Him by faith."[3] The branches are growing out of him, drawing their life from him. They are morally and religiously "clean" because of "the life of the vine pulsating through the branches."[4]

Jesus urges them to abide (*meinate*, to stay or remain) in him, because if they do, they will bear fruit. But if they do not—here is the warning—they will be thrown away, will wither up, and will be thrown into the fire and burned. Obviously, being thrown away means that the vinedresser, God the Father, removes them from Christ the vine. They are no longer in union with Christ. They wither up and die and are burned. As Cyril remarked, if a believer gets into this condition, "we are wholly cut off, and we shall be given to the flames, and shall

---

2. James A Swanson, *Dictionary of Biblical Languages with Semantic Domains: Greek (New Testament)*, 2nd ed. (Bellingham, WA: Lexham, 2001), 99.

3. Cyril of Alexandria, *Commentary on the Gospel according to S. John* (London: Walter Smith, 1885), 2:375

4. D. A. Carson, *The Gospel of John*, Pillar New Testament Commentary (Grand Rapids: Eerdmans, 1991), 515.

have lost besides that life-giving sap . . . we once had from the vine."[5] Thus they can never be reconstituted as branches and placed back into union with the vine. Having once been in union with Christ, and having been taken out of that union with Christ by the Father, they cannot once again be placed into union with Christ, since it is impossible "to reproduce a living branch from its ashes."[6]

This is one of the strongest texts in the New Testament teaching the possibility of apostasy. The only reason one would see this passage as teaching anything other than the possibility of apostasy would be if he or she imported something into the text from elsewhere. There is simply no loophole, within the text, to mitigate this natural reading.

Calvinist Interpretations and the Arminian Response

There are only two other ways to interpret the text. Some Calvinist interpreters argue that the unfruitful branches are believers who are merely being chastened. This is the position of A. W. Pink, which D. A. Carson convincingly refutes.[7] The only other possible interpretation is that the unfruitful branches are professed believers who have never really been in union with Christ. This was Calvin's view and is the majority opinion of Calvinists.[8] Calvin states that "there are many hypocrites who, in outward appearance, flourish and are green for a time, but who afterwards, when they ought to yield fruit, show the very opposite of that which the Lord expects and demands from his people." He also says that "many are supposed to be in the vine, according to the opinion of men, who actually have no root in the vine."[9]

The trouble with this view is that it is at variance with what the text explicitly states. Saying "they have no root in the vine" directly contradicts the text. Jesus does not say, "I am the vine, and according to people's opinion, you are the branches." He does not say, "I am the vine, and you appear to be the branches." He does not say, "I am the vine, and you profess to be the branches." He says, "I am the vine, and you *are* the branches."

He says they are "already clean." He states that they as branches are in union with Christ the vine and are receiving their life from him, a life which they will lose if they do not remain in union with him. They will lose that life because

---

5. Cyril of Alexandria, *Commentary on the Gospel according to S. John*, 2:375.

6. Nash, *Perseverance and Apostasy*, 205.

7. A. W. Pink, *Exposition of the Gospel of John* (Cleveland: Cleveland Bible Truth Depot, 1929), 3:337; cf. Carson, *Gospel of John*, 515.

8. This is the position, e.g., of Carson, *Gospel of John*; Sam Storms, and J. Carl Laney. See Carson; Sam Storms, *Kept for Jesus: What the New Testament Really Teaches about Assurance of Salvation and Eternal Security* (Wheaton, IL: Crossway, 2015), 50 (see also his blog post on the subject, https://www.samstorms.com/all-articles/post/john-15:1-6-and-the-security-of-the-believer); J. Carl Laney, "Abiding Is Believing: The Analogy of the Vine in John 15:1–6," *Bibliotheca Sacra* 146 (1989): 55–66.

9. John Calvin, *Commentary on the Gospel according to John*, trans. William Pringle (Edinburgh: Calvin Translation Society, 1847), 2:108

the Father will take them out of the vine, and they will die and wither and be burned in the fire. How can individuals who, already dead in trespasses and sins, as mere professors are, be described as having life, and then because they are not bearing fruit, be removed from the vine and then die and be burned?

Why would Jesus tell someone, "You are a branch in me, *but you are dead in trespasses and sin*. If you bear fruit, you will be pruned; but if you do not bear fruit, the Father will take you out of union with me, and you will wither and die and be burned!"? Why would Jesus tell unregenerate people any of these things? Why would he tell them that there are fatal consequences for not bearing fruit, though they necessarily cannot bear fruit if they are unregenerate? Why would he warn them that they will be removed from the vine and hence die if they are dead already? Why would he explicitly tell them that they are branches in the vine if they are branches only in appearance and not in reality? Why would Christ tell them to remain if they are not already in the vine? Or why would Christ tell them to remain if they cannot leave?

Albert Nash summarized the fallaciousness of such an argument: "It is impossible for a man dead in trespasses and sins to be cut off from Christ and withered. *The killing of a dead man, the excision of a branch from a tree to which it was never united, and the withering of an already dead and dry branch, are simple impossibilities.*"[10]

When Arminians read John 15:1–6 in its context and then read the Calvinist interpreter who says, "Obviously these fruitless branches are merely professing faith but were never truly regenerate," they go back and reread the text, scratch their heads, and ask themselves, "Am I missing something?" When they read Calvinists who say this text is describing "unsaved believers" who have "fickle faith," who merely "claim to be Christ's" but are "not bearing fruit,"[11] they have to go back and reread the passage, only to remind themselves that it is Jesus himself who says these genuine, living branches being given life by the vine can either be pruned by the Father and bring forth more fruit or can be taken out of union with the vine and burned. Arminians conclude that this is the only way to read this text unless one imports knowledge from other texts that eternal security is true.

2 Peter 2:20–22

Second Peter 2:20–22 reads:

> For if, after they have escaped the defilements of the world through the knowledge of our Lord and Savior Jesus Christ,

---

10. Nash, *Perseverance and Apostasy*, 206 (italics added).
11 The first two phrases are from Storms's blog; the latter two phrases are from Laney, "Abiding Is Believing," 64.

they are again entangled in them and overcome, the last state has become worse for them than the first. For it would have been better for them never to have known the way of righteousness than after knowing it to turn back from the holy commandment delivered to them. What the true proverb says has happened to them: "The dog returns to its own vomit, and the sow, after washing herself, returns to wallow in the mire."

The Arminian Interpretation

The first question to ask about the people described in these verses is, Were they regenerate? That they were is obvious from the fact that they had escaped the world's defilements, and they had done so through the knowledge of Jesus Christ. The word "knowledge" (*epignōsis*) here is significant. Verse 20 says that these people had escaped the world's defilements through knowledge, and verse 21 uses the verb with the same root as *epignōsis* twice to indicate they had known "the way of righteousness." *Epignōsis*, as Robert Picirilli convincingly shows, is a technical term Peter uses throughout 2 Peter to denote "the saving knowledge one gains at conversion."[12] They were also "washed," a metaphor universally used in the New Testament to refer to regenerate people.

The "if" clause in 2:20 also indicates that they were regenerate because they are entangled in the defilements of the world *again*. Furthermore, they "have known the way of righteousness" and have "*turned back* from the holy commandment given to them." The text thus presents as clear a picture as possible of a regenerated individual who turns back from his regenerate state.[13]

They are being warned against turning back from Christ's truth to the heresy of false teachers, which is the subject of chapter 2.[14] Peter warns them that, if they turn back, their state will be worse than before they came to know Christ. It would have been better for them never to have known Christ than, after having had that knowledge, to turn back from it. He then undergirds his declaration by a proverb about the dog returning to its vomit (cf. Prov. 26:11) and the sow returning to wallowing in the mud. There could be no more vivid

---

12. Robert E. Picirilli, *Grace, Faith, Free Will: Constrasting Views of Salvation: Calvinism and Arminianism* (Nashville: Randall House, 2002), 230. See Picirilli's detailed study of this in "The Meaning of 'Epignōsis,'" *Evangelical Quarterly* 47 (1975): 85–93. See Matthew McAffee, "Apostasy in 2 Peter: Its Literary Setting and the Role of Spiritual Immaturity," an unpublished paper that probes this text in light of Picirilli's scholarship.

13. F. Leroy Forlines, *Classical Arminianism: A Theology of Salvation* (Nashville: Randall House, 2011), 333.

14. Whether this text refers to the false teachers or those they have led astray is immaterial, since the text still describes them as having been, at one time, believers.

portrayal of a true believer for whom it is possible to turn back from Christ and become an unbeliever, being in a worse state than before conversion.

It is also clear from Peter's statements here that there is no recovery from this turning back. He does not say that the one who turns back is in the same state as before conversion. He states emphatically, twice, that those who turn back are in a *worse* state than before they came to a knowledge of Christ: Their last state is worse than their preconversion state, and it would have been better for them never to have known Christ than to know him and then turn back from him. The only way these statements have any force is if there is no return from this apostate condition. The only thing worse than being unregenerate with a possibility of coming to know Christ is being in an unregenerate state without that possibility.

The Calvinist Interpretation and the Arminian Response

Most Calvinists interpret the individuals spoken of in this text as professed, not genuine, believers. Amazingly, Wayne Grudem states that this passage speaks of false teachers who escaped the world's defilements through a knowledge of Christ but then "turned back to their previous ways." Then he simply says, "Moreover, they had never really been saved, for Peter says, 'It has happened to them according to the true proverb, The dog turns back to his own vomit, and the sow is washed only to wallow in the mire' (v. 22)—in other words, the repentance was only an outward cleansing, and it did not change their true nature."[15]

Yet how does a dog turning back to its vomit or a sow to wallowing in the mire show that repentance is only outward and did not change their true nature? Calvin's own straightforward interpretation is preferable. He explains that Peter meant that "the gospel is a medicine which purges us by wholesome vomiting, but that there are many dogs who swallow again what they have vomited to their own ruin." Similarly, the gospel is "a laver which cleanses all our uncleanness, but that there are many swine who, immediately after washing, roll themselves again in the mud."[16]

Why would the Holy Spirit, through Peter, describe false teachers, who all this while had been unbelievers—the most wicked hypocrites and deceivers—as having through knowledge of Christ escaped the defilements of the world? John Goodwin aptly called this "the first-born of incredibilities."[17]

---

15. Wayne Grudem, "Perseverance of the Saints: A Case Study from the Warning Passages in Hebrews," in *Still Sovereign: Contemporary Perspectives on Election, Foreknowledge, and Grace*, eds. Thomas R. Schreiner and Bruce A. Ware (Grand Rapids: Baker, 2000), 149. See also Thomas R. Schreiner, *1, 2 Peter, Jude*, New American Commentary (Nashville: B&H Academic, 2003), 362–63.
16. John Calvin, *Commentaries on the Catholic Epistles*, trans. John Owen (Grand Rapids: Eerdmans, 1948), 411–12 (italics added).
17. Goodwin, *Redemption Redeemed*, 215–16.

How can the text say these people have "escaped" a life of sin when all along, the entire time after their escape, they have been in bondage to sin and the devil and enemies of God and are putting up a hypocritical front? From what can they be said to have escaped? As Goodwin says, this Calvinist argument requires its adherent to say of these individuals that "all the while they were free from the pollutions of the world, they were still dogs and swine, and if so, as inwardly vile and wicked as ever."[18] The Arminian knows that this is wrenching the text from its obvious meaning because the interpreter already "knows" that certain perseverance is true.

Summary

The plain reading of the passages above is that they teach the possibility of apostasy. The New Testament teaches that continuing in faith is a necessary condition of final salvation but that such continuance is not guaranteed. Thus Scripture warns believers of the consequences of not continuing in faith and gives examples of people who have apostatized. Paul even says that there is a possibility he himself might become disqualified from salvation. Jesus goes as far as to say that branches in union with him, the vine who gives them spiritual life, can die again and be burned. Peter says that even those who have "escaped" from sin's dominion because they came to know Christ can turn back and be in a worse condition than before their conversion. Applying normal rules of exegesis to these passages yields the conclusion that it is possible for a regenerate person to apostatize. Any other interpretation requires the importation of theological conclusions from outside these texts.

REFLECTION QUESTIONS

1. How does Paul's concern of the possibility that he himself might become *adokimos* (unapproved, failing the test, disqualified, reprobate) inform the question of the possibility of apostasy?

2. Which is more tenable Calvinist interpretation of John 15—that the Father's removing unfruitful vines, allowing them to die, and burning them is merely temporal discipline; or that those who are in Christ the vine, drawing spiritual life from him, are mere professors who only seem to be in Christ the vine?

3. If John 15 were only warning mere professors, not genuine believers, of the need to remain in Christ, why would he think it was possible for them to heed his admonition to bear fruit? How could they do so if they were dead already and not truly alive as a branch in Christ the vine?

---

18. Goodwin, *Redemption Redeemed*, 216.

4. How does Peter's remark about apostates' condition being worse than before their conversion affect the debate about whether the individuals he describes could recover from apostasy?

5. What do you think of Calvin's statement regarding the dog returning to its vomit and the sow to wallowing in the mud, that Peter is referring to the gospel as "a medicine which purges us by wholesome vomiting" and "a laver which cleanses all our uncleanness," from which the "godly" can turn away?

Do Arminians Affirm Two Kinds of Apostasy?

The answer to the question of whether Arminians affirm two kinds of apostasy depends on which kind of Arminian you ask.[1] Many Arminians believe that there are two kinds of apostasy: (1) *total and final apostasy*, a rare and severe type of apostasy that comes about through a renouncing of belief and cannot be remedied, and (2) *backsliding*, the most common type of apostasy, which comes about through sinning and can be remedied through penitence. This chapter will refer to these two types as "Apostasy 1" and "Apostasy 2."[2] Many other Arminians (e.g., Reformed Arminians) believe that there is only one kind of apostasy. They hold that Apostasy 1 is the only sort of apostasy taught in Scripture.[3]

---

1. One will notice that, unlike in other sections, the chapters on perseverance do not deal with Arminius. This purposeful omission results from the ambiguity of his thought on this matter. I have given up on ascertaining what his settled thought was on this doctrine, since he says things throughout his career that each non-Calvinist position discussed in these chapters can claim. The most Reformed Arminians, Wesleyan Arminians, or non-Calvinist eternal securitists can say is that their position on perseverance and apostasy is true to the *trajectory* Arminius was on and would have consistently articulated had he lived longer and further fleshed out his system.

2. Some Arminians believe that even the sort of apostasy mentioned in Hebrews 6 and 10 can be remedied. Yet this position has historically been in a tiny minority among Arminians. Even Robert Shank, who sees Hebrews 6 and 10 as not teaching the irremediability of apostasy, believes that the biblical texts regarding the sin against the Holy Spirit give "warrant for believing that only in rare instances (e.g., Eli's sons) may apostasy be irremediable before the occasion of death" (Robert Shank, *Life in the Son: A Study of the Doctrine of Perseverance* [Springfield, MO: Westcott, 1961], 322).

3. Reformed Arminians such as F. Leroy Forlines, Robert E. Picirilli, Stephen M. Ashby, and I have argued for this basic position. Other notable Arminians, such as I. Howard Marshall, Scot McKnight, and Dale Moody, have argued that Apostasy 1 is the only type of apostasy. See I. Howard Marshall, *Kept by the Power of God: A Study of Perseverance and*

Those Who Affirm Both Apostasy 1 and 2

Most Arminians (and Lutherans) believe that Apostasy 1 is spoken of in passages such as Hebrews 6 and 10, as well as passages referring to the sin against the Holy Spirit or the unforgivable sin (Matt. 12:31; Mark 3:29; Luke 12:10). Thus they see Apostasy 1 as an irremediable defection from grace through unbelief.

	Calvinists	Eternal Securitists	Reformed Arminians	Most Arminians
Apostasy 1	No	No	Yes	Yes
Apostasy 2	No	No	No	Yes
No Apostasy	Yes	Yes	No	No

However, most Arminian (and Lutheran) theologians would say that most cases of apostasy are *not* of the Apostasy-1 type referred to in Hebrews 6 and 10 and the passages on the sin against the Holy Spirit. The other type of apostasy, Apostasy 2, results from sinning, not lapsing into a state of unbelief, and is remediable.[4] Sometimes, depending on the interpreter, Apostasy 2 is caused by one unconfessed sin, sometimes by several. In his essay on the Wesleyan Arminian doctrine of perseverance, for example, Steven Harper argues that Wesley "proposed another alternative—one that differentiated between involuntary and voluntary sin. Involuntary transgressions (i.e., sins we commit without the awareness that we have done so) are not held against us by God, unless we discover them and do nothing about them." Harper explains that, for Wesley, "voluntary sins—deliberate violations of known laws of God—do, however, become mortal if we do not repent of them. The subject of eternal security rests (in both categories of sin) on the matter of ongoing repentance. . . . As long as we live in faith (i.e., the moment-by-moment unfolding of our lives in both attitude and action), we are not committing sin."[5]

Falling Away (Eugene, OR: Wipf and Stock, 2008); Scot McKnight, *A Long Faithfulness: The Case for Christian Perseverance* (Denver: Patheos, 2013); Scot McKnight, "The Warning Passages in Hebrews: A Formal Analysis and Theological Conclusions," *Trinity Journal* 13 (1992): 33 n. 39; Dale Moody, *Apostasy: A Study in the Epistle to the Hebrews and in Baptist History* (Macon, GA: Smyth and Helwys, 1997); and Dale Moody, *The Word of Truth* (Grand Rapids: Eerdmans, 1981), 348–65.

4. Wesley's intellectual progenitor John Goodwin referred to such individuals as "twice regenerate," saying that regeneration can be "reiterated" or "repeated." See Jesse F. Owens, "Scripture and History in the Theology of John Goodwin," paper presented at the Evangelical Theological Society Annual Meeting, November, 2015.

5. J. Steven Harper, "Wesleyan Arminianism," in *Four Views on Eternal Security*, ed. J. Matthew Pinson (Grand Rapids: Zondervan, 2002), 240. Some who affirm Apostasy 2 would even say that every sin, or several unconfessed sins, represents a "loss of faith," essentially saying

"It is remarkable," declared Wesley in his sermon "A Call to Backsliders," "that many who had fallen either from justifying or sanctifying grace . . . have been restored . . . and that very frequently in an instant, to all that they had lost. . . . In one moment they received anew both remission of sins, and a lot among them that were sanctified."[6] In his sermon "The First Fruits of the Spirit," Wesley asked believers,

> Wilt thou say, "But I have again committed sin, since I had redemption through his blood?" . . . It is meet that thou shouldst abhor thyself. . . . But, dost thou now believe? . . . At whatsoever time thou truly believest in the name of the Son of God, all thy sins antecedent to that hour vanish away. . . . And think not to say, "I was justified once; my sins were once forgiven me:" . . . "He that committeth sin is of the devil." Therefore, thou art of thy father the devil. It cannot be denied: For the works of thy father thou doest. . . . Beware thou suffer thy soul to take no rest, till his pardoning love be again revealed; till he "heal thy backslidings," and fill thee again with the "faith that worketh by love."[7]

Woodrow Whidden has encapsulated this approach in his *Asbury Theological Journal* article, "Wesley on Imputation": "Forgiveness of sins (both of nature and acts) is constantly available, but must somehow be constantly applied for by penitent ones experiencing salvation. . . . They must continuously apply for pardon or face the loss of their salvation." Believers struggling with sin are like "high wire or trapeze artists" in that they can perform "with or without a safety net underneath." In the Reformed model, "the safety net is always underneath the faithful and one has to consciously move out of faith relationship with Christ to have such a net removed." In the Wesleyan model, "the incidentally falling performers must somehow appeal for the safety net to be put in place before they crash (through sin)."[8]

---

that sin and saving faith cannot coexist. There is a great deal of ambiguity and diversity from author to author.

6. "A Call to Backsliders," in *The Works of John Wesley*, 3rd. ed., ed. Thomas Jackson (Grand Rapids: Baker, 1986 [1872]), 5:526.

7. "The First Fruits of the Spirit," in *Works*, 5:95–96.

8. Woodrow W. Whidden, "Wesley on Imputation: A Truly Reckoned Reality or Antinomian Political Wreckage?" *Asbury Theological Journal* 52 (1997). 66. A similar approach is also found among Lutherans, all of whom teach the doctrine of "reconversion." See Francis Pieper, *Christian Dogmatics* (St. Louis: Concordia, 1957), 2:575, 3:90. 4:188. All Lutherans, even Missouri Synod and other contemporary Lutherans who are closer to Calvinism on the doctrine of unconditional election, believe in the possibility of apostasy and reconversion.

Those Who Affirm Only Apostasy 1

Unlike most Arminians, Reformed Arminians affirm that Scripture teaches only Apostasy 1. Why do Reformed Arminians believe this? First, they argue that the New Testament makes no distinctions between two different types of falling from grace but presents only one—a complete, irremediable "shipwreck of faith." Second, they argue that justification by faith is a once-for-all category that incorporates the believer into a status of being "in Christ" rather than a fragile possession one is carrying in one's hands.[9] Third, they argue that Apostasy 2 is an implicit denial of the doctrine of justification by the imputed righteousness of Christ apprehended through faith.

Reformed Arminianism agrees with the Reformed tradition's understanding of justification by faith as *the once-for-all appropriation of the finished work of Christ in atonement*. When individuals place their faith in Christ, they are brought into union with Christ, and in that union they receive the benefit of his death and righteousness; they are imputed with his active and passive obedience. Justifying faith does not come and go, wax and wane, as believers sin and receive forgiveness for their sins. That is the way many Arminians see justifying faith. They think that, when an unbeliever gets into a condition of unconfessed sin, that indicates the absence of faith. Thus, again, for many Arminians, justification is more like a substance one possesses rather than a forensic status into which one is incorporated.

Reformed Arminians do not view justifying faith and its relation to sin in the believer's life in this way. Rather, they see justification by faith as a decisive, once-for-all *status* into which the believer is incorporated. Thus, even when believers are in a condition of sin of which they have not repented, they remain in union with Christ, they retain their "in Christ" status (1 Peter 1:5). Their justifying faith is still intact, which maintains their union with Christ. Union with Christ is a status into which the believer has been incorporated. As long as the believer is in union with Christ, his or her sins are covered.[10]

Thus one might say that the difference between Reformed Arminians and Calvinists is not on the *nature* of justifying faith but its *extension*. Calvinists believe that if one experiences justifying faith, that faith will, of necessity, *extend* to the end of life. Reformed Arminians believe, on the contrary, that the *extension* of one's justifying faith to the end of life is not guaranteed. Yet Reformed Arminians still agree with Calvinists on the *nature* of justifying faith: While in union with Christ through justifying faith, believers' sins are imputed to Christ, not to them. Recall the statement above by Wesleyan theologian Steven Harper: "As long as we live in faith (i.e., the moment-by-moment

---

9. Robert E. Picirilli, *Perseverance* (Nashville: Randall House, 1973), 14–15.

10. Thus, e.g., contemporary Reformed Arminians agree with everything the fifth head of Doctrine of the Canons of Dort (e.g., on sin in the life of the believer and assurance) except the doctrine of perseverance and apostasy.

unfolding of our lives in both attitude and action), we are not committing sin." This view of the *nature* of justifying faith is much different from that of Reformed theology.

In Reformed theology, justifying faith does not consist in the attitudes and actions of the moment-by-moment unfolding of our lives. Justification is not a substance we hold in our hands, in greater or lesser measure. It is not a waxing-and-waning, "off-again, on-again" dynamic. Instead it is a forensic standing into which we are incorporated. The attitudes and actions of the moment-by-moment unfolding of our lives is, according to Reformed theology, about sanctification, not justification. This difference, of course, flows out of divergent views of justification. The Reformed tradition ties *imputation* of the righteousness of Christ to justification and *impartation* of the righteousness of Christ to sanctification. Many Arminians, however, emphasize impartation, believing imputation to be a legal fiction, and thus conflate justification and sanctification (see Question 11).

In Reformed theology, while individuals are in union with Christ through justifying faith—credited with the once-for-all, finished work of Christ in atonement—they cannot fall. But unlike Calvinists, Reformed Arminians believe it is possible for a believer to become an unbeliever. When that happens, when justifying faith comes to an end, to quote Leroy Forlines, God "takes the believer out" of union with Christ.[11] Thus, once outside of justifying faith and union with Christ, apostates can no longer appropriate that once-for-all, finished work of Christ in atonement. His active and passive obedience are no longer imputed to them.

Forlines's notion of the apostate being "taken out of" union with Christ flows out of his exegesis of John 15. The imagery there is of God the father being the vinedresser, Christ being the vine, and believers being branches in the vine (see Question 39). This passage is a vivid illustration of the concepts of the nature and extension of justifying faith. Believers, as Christ's branches, are organically connected to Christ the vine. They are "growing out" of Christ the vine. They are not severed from the vine and then regrafted into it every time they sin or go through a period of unconfessed sin, every time their faithfulness waxes or wanes. This is where Reformed Arminians and other sorts of Arminians disagree on the nature of justifying faith. However, believers, as Christ's branches, are still capable of being severed from Christ the vine. When they cease abiding in Christ, there is no regrafting. Instead, they are thrown away and they dry up. They are then cast into the fire and burned, and it is impossible "to reproduce a living branch from its ashes."[12] This is where

---

11. Forlines, *Classical Arminianism: A Theology of Salvation* (Nashville: Randall House, 2011), 239, 317, 335–36, 355.

12. Albert Nash, *Perseverance and Apostasy: Being an Argument in Proof of the Arminian Doctrine on That Subject* (New York: N. Tibbals and Son, 1871), 205.

Reformed Arminians disagree with Calvinists as well as other Arminians on the *extension* of justifying faith.

Summary

Reformed Arminians concur with Calvinists on the nature of justifying faith (what it is) but disagree on the extension of justifying faith (how long it necessarily lasts). Most Arminians, however, disagree with Calvinists on *both* the nature *and* extension of justifying faith. They see it more as a moment-by-moment "faithfulness" rather than a forensic standing in the once-for-all finished work of Christ in atonement, appropriated by enduring faith.

This distinction helps explain why Reformed Arminians believe that apostasy occurs through the renouncing of faith-alone and thus cannot be remedied. One can see how Arminians who agree with Calvinists on the *nature* of justifying faith as an appropriation of the once-for-all, finished work of Christ in atonement, yet agree with Arminians that the *extension* of justifying faith until the end of life is not guaranteed, would affirm only one type of apostasy, Apostasy 1. This apostasy is like that described in Hebrews 6 and 10 and the texts on the sin against the Holy Spirit. It is the "total and final" type that most Arminians (as well as Lutherans) believe is a rare kind of apostasy that is nevertheless possible.

If apostasy is defined only as the rejection of justifying faith—not as losing salvation because one sinned and failed to confess it—then passages like Hebrews 6 and 10, and those referring to the unforgivable sin or the sin against the Holy Spirit, which obviously refer to an apostasy that cannot be remedied, make sense. Reformed Arminians, while believing that apostasy is possible, still agree with Calvinism on the *nature* of justifying faith. Thus they emphasize the once-for-all character of the finished work of Christ, whose active and passive obedience are imputed to believers through justifying faith and union with Christ. If an Arminian believes the Bible teaches both these things, then if follows that sins committed while one is in union with Christ are covered by the imputed active and passive obedience of Christ. Thus there *cannot* be an Apostasy 2, in which the believer can repeatedly fall out of a state of grace because of sin and must confess that sin before he can be reconverted or restored to justifying faith.

REFLECTION QUESTIONS

1. What is Apostasy 1?

2. What is Apostasy 2?

3. How does a Reformed approach to the nature of justifying faith inform the perspective that affirms only Apostasy 1?

4. How does seeing one's moment-by-moment faithfulness as a matter of justification rather than sanctification affect one's answer to this question?

5. How does one's approach to the imputation of Christ's righteousness affect one's answer to this question?

Scripture Index

Name Index

Subject Index

F

40 QUESTIONS SERIES

40 QUESTIONS SERIES

Erratum

Page 18, paragraph 2, last sentence: The person described in verses 14–24 was <u>unregenerate</u>.

40 Questions About Arminianism